STUDIES IN THE EARLY HISTORY OF BRITAIN

General Editor: Nicholas Brooks

The English Peasantry and the Growth of Lordship

To Rodney Hilton

The English Peasantry and the Growth of Lordship

Rosamond Faith

Leicester University Press
London and Washington

Leicester University Press
A Cassell Imprint
Wellington House, 125 Strand, London WC2R 0BB
PO Box 605, Herndon, VA 20172

First published 1997

British Library Cataloguing in Publication Data

A catalogue record for this book is available from the British Library.

ISBN 0-7185-0011-3

Library of Congress Cataloging-in-Publication Data

Faith, Rosamond, 1935–
    The English peasantry and the growth of lordship / Rosamond Faith.
        p.   cm.–(Studies in the early history of Britain)
    Includes bibliographical references and index.
    ISBN 0-7185-0011-3 (hardcover)
    1. Peasantry–England–History.   2. Landlord and tenant–England–
History.   3. Social history–Medieval, 500–1500.   I. Series.
HN398.E5F35   1997
305.5′633′0942–dc20   96–34990
                                                                                              CIP

Typeset by BookEns Ltd., Royston, Herts.
Printed and bound in Great Britain by Biddles Ltd, Guildford and King's Lynn

Contents

List of figures

Foreword

The aim of the *Studies in the Early History of Britain* is to promote works of the highest scholarship which open up new fields of study or which straddle the barriers of traditional academic disciplines. As scholarship becomes ever more specialized, interdisciplinary studies are needed not only by scholars but also by students and laymen. This series therefore includes research monographs, works of synthesis, and also collaborative studies of important themes by several scholars whose training and expertise has lain in different fields. Our knowledge of the early middle ages will always be limited and fragmentary, but progress can be made if the work of the historian has secure foundations in philology, archaeology, geography, literature, numismatics, art history and liturgy – to name only the most obvious. The need to cross and to remove academic frontiers also explains the extension of the geographical range from that of the previous *Studies in Early English History* to include the whole island of Britain. The change would have been welcomed by the editor of the earlier series, the late Professor H.P.R. Finberg, whose pioneering work helped to inspire, or to provoke, the interest of a new generation of early medievalists in the relations of Britons and Saxons. The approach of this series is therefore deliberately wide-ranging. Early medieval Britain can only be understood in the context of contemporary developments in Ireland and on the continent.

A century has passed since Seebohm, Maitland and Vinogradoff first established the study of the origins of the structures of English rural society upon a broad understanding of European social institutions and law. Since that time much detailed work has transformed our interpretation of key texts and documents, while two generations of medieval archaeologists and one of landscape scholars have massively increased the volume and the range of evidence to be considered. But hitherto no one has dared to take up the challenge of meeting the need for reinterpretation of the origins of our society. Yet since the vast bulk of the early medieval population derived their livelihood from the land, there is no more important subject in English history than the evolution of the peasantry and of the ties that bound them to the soil and to their lords. Unless we understand that aright we shall distort the balance and misinterpret the development of English history. Dr Rosamond Faith comes to the early Middle Ages having made many contributions to the study of the later medieval English peasantry and their status. She is therefore particularly well placed to comprehend the trajectory of medieval social history and to appreciate the rich complexity and variety of arrangements that the fragmentary evidence suggests were already to be found in the early middle ages. This volume departs from the pattern of the series in that its chronological range includes the whole of the twelfth century, rather than ending with the Norman Conquest and Domesday Book. From the thirteenth century the huge bulk of surviving estate records means that the history of rural social relations is thereafter much more fully known. It is a great delight, therefore, to welcome to the series a major new synthesis of the earlier 'dark-age' development. Dr Faith's elucidation of the changing fortunes of the peasants of the 'inland' and the 'warland' over almost a millennium sets out much that was distinctive and much that was common to western Europe in English history. In particular her new analysis explains and defines the traditional individualism, and the claims to ancient freedom, of the English countryman. I am confident that it will deservedly be ranked alongside the late nineteenth-century classics of English social history and will come to have an equally seminal influence upon our understanding.

N.P. Brooks
University of Birmingham
May 1996

Acknowledgements

A glance at the footnotes will reveal the very great extent to which this book is based on the published work of others. It rests also on the unpublished work of younger scholars, among whom Phillip Schofield, Chris Thornton, Andrew Wareham, Mark Gardiner, Debby Banham and Dawn Hadley generously lent me their theses: I have had fruitful discussions with all of them. What may not be so apparent, and I should like to record here, is the debt I owe to two groups: the Birmingham University Medieval Graduate Seminar and the West Oxfordshire Charter Boundary Walkers. Discussions with their members have over the years brought me the chance to benefit from others' knowledge, to try out new ideas and, best of all, many friendships. Chris Dyer, Zvi Razi and John and Sarah Blair have read the entire text at different stages, Niall Brady and Nick Higham part of it, and I hope they will agree that the final version is the better for their comments. Parts have been given as papers at seminars and conferences in Leicester, Oxford, Cambridge, Cardiff and Birmingham and I am grateful for the comments that arose on those occasions. Most first books are written when the author's children are only old enough to warrant an indulgent nod in a preface: I have had the pleasure of discussing this one with mine as adults. I have treated Ralph Evans's books, and many of his ideas, as my own. Sam Rothenstein and Nicholas Faith have by their financial support given me the leisure to research and write which is denied to so many of today's overworked academics, and Wolfson College, Oxford hospitably granted me membership of its Common Room. The University of Oxford gives its alumni the benefit of access to its lectures, seminars, and libraries: the staff of the History Faculty Library have been particularly helpful. David Howlett, editor of the *Dictionary of Medieval Latin from British Sources* kindly gave me access to this valuable resource. The Marc Fitch Fund underwrote the cost of the maps. I am most grateful to Nicholas Brooks for his careful editing and to Harry Buglass for his elegant and lucid map-making. Both helped to tell my story infinitely more clearly than I could have done unaided.

Abbreviations

Ag. Hist. I.I	S. Piggott, ed., *The Agrarian History of England and Wales* I.I, Prehistory (1981)
Ag. Hist. I.II	H.P.R. Finberg, ed., *The Agrarian History of England and Wales* I.II, *A.D. 43–1042* (1972)
Ag. Hist. II	H.E. Hallam, ed., *The Agrarian History of England and Wales 2 1042–1350* (1988)
AgHR	*Agricultural History Review*
ASSAH	*Anglo-Saxon Studies in Archaeology and History*
BAR	British Archaeological Reports
BCS	W. de G. Birch, *Cartularium Saxonicum* (3 vols. 1885–93)
BL	British Library
Bosworth and Toller	T.N. Toller, ed., *An Anglo-Saxon Dictionary Based on the Manuscript Collections of the late Joseph Bosworth* (1898); *Supplement with Revised and Enlarged Addenda by Alistair Campbell* (1921)
DB	*Domesday Book* (cited from Phillimore edition)
EcHR	*Economic History Review*
EHD I	D. Whitelock, ed., *English Historical Documents, I, c 500–1042* (1955)
EHD II	D.C. Douglas and G.W. Greenaway, eds, *English Historical Documents II 1042–1189* (1953)
EHR	*English Historical Review*
Ekwall, *English Place-Names*	E. Ekwall, *The Concise Oxford Dictionary of English Place-Names* (4th edn, 1960)
EPNS	English Place-Name Society
HE	*Bede's Ecclesiastical History of the English People*, ed. B. Colgrave and R.A.B. Mynors (1969)
Liebermann	F. Liebermann, *Die Gesetze der Angelsachsen* (3 vols, 1903–16)
Robertson, *Charters*	*Anglo-Saxon Charters*, ed. A.J. Robertson (2nd edn, 1956)
S	P.H. Sawyer, *Anglo-Saxon Charters: an annotated list and bibliography* (1968)
TRHS	*Transactions of the Royal Historical Society.*
VCH	*Victoria County History*

Introduction

This book is a study of the relationship between two kinds of people: on the one hand the peasantry, the men, women and children who supported themselves by farming, and who 'as in the past, so in the present ... are the majority of mankind', on the other hand their lords.[1] The term 'peasant' is stretched to its limits in the course of the book, for it is used to describe small farmers as well as substantial independent yeomen. I follow Theodor Shanin in defining peasants as cultivators and pastoralists who depend mostly on family labour to work a farm which is in some way a possession of the family and which provides for most of its needs. But where Shanin includes as a defining characteristic of peasants that they are 'underdogs', 'kept at arm's length from the social sources of power', I part company from him, for a major theme of this book is the role that some of the peasantry played in the working of the early 'state' and the implications that this had for their social and legal status. I define 'lords' as people and institutions with power over others, and this term too is stretched to its limits for the nature of lordship changed profoundly over time. Although it is concerned with the changes in rural life, in agriculture and in forms of settlement that took place over a very long period indeed, from the Anglo-Saxon settlements to the end of the twelfth century, this is not primarily a work of agrarian history. Throughout, these changes are perceived as a product of political and social developments as much as endogenous features of the rural economy.

---

1. T. Shanin, ed., *Peasants and Peasant Societies* (1971), 14–17.

1 Extensive lordship

While living within the Roman empire brought many common experiences to the people of its provinces, in their varied experiences of 'after Rome' they took distinct paths. Between the effective end of Roman rule and the onset of large-scale Germanic settlement Britain experienced a hiatus unique in Europe. Later developments and arrangements constantly turn out to have their roots in this period. The early Middle Ages in Europe have been seen as the period of 'the other transition', between the economy of the ancient world, where surplus was transferred to the state as tax, and that of feudalism, where it was transferred to landowners as rent.[1] In England – for the focus of most of this book is narrowed down to what can be said of England, not Britain as a whole – the transition from 'the ancient world' to 'feudalism' was an indirect and long-drawn-out process. In the early stages of this process social arrangements and forms of power emerged which were neither 'ancient' nor 'feudal'.

The reasons for this lie far back, 'before Rome'. In late Iron Age Europe it was neither tax nor rent but tribute, a transfer sanctioned by political power, that expressed relationships between rulers and peoples. This reflects an important characteristic of early European politics: the circulation of valuable goods, in the form of tribute and gifts, as the articulation of power relationships between peoples. Within elites, wealth circulated by means of gift exchange. Such movements of wealth for political purposes 'ran largely parallel to and independent of the normal "economic" circulation of goods'.[2] Largely controlled by rulers, this process allowed some wealth to 'trickle down' to members of military elites, but probably little further. Such wealth was not immediately derived from the 'real' agricultural economy – it is doubtful if peasant farming was capable of providing a tradable

---

1. For social relationships in tribute- and tax-paying societies contrasted with those in 'feudal' societies: C. Wickham, 'The other transition: from the ancient world to feudalism', *Past and Present* 103 (May 1984), 3–36; P. Anderson, *Passages from Antiquity to Feudalism* (1974), 107–42. For an analysis of feudal rent which would include in it tribute: K. Tribe, *Land, Labour and Economic Discourse* (1978), ch. 2.
2. T. Reuter, 'Plunder and tribute in the Carolingian empire', *TRHS* series 5th series 35 (1985), 75–94, at 85; T.M. Charles-Edwards, 'Early medieval kingships in the British Isles' in *The Origins of Anglo-Saxon Kingdoms*, ed. S. Bassett (1989), 28–39.

surplus which could have produced the expensive items found at royal and aristocratic sites. The wealth of rulers in the Celtic Iron Age could not have been sustained merely by extracting the surplus of a dependent subsistence peasantry. The sources of the wealth of the upper class thus lay elsewhere than in the direct exploitation of land as a productive resource.

The elites who were the beneficiaries of these processes were thereby made yet more powerful within their own territories, able to extract supplies from their own peoples, but in late Iron Age Britain the link between the peasantry and their rulers was likely to have been an indirect one. It lay not in the transfer of peasant labour to work on great estates, nor in the transfer of surplus in cash or kind in return for land.[3] Tribute in the form of foodstuffs was transferred from farmers to rulers and other lords, not because lords owned the land but because they ruled the people. It is tribute drawn from a wide area of subordinate territory, rather than the direct exploitation of the land, that is likely to have been the mainstay of the economy of the late Iron Age hillfort. As the impressive amounts of cattle bones found at some of them testify they are 'consumption sites' rather than centres of agricultural estates.[4] If Iron Age rulers were supported from the immediate countryside it was likely that they took that support in the form of fighting men, 'their harvest as warriors'.[5] This must have disrupted rural society, but need not have entailed a debasement of the peasantry: a concept at the heart of the moral economy of such a society was that participation in battle conferred free status and membership of the people. This was an idea with a long life before it.

The experience of later centuries was to show that the small regional political entity, whether we call it *pays*, region, or small kingdom was always a lively geopolitical reality. Much the same pattern of small territories as the *pagi* of Celtic Gaul may have

---

3. Agrarian economy: P.J. Fowler, *The Farming of Prehistoric Britain* (1983), first published as 'Later prehistory' in *Ag. Hist.* I.I (1981), 63–298; land-units and communal organization: M. Todd, *The South-West to AD 1000* (1987), 115–25; H.C. Bowen and P.J. Fowler, eds, *Early Land Allotment in the British Isles*, BAR British series 48 (1978); B. Cunliffe, *Iron Age Communities in Britain* (1974).
4. H. Gent and C. Dean, 'Catchment analysis and settlement hierarchy: a case study from pre-Roman Britain' in *Central Places, Archaeology and History*, ed. E. Grant (1986), 13–26.
5. P.J. Geary, *Before France and Germany: the creation and transformation of the Mediterranean world* (1988), 113; D. Nash, 'Celtic territorial expansion and the Mediterranean world' in *Settlement and Society: aspects of west European prehistory in the first millennium BC*, ed. T.C. Champion and J.V.S. Megaw (1985), 45–67 at 46.
6. T.M. Charles-Edwards, 'Native political organization in Roman Britain and the origin of MW *brenhin*' in *Antiquitates indo-germanicae*, ed. M. Mayrhofer *et al.* (Innsbruck 1974), 35–45; Charles-Edwards, 'Early medieval kingships', 28–39; M. Richter, *Medieval Ireland: the enduring tradition* (1988), 17–19; Caesar, *de bello gallico*, V.xxi, xxii; B.R. Hartley and R.L. Fitts, *The Brigantes* (1988), 2–4; G. Webster, *The Cornovii* (1975), 17–20; J.L. Bruneaux, *The Celtic Gauls: gods, rites and sanctuaries*, trans. D. Nash (1988), 99–100.

underlain the political map of pre-Roman Britain.[6] This was already a country in which, not only in their geography and farming practice but also in their political economy, regions had already developed strong identities. Regional factors are likely to have influenced the extent to which 'Romanization' affected the status of the peasantry. Where the demands of the state for taxation drove peasants into dependence on landowners they are likely to have lost their independence.[7] Yet many peasants in areas outside the range of the villa estate economy and inaccessible to the tax collector may have lived virtually untouched by the Romanized economy.[8] Romanization brought new ideas about land, as something that can be transferred to individuals whose rights are protected at law. Nevertheless a peasant culture persisted in which membership of a family was very important, and the family's rights over a particular piece of land continued over time.[9]

From the point of view of the relationship which is the theme of this book, England after Rome saw the beginnings of a crucial combination. On the one hand autonomous powers exercised control over substantial territories; on the other a self-sufficient peasantry practised a mixed subsistence agriculture in small scattered settlements. Essentially, the

---

7. Wickham, 'Other transition'; for the experience of the peasantry elsewhere in the empire: A.H.M. Jones, *The Later Roman Empire AD 284–602: a social, economic and administrative survey* (2nd edn, 2 vols 1973); M. Rostovtzeff, *The Social and Economic History of the Roman Empire* (2nd edn, 1963); E. Baudoin, *Les grandes domaines dans l'empire romain* (Paris, 1899); N.D. Fustel de Coulanges, *Histoire des institutions politiques de l'ancienne France* (6 vols, 1888–92), I; P. Garnsey and R. Sellar, *The Roman Empire: economy, society and culture* (1987); R. Clausing, *The Roman Colonate: the theory of its origin* (New York, 1925); A.H.M. Jones, 'The Roman colonate', *Past and Present* 13 (April 1958), 1–13; J.C. Percival, 'Seigneurial aspects of late Roman estate management', *EHR* 84 (1969), 449–73.
8. Romanization: P. Salway, *Roman Britain* (1981); C. Thomas, ed., *Rural Settlement in Roman Britain*, CBA Report 7 (1966); R. Hingley, *Rural Settlement in Roman Britain* (1989); M. Millett, *The Romanization of Britain: an essay in archaeological interpretation* (1991). Villa estate economy: A.L.F. Rivet, ed., *The Roman Villa in Britain* (1969); Salway, *Roman Britain*, 109–24; M. Todd, ed., *Studies in the Romano-British Villa* (1978); W. Davies, 'Roman settlements and post–Roman estates in SE Wales' in *The End of Roman Britain*, ed. P.J. Casey, BAR British Series 71 (1979), 153–73; J.T. Smith, 'Villas as a key to social structure' in *Studies in the Romano-British Villa*, ed. M. Todd (1978), 149–85; S. Applebaum, 'Peasant economy and types of agriculture' in *Rural Settlement in Roman Britain*, ed. Thomas, 99–107; N. Higham, *Rome, Britain and the Anglo-Saxons* (1992), 86–97.
9. Property and Roman law: E. Levy, 'The vulgarization of Roman law in the early middle ages', *Medievalia et Humanistica* 1 (1943), 14–40. Family joint occupation seems to be the implication of 'aisled buildings': P. Morris, *Agricultural Buildings in Roman Britain*, BAR British Series 70 (1979); J.T. Smith, 'Romano-British aisled houses', *Archaeological Journal* 120 (1963), 1–30; S. Applebaum, 'Roman Britain' in *Ag. Hist.* I. II, 3–277 at 20–6; G.R.J. Jones, 'Post-Roman Wales', *ibid.*, 299–349 at 320–34; W. Davies, *Wales in the Early Middle Ages* (1982), 76ff. and 203–5; T.M. Charles-Edwards, 'Kinship, status and the origin of the hide', *Past and Present* 56 (August 1972), 3–33. There was possibly a parallel syncretic legal culture in early Brittany: L. Fleuriot, 'Les tres anciennes lois bretonnes: leur date, leur texte' in *Landevennec et la monachisme breton dans le haut moyen Age* (Landevennec 1985).

former were supported from the surplus of the latter, but the social form in which this transfer took place cannot usefully be summed up either as 'tax' or as 'rent'. The dominance of considerably developed local political authorities over a society based on a still relatively undeveloped agrarian economy took the form of a complex of rights to services and renders from the people of a given territory. G. Barrow has given the name 'extensive lordship' to this kind of dominance and there is surely no better term.[10] In England extensive lordship forms a link between the social organization of the ancient world, where the state had power, and 'feudalism', where landowners did.

The relationships between lords and peasants inherent in extensive lordship continued to be an important form of social organization governing the lives of many peasant families in Anglo-Saxon England, and are one recurrent theme in this book. But they co-existed with another set of relationships of a very different nature: those between lords and a very dependent servile stratum of the peasantry. These dependent people and their history are a parallel theme. Chapters 2 and 3 are devoted to them.

After the collapse of Roman state power in Britain, political authority, which was already in the fourth century beginning to shift from the *civitas* capital to the countryside, fragmented into a multitude of small kingdoms.[11] The combination of this atomized political power with the remnants of the bureaucratization inherited from Rome may have intensified exploitation of the peasantry. Grain supplies from the surrounding countryside, raised by taxation and applied to the purposes of the Roman state while that state endured, as it gradually collapsed were transferred into the hands of a local nobility who 'emerged as kings when the Imperial superstructure was removed'.[12] Some kind of continuity along these lines is also possible in the smaller 'sub-Roman' territories, some related to towns, which retained their

---

10. G.W.S. Barrow, *The Kingdom of the Scots: government, church and society from the eleventh to the thirteenth century* (1973), 25.
11. L. Alcock, 'The activities of potentates in Celtic Britain' in *Power and Politics in Early Medieval Britain and Ireland*, ed. S.T. Driscoll and M.R. Nieke (1988), 22–46; E. James, 'The origins of barbarian kingdoms: the continental evidence' in *Origins of Anglo-Saxon Kingdoms*, ed. Bassett, 40–52; N.P. Brooks, 'The creation and early structure of the kingdom of Kent', *ibid.* 55–74; N. Higham, *The Northern Counties to AD 1000* (1986), ch. 6; S. Esmonde Cleary, *The Ending of Roman Britain* (1989), ch. 5; N. Higham, *Rome, Britain and the Anglo-Saxons* (1992), 69–152; D. Dumville, 'The origins of Northumbria: some aspects of the British background' in *Origins of Anglo-Saxon Kingdoms*, ed. Bassett, 213–22 and 'Sub-Roman Britain: history and legend', *History* 62.205 (June 1977), 173–92 for a criticism of the sources and their use by historians.
12. Davies, 'Roman settlements'; K. Pretty, 'Defining the Magonsaete' in *Origins of Anglo-Saxon Kingdoms*, ed. Bassett, 171–83 at 174. For the (disputed) survival of Roman taxation in Gaul: W. Goffart, *Rome's Fall and After* (1989), 168ff.; R. Doehaerd, *The Early Middle Ages in the West: economy and society*, trans. W.G. Deakin (1978), 248–50; in Britain: Applebaum, 'Roman Britain', 251–2; H.P.R. Finberg 'Anglo-Saxon England to 1042' in *Ag.Hist.* I.II, 385–525 at 400.

identity into the period of Anglo-Saxon settlement. S. Bassett has
drawn attention to examples of such areas which survived as socially
recognized units, and we should consider the possibility that the
reason they survived was because they were organized for the
collection of revenues, run by 'bureaucrats of a Roman sort'.[13] The
post-Roman Britain that emerged in the fifth century thus preserved,
or recreated in a new form, some very important elements of the late
Iron Age world. At the political level were local autonomous powers. A
culture re-emerged in which the obligation and capacity to bear
weapons were essential qualifications for free status and membership
of a polity. In the rural economy at every level family structures and
attitudes to land provided for a group wider than the nuclear family.

To the extent that social rank can truly be said to show up
archaeologically, early Anglo-Saxon communities of the period of
migration look rather *flat* little societies.[14] In so far as this would be
revealed by richer burials, the fourth- and fifth-century cemeteries do
not show great extremes of rank. Differentiation begins to appear in
the sixth century and great riches in the seventh. Yet the small farming
communities whose settlements have so far been investigated do not
look as if they were capable of gradually producing from their own
ranks emergent ruling families who eventually became so dominant
that we can call them kings. Moreover, far from producing a
transferable surplus, agriculture in the settlement period may have
been through a period of fall-back, if not outright recession.[15] Yet out of
this 'flat' society emerged the kingships whose rivalries dominate the
political history of Anglo-Saxon England.[16]

In understanding the emergence of kingship in early Anglo-Saxon
England it is relevant to recall the relationship of political power to the
agrarian economy which has been suggested as characteristic of late
Iron Age polities. In this society too, it was not the surplus agricultural
produce of their own estates but produce and tribute from their own

---

13. S. Bassett, 'Churches in Worcester before and after the conversion of the Anglo-
    Saxons', *Antiquaries Journal* 69 (1989), 225–56 at 244.
14. C.J. Arnold, *An Archaeology of the Early Anglo-Saxon Kingdoms* (1988); P.J.
    Fowler, 'Agriculture and rural settlement' and P. Rahtz, 'Buildings and rural
    settlement', both in *The Archaeology of Anglo-Saxon England*, ed. D.M. Wilson,
    (1976); R. Hodges, *The Anglo-Saxon Achievement: archaeology and the beginnings
    of English society* (1989), 34–42; C. Scull, 'Archaeology, early Anglo–Saxon
    society and the origins of Anglo-Saxon kingdoms', *ASSAH* 6 (1993), 1–18 at 8–11;
    H. Uhlig, 'Old hamlets with infield and outfield systems in western and central
    Europe', *Geografiska Annaler* 43 (1961), 285–307.
15. M. Bell, 'Environmental archaeology as an index of continuity and change in the
    medieval landscape' in *The Rural Settlements of Medieval England*, ed. M. Aston,
    D. Austin and C. Dyer (1989), 269–86. Population: S.C. Hawkes, 'The early Saxon
    period' in *The Archaeology of the Oxford Region*, ed. G. Briggs, J. Cook and T.
    Rowley (1986), 64–108 at 75–6. Out-migration: F.M. Stenton *Anglo-Saxon
    England* (1947), 4–8. Plague in 549: Dumville, 'Sub-Roman Britain', 189; in 547
    and 682: Higham, *Northern Counties*, 245.
16. Scull, 'Archaeology'.

Figure 1   Hallamshire, Yorkshire, also known as the soke of Sheffield or the soke of Ecclesfield. The freemen of Hallamshire still attended its sokemoot and attended at the lord's hunt at the close of the twelfth century. *Source*: after G.W.S. Barrow, *The Kingdom of the Scots* (1973), map 1.

people and from the people of subject territories that supported ruling elites. The outright ownership and direct exploitation of land by elites were slow to develop. In a period when kingship grew from the exercise of physical power, leadership in battle was an important legitimization of other kinds of rule. This has implications for the delegated or subaltern rule which, I will argue, lay at the origins of lordship, rooting it in the exercise of force, rather than in an economic development endogenous to the economy.

Studies of individual kingdoms bear out the picture of kingship as an institution that was only emerging in the sixth century, that is to say in a country long settled.[17] Some central themes have emerged which S. Bassett has recently used as the basis for an important model of the emergence of small kings and kingdoms. He proposes two possible scenarios. In one, Germanic settlers moved into existing Romano-British estates and merged with the existing farming population. Over

---

17. B. Yorke, *Kings and Kingdoms of Early Anglo-Saxon England* (1990), 9–19; C.J. Arnold, 'Territories and leadership: frameworks for the study of emergent polities in early Anglo-Saxon southern England' in *Power and Politics in Early Medieval Britain and Ireland*, ed. S.T. Driscoll and M.R. Nieke (1988), 111–27.

several generations a mixed British-Germanic people developed, leading in time to 'the emergence of a tribe (i.e. extended family) identifiable as the dominant group within that district'. Over time, tribe and territory became identified. The dominant extended family became internally more and more hierarchical, producing leading members from its own ranks who installed themselves as heads of their own 'tribal communities' by inheritance and of other people's by force. By extending their territory the 'process of state formation ... began in earnest'. The leaders of these extended areas became recognizably kings and their families recognizably dynasties. Bassett's second, exogenous, path to kingship lay via the 'takeover of an existing ... British territory of one sort or another by an outside group'. As a result of such takeovers, some centres of sub-Roman kingdoms became important Anglo-Saxon royal centres.[18] Struggles between kings produced hierarchies of territories and rulers, in which the subordinated eventually lost identity and autonomy. Subject kingdoms had subaltern status and their rulers declined over time from kingly or sub-kingly rank to exercising a kind of delegated authority as ealdormen.[19]

The cultural values of the Anglo-Saxons were deeply imbued with violence, its pleasures and its rewards. Service in war called for young and fit men. This made it a stage in life, not a permanent career.[20] Kings needed to provide for sons and brothers, to raise armies and money. *Realpolitik* and the demands of reciprocity demanded that they reward those who had claims on them from ties of blood or the provision of service. They rewarded them, or bought their support, in a variety of ways: by marriage alliances, by gifts of the traditional kind, by support in war, by fostering their sons at court, by the spiritual fosterage of godparenthood. But the prime currency of reward came to be a grant of territory.

At the highest level, within the royal family, what was given was a kingdom. Royal kinsmen were granted authority over wide areas which were, or thus became, in effect sub-kingdoms.[21] Others who had claims on the king based on service of an unmilitary kind could also expect tangible reward in the form of land, as well as the less tangible esteem

---

18. S. Bassett, 'In search of the origins of Anglo-Saxon kingdoms' in *Origins of Anglo-Saxon Kingdoms*, ed. Bassett, 3–27 at 22, 23, 24; G. Foard, 'The administrative organisation of Northamptonshire in the Saxon period', *ASSAH* 4 (1985), 185–222 at 210; J. Campbell, 'Bede's words for places', *Words, Names and Graves: early medieval settlement*, ed. P.H. Sawyer (1979), 34–53 at 50 n. 20; J. Blair, *Early Medieval Surrey: landholding, church and settlement before 1300* (1991), 24 and n. 74.
19. Charles-Edwards, 'Early medieval kingships', 31–9; Bassett, 'Origins of Anglo-Saxon kingdoms', 6–17.
20. T.M. Charles-Edwards, 'The distinction between land and moveable wealth in Anglo–Saxon England' in *English Medieval Settlement*, ed. P.H. Sawyer (1979), 97–104 at 99–101.
21. J. Campbell, *Bede's Reges and Principes* (Jarrow 1979); Charles-Edwards, 'Early medieval kingships', 31–2.

that came from proximity to the king and a right to participate in political and legal decision-making. The political order of early Anglo-Saxon England was thus to a very great extent based on delegated authority. Sub-kings and ealdormen had powers over regions akin to those that kings had over kingdoms: powers to command loyalty and exact surplus.

The physical support system of Anglo-Saxon kings was the formalized delivery of supplies to royal centres, to which the king and his entourage travelled on circuit. The granting away of territory was often accompanied by the granting away of rights to this collected surplus, and this was an important factor in establishing the economic base of the aristocracy. Chapter 4 discusses this. That this localizat-ion of authority did not bring about its total fragmentation was due to the exceptional sophistication and centralization of the Anglo-Saxon state.

It surely cannot be right, however, to think of *all* political power – essentially in this period the ability to command supplies and fighting men – as delegated 'from above'. Regional aristocracies, Bassett's 'dominant families', of which we know little or nothing may well have had, and retained over long periods of time, power bases in their localities which owed nothing to authority handed down by kings and everything to their personal and inherited ability to command men and resources from 'their' territories.

Although Anglo-Saxon history has traditionally been written in terms of the major kingdoms that eventually emerged, it is the small region that is now seen as vital to our understanding of the political and social structure of early England. The extent to which these regions have been recognized and identified, and the terms in which they have been described, has necessarily been to some extent dictated by the kind of evidence available. Some of these smaller units are recorded in the Tribal Hidage, a document of the seventh or eighth century, which lists various peoples and gives for each an assessment in round hundreds of hides. Others have been traced from their later manifestations as other forms of territorial unit, as sokes, as the land attached to major minsters, as groups of hundreds, as ecclesiastical divisions, or as post-Conquest baronies. That this has been possible is testimony to their strong identity and viability.[22]

One analysis emphasizes the geographical and economic rationale of small regions. This approach is critical of the idea that Germanic

---

22. For example: for the emergence of the ancient secular divisions of Cumbria as the deaneries of the diocese of Carlisle see A.J.L. Winchester, *Landscape and Society in Medieval Cumbria* (1987), 89–90; for the identification of minster territories with former land-units see D. Hadley, 'Danelaw society and institutions: east midlands phenomena' (Ph.D. thesis, University of Birmingham, 1992), part 5; for hundreds see H.M. Cam, 'Early groups of hundreds' in her *Liberties and Communities in Medieval England: collected studies in local administration and topography* (1944), 91–106; for baronies see R. Reid, 'Barony and thanage', *EHR* 35 (1920), 161–99; D. Roffe, 'From thegnage to barony: sake and soke, title and tenants-in-chief', *Anglo-Norman Studies* 12 (1989), 157–76.

settlement was related to previously existing political divisions or to the settlement patterns of the indigenous British population. It identifies the territory of the smaller peoples in the Tribal Hidage as 'primary settlement areas'.[23] Similar 'resource territories' which combined the essential elements necessary for a group to survive have been identified via the links between different settlements, natural boundaries and place-names.[24] The physical essential of such a territory was an area of land, not necessarily physically integrated or with fixed boundaries, with which its inhabitants identified themselves. Its economic basis was an agrarian economy of low-intensity mixed agriculture based on self-sufficient farms, combined with transhumant stock-raising. D. Hooke has shown how 'folk-areas' in the west midlands were defined by this dual economy. Typically they combined 'developed regions, usually located in riverine situations, linked to areas of outlying woodland surviving along major watersheds in a pattern of seasonal transhumance'. These elements survived to influence the composition of later land-units which she is able to reconstruct from the evidence of boundary clauses in Anglo-Saxon charters.[25] That their important central places were often at or near important Roman or pre-Roman sites, cemeteries and socially acknowledged frontiers shows that small regions had a sense of, perhaps even a continuity with, their historic past.[26] These central places can be seen as the headquarters of the 'dominant families' of Bassett's account.

It is members of such families we might envisage ruling the kind of land-unit which has come to be known as the 'small *scir*'. (This is the same word as our modern 'shire', but its Old English form is used throughout to distinguish it from that later, larger administrative unit.) The 'small *scirs*' which persisted into medieval England and lowland Scotland are a widely occurring and long-lasting form of these small regions. They were a more meaningful focus for group identity than was a kingdom: as late as the nineteenth century Oxfordshire people still spoke of 'Banbury-shire'.[27] Such evidence as we have about the

---

23. W. Davies and H. Vierck, 'The contents of the Tribal Hidage: social aggregates and settlement patterns', *Frühmittelalterliche Studien* 8 (1974), 223–93. The information in the Tribal Hidage is discussed in *Origins of Anglo-Saxon Kingdoms*, ed. Bassett, *passim*, the text itself in D. Dumville, 'The Tribal Hidage: an introduction to its texts and their history', *ibid.* 225–30.

24. A. Everitt, *Continuity and Colonization: the evolution of Kentish settlement* (1986); Blair, *Early Medieval Surrey*, ch. 1; Brooks, 'The creation and early structure of the kingdom of Kent'; N. Higham, *The Origins of Cheshire* (1993), 127–81; M. Costen, *The Origins of Somerset* (1992), 61–70, 87–100.

25. D. Hooke, *Anglo-Saxon Settlements of the West Midlands: the charter evidence*, BAR British Series 95 (1981), ch.3 at 48.

26. For example Blair, *Early Medieval Surrey*, 24 and n. 74; Everitt, *Continuity and Colonization*, 331–2.

27. For example R.B. Smith, *Blackburnshire* (1961); Banburyshire: A. Howkins, *Reshaping Rural England: a social history 1850–1925* (1991), 30; Hallamshire: W. Farrer, ed., *Early Yorkshire Charters* (3 vols, 1914–16), I, viii.

early identity of small *scirs* is all the more important because the identity of many can only be reconstructed from evidence that comes almost entirely from a period very late in their history, when they may have lost much of their original character. This evidence, whose study was pioneered by Maitland and Jolliffe, is the body of apparently archaic obligations and customs that survived, principally in northern and east Anglian society, after the Norman Conquest.[28] Fig. 1 shows 'Hallamshire', Yorkshire, one of the many small *scirs* reconstructed by G. Barrow. Echoes, though much less well-documented, from other regions are accumulating to the extent that the *scir* now appears as a widespread form of social organization.[29] We now have some idea of the social relationships which bound it together: it is not too fanciful to call it the political economy of the small *scir*. The *scir*, in J. Bossy's telling phrase, can be seen as a 'landscape of obligation' rather than a landscape of ownership.[30] At its head were recognized authorities, 'ealdormen' in the laws, with considerable powers, backed by military force but socially sanctioned. These authorities received tribute at important centres which were also centres for the political process and the settlement of disputes and at which a variety of duties were owed. The *scir* may once have had a complex cultural identity of which we can only study the vestiges in the written record. Social gatherings such as the fairs and horse-races which appear in Norse literature as such important parts of the social fabric, while they are the most ephemeral kind of activity, may once have been what gave people the liveliest sense of identity. What has a better chance of survival in the written record are rights and obligations, and our records show us the vestiges of what were once surely elaborate networks of these. Authority over the *scir* was based not on the ownership of land but on the 'extensive lordship' invoked at the beginning of this chapter: the power to command goods and services from the population of an area. From the obligations of the people of the *scir* to provide supplies and military service there stemmed their corresponding rights to socially recognized free status as members of a people, with access to the law. In so far as they affected the peasantry, the social relationships within *scirs* are the subject of Chapters 4 and 5.

Subsequent chapters examine the social organization that came to replace the *scir*. One such was the estate, a term which will be used to imply full ownership of land by an individual or family. The growing

28. Barrow, *Kingdom of the Scots*, ch. 1; F.W. Maitland, 'Northumbrian tenures', *EHR* 5 (1890), 625–32; J. Jolliffe, 'Northumbrian institutions', *EHR* 41 (1926), 1–42; D.C. Douglas, *The Social Structure of Medieval East Anglia*, Oxford Studies in Social and Legal History 9 (1927); F.M. Stenton, *Types of Manorial Structure in the Northern Danelaw*, ibid. 2 (1910); W.E. Kapelle, *The Norman Conquest of the North: a region and its transformation 1000–1135* (1979), ch. 3.
29. T. Williamson, *The Origins of Norfolk* (1993), 83–104; Higham, *Origins of Cheshire*, 176–81; Costen, *Origins of Somerset*, 86–93; D. Kenyon, *The Origins of Lancashire* (1991), 70–5, 89–97, 105–8.
30. Prof. J. Bossy, pers. comm.

importance of private landlordship brought changes in the social and legal status of the peasantry. These are discussed in the context of the bookland estate of late Anglo-Saxon England in Chapter 6 and in the context of the impact of the new Anglo-Norman landowning class in Chapters 7, 8 and 9. Yet ideas about free status which stemmed ultimately from the political culture of the era of the 'extensive lordship' of the *scir* were extraordinarily long-lasting. They are found recurring as part of a social theory which was still an influence on the peasantry after the Conquest: Chapter 10 looks at these ideas.

Multiple estates

Early units of landholding have come to be known as 'multiple estates'. A body of very influential work by G.R.J. Jones has shown the importance of the concept of the 'multiple' (sometimes the 'composite', 'federal', 'complex' or 'discrete') estate to the study of rural Britain. Multiple estates are sometimes treated as if they were identical with the *scir*, and the term 'estate' is widely used of any discernible early land-unit. Yet while there are many physical continuities, it will not help us in understanding either to conflate the two. The *scir* was a political unit; the multiple estate was essentially a unit of ownership and production, and we should be cautious of using the term in contexts where these are anachronistic concepts. Rule and control over people only gradually evolved into the ownership of land, and the stages by which this happened are one of the themes of this book.

Jones described the multiple estate as a highly regular arrangement.[31] He drew heavily on the descriptions of royal estates in the Welsh laws, and this has opened his model to a variety of criticisms, for the laws present an ideal of how society should be organized, and the prime concern of the passages in them which refer to royal estate organization may have been with collecting tax.[32] Many of Jones's examples of multiple estates come from the later medieval period, when the relationships within them had been transformed by post-Conquest changes in the status of the peasantry and the nature of

---

31. G.R.J. Jones, 'Post-Roman Wales'; 'Multiple estates and early settlement' in *English Medieval Settlement*, ed. Sawyer, 11–40; 'Multiple estates perceived', *Journal of Historical Geography* 11 (1985), 352–63 at 354; 'Early territorial organization in England and Wales', *Geografiska Annaler* 43 (1961), 174–81; 'Basic patterns of settlement distribution in northern England', *Advancement of Science* 18 (1961), 191–200; 'The portrayal of land settlement in Domesday Book', in *Domesday Studies*, ed. J.C. Holt (1987), 183–200. A critique is N. Gregson, 'The multiple estate model: some critical questions', *Journal of Historical Geography* 11 (1985), 339–51. See too D. Hooke, 'Early medieval estate and settlement patterns: the documentary evidence' in *Rural Settlements of Medieval England* ed. Aston, Austin and Dyer, 9–30; *Anglo-Saxon Landscapes of the West Midlands*, chs 3 and 4.
32. Davies, *Wales in the Early Middle Ages*, 43–7.

lordship: his reconstruction of a multiple estate centred on South Malling, Sussex was based on a thirteenth-century custumal.[33] Nevertheless his analyses of a wide range of land-units have shown how widespread are the principal component elements of his multiple estates.[34] These components will figure as important categories in the analysis of rural society that follows, but they are not seen as necessarily indicating the existence of a multiple estate in the sense of a recognized unit of land ownership and exploitation. We can single them out as follows. The essential territorial features of the multiple estate are 'hierarchies of settlement', in Jones's words. Links between outlying settlements and important central places, sometimes enduring over very long periods of time, reveal a landscape organized in the interest of a minority able to control and exploit groups of its inhabitants. Their central foci are prestigious headquarters. Associated with these, and devoted to supplying them, are settlements of dependent tenants and/or slaves. Chapter 2 discusses a range of such centres of production, mainly those associated with minsters and royal lands, and Chapter 3 describes their distinctive populations. A network of outlying settlements, grouped into units, supplied the headquarters with food renders and specialist services, some agricultural, some concerned with hospitality. Fig. 2 shows N. Higham's interpretation of the place-names of outlying settlements in the early land-unit which is now the large parish of Malpas, Cheshire: among them were places which supplied honey, beef, wood and milk.

A very characteristic group of obligations within a multiple estate were ploughing and harvest work at the centre, and attendance and service at the lord's hunt. While Jones incorporated them into his multiple estate model, these dues are treated here instead as 'privatized' relics of early *scir* organization, for such obligations seem to be emblematic of the relationship of the people of a *scir* to its rulers. The growing sophistication of the 'state' in later Anglo-Saxon England imposed a further network of 'public' obligations: military service and related duties, and the payment of tax are the most important of these. Obligations of this type came to be seen as essentially connected with personal freedom: Chapter 4 describes them and Chapter 5 the peasants among the populations that owed them, while they recur in the concluding chapters as relics surviving into Anglo-Norman England of the social relations of pre-Conquest society.

It is useful to see the multiple estate less as a relic of antique social organization – a fixed entity enduring over time, although some may have been just that – than as part of a process. Its component centres and dependencies were a widespread and evolving series of responses to the realities of politics, agriculture and settlement. Wales may have

33. Jones, 'Multiple estates and early settlement', 22–9.
34. E. Miller, 'La société rurale en Angleterre (x[e] au xiie siècles)', in *Agricoltura e mondo rurale in occidente nell' alto medioevo*, Settimane di Studio del Centro Italiano di Studi dell' Alto Medioevo 13 (Spoleto 1966), 111–34.

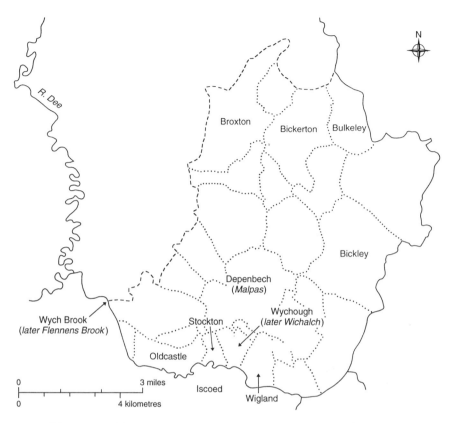

Figure 2 Malpas parish, Cheshire, with township names indicating renders of honey (Bickerton, 'beekeepers' farm'), cattle (Bulkeley, 'bullocks' *leah*'), dairy products (Stockton, 'enclosure at a dairy hamlet') and salt (Wychurch, 'valley at a *wic*'). *Source*: after N. Higham, *The Origins of Cheshire* (1993), fig. 5.2.

been different, but as we can observe it in Anglo-Saxon England the multiple estate seems to represent a stage in the evolution of extensive lordship. It may have arisen when power to command goods and service from wide areas became more organized and systematized as these larger areas fragmented into smaller landholdings. Its structure was not only appropriate to the lands of great powers like the Welsh kings. Analyses of some quite small 'estates', even single manors, of which Chapter 9 contains a handful of examples, show that they have the same structure in miniature. Fig. 3 shows a small such estate in Northamptonshire reconstructed by D. Hall. Breaking down estates into their component parts and attempting some explanation of how and when these components came into existence brings out the extent to which they were functional responses to economic

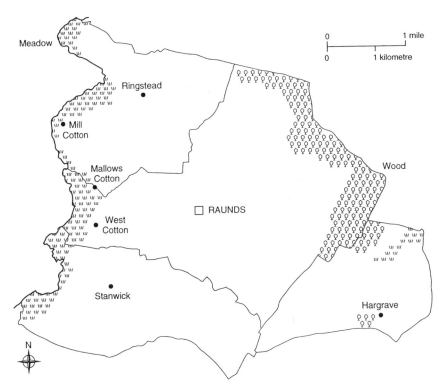

Figure 3   The manor of Raunds, Northamptonshire, a small multiple estate consisting of Raunds plus the three neighbouring hamlets of Stanwick, Hargrave and Ringstead, and small settlements at West Cotton, Mallows Cotton and Mill Cotton. *Source*: after D. Hall, 'The late Saxon countryside: villages and their fields' in *Anglo-Saxon Settlements*, ed. D. Hooke (1988), 99–122, fig. 5.4.

necessities, responses which developed over time. One of these components, its 'inland', was at the heart of the estate, and that is where we will begin.

2 Inland

The previous chapter indicated the importance of large-scale organization of the countryside, whether into *scirs*, royal circuits or multiple estates, to provide for the needs of powerful and prestigious consumers. When we come to examine more closely the working of early estates we find that most of what we know has to do with those in the hands of major minsters. While the law codes provide us with some invaluable information about the provisioning of kings, we know very little about the lands of the early aristocracy. This may have produced an important bias, leading to the ecclesiastical estate becoming taken as a model for large estates generally. Yet the church's lands may not have been typical, for ownership might well have influenced organization. The most obvious contrast is that between religious communities and kings. Regular supplies for the table were a basic need of any large household. But the needs of the church differed from those of the king. While the kings of Wessex were often on the move the Winchester clergy stayed in one place and needed supplies delivered to Winchester from their properties. Bishops, who could travel round their dioceses and should do so, according to Bede, who stressed their pastoral role, perhaps had a different supply system from that of the minster clergy.[1] Among lay lords the size of the estate and the political authority and organizational powers of its owner also made a difference. Food 'farms', as regular renders came to be called, needed considerable organization, as well as the authority to ensure that goods were regularly delivered in the right quantities and of good enough quality. A king might command a supply of perishable foods: Ine's subjects were obliged to supply him with bread and ale.[2] To ensure regular deliveries of these staple commodities in a usable condition from a far-flung estate must have required a more efficient delivery network than most small lords could command.

However, although they may not be representative of estates as a whole, minsters, their lands and resources must nevertheless, from their superior documentation, be our starting point. And in their

---

1. A.W. Haddan and W. Stubbs, eds, *Councils and Ecclesiastical Documents Relating to Great Britain and Ireland* (4 vols, 1871), 314–25 (letter of Bede to Egbert) at 316.
2. Ine 70.1: Liebermann, I, 118–19.

essential relationship to the primary producers the minsters as consumers were like other major lords: they needed to command regular supplies of foodstuffs. It was this need that brought into being an essential element in their estates: a directly exploited core area. These early core areas represented a transition between an economy based purely on tribute and the manorial system.[3] They came to be called the 'inland' of estates, and this term is so useful that it will be used throughout.

Inland is an entity crucial to the understanding of the rural social structure of early England. As will appear, it took many forms: the diversity and development and internal arrangements of these forms is a major theme of this book. It is not a simple geographical term, but one deeply connected with landholding. Its essential – and presumably its earliest – meaning is 'inner estate'.[4] But inland was not simply part of an estate, it was an area which had particular functions and which was recognized as privileged, in the sense of being exempt from a wide range of public service and eventually from the payment of geld. Such areas, often enclosed or marked by long-enduring boundaries, survived, although often in a vestigial form, to appear as geld-exempt areas in Domesday Book, and the last part of this chapter outlines the picture we get of them from Domesday. First we need to explore their origins. Some may be early indeed, raising the possibility of continuities from the British church.

Monastic sites

The 'Celtic' monastic foundations in early post-Roman Britain depended for their survival on efficient farming and land management. J. Morris drew attention to the fact that 'the accounts of the first monks are shot through with a conscious enthusiasm for pioneering agriculture', and while some of these stories are late fabrications written to enhance the prestige of the house to which they were related, it does seem true that part of the process of founding a monastery in sixth-century Wales, Ireland and Brittany was to enclose a substantial area around the monastic site within which intensive agriculture was carried on. The monks often used new techniques like corn driers and grew new crops which made them an object of wonder, and enclosed their fields with stone walls which made them a target for resentment by the local peasantry. The Irish monks introduced water-mills to their lands in the west country and Brittany, experimented with new imported fruits and improved plough teams. St Congar, reputedly the founder of a minster at Congresbury, Somerset, had the

---

3. C. Wickham, 'The other transition: from the ancient world to feudalism', *Past and Present* 103 (May 1984), 3–36 at 31–2 and n. 34.; F.M. Stenton, *Anglo-Saxon England* (1947), 477 and n. 1.
4. Bosworth and Toller, s.v. *land* III.4.

reputation of a pioneer of land reclamation: 'places covered with water and reeds, which surrounded his dwelling and were at that time no use to man, were converted into fields most suitable for reclamation, and into flowering meadows'.[5] St Illtyd is said to have invented a new ploughing technique, using an improved form of plough which was still known by his name in nineteenth-century Wales.[6] Such technological 'culture-bearers' were not simply a hagiographical *topos*: the monastic site at Whithorn, which has strong archaeological links with Ireland, shows that 'the mouldboard plough was used by the original British community and ... was potentially available elsewhere in the Celtic west' at a time when the mouldboard was not apparently known in Anglo-Saxon England. The ploughs used had their wooden parts protected by 'plough-pebbles', a simple but effective piece of technology which may have been imported from Ireland and is also found on other British sites. Intensive cultivation with cross-ploughing was possible with these ploughs and from the earliest stages of cultivation at Whithorn, from the sixth century, the land was improved by manuring.[7] Much of the labour on the lands of the British church was evidently done by the monks themselves. The 2,100 'monks of Bangor in Wales, who according to Bede 'were all accustomed to live by their own labour' had first-hand knowledge of farming.[8]

However, monasteries where the monastic ideals of poverty and labour held sway may have co-existed with others which were run much more on the lines of the estates of traditional Romano-British landlords. This after all was the milieu of the first generation of British church founders, who, like Patrick, Samson and David, came from landowning families with slaves or servile tenants. One of the assets of the better-off British church was a tied labour force. Some were slaves, whether born unfree or reduced to servitude as a punishment, given as pious gifts. Monasteries may also have been able to call on a group of bond tenants for labour and food rents, and although the existence of such a group before the eleventh century is not attested by any very firm evidence, W. Davies believes that church lands in Wales were worked by 'a sort of hereditary colonate' and T. Charles-Edwards points out that Irish 'monks' may often have been in fact 'essentially peasants normally owing food renders to the church', and Bangor's large number of monks may have included people like this.[9]

5. J. Morris, *The Age of Arthur* (3 vols, 1977), III, 432ff. at 432, 458–9; S. Rippon, 'Medieval wetland reclamation in Somerset' in *The Medieval Landscape of Wessex*, ed. M. Aston and C. Lewis (1994), 239–53 at 244.
6. F. Arnold–Forster, *Studies in Church Dedications* (3 vols, 1899), II, 178.
7. P.H. Hill and K. Kucharski, 'Early medieval ploughing at Whithorn and chronology of plough pebbles', *Trans. Dumfriesshire and Galloway Natural History and Antiquarian Society*, 3rd series 65 (1990), 73–83.
8. *HE*, II.2.
9. T. Charles-Edwards, 'The pastoral role of the church in the early Irish laws' in *Pastoral Care before the Parish*, ed. J. Blair and R. Sharpe (1992), 63–80 at 67; H. Price, 'Ecclesiastical wealth in early medieval Wales' in *The Early Church in Wales and the West* ed. N. Edwards and A. Lane (1992), 22–32 at 28–9; W.

How much of the organization of the British church survived into Anglo-Saxon England? P. Hase has recently argued that in areas of the west country such as Dorset, Somerset, Devon and Cornwall, where Saxon conquest took place after the West Saxon kings had become Christian, the monastic foundations of the fifth and sixth century were well embedded and the West Saxons 'are likely to have taken over districts with a residential church of some vigour'.[10] The aristocratic milieu of British Christianity is evoked by S.M. Pearce as a context for some possible links. She suggests that there were continuities between the villa estates of Christian Romano-British aristocratic families and early Anglo-Saxon churches: Shaftesbury and Iwerne, Dorset, Cheddar, Somerset and Deerhurst, Gloucestershire are among her examples. She sees the British church in this area as persisting under Saxon occupation in the seventh century. The primary attraction of the villa sites chosen seems to have been the existence of a cemetery which could be used, but Pearce thinks that it is possible that some early minsters in the west country founded on or near the sites of Roman villas also took over their albeit 'somewhat run-down estates', whose boundaries remained intact.[11] If the villas with cemeteries were also estate centres, it is tempting to suggest that the new minsters also took over the labour of a tied peasantry or slave force at work there, but there is no evidence that would establish this. Certainly the evidence, if not for continuity, at least for the Anglo-Saxon church building on an existing British foundation, is nearly all from western England. It has been suggested that both Sherborne and Glastonbury were early Anglo-Saxon foundations on British monastic sites, so their lands deserve as close an examination as the documentation will allow.

Sherborne[12]

Medieval tradition at Sherborne Abbey preserved a story that Cenwalh, king of Wessex (643–74) had given it 100 hides at *'Lanprobi'*

---

contd.
>Davies, *An Early Welsh Microcosm: studies in the Llandaff charters* (1978), 47; W. Davies, *Wales in the Early Middle Ages* (1982), 164–6.

10. P. Hase, 'The church in the Wessex heartlands' in *Medieval Landscape of Wessex*, ed. Aston and Lewis, 47–81 at 51.
11. S.M. Pearce, 'Estates and church sites in Dorset and Gloucestershire: the emergence of a Christian society', in *The Early Church in Western Britain and Ireland: studies presented to C.A. Ralegh Radford*, ed. S.M. Pearce, BAR British Series 102 (1982), 117–37. H.P.R. Finberg, 'Roman and Saxon Withington' in his *Lucerna: studies of some problems in the early history of England* (1964), 21–65, and R.J. Faith, 'Tidenham, Gloucestershire, and the origins of the manor in England', *Landscape History* 16 (1994), 39–51 at 40–1, propose similar continuities.
12. L. Keen, 'The towns of Dorset' in *Anglo-Saxon Towns in Southern England*, ed. J. Haslam (1984), 203–47 at 208–12, 216–21, 230–1, 238; H.P.R.Finberg,

at the foundation of the West Saxon minster.[13] It seems that what he gave may have been the endowment, or part of the endowment, of a much older institution. *'Lanprobi'* combines the personal name Probus, a Celtic saint whose cult was restricted to Dorset and Cornwall, with the element *lan*, which in the context of Celtic Christianity means a church or religious community within some kind of enclosed and/or cleared space.[14] Probus's church itself, it is now thought, was to the east of the present town of Sherborne.[15] Lanprobus already had a long history as a centre of some importance. There was a major Romano-British settlement there, and K. Barker has made out a case for the surrounding Yeo valley parishes being part of a large estate centred on Sherborne.[16] J. Campbell, too, sees it as the centre of a large multiple estate, whose existence influenced the decision to establish the West Saxon see at Sherborne in 705.[17] If the Cenwalh story is correct – and it perhaps originated in an attempt to establish an ancient provenance for Sherborne's possessions – then Lanprobus was likely to have still been an active British church at the time when Cenwalh was pushing the hegemony of Wessex westward. Keen's view is that 'the British church continued to function under Saxon government', and Cenwalh may have transferred Lanprobus's land and its cultivators, now part of the possessions of the kings of Wessex, to the new foundation as a going concern.

If it was a going concern, can it have continued to be organized in much the same way? The topography of early medieval Sherborne is thoroughly debated ground but some kind of defined central core area seems to have had a long history there. Fig. 4 shows the principal features through which this has been reconstructed by L. Keen. This history has to be traced retrospectively. When the West Saxon see was established in 705 its church was built on a new site in what is now Sherborne town. Later evidence of the internal organization of the church's land shows that it contained an area known as its 'stocland' or 'stokland'. A charter of Ethelred of 998, sanctioning the refoundation of the minster, states that there were in Sherborne 'a hundred *agelli* in

---

contd.

    'Sherborne, Glastonbury, and the expansion of Wessex' in *Lucerna*, 95–115; M.A. O'Donovan, ed., *The Charters of Sherborne* (1988), app. 2, 83–8; D. Hinton, 'The topography of Sherborne: early Christian?', *Antiquity* 55 (1981), 222–3; K. Barker, 'Sherborne in Dorset: an early ecclesiastical settlement and its estate', *ASSAH* 3, (1984), 1–33. Barker's reconstruction of the estate has been questioned by C.C. Thornton, 'The demesne of Rimpton 938 to 1412, a study in economic development' (Ph.D. thesis, University of Leicester, 1988) at 34–47.

13. BL MS Cotton Faustina Aii, fo 24; W. Dugdale, *Monasticon anglicanum* (6 vols, 1817–30), I, 337.
14. Arnold-Forster, *Dedications*, II, 542; Keen, 'Towns', 209–10.
15. Keen, 'Towns', fig. 73 at 217.
16. *Ibid.*; Barker, 'Sherborne'.
17. J. Campbell, 'The church in Anglo-Saxon towns' in his *Essays in Anglo-Saxon History* (1986), 139–54 at 140.

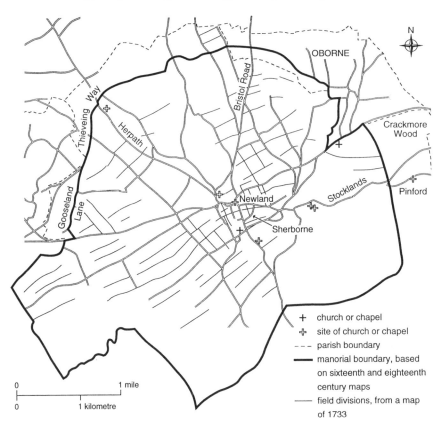

Figure 4   The manor of Sherborne, Dorset. The track which forms part of the manorial boundary may have originated in Wulfsige's enclosure of the monastic *praedium* 'with hedges and ditches'. *Source*: after K. Barker, 'Sherborne in Dorset: an early ecclesiastical settlement and its estate', *ASSAH* 3 (1984), 1–33, and L. Keen, 'The towns of Dorset', in *Anglo-Saxon Towns in Southern England*, ed. J. Haslam (1984), 203–47, fig. 73 at 217.

a place called Stockland'. Stockland has been identified as the area around the British church, and in what may have been a much-diminished form it survives in fourteenth-century field names.[18] 'Stockland' seems to have been a distinct category of land, not confined to Sherborne. Many 'Stockland' place-names take their first element from OE *stoc*. Two meanings are suggested for this word by the most recent experts. One is 'monastery, cell' and the other 'cattle-farm, dairy-farm'. An earlier suggestion was 'a place fenced in'.[19]

18.   Dugdale, *Monasticon*, I, 337 no. 2; S 895; Keen, 'Towns', 211–12.
19.   Bosworth and Toller; Ekwall, *English Place-Names* s.v. *stoc*.

Ekwall points out that places with this element in their names are often found linked to neighbouring villages; Chardstock with nearby Chard is a good example of such a linkage. Milton Abbey in Dorset had a manor called Stockland which was assigned to supply the monks with food and clothes.[20] Stocklands generically were inhabited land, not simply farmland. Possibly the 'hundred *agelli*' or small plots of land in Stockland were the fields or plots of the Stockland tenants, and even of their predecessors the 'monk-tenants' of Lanprobus. What may be their relics are found in the traces of a grid of small rectangular fields in and near Sherborne surviving in the field boundaries of the eighteenth century.[21] If this interpretation seems to stretch the evidence beyond what it will safely bear, it should be seen in the context of the fact that a large population of dependent smallholders, closely associated with an ecclesiastical community and physically clustered around it, is exactly what we find in later monastic centres. Stockland may even be a term which implied something about its inhabitants: 'stockikinde' land is found contrasted with distinctively free 'gavolkinde' land in a twelfth-century description of the lands of Bilsington Priory, Kent.[22]

When Bishop Wulfsige refounded the minster at Sherborne between 992 and 1001 and installed a community of monks he enclosed an area known as the *praedium* of the monastery 'with hedges and ditches'. Was the *praedium* simply the enclosure comprising the buildings of the minster? Or was it the larger area, the Stockland described above?[23] Ethelred's charter, which gives us this information, emphasizes that Wulfsige marked out the boundary of an area of agricultural land because of disputes and incursions in a period of rural shortages and 'growing greed' – in other words there was local pressure on agricultural land and it would be a wise move for the minster to define and protect its territory with a substantial barrier. A long curving track encloses an area around Sherborne, delineating an area slightly smaller than the present parish. It does not correspond with the parish boundaries but was sufficiently revered as a boundary to be part of a sixteenth-century processional route. Possibly this marks the edge of the *praedium* so carefully ring-fenced by Wulfsige.[24] The Stockland was included within the *praedium* and, although the term is

---

20. *DB* I, 77a, 78b. Stockland, Devon already had its name by 934, the date of its grant to Milton Abbey recorded in S 391, but Robertson, *Charters*, 300–4, and Sawyer consider this charter late and spurious. The small soke of Gimingham, Norfolk, had in the later middle ages 'stokeland' at an area formerly known as Oldbereye: C. Hoare, *The History of an East Anglian Soke: studies in the original documents* (1918), 178, 181.
21. Keen, 'Towns', fig. 73 and 238, dates this as mid–Saxon.
22. *Cartulary and Terrier of the Priory of Bilsington*, ed. N. Neilson, British Academy Records of the Social and Economic History of England and Wales 7 (1928).
23. J. Blair, 'Anglo–Saxon minsters, a topographical review' in *Pastoral Care Before the Parish*, ed. Blair and Sharpe, 226–66 at 233; Barker, 'Sherborne', claims to find a ditched enclosure around the abbey site.
24. Keen, 'Towns', 221.

not used in any of the Sherborne documents, I think it is fair to consider the *praedium*, with Stockland within it, as Sherborne's inland.

The minster estate swelled as kings added on more land from the royal estate, but the identity of its core area was preserved. The 'inner–outer' structure of Sherborne's lands shows up in Domesday Book. A substantial area of Sherborne was exempt from geld and 'had never been divided into hides': sixteen ploughlands held by the bishop of Salisbury in demesne and nine and a half held by the monks in demesne.[25] Tax-exempt status is characteristic of monastic and royal inlands, and it is discussed more fully below in the context of the tax system. If, as is probable, Sherborne's exempt land was identical with the area later known as the 'in-hundred' it may represent a relic of the Saxon church's seventh-century endowment and possibly the land that supported the monks of the British church.[26] By the fourteenth century Sherborne's stockland was part of the abbey's Barton Farm and was mostly down to grass.[27] Thus the abbey's demesne land had a long history: evolving from the inland of the Saxon bishops and their successors, which in turn had been the land near the British church, and that in turn part of a Romano-British prestigious centre.

There are Cornish parallels for such an enclosed area of an estate, and to wall, hedge or fence it was certainly a practice in the Cornish church. In Cornwall both early churches and secular settlements have the element *lann* in their names: the term originally meant simply 'enclosure'. Churches with this element were 'sites of importance from their foundation', frequently on favourable valley-bottom sites, with access to navigable waters and prime natural harbours. One of their features is that a number have an outer enclosure or enclosures. A. Preston-Jones has mapped three of these outer boundaries and from her maps it can be seen that at Mabe, St Mawgan and Padstow they enclose a D-shaped area about 500 metres across from the respective churches and their related settlement. Padstow had a second boundary as well, yet another 500 metres out from the first (Fig. 5). The fourteenth-century life of St Petroc tells us that he 'surrounded the limits of his lands with very long ditches dug deep like valleys, the ruins of which remain to this day' and can still be traced. Wulfsige would have been doing just the same thing.

There is some speculation as to whether these enclosed areas around Cornish churches – too large to be simply the area occupied by the church and its burial ground – were 'the ... enclosed agricultural land about the settlement' or sanctuaries. Athelstan's gift to St Buryan of land 'in seven places' was encompassed by two separate boundaries. Within one was the area which included the entire village around the

---

25. *DB* I, 77a.
26. For the contrast between the in-hundred and the out-hundred see Keen, 'Towns', 218–21 and fig. 74 at 219.
27. Dugdale, *Monasticon*, I, 335.

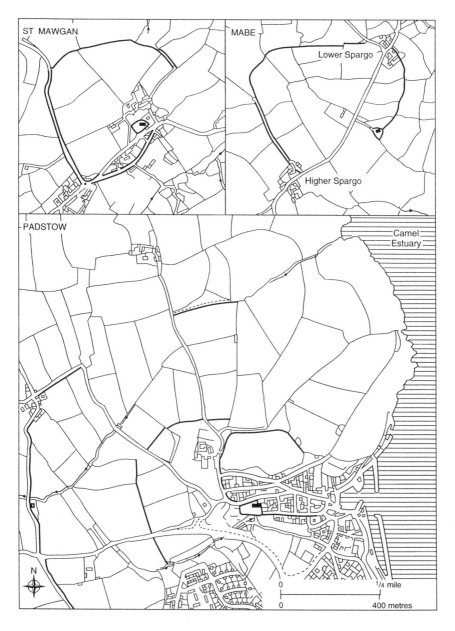

Figure 5 Monastic enclosures at St Mawgan, Mabe and Padstow, Cornwall. *Source*: after A. Preston-Jones, 'Decoding Cornish church-yards' in *The Early Church in Wales and the West*, ed. N. Edwards and A. Lane (1992), 104–24, fig. 11.11 at 121.

church. This was 'a privileged sanctuary'.[28] If we do not insist too heavily on the difference between a 'sanctuary' and an enclosed area, considered particularly the possession of the church and devoted to its support, privileged by exemptions from taxation, then we may see in these Cornish examples much the same kind of enclosed inland as emerges from the evidence elsewhere. Its privileged status was recognized by tax exemption recorded in Domesday Book: the lands of St Buryan, like those of many Cornish churches with Celtic dedications, 'never paid geld' or 'only paid geld to the saint'.[29]

Glastonbury

At Glastonbury we find several of the same features as at Sherborne: a donation from Cenwalh, a tradition of continuity with a British church, an inner area marked off by a boundary treated with great respect by local people, a tax-exempt area in Domesday Book. What we do not yet have is the body of topographical analysis which has begun to illuminate Sherborne. While the existence, still less the actual position, of the Celtic church at Glastonbury is not established, it is agreed that the Saxon monastery established there in the late seventh century was endowed with lands which were already part of major high status post-Roman estates of the multiple or federated type. M. Costen portrays the Saxon 'conquest' of Somerset as a matter of accommodation to and adaptation of these existing structures rather than a wholesale remodelling of society, so it is possible that Glastonbury, like Sherborne, was given an inland which was already the centre of such an estate.[30] However, little is known about its early endowment. Its first known grant was of six hides on Glastonbury island itself, and a slightly later one gave land at *Lantocal* or *Lantocay*, now Leigh in Street, on the Roman road leading south from the present town.[31] These charters are only known through post-Conquest summaries which the Glastonbury monks may simply have fabricated to provide an impressively early provenance for the landholdings of their house, but if so it was clever of them to have used such an archaic and Celtic form in the grant of *Lantocal*. This is the same kind of place-name as Lanprobus, and if it was a Celtic church its situation in relation to the site of the Saxon minster is much the same as Lanprobus church was

---

28. A. Preston-Jones, 'Decoding Cornish churchyards' in *The Early Church in Wales and the West*, ed. Edwards and Lane, 104–24 at 115–21, fig. 11.11, quotations at 115, 120; Athelstan's grant to St Buryan is BCS 785 (S 450).
29. W.L.D. Ravenhill, 'Cornwall' in *The Domesday Geography of South–West England*, ed. H.C. Darby and R.W. Finn (1967), 296–308.
30. M. Costen, *The Origins of Somerset* (1992), 64–5, 77–8, 82ff.
31. *De antiquitate glastoniensis ecclesie* by William of Malmesbury, printed by T. Hearne, ed., *Adami de Domerham historia de rebus gestis glastoniensibus* (2 vols, 1727) (S 1666); BCS 47 (S 1249); H.P.R. Finberg, *The Early Charters of Wessex* (1964), 49–50, nos. 356, 357, at 109–10.

to the Saxon minster at Sherborne. An early endowment which combined land near the minster site and an outlying area with connections with a British church may have been the embryo, added to by later donations, of the privileged area later known as Glastonbury abbey's 'Glaston twelve hides'. This was an inner area similar to the *praedium* at Sherborne, tax-exempt in Domesday, and marked by distinctive boundaries still visible in the sixteenth century.[32]

Episcopal sites

To the extent that the episcopal structure of late Roman Britain was part of the Romano-British polity it is likely to have shared in its collapse, and in the collapse of urban life. Nevertheless the British episcopate seems to have left its mark on the landscape of the west midlands. At Worcester, Gloucester and Lichfield S. Bassett has demonstrated continuities between the *parochia* of British Christian bishops and the territories of major early Anglo-Saxon churches.[33] Bassett proposes that Roman Gloucester had been 'an important political centre which controlled a substantial hinterland and was an episcopal see'. St Mary de Lode, Gloucester, is now seen as having originated in a British church, built on the remains of a large Romano-British courtyard house. It provides the link with the Anglo-Saxon church. In *c.* 679 Osric, king of the Hwicce, founded a minster at Gloucester dedicated to St Peter, giving it a large territory which may have included the whole hinterland of the Roman city, what one (rather suspect) charter calls 'the city with its territory' (*illam civitatem cum agro suo*), an area of 300 hides which became the three hundreds of Gloucester, Dudston and Kings Barton.[34] Soon afterwards, seemingly through the agency of the king's sister Cyneburh, the first abbess of the new foundation, the land was handed over to St Mary's, which remained the mother church of Gloucester and its hinterland. In the early tenth century a substantial part of St Mary's parish was carved out for the new royal foundation of St Oswald's, established next to the royal palace (also on a Roman site) at Kingsholm and closely

---

32. M. Aston, 'The towns of Somerset' in *Anglo-Saxon Towns in Southern England*, ed. Haslam, 167–247; N. Neilson, 'English manorial forms', *American Historical Review* 34 (1929), 725–39; S.C. Morland, 'Glaston Twelve Hides' in his *Glastonbury, Domesday and Related Studies* (1991); *DB* I, 90a.
33. S. Bassett, 'Church and diocese in the west midlands: the transition from British to Anglo–Saxon control', in *Pastoral Care Before the Parish*, ed. Blair and Sharpe, 13–40, at 26–9.
34. H.P.R. Finberg, 'The early history of Gloucester abbey' in his *Early Charters of the West Midlands* (1961), 153–66 at 158; C. Heighway, 'Anglo-Saxon Gloucester, c680–1066', in *VCH Gloucestershire*, IV (1988), 5–12; N.M. Herbert, 'Medieval Gloucester', *ibid.* 13–22; Hundreds: C. Heighway, 'Saxon Gloucester' in *Anglo-Saxon Towns in Southern England*, ed. Haslam, 359–83 at 375 and n. 24.

associated with it.[35] St Peter's, the earlier church, had no parish of its
own and it was not until the eleventh century that it received lands and
eventually eclipsed St Mary's in importance, reversing their earlier
relationship.[36]

The continuities of church life and church landholding at Gloucester
encourage the search for any signs of the continuity found at
Sherborne between the early territory of the British church, the
geld-free inland of the Saxon minster, and the barton or home farm of
the later monastery. We may be able to discern vestiges of the inner
core of the inland of St Mary's in the concentration of its property
around the church revealed in the post-Conquest town. By the late
eleventh century Gloucester was once again a thriving and important
urban and royal centre. The 'Wood Barton' there is very unlikely to
have been established in a built-up area, so the name may perpetuate
an early barton.[37] Confusingly, St Mary's lands are entered in
Domesday Book as the property of St Peter's, and St Mary's was by
this time simply the 'church of the abbey demesne'. But what had
surely been St Mary's inland appears as the abbey's manor of Abbots
Barton, an area 'which was always quit of geld and all royal service'.
This was an extensive manor with 'members' in the outlying parishes
of Barnwood, Tuffley and Morwents End, a large hidage (23 3/4 hides)
and nine plough teams at work on the demesne arable.[38]

The church of St Helen, Worcester, had as its parish a 'discrete
territory around the former Roman city which had been 'the focus of a
British *provincia*' and 'all the hallmarks of ... the mother-church in the
Celtic system ... which held pastoral responsibilities for a wide but
defined area'. St Michael's, Lichfield, was possibly the seat of a British
bishop and already in the seventh century the centre of a vast multiple
estate. They are two further examples of rich British churches which
were the antecedents of well-endowed Saxon minsters, but the
topographical research has not yet been undertaken which might
reveal whether there were continuing minster inlands at Worcester
and Lichfield.[39] Still in Mercia, the 'core estates' of Evesham Abbey
were 'originally a single estate granted to the abbey in the early 8th
century, which may itself have been made up from a nucleus of one or

---

35. Heighway, 'Saxon Gloucester', 371–5.
36. Bassett, 'Church and diocese', 27–8; Heighway, 'Saxon Gloucester', 375.
37. Herbert, 'Medieval Gloucester', 66. Bartons are discussed at pp. 36–8 below.
38. *DB* I, 165c; Heighway, 'Saxon Gloucester', 375; Finberg, *Early Charters of the West Midlands*, 41 for a charter of 777 x 790 granting 120 hides outside the city of Gloucester noted in the Gloucester cartulary as 'where Barton now is'.
39. Worcester: Bassett, 'Church and diocese', 26; 'Churches in Worcester before and after the conversion of the Anglo-Saxons', *Antiquaries Journal* 69 (1989), 225–56 at 243, 233–5; C.J. Bond, 'Church and parish in Norman Worcestershire' in *Minsters and Parish Churches: the local church in transition 950–1200*, ed. J. Blair, Oxford University Committee for Archaeology Monograph 17 (1988), 119–58 at 130. Lichfield: Bassett, 'Church and diocese', 29–35.

more estates of Roman origin'. The entire town of Evesham was free of geld by 1086 and may represent the abbey's inland.[40]

The examples discussed so far were important landholdings of major British churches or sees. What of the endowments of smaller churches? The dedication of the church at Warrington, Lancashire, to the sixth-century St Elphin, an aristocrat from the highly educated circle of St Illtyd, and its high status as the head of a hundred with a geld-free core of land in Domesday Book, may indicate one example among many of surviving small British minsters, or it may be a rare example of a rare category.[41] In this context it would be of great interest to know more about the 'holy places in divers regions which the clergy of the Britons deserted' in their flight from the advancing Anglian forces in Northumbria and which early in the seventh century came into the possession of the Northumbrian church.[42] The land along the Ribble (*iuxta Rippel*) granted to Wilfrid's minster at Ripon was part of this windfall: it may have been 'a small British kingdom or lordship'.[43] Ripon became the centre of Wilfrid's Northumbrian diocese. Bede describes the church there as 'a minster of forty hides' (*monasterium XL familiarum*) and Wilfrid secured its liberties by papal privilege.[44] We do not know the origins of a well-defined central area at Ripon, known as 'St Wilfrid's League', but it is tempting to see it as the inland of the church. It appears in Domesday Book as the property of Wilfrid's successors, the archbishop and canons of York. It was an area exempt from geld, a manor with its own demesne and tenant land, and the centre of a large complex estate to which belonged fourteen separate berewicks.[45] Like Sherborne and Glastonbury, Ripon's privileged area was marked by a respected boundary, 'anciently laid down and marked out by watercourses, ditches and great stones', believed to date from the time of St Wilfrid and said in late fifteenth-century Ripon to have been 'continuously known and used by us' ever since.[46]

Probably a note of caution is in order here, reminding us that it would be perfectly possible for a Saxon minster at any date to develop its own inland from scratch, with no continuities from older landholdings. Wulfred, archbishop of Canterbury (805–32) provides

---

40. Bond, 'Church and parish', 133; H.B. Clarke, 'The early surveys of Evesham Abbey: an investigation into the problem of continuity in Anglo–Norman England' (Ph.D. thesis, University of Birmingham, 1978), 379–81.
41. Arnold-Forster, *Dedications*, II, 182–4; *DB* I, 269b. I am grateful to Dr J. Blair for information on St Elphin's as a minster.
42. *Eddius (alias Stephanus), Life of Bishop Wilfrid*, ed. B. Colgrave (1927), xvii.
43. D. Kenyon, *The Origins of Lancashire* (1991), 73–4.
44. *HE* III, 25; Stenton, *Anglo-Saxon England*, 136; M. Roper, 'Wilfrid's landholdings in Northumbria' in *Saint Wilfrid at Hexham*, ed. D.P. Kirby (1974), 61–79.
45. *DB* I, 303c; D.M. Palliser, 'An introduction to the Yorkshire Domesday' in *The Yorkshire Domesday* (1992), 1–38 at 28.
46. BL Add MS 37770, fo. 362. For Ripon's claims to privileged status see p. 38 below.

one example. Part of his estate management policy was to build up, by purchase and exchange, pieces of land – some probably individual farms – and consolidate them into larger units. He made one such accumulation at Eastry, where there was a 'mother church', and had it enclosed by a boundary hedge.[47] This is just what Wulfsige is said to have done at Sherborne, and it may well have been part of good late Anglo-Saxon estate management to put a ring fence around the inland. Examples like this are a salutary warning against *assuming* continuities between the estates of an early British church and the inland of an Anglo-Saxon minster.

If we turn to minsters outside the west country, the north-west and the west midlands we move outside the area where there are slim indications of continuity between British and Anglo-Saxon church lands to those where there are virtually none. This may be a problem of evidence, rather than a sign that continuity was absent. Nor is it to say that Romano-British land use did not affect early minster estates. Quite the reverse. To take Kent: A. Everitt shows that the majority of early minsters here were founded in 'seminal settlements ... where the evidence for Romano-Jutish continuity is especially apparent'.[48] But the link is with high status sites (which may well have had churches), taken over by kings, out of whose territories they endowed minsters. This endowment from the fisc, rather than the continuation of British churches as such, is where the future of minster endowment lay.

That being so, we need now to examine whether the structure of early royal estates influenced the minsters endowed from them. Here the main elements of Jones's multiple estate are a useful framework: a core area, or several such, and a collection of outlying holdings. Royal patronage and endowment by Oswiu of Northumbria, in thanks for victory in battle in 654, shows a likely pattern, although no kind of continuous history exists to confirm it. Oswiu gave twelve 'small properties' on which to found minsters, six in Deira and six in Bernicia, each of ten hides. The nunneries founded with this endowment included Hartlepool and Whitby.[49] Whitby was the administrative centre of an extensive estate in the eleventh century, and though the minster itself was in ruins, the church of St Mary at Whitby, which may have been in some way its successor, was the ecclesiastical centre for a large area with at least six settlements. This centre-plus-dependencies structure may have been built into its early endowment.[50]

Bede's history of his own monastery at Jarrow and its companion at Wearmouth contains a good description of an early monastic estate. It

47. N.P. Brooks, *The Early History of the Church at Canterbury: Christ Church from 597 to 1066* (1984), 138.
48. A. Everitt, *Continuity and Colonization: the evolution of Kentish settlement* (1986), 192–3.
49. *HE* III, 24.
50. W.E. Kapelle, *The Norman Conquest of the North: a region and its transformation 1000–1135* (1979), 79; *DB* I, 305a.

combined both these elements, centre and scattered property. The monastery at Wearmouth was built in 674 and Egfrid king of Northumbria gave the founder-abbot Benedict Biscop 'from his personal property an area of land comprising seventy hides'. In 682 a second, smaller, monastery was founded, at Jarrow, for which Egfrid gave 40 hides, all free (as the earlier donations are likely to have been) from military service.[51] We do not know exactly where any of these properties were, but it is likely that the gifts to Wearmouth and Jarrow were, like those to Hartlepool and Whitby, an entire area containing scattered 'small properties' rather than a block of land. Other early minsters had similarly dispersed properties. The scattered donations of Mildburg to Wenlock in Shropshire, in all consisting of 'sixty three hides in diverse places', were made up of properties as small as three or four hides.[52] The amount of agricultural surplus that three or four hides could provide was very small – a sizeable community would need a large accumulation of these small units. Collecting rents or renders from an estate like this in a region of scattered upland farmsteads could pose problems of management.

By contrast with the collections of separate properties given to the Northumbrian monasteries, a minster estate might consist of an entire *regio* already enclosed by an ancient boundary well known locally. The '*villa* with the surrounding region' given to Wilfrid's minster at Hexham may have consisted of the entire *scir* of 'Hexhamshire' with the *villa* as its centre.[53] The earliest endowment of Ely was thought by Ely's medieval (though not by its modern) historian to have been a region which had been an Anglian princess's dowry.[54] Frithuric's endowment of Chertsey, Surrey, was a recognizable area which corresponded to the later Godley hundred and had as boundaries the Thames, the land of the *Sunningas* people, and an ancient dyke called *Fullingadic*.[55] Within such *regiones* with their recognized perimeters there might be large blocks of land, but within these blocks there are likely to have been dispersed settlements. Cædwalla of Wessex endowed Eorkenwald's minster at Barking with an estate in Surrey which comprised three contiguous blocks of land along the Thames, the later parishes of Battersea, Wandsworth and Putney. Œthelred, a member of the East Saxon royal family, gave 40 hides for the new nunnery near the end of the seventh century. This estate was enclosed by a boundary, and comprised land at four separate settlements, and an area of cleared woodland.[56] Royal lands given to found minsters in

---

51. *Historia abbatum auctore Baeda* in *Venerabilis Baedae opera historica*, ed. C. Plummer (1896), 367–8, 370.
52. Finberg, *Early Charters of the West Midlands*, 204–6.
53. M. Roper, 'The donation of Hexham' in *Saint Wilfrid at Hexham*, ed. Kirby, 169–71.
54. E. Miller, *The Abbey and Bishopric of Ely: the social history of an ecclesiastical estate from the tenth to the early fourteenth century* (1951), 8–15.
55. BCS 34 (S 1165); J. Blair, *Early Medieval Surrey: landholding, church and settlement before 1300* (1991), 14, 25.

Derbyshire and Nottinghamshire in the seventh century survived in the form of the *parochia* of the minster, generally in contiguous blocks of land which later became separate parishes. Nevertheless, within these large blocks of territory dispersed settlement was still the predominant pattern.[57]

While bounded by a recognized perimeter, a property may effectively have consisted of an 'archipelago' of rights to tribute from only *some* of the settlements within that area. An estate at Bexhill, Sussex, was purportedly given by Offa of Mercia in 772 to Bishop Oswald of Chichester to found a minster. There are many features of the charter which make this date impossible, and the Old English clauses describing the land involved may date from the tenth or eleventh century when it was becoming the rule to define landholdings in more detail. This means that although we cannot be sure that Bexhill's lands looked like this as early as the eighth century, they had acquired their structure by about 1000.[58] The land given by Offa had two quite distinct elements. There were eight hides of *inland* defined by a boundary containing ancient boundary features, an 'old boundary ditch (or dyke)' and 'the boundary' which may have outlined an existing unit. This area is called 'the inland of the *Bæxwarena*', the 'Bexhill people'. This raises the possibility that the Bexley inland represented the land of a primary settlement, which had been diverted to support first the kings of Sussex and then the community of an early minster. There were 20 hides of *gavolland* or *utland* in nine outlying settlements. Fig. 6 shows the division between the two components of the Bexhill estate. The early church at Bexhill was probably not on the site of the present parish church, but near the area of the inland. This minster did not survive, its land being taken over by Selsey, and no more is heard of it, but it has left us some very valuable information about the topography and size of an early inland, which can be mapped.[59]

Kings gave valuable assets in the form of grazing rights, fisheries and woodland. The endowment of the minster, probably a double house, founded at Lyminge, Kent, by Ethelburga, daughter of Ethelbert of Kent (d. 647), shows what a mixed 'portfolio' a royal foundation could accumulate. The minster was founded at the centre of a royal

---

56. BCS 82 (S 1248); BCS 81 (S 1171); C.R. Hart, *The Early Charters of Eastern England* (1966), 117–45, places identified at 144–5, 130–1.

57. D. Hadley, 'Danelaw society and institutions: east midlands phenomena' (Ph.D. thesis, University of Birmingham, 1992), ch. 5.

58. BCS 208 (S 108); Stenton, *Anglo-Saxon England*, 207 n. 4. I am grateful to Prof. N. Brooks for his help here.

59. E. Barker, 'Sussex Anglo-Saxon charters', *Sussex Archaeological Collections* 86 (1947), 42–101 no. 14, 90–5; J.E. Ray, 'The church of SS Peter and Paul, Bexhill', *ibid.* at 53 (1910), 61–108; P. Brandon, *The Sussex Landscape* (1974), 78–80 and fig. 6 at 80; M. Gardiner, 'Some lost Anglo-Saxon charters and the endowment of Hastings College', *Sussex Archaeological Collections* 127 (1989), 39–48 argues for a genuine charter as the basis for BCS 208 (S 108).

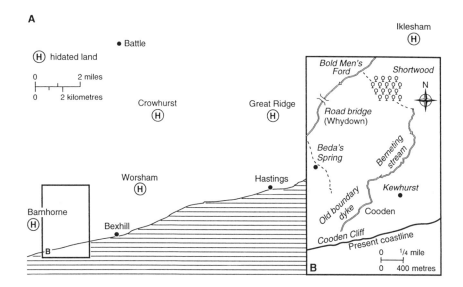

Figure 6 Bexhill, Sussex, from a charter of *c.* 1000:
A   Hidated land, marked H, at some of Bexhill's *utland* settlements.
Not all the settlements can be identified.
B   Elements (italicized) in the boundary of the inland.
Source: from BCS 208 (S 108) and E. Barker, 'Sussex Anglo-Saxon charters', *Sussex Arch. Collections* 86 (1947), no. 14, 90–5.

estate next to a royal 'court' where the kings of Kent enjoyed good hunting, and the church itself is on a site which has links with the Roman and Jutish past. Its lands were a block of traditionally recognized territory based on Lyminge itself, but it had in addition a salt works and the wood – now Saltwood – to provide its essential fuel, large tracts of grazing for sheep and oxen on Romney Marsh, fisheries, and land yielding iron pyrites which were worked on the minster site.[60] It must always have been difficult to secure regular deliveries from the dispersed farms and settlements of a large estate. It is worth remembering in this context that medieval English people took much of their cereal intake in the form of drink. This meant that some of the principal components of *feorm* were perishable, such as malt which figures in the renders recorded in wills and charters relating to twelve different estates. The earliest is the will of Abba, 833 × 839, directing that his beneficiary shall give 50 ambers of malt to the nuns of

---

60.   BCS 73 (S 12); BCS 97 (S 19); BCS 98 (S 21); BCS 148 (S 23); BCS 160 (S 24); BCS 289 (S 153); BCS 419 (S 286); Everitt, *Continuity and Colonization*, 191–3; Brooks, *Canterbury*, 183–4; R.C. Jenkins, *Some Account of the Church of St Mary and St Eadburg in Lyminge* (1859); R.C. Jenkins, *The Chartulary of the Monastery of Lyminge* (1889), 17–40.

Folkestone, along with bacon, cheese, loaves, sheep and an ox.[61] Malt had to come to Canterbury from Brabourne, Kent, a good day's journey away (fifteen miles) as part of a food rent given to St Augustine's by the will of Ealhburg in 844 × 864.[62] Beer or ale is another, perhaps even more perishable, commodity. Beer 'could be found in an Anglo-Saxon household at practically any time' and it is likely that it was a regular part of monastic diet. It figures in the earliest recorded food rent, in the laws of Ine (?694) and it is a very frequent component of food rents.[63] That grain was eaten by high-status people in the form of bread, rather than in the pottage which was so characteristic of medieval peasant diet, is suggested by the regularity with which loaves appear in food farms, sometimes two or three different qualities of loaf being specified, wheaten being preferred.[64]

In spite of the theological commitment to asceticism important in early monasticism, minsters were not founded in the wilderness but are likely to have been on the best land available, some on sites fit for kings.[65] The king retained some rights in land he had granted away, and a minster was likely to have holdings in places where the king had land too. Names deriving from 'bishop's *tun*' and 'king's *tun*', such as Bishton and Kingston, denote property devoted to the support of king and bishop, not necessarily their residences. They are common names and can be found near each other, as for instance at the bishop's *tun* and the king's *tun* at Tidenham, Gloucestershire, where both the kings of Wessex and the bishops of Hereford had had land in adjacent vills.[66]

The idea of enclosure, whether as barrier or boundary, is important in expressing the status of a prestigious site and many terms associated with inland have to do with boundaries. One is 'worthy'. A 'worthy', from OE *worthig* (an enclosure, a dwelling with surrounding land), is very often, particularly in the west country, simply a farmstead with its lands, but the many worthys associated with minsters and the fact that the place-name 'Worthy', as Gelling argues, often has the connotation of a headquarters or place of status, suggests something more imposing.[67] D. Hadley suggests Brixworth

---

61. D. Banham, 'The knowledge and use of food plants in Anglo-Saxon England' (Ph.D. thesis, University of Cambridge, 1990), ch. 5; Abba's will, *ibid.*, 92.
62. BCS 501 (S 1198).
63. Banham, 'Food plants', 102–6 (social importance of beer), 96–7 (spoiled beer), 97 (beer allowances in the Rule of Chrodegang), 81–4 (food rents).
64. *Ibid.*, 71–86.
65. Blair, 'Anglo-Saxon minsters', 230–1.
66. Kingston' names are interpreted as royal residences by P.H. Sawyer, 'The royal *tun* in pre-Conquest England' in *Ideal and Reality in Frankish and Anglo-Saxon Society*, ed. P. Wormald, D. Bullough and R. Collins (1983), 273–99 at 278 n. 30, or as simply implying royal ownership by M. Gelling, *Signposts to the Past* (1978), 184–5; J. Bourne, 'Kingston place-names: an interim report', *Journal of English Place-Name Soc.* 20 (1987–8), 10–37. Finberg, 'Charltons and Carltons', in his *Lucerna*, 144–60; Faith, 'Tidenham, Gloucestershire', 42.
67. Bosworth and Toller, s.v. *worth, worthig*; M. Gelling, *The Place-Names of Berkshire*, EPNS 49 (1973), 917, 943–4.

Figure 7 The manor of Chilcomb, Hampshire: its constituent vills at the time of Domesday Book. *Source*: after H.C. Darby, *Domesday England* (1986), fig. 3 at 17.

(Northamptonshire), Tamworth (Staffordshire), Wirksworth (Derby-shire), and the 'north worthy' at Derby as examples of minsters situated at the centres of important estates, and she suggests 'monastic enclosure' as one interpretation of the 'worthy' element.[68] Alternatively, we could intepret them as a particular category of enclosed home farm, one belonging to a prestigious ecclesiastical centre, to which it gave its name.

Worthys of this sort are found on the lands of the see of Winchester. The minster founded at Winchester in 662 by Cenwalh of Wessex became the seat of his bishops, the burial place of his people's kings and in some sense his people's capital. Cenwalh endowed it with land around the Roman city.[69] Within this area the old minster had a central core of land which became known as its 'worthy' and so too did the king. The New Minster and Nunnaminster were later to be endowed from this same block. The area still contains the villages of King's Worthy, Abbots Worthy, Headbourne Worthy and Martyr Worthy.[70] This entire territory – the inner core of the 'worthy' and the outer ring of hamlets – containing 28 modern parishes came to be known as the double hundred of Chilcomb, shown on Fig. 7. Although its component properties amounted to 95 hides, Chilcomb was rated in Domesday at only one – a valuable tax concession if not an outright exemption. It was described in a tenth-century document as 'land cultivated by the bishop and which *coloni* inhabit'.[71] It would be hard to better this as a description of inland.

By the Conquest this huge central holding had broken down into component manors with their own churches.[72] Domesday's description of these gives us an insight into the social structure of the inland. Some of the minster's land had been leased. (Headbourne) Worthy, was held by Ralph Mortimer in 1086 as the third heir of a lease for three lives. The manor bears the characteristic marks of a minster inland: tax-exemption and a dependent tenantry. It had a large tied workforce of 24 slaves and 27 bordars, but was rated at only one hide.[73]

Not all minster inlands have names by which they can be identified. The Worcestershire minster of Hanbury, founded in the seventh century with a handsome 50 hides, had an area of what seems to have been inland near the minster itself on steep Church Hill, but this does

---

68. Hadley, 'Danelaw society' 244–5, 246 n. 11.
69. BCS 1159, 1160 (S 818, 1820); P.H. Hase, 'The mother churches of Hampshire' in *Minsters and Parish Churches*, ed. Blair, 45–66 at 48.
70. BCS 389 (S 273) (Worthy); BCS 473 (S 309) (Headbourne Worthy). Both these charters are discredited, but the bounds of three hides at 'Worthy' may delineate a genuine unit: BCS 520 (S 340) (Martyr Worthy) BCS 652 (S 1491). H.P.R. Finberg, 'The Winchester cathedral clergy, their endowments and their diplomatic crimes' in his *Early Charters of Wessex*, 214–48 at 215–17.
71. H.C. Darby, *Domesday England* (1986 edn), fig. 3 at 17; BCS 620 (S 376); Finberg, 'Winchester cathedral clergy', in *Early Charters of Wessex*, 230–2 at 231; *DB* I, 41a.
72. Hase, 'Mother churches', 49.
73. *DB* I, 46d.

not seem to have had a distinctive name which has survived.[74] The existence of the inlands of many Anglo-Saxon minsters can only be deduced from Domesday evidence of geld-exemption – evidence which is discussed at the end of this chapter. More controversially, post-Conquest evidence of the social structure of minster estates can be shown to reflect the old inland/outland division – discussion of this too is reserved to a later section of this book.

Bede's account of the early monks at Jarrow shows that an intensively exploited inland was an essential part of the organization of early minsters. Their ambitious standards of building and provision of books, although owing much to Biscop's generous gifts, may also reflect the production of a marketable surplus. The Northumbrian monasteries were founded in the spirit of early monasticism which enjoined asceticism and manual work. Wearmouth and Jarrow soon had 600 monks between them: a large number of mouths to feed. Such a large number, in fact, that it raises the possibility that these were 'monk-tenants' on the lines of an Irish monastery. Whitby's own shepherd – we know he was called Hadwald – was described as a 'brother' from the abbess's *familia*, and in continental monasteries the *familia* meant not just the monastic community but the workers on the monastic inland as well.[75] Both monasteries had some kind of home farm and to build it up Abbot Ceolfrid of Jarrow negotiated to obtain land near to hand.[76] There was arable the brothers themselves ploughed, and the dairy herd of sheep and cows essential to provide milk and cheese for a religious body likely to be observant about dietary laws which forbade meat in Lent and on Fridays.[77] The brothers did routine smithing, winnowed the corn and baked their own bread.[78] Bede does not say anything about reaping, and possibly, just as at Bury St Edmunds centuries later where 'all ought to cut the saint's corn', a seventh-century minster could perhaps call on the local peasantry for help with this essential task which required a large amount of labour in a short time. In giving parts of their kingdoms Oswiu and Egfrith had given the rights they themselves had over those lands, and harvest work was a traditional *scir* obligation.

At Christchurch, Hampshire, a minster founded in the seventh century, the 'lands near the church', amounting to five and a half hides, were 'for food and drink' for the resident clergy there, in contrast to the 'external estates'.[79] This functional way of describing the inland of a monastic estate, which comes from Christchurch's twelfth-century *History*, is found quite commonly in Domesday, generally in phrases such as land *ad victum monachorum* or *ad vestitum monachorum*. We

---

74. C.C. Dyer, *Hanbury: settlement and society in a woodland landscape* (1991), 24–5.
75. A. Thacker, 'Monks, preaching and pastoral care', in *Pastoral Care Before the Parish*, ed. Blair and Sharpe, 137–70 at 141–2.
76. Bede, *Historia abbatum*, ch. 15.
77. *Ibid.*
78. *Ibid.*, ch. 8.
79. Hase, 'Mother churches', 52–3.

may suspect that with these stock phrases the Domesday clerks were finding Latin equivalents for English terms like 'fostorland', 'scrudland' and 'shoeland'. The *solanda* of the canons of St Pauls – a very early endowment indeed – may have been 'shoelands' in origin.[80] Land designated to supplying particular needs of the clergy, like shoes and clothes, may have delivered it in the form of rents which went to their purchase.

Bartons

'Bartons' are an important form of specialized inland. They were an important part of the later monastic economy and many places so named are still found near monastic and seigneurial sites. These large minster bartons were not simply farmyards and fields but populated areas, as were the Barton manors already noted at Gloucester. They are very frequently noted in Domesday as not simply exempt from geld, but *traditionally* geld-free – a privilege marking ancient inlands.[81] The barton came to mean a home farm or grange. However, 'barton' (from *bere-tun*, 'barley-*tun*') originally meant a specific kind of *tun*, one devoted to barley or more generally grain production, and *tun* in an Anglo-Saxon place-name is generally taken to indicate not simply a farm but a settlement. Among the earliest endowments of the see of Hereford are Bartonsham and Barton in Colwall, and among its Domesday holdings, some of which may also be early, is *Bertune*.[82] Modern 'Barton Farms' can be pointers to the existence of earlier barton settlements: Barton Farm in the Stockland at Sherborne is a good example. Bartons are unlikely to have been created near minsters in areas that were already urbanized, so when we find a 'Barton' in a built-up area surrounding a minster, and when it is large enough to have supported a population of workers and tenants, it is likely to be early. Abingdon, Berkshire, a Roman site which has a tradition of a seventh-century church, had also a large parish of St Helen, large enough to contain several modern parishes. Within this parish, and just outside the abbey's gates, was Barton Court Farm, itself on the site of a Roman villa-farm. This was one of its two major home farms in the eleventh century and gave its name, Barton, to one of the two huge manors into which the hundred of Hormer, in which Abingdon abbey

---

80. M. Gibbs, ed., *The Early Charters of the Cathedral Church of St Paul, London*, Camden 3rd series 53 (1939), xx–xxvi.
81. See pp. 44–85 below.
82. J. Barrow, 'A Lotharingian in Hereford: Bishop Robert and the reorganisation of the church of Hereford 1079–1095' in *Hereford: Proceedings of the 1990 British Archaeological Association Conference*, ed. D. Whitehead (forthcoming). For Barton place-names see Ekwall, *English Place-Names* s.v. *Barton*; Banham, 'Food plants', 27–8; G. Rosser, *Medieval Westminster 1200–1540* (1989), fig. 5, shows farm buildings on the almonry site at Westminster Abbey. There is a Barton Street near the abbey.

lay, was divided by 1086. It contained extensive and valuable Thames-
side river meadows as well as arable.[83] Identifying genuinely early
bartons is a difficult matter, and only archaeological evidence, or a
genuinely early place-name with this element, is firm evidence.

Wheat was the superior bread grain and 'wheatlands' and 'wheat
garstons' near minsters are versions of bartons – areas of inland
devoted to producing wheat. The banlieu, or privileged inner area of
Bury St Edmunds, we learn from a charter which gives its boundaries,
included a smithy and a 'barton', translated in another version of the
charter as *villa frumentaria* or 'wheat farm'.[84] This must have been
much the same kind of establishment as Bishop Oswald of Worcester
made at Kempsey, Worcestershire, where there were 'two hides less
sixty acres which the bishop has attached to his farm (*ham*) as his
wheat land'.[85] Special arrangements like this strengthen the impression that the field system of an inland was often quite separate from
those on land worked by the peasants of the district. This is one of a
range of important and deep-seated dichotomies to which the inland/
outland structure gave rise.[86]

As the areas that grew up around some minsters developed in late
Anglo-Saxon England into major towns their inlands, while ceasing to
be working bartons, retained their identity in the form of privileged
areas. St Pauls' 'shoelands' became 24 geld-free hides around the
cathedral.[87] The banlieu or inland at Bury St Edmunds was traditionally
exempt from payments to the king and 'scotfree from *heregeld*', the tax
levied to pay the army. Its inhabitants in the eleventh century swore
that 'they would never be the taxpayers of anyone, save the saint
[Edmund] alone'.[88] Some of these urban ecclesiastical inlands were
perpetuated after the Conquest in the form of an area of privileged
jurisdiction. There were distinct 'in-hundreds' and 'out-hundreds', each
of which contained tithings and hamlets, at Axminster, Sherborne,
Reading, Bath and Wells, and Beaminster. At Reading in the thirteenth
century the abbey had the right to suit of court in the 'intrinsec
hundred' from 'the men of the surrounding manors according to the
custom of time past'.[89]

Of course, not all these privileged districts are ancient: some may

---

83. *DB* I, 58cd; D. Miles, *Archaeology at Barton Court Farm, Abingdon, Oxon*,
   Council for British Archaeology Research Report 50 (1986).
84. BCS 808 (S 507). Scholarly opinion is against the authenticity of this charter,
   except for Hart, *Charters of Eastern England*, no. 74 at 54–8. Wheat place-
   names: Banham, 'Food plants', 20–2.
85. Kempsey: Robertson, *Charters*, LV at 114–15.
86. See p. 36 above.
87. Gibbs, *Early Charters*, xxiv, nos 8, 11.
88. Hart, *Charters of Eastern England*, no. 114 at 72; F.E. Harmer, *Anglo-Saxon
   Writs* (1952), no. 15 at 158–9; *The Kalendar of Abbot Samson of Bury St.
   Edmunds and Related Documents*, ed. R.H.C. Davis, Camden 3rd series 84
   (1954), xlv, xxv–xxvi.
89. H.M. Cam, '*Manerium cum hundredo*: the hundred and the hundredal manor',
   EHR 47 (1932), 353–76.

simply represent an attempt by a religious house to claim for itself a valuable exemption from geld and an area of private jurisdiction. This would be particularly likely to happen in the case of towns which wished to buttress their claims to independence by appeal to supposedly ancient privileges. Medieval Ripon had a strong, but not necessarily well-founded, belief in the antiquity of its own liberties. Its privileges were claimed after the Conquest by a spurious charter of Athelstan and a rhyming version of it, both of which take us well into the realm of 'the invention of tradition', but the parallel between 'St Wilfrid's League' and Glastonbury's privileged twelve hides is worth noting:

> Wittyne all that is and is gan
> Yat ich Kynge Attelstane
> Has given as frelich as ich may
> To Kyrke and Chaptel of Seynt Wylfray
> Of my fre devocoun
> Thar pees at Rypone
> On ilke syde ye kyrke amile
> For al ille dedes and ilke Gyle ...
> And alle the land of Seint Wilfray
> Of ilkyne Gelde fre shal bene ay ...[90]

Royal estates

Minster inlands evolved to meet the needs of a settled community: the centres of royal estates, arranged to suit the needs of an itinerant court, may have been administered rather differently. The obligations typical of extensive lordship outlined in the previous chapter, in which service in the hunting field and occasional agricultural work at a centre, coupled with money payments, were the most important elements, remained in being on kings' lands. The supply of royal food renders, *feorm*, may have ensured that many royal vills remained collecting centres rather than agrarian enterprises. By the late seventh century the kings of Wessex had regularized their support systems to the extent that a law of Ine had fixed a rate at which *feorm* was charged. They expected to receive from every ten hides '10 vats of honey, 300 loaves, 12 ambers of Welsh ale, 30 ambers of clear ale, 2 full grown cows or 10 wethers, 10 geese, 20 hens, 10 cheeses, a full amber of butter, 5 salmon, 20 pounds in weight of fodder and 100 eels'. Three hundred loaves, for what the calculation is worth, represents rations for a slave and his family of 150 days. 'Twenty pounds in weight of fodder', even if 'hard food' not hay is meant, would not feed many horses. Grazing was probably also made available for the royal party's

---

90.   W. Farrer, ed., *Early Yorkshire Charters* (3 vols, 1914–16), I, no. 114 at 107–8.

mounts. There is much that we do not understand about this often-quoted text: this seemed to Stenton a 'formidable rent' from a privately owned estate organized for a lord's profit.[91] Its opening phrase, 'for food render (*fostre*) from every ten hides' and the fact that fodder is included might equally well suggest supplies for an itinerant royal household (although we do not know for how long it was expected to support the king and his retinue). It is the variety, specificity and the level of organization implied that are formidable about this collection of supplies, not its size. Ine's ruling about *feorm*, taken together with other laws in his code relating to tax liability (using 'tax' in the sense of the obligation to pay dues or tribute of various kinds to the king), shows that at least in Wessex the king's support system was becoming more organized in the seventh century. An area whose people were subject to the political hegemony of a ruler and the obligation to provide him with hospitality was becoming more like an estate organized to support its royal landlord with specified products produced explicitly for his benefit. This involved a definite intervention in the rural economy.

Feorm was, and remained, the basis of royal support. It was still so in the eleventh century, when its assignment and collection were reorganized and the unit known as 'the *feorm* of one night' became standardized and extensively commuted into cash payments.[92] An early stage in rationalizing the system was the establishment of regular circuits based on royal vills. Granting land at Westbury and Henbury, Gloucestershire, to the bishop of Worcester in the 790s, King Offa of Mercia reserved to himself food rent in ale (some 'Welsh' some 'mild' and some 'pure'), oxen, sheep, cheese, corn and meal to be delivered *ad regalem vicum*, to the royal vill.[93] The huge estate at Westbury on Trym, Somerset, must have consisted of many scattered farms and perhaps small villages when Offa's tribute due from it was listed: only a considerable feat of organization could have made sure that he received what was due to him when and where he required it.

To organize the countryside to supply a king with his needs involved standardization of two kinds. Unless every part of the royal lands were to be allotted a specific and separate assignment of the *feorm* to be produced, there must be at least a rough notion of a standard rate of burden. Ine's law setting the rate for ten hides can be seen as part of this process of setting the rate. The minsters Oswiu endowed in Northumbria with twelve 'small properties each of ten hides' may represent farmers organized to provide ten hides' worth of provisions – the kings and people of Northumbria knew what was due from ten

91. Liebermann, I, 119–20: Ine 70.1; Stenton, *Anglo-Saxon England*, 285; T.M. Charles-Edwards, 'Early medieval kingships in the British Isles' in *The Origins of Anglo-Saxon Kingdoms*, ed. S. Bassett (1989), 28–39 at 29–30.
92. P. Stafford, 'The farm of one night and the organisation of King Edward's estates in Domesday Book', *EHR* 33 (1980), 491–52.
93. *EHD* I, no. 78 at 467–8.

hides just as the kings and people of Wessex did, although the amounts
may well have been different in the different kingdoms.[94] The second
kind of standardization involved assigning to various parts of a
terrritory its share of the overall obligations in *feorm*. When Ine laid
down what he expected to receive from his lands, the Wessex
settlements which would have supplied it were likely to have been
small, scattered clusters of farms or single farmsteads, not nucleated
villages. There was evidently a system of procurement based on the
hide, the unit by which land was assessed for tax. When between 685
and 687 Cædwalla, king of Wessex, gave 60 hides at Farnham, Surrey,
for a minster they were already 'assigned to their own places and
names'. Ten hides were at Binton – that is to say ten hides' worth of
the *feorm* for Farnham came from Binton, two hides' worth from Churt,
the rest from a place called *Cusanweoh* and from other neighbouring
places. To allot the hidage in this way was to single out individual vills
or farms in an area perhaps as large as 25,000 acres.[95] It is not
uncommon for charters to indicate the location of the hidage of an
estate among its constituent parts: the Bexhill charter already cited
does just this.[96] Cædwalla's charter is only unusual, and unusually
revealing, because it shows a deliberate process of 'assigning' hides to
places.

The *feorm* from royal supply networks was supplemented by the
produce of sizeable inlands at some royal centres. Domesday Book
reveals some royal manors which had large inlands intensively
exploited by large forces of agricultural workers: 30 teams and 82
slaves were at work on the Leominster arables, and labour was owed
by outlying tenants as well. Royal *tunas* in Somerset, some of which
'date from the earliest phase of English occupation' and were
successors to early Old Welsh estates, were at the centres of extensive
territories.[97] South Petherton, for instance had land for 28 plough
teams in 1086, and a workforce which included 22 freedmen
(*colibertos*) and five slaves.[98] In 1086 among the king's lands in
Hampshire were Barton (Stacey) and its berewick (Kings) Worthy,
which had supplied King Edward with half a day's *feorm* and now
supplied King William – a large and valuable manor with a large
workforce. It belonged to the remaining part of the large royal territory
from which Cenwalh had carved out the Winchester minsterland
described above.[99]

The king's inland, like the minsters', was a privileged and geld-free
area – land given at Ashwick and Evesty, Somerset, between 1061 and

---

94. *HE* III, 24.
95. BCS 72 (S 235); P.H. Sawyer, *From Roman Britain to Norman England* (1978),
     143–4; Blair, *Early Medieval Surrey*, 25 and notes 83–5, fig. 9 at 6. The assigning
     of hidage is discussed more fully below, at pp. 51–4.
96. See pp. 30–1 above.
97. *DB* I, 180a; Costen, *Origins of Somerset*, 88–93.
98. *DB* I, 86b.
99. *DB* I, 38c; p. 34 above.

1082 was to be 'just as free in all things as the king's own inland'.[100] Exempt lands in Domesday reveal its existence. In Colchester in 1086 the king had 102 exempt acres as his *dominium*, later called the 'inland'.[101] Vills, sometimes groups of vills, which were responsible for supplying *feorm* to the king, especially in Dorset, Hampshire, Somerset and Wiltshire are noted in Domesday as being geld-free or unhidated.[102] These are examples of a widespread exemption from tax of the land which supplied the king's needs.

Whatever the form in which it was collected, royal tribute necessitated a resident bureaucracy of royal reeves or officials, household staff, supervisors of the royal lands, and so on. We know of this mainly from Domesday Book, but something of the same kind of organization must always have been necessary to co-ordinate and arrange for the collection of, for instance the 20 cows, 20 pigs, and 3000 'dogbreads' (hard-baked bread was given to both horses and dogs in the middle ages) due at Cheltenham, or the wheat, malt, honey and again dogbread at Cheltenham and Cirencester.[103] S.P.J. Harvey and J. Campbell have highlighted the service bureaucracies resident on royal estates: the eight reeves, eight bailiffs, and eight riding-knights – 'numbers which suggest eight working teams of three officials' – at Leominster, for instance. Tewkesbury and Berkeley, Gloucestershire had similar large estate staffs.[104]

S.P.J. Harvey has found that, in the eleventh century at least, it was typical for royal estates to be less 'demesne oriented' than ecclesiastical ones. The situation had no doubt changed in many respects by the eleventh century, but the emphasis on royal manors on cash income from jurisdictional profits and commuted food rents, extracted and managed by royal officials, rather than on the profits of agriculture, may well reflect a divergence between royal and ecclesiastical estates which had originated much earlier. We might expect both the land and the people of royal inlands to have been less intensively exploited than those of the church. There is evidence that this view was shared by many medieval people.[105]

---

100. Harmer, *Writs*, no. 6 at 134–5.
101. J.H. Round, 'The Domesday of Colchester', *The Antiquary* 6 (1882), 5–9, 95–100, 251–6. I am grateful to Dr C. Thornton for this reference.
102. Darby, *Domesday England*, 217.
103. *DB* I, 162d.
104. J. Campbell, 'Some agents and agencies of the late Anglo-Saxon state' in *Domesday Studies*, ed. J. Holt (1987), 201–18 at 215–16; S.P.J. Harvey, 'Domesday England' in *Ag. Hist.* II, 45–136 at 88–9; *DB* I, 163a.
105. Harvey, 'Domesday England' 87–95; R.J. Faith, 'The "great rumour" of 1377 and peasant ideology' in *The English Rising of 1381*, ed. T.H. Aston and R.H. Hilton (1984), 43–73.

Berewicks

Specialized production for important consumers played an important role in estate formation, giving rise not only to intensively exploited areas at centres but also to detached dependencies where production was dedicated to the supply of those same centres. In the case of the king's lands, the production and collection of surplus to supply large amounts of *feorm* gave rise to outlying settlements whose sole function this was. Although geographically scattered they were functionally his inland. 'Kingston' and 'Kington' place-names have, it is true, been interpreted by P.H. Sawyer as 'royal *tuns*' in the sense of royal residences. But it makes the structure and working of royal estates much easier to understand if they are seen simply as places owned by the king. If, as seems reasonable, we extend this to mean places whose inhabitants were directed to *supplying* the king – places 'where the king's own husbandmen live' in Finberg's words – they fall into place as a network of discrete inlands.[106] We cannot be sure, from their Domesday descriptions, that the very large royal estates like South Petherton and Leominster, cited above, had inland in a single consolidated area, rather than distributed among a number of separate centres in this way. Like central inlands, places which supplied royal *feorm* were tax-exempt, as Domesday shows, 'the king's *ahne feorm land*' in the terminology of the Geld Rolls.[107]

'Kingstons' are a royal form of the kind of settlement known as the berewick. Berewicks have much the same semantic history as bartons.[108] As the barton or *bere-tun* was originally a barley growing *tun*, so a berewick was an outlying farm or *wic* where barley was grown. Just as a 'barton' became a generic name for a home farm, so 'berewick' became a widely used term for a dependent farm or settlement. Berewicks and bartons related to a centre are sometimes named from their geographical relationship: Norbiton and Surbiton being the northern and southern *beretuns* of the king's manor of Kingston, Surrey.[109] The very large numbers of such settlement names – north, south, west and east *tuns* – have shown how widespread the estate organization of centre-plus-berewicks actually was.[110] Royal

---

106. Bourne, 'Kingston place-names' n. 51. This was Finberg's interpretation of 'Charltons': Finberg, 'Charltons', 158 but see also pp. 150–1 below. Sawyer, 'The royal *tun*', 278 and n. 3; Gelling, *Signposts*, 184–5.
107. Tax exemption: Stafford, 'Farm of one night', 493; also pp. 48–53 below.
108. Gelling, *Signposts*, 165; Ekwall, *English Place-Names*, xxxii and s.v. *berewic* and *barton*.
109. J. Blair, 'An introduction to the Surrey Domesday' in *The Surrey Domesday* (1989), 1–17 at 13.
110. See especially D. Hooke, *Anglo-Saxon Settlements of the West Midlands: the charter evidence*, BAR British Series 95 (1981), e.g. 73; T.H. Aston, 'The origins of the manor in England', *TRHS* 5th series 8 (1958), 59–83, reprinted with 'The origins of the manor in England: a postscript' in *Social Relations and Ideas: essays in honour of R.H. Hilton*, ed. T.H. Aston, P.R. Coss, C. Dyer and J. Thirsk (1983), 1–43 at 36–7.

centres on the king's lands in Worcestershire seem to have been serviced not by a large inland but by widely scattered berewicks where lived the labour force producing his supplies.[111] On the large manor of Helstone in Cornwall, held by the count of Mortain in 1086, the terse Domesday description conceals a large estate with a centre and a penumbra of the small scattered hamlets so characteristic of the county, each with its own *inland* worked by slaves and bordars.[112] Such a structure is also found at the bishop of Winchester's huge manor of Taunton, presently being investigated by H. Fox and C. Thornton. The land the bishop controlled directly became known as the 'in-faring', the land leased or sub-enfeoffed as the 'out-faring'. Within the 'in-faring', individual barton farms with an associated workforce developed: these were a post-Conquest development, but the distinct inner/outer structure of the manor, with individual centres inside the inner estate, may well be earlier.[113]

In the counties of Danish England so many estates were organized into centre-plus-berewicks that the compilers of Domesday Book in those counties were forced to devize particular formulae by which to record the answers in order to reflect this form of estate structure. In Lincolnshire and Yorkshire they tackled the formidable task of recording tax liability by giving separately the name of each manor and the names of its berewicks and its sokelands, indicating each by a marginal rubric and giving each an individual tax liability in terms of 'carucates to the geld'. When we are told of a detached piece of land that 'it is inland of' such and such a manor, this land too may be reckoned as a berewick, even if not rubricated as such.

F.M. Stenton used this information to show a distinctive structure in the Danelaw: a manorial centre with its constellation of dependent vills.[114] As we have seen, this structure is widely accepted as typical of – indeed it virtually constitutes the common denominator of – the multiple or complex estate. But Stenton's analysis went deeper than the geography of the estate, and penetrated into its social structure. He proposed a basic division between land which belonged to the lord and land from which he was only entitled to claim rents and services of various kinds. In the first category was inland. This included the manorial centre, the land of the peasantry who farmed there, *and* the peasantry of the dependent berewicks. The inland was 'that portion of an estate over which the lord had most immediate and direct control, the land of villeins and bordars in contrast to the lands of the sokemen'. The berewick was 'a detached portion of inland, a holding geographically separate from the chief manor of which it formed part,

111. J.D. Hamshere, 'Domesday Book: estate structures in the west midlands' in *Domesday Studies*, ed. Holt, 155–82 at 163.
112. G.R.J. Jones, 'The portrayal of land settlement in Domesday Book', *ibid.*, 183–200 at 196.
113. Pers. comm. Dr C. Thornton.
114. F.M. Stenton, *Types of Manorial Structure in the Northern Danelaw* in Oxford Studies in Social and Legal History 2 (1910).

but owned, as to its soil, by the manorial lord'. Sokeland, by contrast, was 'land regarded as belonging to the men seated upon it, but carrying a liability to services and dues to be rendered at the manorial centre to which it was appendant'.[115]

In any area where scattered settlement was the natural agricultural form, inland must often have consisted of scattered single farms. We have a description of the inland of a 20-hide estate at Sherburn, Yorkshire, a collection of individual farms up to ten miles away from Sherburn:

> half a hide at Hibaldestoft, one hide at Fryston, two oxgangs at Hillam, two oxgangs at Lumby, one and a half hides at Milford and at Steeton one hide and at Mickleford two hides and all at Latherton except one hide and another half hide at Fenton and another half hide at Cawood

The archbishop of York's manor at Southwell, Nottinghamshire, consisted in 956 of eleven vills, but within them his ownership was restricted to the holdings of individual peasants: 'in Farnsfield two manslots belong to Southwell, in Hallam sixty acres and three manslots, in Normanton every third acre, in Fiskerton two shares (dales) and four manslots out of all that land'.[116]

Berewicks were such a prominent feature of agrarian organization in Lincolnshire and Yorkshire that the Domesday clerks had to evolve a particular way of recording them which was unique to that circuit. Yet berewicks were not peculiar to Danish England nor to counties where Domesday specifically records their existence. The *geburland* of Abingdon Abbey's manor of Cumnor is described in a tenth-century charter. It consisted of three contiguous areas of land, later the parishes of Hinksey, Wytham and Seacourt, and these were later referred to as its *appenditias* or berewicks. Fig. 8 shows the bounds of Abingdon's *geburland* as recorded between 955 and 957. Features in the boundary show that there were then evidently scattered home-steads surrounded by their own land in this area, and there is no sign of the nucleated settlements which were there in the twelfth century.[117] The inland of Bexhill already referred to, although it was a compact area with known boundaries, nevertheless lay in an area of much the same kind of dispersed settlement. Widely dispersed inland is found in Kent, where scattered farmsteads remained characteristic of rural settlement. Fig. 9 is derived from Jolliffe's map of the inland of

---

115.   *Ibid.*, 11, 13–14; P. Vinogradoff, *English Society in the Eleventh Century: essays in English mediaeval history* (1908), 366.
116.   BCS (S 712); BCS 1029, 1348 (S 659); Farrer, *Early Yorkshire Charters*, I, no. 6 at 18–21, no. 2 at 5–10. The 'manslot' was a peasant holding.
117.   BCS 1002 (S 663); bounds: Gelling, *Place-Names*, 729–31.

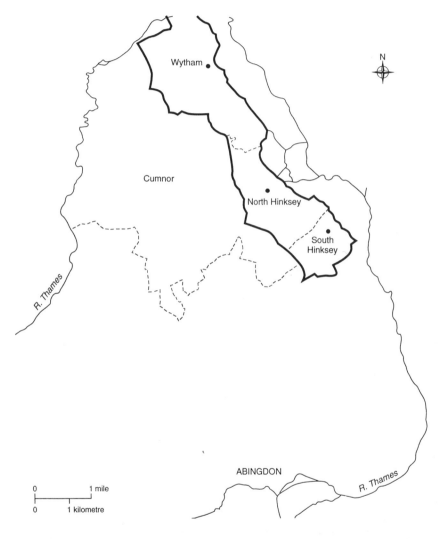

Figure 8 The manor of Cumnor, Berkshire. The heavy line marks the boundary, at some places conjectural, of the *geburland*, a distinct area within Abingdon Abbey's large manor of Cumnor which comprised the parishes of Cumnor, Seacourt, Wytham and Hinksey. *Source*: after BCS 1002 (S 663) and M. Gelling, *The Place-Names of Berkshire*, EPNS 51 (1974), 729–31.

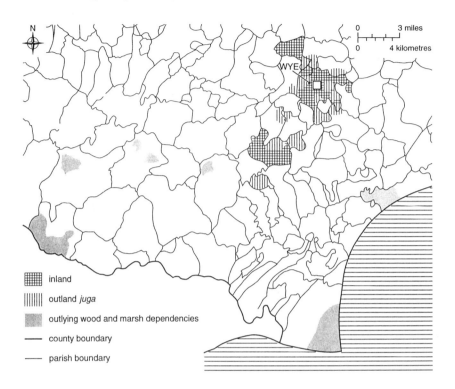

inland

outland *juga*

outlying wood and marsh dependencies

county boundary

parish boundary

Figure 9   The inland and outland of the manor of Wye, Kent. *Source*: after J. Jolliffe, *Pre-Feudal England: the Jutes* (1933).

the great manor of Wye in Kent, which belonged to the abbots of Battle: it is distributed among some 20 modern parishes.[118]

The huge manor of South Malling in East Sussex plays an important part in Jones's model of the multiple estate and he has closely analysed its make-up.[119] His information about the various tenancies on the estate comes from the thirteenth century, by which time it had been subject to many generations of seigneurial management strategy. Nevertheless, it still then consisted of 'a multiplicity of vills and dependencies and settlements' reaching from the fertile lowlands near South Malling itself far up into the Weald. Malling lands consisted of settlements 'within the wood' (the Weald) and 'without the wood'. They were later known as tithings. Before the Conquest the settlements in the tithings 'within the wood', if they were permanent

---

118. J. Jolliffe, *Pre-Feudal England: the Jutes* (1933), map 1, x, 4–8.
119. Jones, 'Portrayal of land settlement', 185–6; 'Multiple estates and early settlement' in *English Medieval Settlement*, ed. P.H. Sawyer (1979), 11–40 at 20–9.

settlements at all, were separate farmsteads or at most hamlets, and were more likely to have been summer pastures or denns.[120] Tenants here in the thirteenth century owed the same mixture of hunting service and occasional work at the estate centre as was typical of the sokemen of the northern and eastern *scir*. 'Without the wood' in the area round Malling, where place-names suggest that settlement was more nucleated, an inner core can be discerned where the best agricultural land is to be found, with a service tenantry to work it, but this inland too was scattered over a number of vills.

Deerhurst, Gloucestershire, was the centre of a huge and complex estate by 1086, part of the structure of which had already been laid down in the early eighth century. By 1086 Deerhurst had been given to Westminster Abbey but it had originally been a minster in its own right, founded early in the ninth century when the thegn Æthelmund's son Æthelric, wishing to be buried there, gave it land from his ancestral property at four different places. One at least of these, Todenham, was one of Deerhurst's four berewicks listed in 1086: Todenham, Hardwicke, Bourton on the Hill, Gloucestershire, and Sutton under Brailes, now Warwickshire.[121] Throughout the middle ages Westminster Abbey kept these berewicks as part of its 'demesne'; that is to say as that part of its estate directly exploited for the abbey's own use. To use pre-Conquest terminology, they remained part of its inland.[122] Deerhurst also had scattered lands held by radmen, 'free men ... all of whom however in the time of king Edward ploughed and harrowed and mowed and reaped for the lord's use'. In other words, Deerhurst had much the same mixture of dependent berewicks and freeholdings which, had it been in eastern England, would have caused the Domesday commissioners to have described it as *manerium ... berewica soca* ('manor, berewick sokeland').

Specialized production centres

Although tribute in cattle was probably the oldest and most 'royal' kind of tribute, cattle do not in fact figure very largely in what scanty references we have to actual food renders, mutton and bacon being much the most common forms of meat.[123] (Even King Ine's *feorm* from ten hides, we recall, gave him the option of ten wethers in place of two cattle.) Mutton and bacon, poultry, bread and ale, honey and cheese were the staple aristocratic foods and figure largely in recorded reference to *feorm*, while honey in large quantities recurs in food rents from Welsh manors recorded in Domesday Book. To obtain a varied

---

120. Everitt, *Continuity and Colonization*, 54–5.
121. *EHD* I, no. 81 at 471–3; Blair, *Minsters and Parish Churches*, 2–3.
122. B.F. Harvey, *Westminster Abbey and its Estates in the Middle Ages* (1977), 344–5, 360.
123. Charles-Edwards, 'Early medieval kingships', 29–31.

diet entailed a certain amount of specialization among supply centres. In pastoral regions with large remote hill farms, such as much of Northumbria was in Bede's day, a minster may have grown its own corn on its inland and taken its supplies from individual farms in the form of cattle or cheese. Other dues, like the hounds from (or kennelled at) *Hundatun,* have left their mark in place-names derived from particular products or crops, flax at Linacre and Halifax, for instance, and important elements in diet like cereals (Wheathampstead, Rycote), leeks (Laughton, Latton) and legumes (Peasenhall, Pishill, Banham).[124] The process of specialization is hard to date but place-names may occasionally give a clue to its chronology. In the area which became the Lancashire hundred of Salford, for instance, there was very little Anglian settlement before the mid-seventh century and spoken British did not give way to Anglian until well into the eighth. Consequently it may be very significant that places in the Salford district that took their names from centres and churches have British names, while places that were fixed supply centres, such as Gressingham ('grazing-place') and Barton ('barley farm') have Anglo-Saxon names: the suggestion here is that these were an Anglian innovation, new suppliers for old-established centres.[125]

Inland as a tax-exempt area

One of the characteristics already noted of early minster inlands is their exemption from geld. Does this derive from an early exemption of church lands from public service of all kinds? Kings, in giving land to the church, conveyed to it the entitlement to *feorm* that was primarily what made the gift worth having. They conveyed to the new owner the rights to the services they themselves had enjoyed. Other forms of obligation laid on the land may have only gradually been defined in the period when the early Anglo-Saxon minsters were getting their lands. The obligation we know most about is military service. It came to be a universal obligation on 'folkland' and from the late seventh century anyone of *ceorl* rank and above was liable to the fine called *fyrdwite* for 'draft-dodging'.[126] The extent to which the church's land was exempt from providing military service at this early date is a little ambiguous. The religious themselves were not obliged to bear arms (although at least one tenth-century bishop left an impressive collection of war-gear in his will), but were the tenants on their lands obliged to do so?[127]

124. H.E. Hallam, 'England before the Norman conquest', *Ag. Hist.* II, 45–136 at 23–40 gives many examples of similar place-names but the explanation given at 23 is doubtful.
125. Kenyon, *Origins of Lancashire,* 92–100.
126. Liebermann, I, 112: Ine 51.
127. N.P. Brooks, 'The development of military obligations in eighth and ninth century England' in *England before the Conquest: studies in primary sources presented to Dorothy Whitelock,* ed. P. Clemoes and K. Hughes (1971), 69–84.

This mattered to the church. Men leaving the land to fight were a loss to the landowner: the church of Tours tried unsuccessfully to establish exemption for its men in the sixth century.[128] Bede's distress at the transfer of so much property into the hands of aristocratic founders of minsters was in part due to the fact that this was a loss to the Northumbrian state, land held by the religious being no longer available to set up aristocratic young warriors. His concern also rather suggests that land booked to the church was exempt from military service, at least *de facto*. It was this potential loss of military resources that led to the insistence of kings from not long after Bede's time that the three 'common burdens' of military service, bridge work and fortress work were to be demanded from holders of bookland, among whom the church was prominent. This more closely regulated exaction of public service may in turn have led to a more clearly formulated recognition of certain land from which it was thought unreasonable to demand such service. The immediate supply-lands of major churches and of the king himself are prime candidates for such a privilege, but by extension the inlands of other landowners could have begun to be seen in this light.

Most references to inland come from late Anglo-Saxon England, and thus from a period when it had been subject to centuries of change. Moreover, many of these occur in a specific context: the exaction of geld as a regular tax. To look at inland from this point of view is inevitably confusing: it is to study a real entity within the limited perspectives and with the specialized vocabulary of a fiscal system. There is another problem. Many of our references to inland come from Domesday Book (although, as we shall see, it is not recorded consistently there: see Appendix 1). Domesday Book is a fixed picture of a society which was going through profound changes. Many of these changes – and it will be the purpose of the second part of this book to look at them more closely – were to do with the exploitation of estates by new landlords. Under the management of their Norman lords the inhabited inland on many estates was evolving into what came to be called land *in dominio*, 'the demesne', an untenanted home farm. Inland differed from land *in dominio* in the sense that it included tenements of a particular type, which are described in the following chapter. But over time inland shed its tenancies and became indistinguishable from land *in dominio*. (Sometimes, and this may have happened where new land was being taken in hand, the two are distinguished. In Oxfordshire the bishop of Lincoln had *in dominio* 'land for ten plough teams and three hides besides the inland' at

---

cont.

    Will of Theodred: D. Whitelock, M. Brett and C.N.L. Brooke, eds, *Councils and Synods with Other Documents relating to the English Church* (2 vols, 1981), I, 77.

128. Brooks, 'Military obligations', 73 n. 2.

Banbury.[129]) This transformation had begun before the Conquest, and it was to gather speed after it. The processes by which this happened are described in Chapter 8. There was a trajectory from inland to demesne, but different estates were at different points on this trajectory when the Domesday commissioners came round.

Although to look at inland in the context of the fiscal system is limiting in many ways, and is certainly far from straightforward, it does show us how Anglo-Norman government took account of this long-standing institution. The first reference to geld is to a levy for a particular purpose – to pay the Danes in 991. Once imposed it survived as a recurrent tax until the late twelfth century.[130] It was charged on the hide or carucate and assessed via the county's various subdivisions: hundreds, groups of vills, vills and manors. (Some areas of land were simply overlooked by the tax system because they were too small, remote, or obscure to be assessed, some because they had never been included in any previous network of public obligation.[131]) Like any tax the geld was subject to exemptions. In the folios of Domesday Book and the small group of documents associated with collection of the geld we can see, although only dimly, the tax system coming to grips with two distinct but overlapping systems of exemption. There was the long-standing privileged position of inland as an area exempt from public burdens of all kinds, a position which may have originated long before the geld itself. And there were the claims of the interest groups and individuals who had been able to negotiate with William or his predecessors a reduction of their tax burden by means of gaining exemption for their inland.[132]

The division of land into exempt *inland* and taxable *warland* is most clearly displayed in the very small amount of surviving documentation of the administration of the geld system apart from Domesday Book. The document known as the Northamptonshire Geld Roll records the overall tax position for the various hundreds of Northamptonshire. It is

---

129. All the Oxfordshire references to inland treat it as if it were a type of land *in dominio*: *DB* I, 155b, 155c, 156d, 158a, 158b, 159a. These and other similar entries are discussed by Vinogradoff, *English Society*, 188 and n. 3; F.M. Stenton, 'Domesday survey' in *VCH Oxfordshire*, I (1939), 373–428 at 393–4.
130. For the history of geld and its collection: J.H. Round, 'Danegeld and the finance of Domesday' in *Domesday Studies*, ed. P.E. Dove (2 vols, 1888, 1891), I, 77–142; Stenton, *Anglo-Saxon England*, 636–7; F.W. Maitland, *Domesday Book and Beyond: three essays in the early history of England* (1960 edn), 546–63; H.R. Loyn, *The Governance of Anglo-Saxon England 500–1087* (1984), 119–22; W.L. Warren, *The Governance of Anglo-Norman and Angevin England 1086–1272* (1987), 35–9, 144–7; Darby, *Domesday England*, 9–10, 137–8; S.P.J. Harvey, 'Domesday Book and its predecessors', *EHR* 86 (1971), 753–73.
131. For example, see *DB* I, 159d for uncultivated land at Swyncombe, Oxfordshire; *DB* I, 157a for land near Oxford of the canons of St Frideswide's 'which never paid geld nor belongs nor belonged to any hundred'.
132. Vinogradoff, *English Society*, section III, ch. ii; S.P.J. Harvey, 'Taxation and the economy' in *Domesday Studies* ed. Holt, 249–64; R.W. Eyton, *A Key to Domesday* (1878), 5–6; R.W. Finn, *The Domesday Inquest and the Making of Domesday Book* (1960), 136–59; Harvey, 'Taxation and the economy', 249–64.

a surviving example of a kind of document which must have been very common, for it was a useful check on what proportion of the total hidage of a county could be expected to render its tax.[133] The Northamptonshire Roll divides the hidage for each hundred into hides *gewered*, hides *inland*, hides of *kynges ahnen ferme land* and hides of *wasta*, waste. The *gewered* hides were those which paid geld, but the other three categories were exempt land. Two are comparatively straightforward. 'Waste', from the tax collector's point of view, was land from which nothing could be collected – whether it was land that had been deliberately devastated and 'wasted', or uncultivated and uncultivable land, or simply land which had never been adequately surveyed and assessed for tax.[134] The *kynges ahne ferme land* (the king's own *feorm* land), the land which supplied the king with *feorm* or food rent as the inland of England's most privileged landholder, appears here as a separate tax-exempt category. Inland, the third exempt category in the geld roll, is the aggregate sum of the hides of all the inland in each hundred.

Like any other component of the tax system, inland could be manipulated. The amount of inland in Northamptonshire, for instance, seems to have been enlarged at a stroke as a means of giving the county as a whole relief from some of its tax burden. We do not know whether this was achieved by allowing an increased share to each manor or simply by upping the total for each hundred.[135] Totals of inland for a county as a whole are recorded in the geld accounts for the south-western counties preserved with Exon Domesday.[136]

It was not in fact part of the instructions to the Domesday commissioners to enquire into inland as such and although they sometimes note it by name the references are unevenly distributed among circuits and counties. Domesday refers to geld-free areas in several counties which 'had never been assessed in hides' or 'never paid geld' and it seems likely that these are inlands, though not named as such. Vinogradoff, interested primarily in their fiscal connotation rather than their role in the economy of the estate, collected an invaluable body of the evidence of geld-free land contained in Domesday.[137] Substantial parts of royal and ecclesiastical estates, particularly in the south-western counties, were exempt, and these exempt portions are often found at their centres. I have already noted that inlands near episcopal seats and minsters such as Gloucester and

133. Robertson, *Charters*, appendix 1.III, 230–7; J.H. Round, *Feudal England: historical studies on the XIth and XIIth centuries* (1895), 147–56; Ravenhill, 'Cornwall', 307, shows that the exempt 'fiscal demesne' or ungelded land recorded in Exon Domesday for Cornwall tallies with the amounts of exempt lands in the Geld Rolls for that county in *DB* IV, 65.
134. Palliser, 'Yorkshire Domesday', 33–8.
135. J.H. Round, 'Introduction to the Northamptonshire Domesday', *VCH Northamptonshire*, I (1902), 257–98 at 259–69.
136. *DB* IV, 65.
137. See appendix 1 below. Vinogradoff, *English Society*, 177–96.

Sherborne appear in Domesday as exempt. The exemption of a portion of the manor is sometimes expressed in Domesday as the obligation of the manorial tenants to pay the entire amount due from the manor, leaving a proportion exempt, as at Tewkesbury, Gloucestershire, where the geld from 45 hides *in dominio* was 'acquitted' by the tenants of the remaining 50 hides.[138] In Hurstingstone hundred, Huntingdonshire, the ploughlands *in dominio* of the great religious houses like Ramsey and Crowland 'are quit of geld' and it is explicitly the villeins and sokemen who pay.[139]

Some, possibly very many, exemptions are concealed by Domesday but revealed in later surveys. In some cases the exempt portion of the manor was not assessed in hides at all. Although Domesday does not reveal this information, later evidence can show that the core settlement or vill within a federated manor may sometimes be found to be unhidated. The entire Domesday hidages of Burton Abbey's manors, for instance, appear in its early twelfth-century surveys to be accounted for by the hidages of the warland or *terra hominum*, the tenants' land, leaving the inland exempt or, as the survey of Appleby, one of the Derbyshire manors of the abbey, puts it, 'without the king's geld'. Yet the Domesday entries for the abbey's lands do not reveal this for they do not show how the hidage was distributed.[140] The exempt portion was still known as inland in the twelfth century, when the term can also still be found in use on the manors of the canons of St Paul's and Ramsey Abbey.[141]

These widespread exemptions for inlands may have obtained on other ecclesiastical estates. This was the case of the Essex manor of 'Adulfsness', centred on Walton on the Naze. Walton itself, the vill where the principal manorial curia and its lands were situated, seems never to have been assessed in hides, the hidage of the manor being distributed among the other vills. It is only from thirteenth-century sources that we learn this: Domesday conceals the situation, as it must have done on many such federated manors.[142] The same situation is revealed by the late twelfth-century surveys of the bishopric of Worcester's estates. At Fladbury, Worcestershire, the hidage of the entire composite manor was distributed between six outlying vills: the

---

138. *DB* I, 163c, d; A. Williams, 'An introduction to the Gloucestershire Domesday', *Domesday Gloucestershire* (1989), 1–39 at 20–1.
139. *DB* I, 203b.
140. *DB* I, 247c; C.G.O. Bridgeman, 'The Burton Abbey twelfth century surveys', *Collections for a History of Staffordshire* (William Salt Archaeological Society, 1918 for 1916), 209–300 at 244.
141. St Pauls: Gibbs, *Early Charters*, 118–21; Ramsey: *Cartularium monasterii de Rameseia*, ed. W.H. Hart and P.A. Lyons, Rolls Series (3 vols, 1884–93) II, 25. Inland can be found under various names in thirteenth-century manorial documents, e.g. the 'Hinlond' at Chippenham, Wiltshire, in 1275: G.L. Gomme, *The Village Community* (1890), 173–6 (I am grateful to Dr H. Fox for this reference).
142. R. Faith, 'The topography and social structure of a small soke in the middle ages: The Sokens, Essex', *Essex Archaeology and History* 27 (1997), 202–13.

minster vill at Fladbury itself and a neighbouring vill of Craycombe apparently had no hidated land. Significant differences in social structure stemmed from these arrangements, and will be considered later.[143]

Inland is overwhelmingly most often noted in Domesday in Lincolnshire and Yorkshire: we have seen how the commissioners adapted their procedures to record the inland that was in dispersed berewicks.[144] In these counties it was calculated in carucates and bovates *ad geldum*, to the geld, and must therefore have been liable to geld, not exempt. This anomaly may be a result of the attempts of the tax system to get to grips with the social structure of the region, with its manorial centres and outlying berewicks and sokelands.[145] So much inland was in berewicks that to allow them exemption would have seriously reduced the tax base. Had Lincolnshire and Yorkshire inlands been originally exempt from geld? It seems not, for practically no area which 'never paid geld' is recorded there, nor for any other part of the Danelaw. A more profound difference, not yet fully understood, between the Danelaw and the rest of England may be reflected in this fact. One explanation may be that the major religious foundations of the Danelaw did not inherit ancient inlands, as their counterparts elsewhere seem to have done.

Apart from Lincolnshire and Yorkshire, whether *ipso nomine* or as traditionally exempt land, inland is noted by Domesday predominantly, although not exclusively, in Wessex: Surrey, Sussex, Hampshire, Somerset, Dorset and Oxfordshire. Are we looking at a real regional distinction here, or a fiscal phenomenon? In other words, were there really more inlands in these areas, or was assessment to the geld more likely to favour inlands there? A fiscal explanation is entirely plausible. Long-established inlands on royal estates and important minsters in Wessex might well have been given more favourable treatment when decisions had to be made about what land was to be subject to tax.

Post-Conquest tax exemptions

The year 1066 brought to England a king eager to exploit the rich tax base and efficient tax system that were his by conquest and a new landholding class equally eager to avoid as much tax as possible. The result was a new series of tax exemptions. There has been much debate about these, and its complexities have been made even more tangled by twelfth-century references to exemption which may have

---

143. *The Red Book of Worcester*, ed. M Hollings, Worcestershire Historical Society (4 vols, 1934–50), II, 145; pp. 240–2 below.
144. Vinogradoff, *English Society*, 186–94, 366–7, 578; Stenton, *Types of Manorial Structure*, 5–11.
145. For the evolving notion of what the 'manor' consisted of in such areas see D. Roffe, 'Domesday Book and northern society: a reassessment', *EHR* 105 (1990), 310–36 at 334–5.

obscured what the earlier position had been.[146] The author of the *Leges Edwardi Confessoris* considered that ecclesiastical demesnes were exempt, the author of the *Dialogue of the Exchequer* that the demesne lands of barons of the exchequer and the sheriffs were exempt. Henry I's coronation charter promised exemption for the demesne lands of 'those knights who defend their lands by their halberks'; that is, who hold by military service.[147]

Modern historians broadly divide between those who think that some general exemption was extended to the land, or part of the land, of an entire class of landholders and those who think that exemption was a privilege given at royal will to favour particular groups or individuals. Thus R.S. Hoyt considered that the demesnes of manors which lords kept in hand and did not sub-let (confusingly known as manors 'in demesne') qualified for general exemption at the time of Domesday, and that this concession was extended to the demesnes of their sub-tenants by Henry I. Stenton thought that demesnes were normally expected to bear their share of the geld for the entire manor.[148] The fact that in some counties land *in dominio* is assessed in hides, the basis for geld assessment, might be thought to bear this out. The entries in the original Domesday returns for Devon in Exeter Domesday, for instance, preserving formulae which were omitted in the exchequer text, record both hides held by the lord *in dominio* and hides held by the *villani*. This is not in itself evidence that demesnes were taxed, however, as the entire inland of Northamptonshire was calculated in hides in the Geld Rolls for that county.[149] J.H. Round thought that there was no general exemption for demesnes of any kind, exemption being a privilege for which individual lords were required and prepared to bargain. S.P.J. Harvey has extended and refined this argument to show that widespread exemption – or a drastically reduced assessment – for entire manors was granted as a political favour to powerful figures like Odo of Bayeux. These exemptions extended only to the manors that they kept in hand and held directly from the king. References in Domesday show that concessions were made by express written grant, sometimes under seal and witnessed in the county court.[150] They were no Norman innovation, as references to the exemption of part of two Bath Abbey manors 'by the grant of kings Edward and William' show. Grants between individuals could also be made geld-free.[151]

The express exemptions of land *in dominio* recorded in Domesday are relics of a much older system which predates the geld. This system

146. I am grateful to Dr A. Wareham for his advice on this topic.
147. Liebermann, I, 627–70 at 634–5; *Dialogus de scaccario*, ed. and trans. C. Johnson (1950), 56; Liebermann, I, 521–3 at 522 (11.1).
148. R.S. Hoyt, *The Royal Demesne in English Constitutional History 1066–1272* (1950), 52–8; Round, 'Danegeld'; Stenton, 'Domesday survey', 393–4.
149. See p 51 above.
150. Harvey, 'Taxation and the economy'; Round, 'Danegeld', 97–9.
151. Round, 'Danegeld', 97–9; Bridgeman, 'Burton Abbey', 264.

exempted all inland from public burdens. When at some point in the tenth century geld liability came to be systematically assessed, many of these long-standing exemptions were carried over into the new system. Inlands on major royal and ecclesiastical lands, particularly in Wessex, were recorded as exempt, or rated at a beneficially low hidage, but in cases where no exemption was expressly recorded the internal arrangement of the hidage of estates shows that it existed none the less. The Domesday clerks found it was not too difficult to express these ancient inlands as ungelded or unhidated in areas where they were coherent entities, and there they retained their exempt or preferentially rated status. But inland in parts of the Danelaw was too fragmented to be individually exempted and it was assessed for and subject to tax.

3 The tenants and workers of the inland

At present the social history of Anglo-Saxon England stands in urgent need of revision. When the task is undertaken it will be advisable to focus attention in the first instance not on the upper ranks of the peasantry, but on the rural proletariat, the *wealas*, *theowas* and *geburas*.[1]

This chapter considers the inland as a working unit and attempts to single out some of the characteristics of the people who lived and worked there, Finberg's *wealas, theowas* and *geburas*. The inhabitants of inlands had characteristics which survived long enough to be noted in the estate surveys of the twelfth and thirteenth centuries. Kent is the best-documented county in this respect: it had groups of tenants called *inmanni* in the thirteenth century, and a class of cottagers on the archbishop's manors were sometimes called 'inlanders'. Jolliffe and Everitt have both drawn attention to the tenants on the inland who were 'within the right of the lord'.[2] Outside Kent there does not seem to have been a general term for the inland population, but there is no doubt of their existence, their common services closely related to serving the manorial curia, and their dependent status.

A handful of texts has dominated discussions of the status of the Anglo-Saxon peasantry and has been used as the basis for some substantial and influential generalizations. Perhaps the best known of these is the treatise known as *Rectitudines singularum personarum*.[3] Over the years opinion has changed about its date and nature. P.D.A. Harvey has recently followed D. Bethurum in seeing it as connected with Bishop Wulfstan of Worcester and York, but with Wulfstan as

---

1. H.P.R. Finberg, 'Roman and Saxon Withington' in his *Lucerna: studies of some problems in the early history of England*, ed. H.P.R. Finberg (1964), 21–65 at 64–5.
2. A. Everitt, *Continuity and Colonization: the evolution of Kentish settlement* (1986), 178; J. Jolliffe, *Pre-Feudal England: the Jutes* (1933), 17–18, 143; R.A.L. Smith, *The Estates of Canterbury Cathedral Priory: a study in monastic administration* (1943), 120; F.R.H. du Boulay, *The Lordship of Canterbury: an essay on medieval society* (1966), 165; *DB* I, 2b.
3. *EHD* II, no. 172 at 813–16; Liebermann, I, 444–53.

collector and reviser of a mid-tenth-century text written as a guide for an estate manager. This text instructs him about what he should expect from the various kinds of people he would meet on an estate and what he should distribute to them in perks and allowances. Harvey would give it a west country provenance, particularly east Somerset and west Wiltshire, areas where the abbey of Bath had property, and, given the migratory tendencies of medieval manuscripts, he leaves room for Glastonbury Abbey as its place of origin.[4] Two other documents which have been used as evidence for the condition of the peasantry at large have elements in common with, and possibly a link with, the *Rectitudines*. A charter of 900 giving to the Old Minster, Winchester land at Stoke next to Hurstbourne Priors, Hampshire, lists the dues that 'the *ceorls* must do at Hurstbourne'.[5] A survey giving the hidage of a property at Tidenham, Gloucestershire, gives the various parts of the estate, the rents and payments due, and the obligations of the *geneat* and the *gebur*. It is undated and we do not know how it is connected with the charter of 956 and lease of 1061 also found in the only (and later) manuscript which preserves it.[6] It is likely that there were once a great many other documents like these, and that: 'We may be looking at three chance survivors of a kind of document that may have been common in the tenth century: the list of tenant obligations which was the precursor of the later manorial custumal.'[7]

The prevailing tendency has been to see Anglo-Saxon rural society as essentially 'manorialized', a view which has drawn heavily on this little group of documents. Tidenham was an illustration of Seebohm's thesis that 'the Saxon "hams" and "tuns" were manors with village communities in serfdom upon them.' Finberg used Hurstbourne and Tidenham as examples of a manorial economy where labour on seigneurial demesnes or home farms was provided by freed slaves and serfs.[8] In his seminal article on the origins of the manor in England, published in 1958, which has become the basis of many interpretations of early English society, T.H. Aston argued that the 'dichotomy between demesne and peasant land which is central to manorial history' was already in place by the seventh century and can be detected in a law of Ine of Wessex concerning tenancy. He too took

---

4. P.D.A. Harvey, '*Rectitudines singularum personarum* and *Gerefa*', EHR 426 (1993), 1–22.
5. BCS 594 (S 359); Robertson, *Charters*, CX at 206–7; *EHD* II, no. 173 at 816–17; H.P.R. Finberg, 'The churls of Hurstbourne', in *Lucerna*, 131–43; 'Anglo-Saxon England to 1042' in *Ag. Hist.* I.II. 385–525, at 452–3.
6. Robertson, *Charters*, CIX at 204–5; *EHD* II, no. 174 at 817–18; R.J. Faith, 'Tidenham, Gloucestershire, and the origins of the manor in England', *Landscape History* 16 (1994), 39–51.
7. Faith 'Tidenham, Gloucestershire', 40.
8. F. Seebohm, *The English Village Community* (1896), 126, 148–59; Finberg, 'Anglo-Saxon England to 1042', 511–14.

Tidenham as an example of a classical 'bipartite' manor.[9] The fact that *ceorl*, a general term for any non-noble person, was used to describe the heavily burdened tenants at Hurstbourne encouraged statements about the status of the peasantry as a whole. In Stenton's view, the Hurstbourne *ceorls* were 'men who, in origin, were unquestionably free' but whom a run of bad luck had induced to surrender their land on hard terms, and he thought that the cottager and the *gebur* of the *Rectitudines* were likewise at least free in origin.[10] For Finberg, Stenton's interpretation was strained. He saw the Hurstbourne *ceorls* as utterly dependent, not trembling on the verge of serfdom, as Stenton had, but 'well over the verge'.[11] Maitland was suspicious of the Hurstbourne document, but he took the *Rectitudines* and the Tidenham survey to be early evidence of the manorial economy, complete with demesne and tenant land. He was cautious about the status of the peasantry at large. Of the Tidenham *geburs*, 'whether they are free men, whether they are bound to the soil, whether the national courts will protect them in their tenure, we are not told'. He was unwilling to generalize from our knowledge of this group, and emphasized that although 'already in Ine's day there were many free men who were needy and had lords above them' this did not imply a universally unfree peasantry and he argued for the existence of 'swarms of free men' in Anglo-Saxon England.[12]

Broadly speaking, Seebohm's and Aston's views have gained wider acceptance than have Maitland's and Stenton's, and many modern works assume that the peasantry of Anglo-Saxon England was essentially unfree and in much the same dependent position *vis-à-vis* their lords as were the villeins of the thirteenth century. If the *geburs*, bordars, freedpeople and other similar worker-tenants who figure in our texts were typical of the peasantry at large, this would undoubtedly be true. A different approach is adopted here. The dependent peasantry – Finberg's 'rural proletariat' – are seen as essentially people of the inland. Whether compact or dispersed in berewicks, inland had a particular function: to provide the landlord with supplies. This shaped the lives and work of the people who lived there. They were a labour force which was mixed, and which changed significantly over time, but was always composed of people of notably dependent and low social status. We cannot take them, or the conditions under which they lived, as typical of the peasantry as a whole, for the inland was only part of an estate, and the Domesday figures, discussed at the end of this chapter, show that they were not half the rural population.

9. T.H. Aston, 'The origins of the manor in England', *TRHS* 5th series 8 (1958), 59–83, reprinted with 'The origins of the manor in England: a postscript' in *Social Relations and Ideas: essays in honour of R.H. Hilton*, ed. T.H. Aston, P.R. Coss, C. Dyer and J. Thirsk (1983), 1–43 at 9, 11, 18.
10. F.M. Stenton, *Anglo-Saxon England* (1947), 469.
11. Finberg, 'Anglo-Saxon England to 1042', 514.
12. F.W. Maitland, *Domesday Book and Beyond: three essays in the early history of England* (1960 edn), 386–97 at 396.

Although no account of Anglo-Saxon society would be convincing which did not give their evidence due weight, as this chapter will attempt to do, there are other reasons for caution in using our handful of texts as the basis for broad generalization. Leaving on one side the actual provenance of the *Rectitudines* itself, whether at Bath, Glastonbury or Worcester, can it be given any wider context? Harvey rules out the Carolingian capitularies, such as the *Capitulare de villis*, as models, either for style or general approach, for it was evidently not written, as they were, for the administrator of a royal estate. The *polyptyques* or estate surveys which survive for some northern Frankish estates from the seventh, eighth and ninth centuries seem too early to have been models, but they may have something to tell us nevertheless. They have been used in the past to construct a model of the 'bipartite' estate: the landholding divided between 'demesne' (*reserve*) and tenant land. This model is increasingly coming under reconstruction, and, what is more relevant here, the documents themselves are being seen in a new light. More than simple descriptions, they were normative statements of the estate owner's – the church's – dues and rights, recorded in order to establish a unified 'estate custom' over widely dispersed properties.[13] It is possible that the impulse behind the *Rectitudines*, and the documents which seem to be linked with it, was just such a policy of establishing the rights and customs of a newly reformed and endowed minster over all its lands. It would not be surprising if the movement under way from the 960s to reconstitute some of the major minsters, and establish others, on a more firmly monastic basis had been accompanied by a review of their estate management policies on more businesslike lines. If it indeed comes out of the world of the great religious landholders of Wessex in reforming mood, despite its very great intrinsic interest *Rectitudines* cannot be taken to be representative of landowners in England as a whole.

Slaves

To start with the first category of Finberg's 'rural proletariat', the *theowas* or *wealas*, slaves. The drift of the classic works on the European rural economy was that there was a gradual replacement of slavery by serfdom, the principal factor in this change being the emancipation of slaves and their housing on small plots of land. Recent work has tended to reverse this view in respect of significant parts of northern Europe, arguing that slavery did not simply fade away but had a longer life than was previously supposed, lasting in Francia into the

---

13. J.P. Devroey, 'Les premiers polyptyques remois, viie–viiie siècles', reprinted from *Le Grand domaine aux époques mérovingienne et carolingienne*, ed. A. Verhulst (Ghent 1985) in J.P. Devroey, *Etudes sur le grand domaine carolingien* (1993), 78-97.

eleventh century. Nor was serfdom, at least the serfdom of the tenth century on, its natural successor: serfdom is now seen as the product of a sudden transformation in the status of the peasantry, so sudden as to be described as a 'revolution' rather than resulting from a gradual evolution from slavery.[14]

While providing slaves and ex-slaves with plots of land is certainly something which can be observed in England, it seems to have produced a class of worker-tenants specific to the inland, rather than the very dependent but still self-sufficient small peasant who is the serf. Nor did slavery die out. Slaves remained an extremely important part of the workforce on large and small estates and in the household economy of many farmers. Their importance in so many and in such a wide range of agricultural enterprises ensured that slavery was still a substantial institution in the eleventh century.[15] Recent work by J.S. Moore has shown by conjecturally filling in the gaps in the Domesday recording of slaves that slavery was a much more important institution in eleventh-century England than was previously thought. Moore's revised figures would put the national percentage at 12 per cent, instead of the earlier 9 per cent, with slaves in some counties reaching nearly 20 per cent of the recorded population.[16]

Slavery may have survived the decline of the great villa estates of Roman Britain, and Gildas says that many British were enslaved as a result of the Anglo-Saxon conquests of the sixth and seventh centuries. The fact that *walh*, originally meaning 'foreigner' and, later, 'Briton', had by the tenth century come to mean 'slave' must signify that many Britons had lost their liberty. In many areas settled by Anglo-Saxons Britons survived in sufficient concentrations to influence English place-names. One name of this type, Walton – *walh-tun* – is considered by Gelling to date from a period when *walh* had come to mean not Briton but 'serf'.[17] 'Serf' may prove not to be the most useful translation, but some Waltons and Walcots do seem to have been places with distinctively low-status populations. They are often found near minsters: Charlbury, Oxfordshire; Eastry and Folkestone, Kent;

14. Marc Bloch's many writings on the subject include *Slavery and Serfdom in the Middle Ages: selected papers by Marc Bloch*, trans. W.R. Beer (Berkeley 1975); *Feudal Society*, trans. L.A. Manyon (2 vols 1961), chs 19, 20. P. Bonnassie, *From Slavery to Feudalism in South-Western Europe*, trans. J. Birrell (1991); G. Duby, *Rural Economy and Country Life in the Medieval West*, trans. C. Postan (1968), 37–8, 41; P. Toubert, 'La part du grand domaine dans le décollage économique de l'occident (viiie–xe siècles)' in *La croissance agricole du haut moyen âge* (Auch 1990), 60; H.-W. Goetz, 'Serfdom and the beginnings of a "seigneurial system" in the Carolingian period: a survey of the evidence', *Early Medieval Europe* 2 (1993), 29–51.
15. D.A.E. Pelteret, 'Slavery in Anglo-Saxon England' in *The Anglo-Saxons: synthesis and achievement*, ed. J.D. Woods and D.A.E. Pelteret (Waterloo, Ontario 1985), 117–33; J.S. Moore, 'Domesday slavery', *Anglo-Norman Studies* 11 (1988), 191–220; H.B. Clarke, 'Domesday slavery (adjusted for slaves)', *Midland History* 1.4 (1972), 37–46.
16. Moore, 'Domesday slavery'; Appendix 2 below.
17. M. Gelling, *Signposts to the Past* (1978), 93–5.

Deerhurst and Tewkesbury, Gloucestershire: all have a Walton or Walcot nearby. Another place-name element deriving from a term for 'Briton' is Comber- or Cumbe(r)- and places with this element are found near four major estate centres in Kent, Faversham, Maidstone, Otford and Lympne, all but Otford being minsters.[18]

Although capture in war must be one of its chief causes, the history of slavery cannot be reduced to one of racial conquest. The low status of some Britons has to be reconciled with the high status of others, with the inter-marriage of Britons with Anglo-Saxon immigrants, even at the level of royalty, and with the possible survival of the British church in some areas. Not all slaves were British. Wars between the Anglo-Saxon kingdoms themselves – and freelance raiding – brought human booty. Slaves were a valuable export: Anglian slaves were on sale in seventh-century northern Francia where they were freed and put to work on the estates of new monastic foundations.[19] If one were to speculate about what commodities might have contributed to England's booming export trade in the eighth-century 'age of emporia', slaves would be an obvious choice, although one which leaves virtually no trace in the archaeological record.

Slavery was essentially the bottom of a long slippery slope which was a hazard for the economically insecure, and the pressures of poverty meant that the stock of slaves was continually being replaced from within Anglo-Saxon society. One strategy for the poorest families in times of dire want is to sell their children into slavery: the law of the church allowed this without the child's consent if it was under seven, with its consent after that, and at fourteen a boy could sell himself into slavery.[20] This desperate measure at least ensured the child a chance of survival and improved the chances of the rest of the family, with one fewer mouth to feed and a little money in hand. A crowd of people who had sold themselves and their children into slavery in the late tenth century were freed by their female benefactor. The transaction is recorded in a book belonging to the church of St Cuthbert at Durham:

> Geatfleda has given freedom for the love of God and for the need of her soul: namely Ecceard the smith and Ælfstan and his wife and all their offspring, born and unborn, and Arcil and Cole and Ecgfert and Ealdhun's daughter and all those people whose heads she took for food in the evil days. And also she has freed those men she begged from Cwaespatric, namely Ælfwold and Colbrand

---

18. Everitt, *Continuity and Colonization*, 124, 189.
19. S. Sato, 'Les implantations monastiques dans la Gaule du nord: un facteur de la croissance agricole au viie siècle? quelques éléments d'hypothèse concernants les régions de Rouen et de Beauvais' in *La croissance agricole du haut moyen âge: chronologie, modalités, géographie*, Centre Culturel de l'Abbaye de Flaran (Auch 1990), 169–77.
20. *Penitential of Theodore* in *Councils and Ecclesiastical Documents relating to Great Britain and Ireland*, ed. A.W. Haddan and W. Stubbs (3 vols, 1869–78), III, 172–213 at 202.

and Ælsige and his son Gamal, Ethelred Tredewude and his stepson Uhtred, Aculf and Thurkil and Ælsige.

As its editor remarks: 'this little text sheds a grim light on conditions in time of famine and upheaval'.[21] Such poverty meant that some fell into debt and sold themselves to pay it off. It was a pious deathbed act for their creditor to forgive the debt and emancipate them, and wills of the ninth and tenth century make provision for this.

In Roman law the slave was the chattel of his master, without rights or legal personality, and post-Roman Britain may have retained some knowledge of this concept, as it did of the Roman law of property. Christian Anglo-Saxon England came into contact with a European tradition in which the existence of slavery was unchallenged. This was partly through the canon law which incorporated parts of the Roman law of slavery. Theodore insisted on conformity with a canon collection, probably that of Dionysius Exiguus, at the council of Hertford in 672. There were other points of contact: Aldhelm was familiar with a Roman law work, probably the *Breviary* of Alaric, and many Anglo-Saxon scholars may have picked up a smattering of law from Isidore of Seville's *Etymologies*. However, the fact of being *owned* is at the heart of the slave's existence and this is such a universal feature of slavery that there is no need to ascribe it to any particular legal tradition. The laws of Ethelbert of Kent, set down in writing 'following the example of the Romans', are a statement of Germanic custom, not an echo of Roman jurisprudence. The early law codes embody the idea of the slave's lack of legal personality. This is closely connected with the notion that he was legally kinless: it is his owner, not his kin, who pays compensation on his behalf and who clears him by oath when accused.[22]

As a major estate owner, the church was also a slave owner. It has been pointed out that on the estates of the bishop of Worcester, the see of the same Wulfstan whose *Sermon of the Wolf to the English* had excoriated those who had sold their countrymen into slavery, there were still over four hundred slaves in 1086.[23] Nevertheless, individual acts of Christian charity undoubtedly improved the lot of some slaves by freeing and housing them. Wilfrid's mission to Sussex was marked by manumission on a grand scale. Having instructed in the Christian faith the slaves on the estate given him to found a minster at Selsey he baptized them and freed 250 people. This had been a royal estate and the slaves part of its tied workforce: did Wilfrid perhaps set up his converts on smallholdings to work for the Northumbrian monks he had brought with him? Manumission and baptism may have gone together. A version of the mission to Northumbria, which credits a British priest

21. *EHD* I, 563–4.
22. Liebermann, I, 3–4: Ethelbert 11, 12, 14, 16.
23. Clarke, 'Domesday slavery', 40.

rather than Paulinus with the conversion of King Edwin, describes the baptism of his daughter 'with all her men and women'.[24]

While the church did not condemn slavery outright, canon law enjoined that a bishop should free some of his slaves at his death for the good of his soul and this came to be seen as part of any Christian's duty.[25] Many late Anglo-Saxon wills of laypeople contain manumission clauses. This may have been a by-product of the extension of bookland, for one of the benefits that holding land by charter conveyed was the power to free the slaves on it, *on hired und on tun*, both those in domestic service and agricultural workers at the curia.[26] Manumissions by individual landowners must have made a considerable impact over time to the composition of the workforce, turning crowds of slaves into settlements of tied smallholders. Æthelgifu, a rich Northamptonshire widow disposing of her lands in her home county and on her late husband's estate in Bedfordshire and Hertfordshire, freed at least 60 individuals, two slave households and six sets of children. By 1086 only 35 slaves remained on all the land she had owned.[27] Some time before 1038 Thurketel of Palgrave, a Danish Suffolk landowner, arranged for his freed slaves to be provided for: 'each is to have his toft and his *metecu* and his *metecorn*', his cow and corn for his support, and another Dane, Ketel, left his slaves 'all the things which are in their possession except the land'.[28] This last clause brings home the insecurity of the existence of the slaves of even a charitable owner.

Some, enslaved by a powerful neighbour, could get their freedom through the intercession of another. This could be expensive. When, late in the tenth century, one Ælfric tried to enslave one Putrael, Putrael went to Ælfric's brother Boia, who may have been a deacon of Exeter, and paid him 60 pence for his advocacy. Boia arranged terms by which Putrael and his family were released from any claims to their freedom by Ælfric and his family: the price was a full team of eight oxen.[29] The possibilities for collusion and oppression in such a situation must have been tempting. But the story shows that slaves could, for a fee, set about claiming freedom on their own account. The ceremony of manumission at the altar gave them the opportunity to make this a public and recorded occasion. The Bodmin Gospels record the manumission of over a hundred and fifty slaves freed at the altar of St Petroc between about 950 and 1050. Most of the manumitted were

---

24. *HE*, IV, 13; E. John, 'The origin of book-right' in his *Land Tenure in Early England: a discussion of some problems*, 13–15; E. John, 'Bede's use of *facultas*' in his *Orbis Britanniae* (1966), 264–71; H. Chadwick, *Studies on Anglo-Saxon Institutions* (1905), 372–3.
25. *Councils and Ecclesiastical Documents*, III, 583 (council of Chelsea).
26. John, 'Book-right' in *Land Tenure*, 15. For this interpretation of *tun* see pp. 173–5 below.
27. D. Whitelock, *The Will of Æthelgifu: a tenth century Anglo-Saxon manuscript* (1968), 35.
28. D. Whitelock, *Anglo-Saxon Wills* (1930), XXIV, XXXIV at 68–9, 88–91.
29. *EHD* I, no. 147 at 562.

Celtic, perhaps merely reflecting the racial mix of the area or possibly because the indigenous Celtic population were more likely to have been slaves than were the Saxons.[30] There was an entirely secular form of manumission too, which echoes forms found in some of the barbarian law codes. This ceremony took place at the crossroads and symbolically gave the freed person the right to travel.

Manumission brought into being, particularly on church estates, a class of servile tenants who were legally free but still dependent. They formed an important part of the agricultural workforce, particularly on the lands of the church: 24 were at work on Abingdon Abbey's barton in 1066.[31] *Colliberti* (sometimes *coliberti*), 'co-freed', were a class of half-free people, presumably freed as a group. They remained subject in important ways to their former owners who retained rights over their property and their children.[32] Three stages of freedom are represented by the 'half-free', slaves and freedmen (*lisingar*) in Wereham, Norfolk, bequeathed in the will of two East Anglian landowners in the late tenth or eleventh century.[33] Freed slaves may have had to pay for their freedom with labour, and wills show that their former owners could impose conditions of where and for whom they could work. They could be shifted round an estate where labour was needed, or given to legatees as a gift. Wulfmaer, a *collibertus* 'oppressed by the work and the name' bought his freedom from St Peter's, Gloucester with the gift of a fishery on the Severn at Framilode.[34] *Colliberti* appear in Domesday Book chiefly in Wessex (where the clerk was not sure whether they were *geburs* or not), but nowhere in large numbers, and it is likely that they were recorded elsewhere under another term.[35]

Although slaves have always been valued as a source of virtually costless labour in a wide range of societies, their housing and upkeep, however poor, represent an outlay on the owner's part and this means that they have to be employed in ways which make the most efficient use of them. The most economical use of slaves is to work them full-time over a long period and to replace them when they are past their optimum. If they are employed in this way it is worth while for the owner to invest time and trouble training them for responsible and semi-skilled tasks. Hence most Anglo-Saxon slaves are more likely to have been skilled workers and specialists rather than general agricultural labourers. (An exception was the hand-grinding done by women slaves in the early laws, work from which the spread of the water-mill, ubiquitous by the late eleventh century, eventually freed

30. H. Jenner, 'The manumissions in the Bodmin gospels', *Journal of the Royal Institution of Cornwall* 21 (1922), 235–60.
31. *DB* I, 58c.
32. Liebermann, I, 13, Wihtred 8; D.A.E. Pelteret, 'The *coliberti* of Domesday Book', *Studies in Medieval Culture* 12 (1978), 43–54.
33. Whitelock, *Wills*, no. XXXVI, at 92–3.
34. Finberg, 'Anglo-Saxon England to 1042', 440–1.
35. See Appendix 2.

them for other tasks.) Living on the premises, perhaps with the stock, slaves could be closely supervised, and like the slave in the classical world flogged for disobedience or theft. Skilled stockmen, tied to the estate, were vital to its economy, for stock was its most valuable capital asset and stock-keeping was *par excellence* the skilled work needing all-the-year-round attention for which slave labour was well suited. Domesday gives us some indication of the work done by slaves, and this is borne out by references in the laws and the *Rectitudines*. On the model estate of the *Rectitudines* the beekeeper, dairymaids and swineherd were all slaves. Other stock workers listed – oxherd, shepherd, goatherd and cheesemaker (a woman) – are not called slaves, but received food allowances and other perks and were very closely associated with the home farm and probably resident on the inland. Slave stockmen and swineherds are found working for Ely Abbey, responsible for the extensive herds of swine on its swine pastures in Hatfield Forest under the overall supervision of an official who kept some kind of account.[36] Land at Beddington, Surrey, belonging to the bishop of Winchester, was leased between 900 and 910 stocked with a small herd of sheep, 9 oxen and 114 pigs: seven slaves and an unspecified number of stockmen went with the estate as its inland workforce.[37] The Ramsey Abbey oxherds, haywards, swineherds and shepherds allotted cotlands on its demesnes in the twelfth century must have been much the same kind of people.[38]

Ploughing, the most skilled and important work on any estate, is consistently associated with slavery, and this is doubtless because the ploughman and his assistant were responsible for the care of the teams as well as the ploughing itself. It was important that they be trusted, or at least very closely controlled: tenants who deliberately mistreat their lord's livestock when ploughing are a topos of medieval stories. Ælfric, abbot of Eynsham at the turn of the eleventh century, describes the work of the seigneurial ploughman, who feeds and waters the beasts and mucks them out, and makes it plain that he is a slave. 'Hey hey, it's hard work because I am not free.'[39] S.P.J. Harvey points out the significance of the formal ceremony of enslavement: the owner put an ox-goad or a bill-hook into the slave's hand, symbols of the work he was to do driving the oxen or clearing new land.[40] It was probably as ploughman that slaves were retained longest. Domesday consistently shows that, where they are present at all, they are present at the rate of two to each seigneurial plough team: the ploughman or *tentor* who drove the plough and the *fugator* who goaded the team or led the lead ox. Ploughmen's houses and holdings remained recognizable, as *encheland* or *terra akermannorum*, long after other specialist inland

---

36. See pp. 82–3 below.
37. BCS 618, 619 (S 1444); *EHD* I, 561.
38. J.A. Raftis, *The Estates of Ramsey Abbey* (1957), 52–3.
39. G.N. Garmonsway, ed., *Ælfric's Colloquy* (2nd edn 1947), 20–1.
40. S.P.J. Harvey, 'Domesday England' in *Ag. Hist.* II, 45–136 at 66–7.

holdings had become a thing of the past. At Stoneham, the major centre of demesne cultivation in the archbishop of Canterbury's Malling estate in the fourteenth century, were the holdings of the manorial oxherds.[41]

The inland smith, essential to maintain the ironwork of the plough, may have been a household servant or slave: he was one of the three workers that a departing lord was allowed to take with him on giving up a lease, and a smith, Ecceard is among the people who had given up their freedom in return for food recorded in the Durham gospels.[42]

The 'sower', who may have been responsible for doling out seedcorn, and the supervisors of the granary, the pasture and the woodland all appear in *Rectitudines* as permanent resident estate staff, probably slaves or near-slaves. These responsible jobs were entrusted to people who were tied to the estate, relied on its owner for housing and food, and thus had the most reason for loyalty to their employer. It is a parallel to this situation that the office of reeve on the post-Conquest estate went with serfdom. These skilled tied workers were all forerunners of the *famuli*, permanent farm servants, who were still 'an important tributary, sometimes the mainstream of the total labour supply on thirteenth-century estates'.[43] Abingdon Abbey in the twelfth century had an inland labour force which would have been immediately recognizable in the tenth: in all 22 oxherds, pigmen, beadles, shepherds, fencers and so on, all with cotlands.[44]

Domestic slavery was important in the seigneurial household, where women slaves were seamstresses and skilled needlewomen and weavers. Æthelgifu's will freed three women whom she had taught to read in her household at Standon in Hertfordshire, for they were to sing the psalter in her memory. One of her priests was a slave and so was her huntsman, Wulfric, whose family were freed by her will and given 'men' of their own.[45]

Although most of the references that we have to slaves show them at work in the high-status household and on the great estate, it would be a mistake to underestimate their important role in the economy of the smaller estate and the family farm. An Essex sokeman employing one slave may have been an example of a very common type, but Scandinavian England is the only context in which slaves at this level have received any attention.[46] The Scandinavian settlers of the ninth century came from a culture in which slaves played a very important

---

41. Du Boulay, *The Lordship of Canterbury*, 132.
42. Liebermann, I, 118: Ine 63.
43. M.M. Postan, *The Famulus: the estate labourer in the twelfth and thirteenth centuries*, EcHR Supp. 2 (1954).
44. *Chronicon monasterii de Abingdon*, ed. J. Stevenson, Rolls Series (2 vols, 1858), II, 301.
45. Whitelock, *Will of Æthelgifu*, 8, 12.
46. R.M. Karras, *Slavery and Society in Medieval Scandinavia* (1988); D.A.E. Pelteret, 'Slavery in the Danelaw' in *Social Approaches to Viking Studies*, ed. R. Samson (1991), 179–88.

part, both as traded goods and as workers. Slavery was an integral part of Scandinavian peasant farming. Slaves were an essential adjunct to the labour of the family on Norwegian farms, in Denmark on farms of all sizes from the 'magnate farmstead' to the family holdings in villages and isolated farms alike. Danish settlers may well have brought slaves with them and established them on the farms they acquired or created in England, possibly freeing them on arrival: the *liesing* or freedman appears in the treaty of Alfred and Guthrum, and freedmen appear to have been able to gain higher status in the Danelaw than elsewhere in England, acquiring land and establishing farms of their own, giving rise to place-names ending in -*lysing*.[47] Slaves did not have any specific role other than general labourer in the Scandinavian homelands, and outside the largest estates this may have been the case in England too. We have almost no information about farmers' slaves in the rest of England, but the laws routinely mention *ceorls* and 'freemen' as slave-owners, with no suggestion that to own slaves indicated elevated status. In fact it is the small landlord who cannot command the services of a large tenantry who must rely proportionately more on slave labour than does the owner of a large estate. The Russian historian A.Y. Gurevich analysed the distribution of slaves recorded in Domesday on large and small manors: on the smaller manors the ratio of slaves to seigneurial plough teams was 7:10, on larger manors it was 4:10.[48] When the church of Worcester leased some of its land at Luddington, Warwickshire, early in the eleventh century with two plough teams and 100 sheep, twelve slaves were evidently thought about the right size of workforce for this small estate, so a substantial family farm with a single plough team may have employed half a dozen slaves.[49]

Of all domestic building types the slave's hut has the smallest chance of appearing in the archaeological record, but one possibility is that they are among the sunken-featured buildings found on early Anglo-Saxon settlement sites. These are found in rather specific circumstances: in association with larger timber structures, and on sites earlier than the seventh century.[50] Figure 10 shows conjectural reconstructions of two such buildings. Chapelot has proposed that some of the sunken-featured buildings on Frankish sites were slave huts. Similar buildings found in Viking Age Denmark have been identified as slave huts, and a *thraelahus* (slave house) in an Icelandic version of a Norse saga shows that such a category was an accepted part of the landscape. Early settlers, both Germanic and Scandinavian, may have brought slaves with them and housed them near their own dwellings where they would be usefully to hand: the early settlers of

---

47. Pelteret, 'Slavery in the Danelaw', 183–4.
48. Cited by E.A. Kosminsky, *Studies in the Agrarian History of England in the Thirteenth Century*, (1956), 281.
49. Robertson, *Charters*, trans. R. Kisch, LXXIX, 154–5, 402.
50. See pp. 129–30 below.

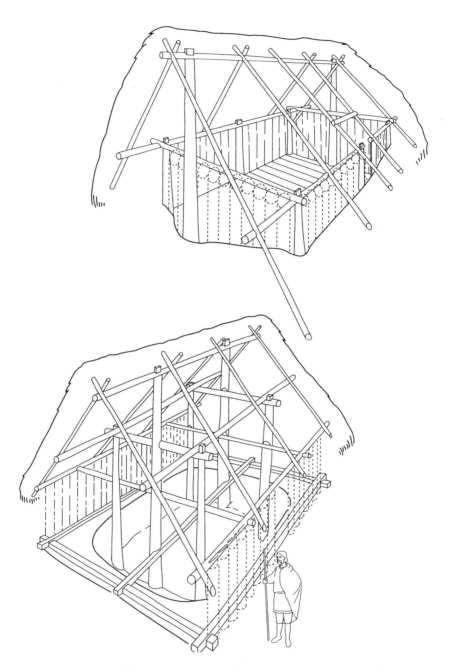

Figure 10 Workers' housing? 'Sunken featured buildings' at West Stow, Suffolk. *Source*: after S. West, *West Stow: the Anglo-Saxon village*, East Anglian Archaeology 24 (2 vols, 1985), II, fig. 290, by permission of Suffolk County Council.

Iceland did just that, bringing ten slaves apiece.[51] The disappearance of the dugout shack from the archaeological record from about the seventh century may have to do with factors unknown to us, but it may reflect the possibility that estate workers and slaves were being better housed. The Domesday commissioners are said to have counted 'those living in *tuguria* as well as those living in houses and owning fields', and *tuguria* may have been cottages and cabins more comfortable than the dugout.[52]

The establishment of inlands, each with its own workforce, must have greatly increased the need for worker housing near the seigneurial curia, minster or royal vill. A Winchester lease obliged the lessee to house, *hamettan*, two peasant families born on the estate.[53] As we shall see, the inland was an area likely to have been crowded with the dwellings of the workers and tenants who lived there. Possibly over time archaeology will reveal some traces of them in the at present unidentified 'earthworks' surrounding many curial sites.

It was probably common to provide slaves and freedpeople with small plots of land when they were housed. The *Rectitudines* recommends that the *kotsetla* should have five acres in return for week work, all slaves a strip of ploughland, a *sulhhæcer*, the beekeeper and ploughman two or three acres, the beadle a 'bit of land', *sum landsticce* and the hayward 'a piece of land nearest the pasture'. This process, for which French provides the useful term *alotissement*, has often seen as the main agent which transformed the slavery of the ancient world into the serfdom of the medieval.[54] However, it is important to make some distinctions here. The housing of slaves brought into being a class of smallholders who were completely dependent on, and tied to, the inland. They were essential to its working, and there is no doubt of their numerical importance, as analysis of their numbers in Domesday will show. But the category of peasants who came to be called serfs in post-Conquest England mostly came into being by quite a different route. The essential distinction is between worker and peasant. The freed slave was a worker who in return for selling his labour as a commodity received a 'wage in land' from the lord, who was his employer and sole purchaser of that labour. The lord, in his capacity as employer, was essential to him. By contrast, the serf was a peasant with a holding, which, however small,

---

51. J. Chapelot, 'Le font de cabane dans le habitat rural ouest-européen: état des questions', *Archaeologie Médiévale* 10 (1980), 5–57; Karras, *Slavery and Society*, 78–82.
52. *EHD* II, no. 198 at 851; W.H. Stevenson, 'A contemporary description of the Domesday survey', *EHR* 22 (1907), 72–84 at 74.
53. F.E. Harmer, *Anglo-Saxon Writs* (1952), XVII.
54. For example, see D. Herlihy, 'The Carolingian *mansus*', *EcHR* 2nd series 13 (1960), 79–89, at 85; M. Bloch, 'How and why ancient slavery came to an end' and 'The *colliberti*: a study on the formation of the servile class', both in *Slavery and Serfdom*; C.E. Perrin, *Seigneurie rurale en France et en Allemagne du debut du ixe à la fin du xiie siècle* (Paris, n.d.)

supported him and his family and provided a surplus which was transferred to the lord in rent paid in cash, kind or labour (or in all these). This transfer of the serf's surplus was only made possible because the lord had control of the land: the lord was not as economically essential to his existence as he was to that of the slave.

Slaves and freedmen were provided with holdings which, like the 'allotments' of the post-enclosure village, were of a size well calculated to prevent them becoming self-sufficient. It is a further sign of their economic dependence that, in addition to their plots and gardens, these inland workers were entitled to food allowances and customary handouts. The *Rectitudines* shows what 'selling one's head for food' could mean on a large and well-run estate. It was not necessarily a bad deal. Slaves were to be provided with a range of traditional perks appropriate to their employment: the herdsman a young pig in the sty, the cowherd the 'beestings' or the first milk from the cow after the birth of a calf for a fortnight, the sower a ration of seed. Beside these, and probably more important, were their basic rations: for a female slave eight pounds of corn, one sheep or three pence for winter food, beans in Lent and whey in summer. All the slaves on the estate were to have food at Christmas and Easter and a 'harvest handful'. A law of Ine states that 'for every labourer a man has he shall pay six weys as *beregafole*': this may be some kind of tax, but it is just possible that it is a traditional dole of barley.[55] Although custom no doubt differed from place to place, it is probable that these perks and rations were widespread. The text known as the *Gerefa*, describing the office of the reeve, probably written late in the tenth or early in the eleventh century, enjoins him not to act despotically, in other words without regard to the rules, but to respect local custom. These customary entitlements may have mitigated the harsh paternalism of the inland labour regime.[56]

Bordars

The Domesday commissioners were instructed to enumerate for each manor the *villani, cottarii et servi*, the villans, cottagers and slaves. But Domesday Book itself includes another category of people not included in this list: the *bordarii* or bordars. The clerks evidently recognized in almost every English county a category of people for whom this seemed to them the most appropriate term. Bordars formed 30 per cent of the total enumerated population. They are unevenly distributed, being between 20 and 40 per cent of the enumerated population in most counties, under 20 per cent in four (Huntingdonshire, Lincolnshire, Rutland and Middlesex) and 40 to 50 per cent in three (Dorset, Hampshire and Worcestershire), and are most

55. *EHD* II, no. 172 at 813–16; Liebermann, I, 116–17: Ine 59.1.
56. Liebermann, I, 453–5 (*Gerefa*).

numerous in Essex where they were half the recorded population.[57]
What were bordars? The term does not appear in any English text
before Domesday and is not common outside its folios. While we can
see the Old English roots of other Domesday terms, like the sokemen
awkwardly Latinized as *sochmanii* or the *cotsetla* who becomes the
cotarius, there is no term like 'bordar' in Anglo-Saxon. So *bordarius*
must be a Latin translation of a Norman French term, and this term is
likely to have been *bordier*. *Bordiers* in northern France in the Middle
Ages were smallholders holding small allotments of land by particularly
servile tenure. L. Mussuet has described the *bordiers* of Normandy,
Maine and Poitou. In Normandy, where there was no slavery, they
were the bottom rank of a strictly hierarchical society. The *bordier*
typically had no plough team of his own and worked with his hands for
the lord at a wide range of low status and dirty work described as *opera
servilia*, from cleaning chimneys to carrying out and spreading
nightsoil, building and general labouring. In spite of his low status
he was a trusted servant and probably lived on the curia, working as
overseer, carrying seed to the sowers and acting as nightwatchman.
Bordars' housing is likely to have been similar to cottars', for the
Domesday clerks on occasion used the terms 'bordar' and 'cottar'
indiscriminately. Perhaps their cottages were among the *tuguria* of
Bishop Robert Losinga of Hereford's account of the Domesday survey.[58]

Bordars' smallholdings seem often to have been grouped together
and known collectively as 'bordland'. They were evidently physically
part of the inland, as the *masurae bordariorum* at Bovecumbe in the
Isle of Wight, or the lands of the 'seven bordars who dwell on the
inland' of St Martin's at Canterbury.[59] A study of Porlock, Somerset,
has identified plots of land used by serfs and bordars for growing
subsistence crops. These plots appear on the tithe map as very small
rectangular fields behind the village. Porlock was the only nucleated
settlement in this area of scattered farms.[60] On what looks very much
like the vestiges of the inland of the royal manor at Isleham,
Cambridgeshire, the holdings of ten 'boarders' were set together away
from the fen, and unlike their freer neighbours, the 'boarders' had no

---

57. See Appendix 2.
58. L. Mussuet, 'La tenure en bordage, aspects normands et manceaux', *Revue
historique de droit français et étranger*, 4th series 28 (1950), 140; R. Carabie 'La
propriété foncière dans le très ancien droit normand (xie–xiiie siècles)',
Bibliothèque d'histoire du droit normand, 2nd series 5 (Caen 1943), 111; G.T.
Beech, *A Rural Society in Medieval France: the Gatine of Poitou in the Eleventh
and Twelfth Centuries* (Baltimore 1964), 103. For another interpretation: S.P.J.
Harvey, 'Evidence for settlement study: Domesday Book' in *English Medieval
Settlement*, ed. P.H. Sawyer (1979), 105–9 at 107–9. *Tuguria*: see p. 69 above.
59. *DB* I, 52b, 2; *The Register of St Augustine's Abbey, Canterbury, Commonly Called
the Black Book*, ed. G.J. Turner and H.E. Salter, British Academy Records of
Social and Economic History (2 parts 1915, 1924), 308, 22.
60. S. Everett, 'The Domesday geography of three Exmoor parishes', *Proc. Somerset
Archaeological and Natural History Society* 112 (1968), 54–60.

rights in that valuable resource.[61] Losinga's phrase 'those living in *tuguria* as well as those living in houses (*domus*) and owning fields', shows that the *domus* went with fields, while *tugurium* did not. Bordar holdings were small and likely to have been measured in acres, typically between five and eight, rather than in yardlands as were the holdings of the *villani*. They were thus distinct from those of the cottars – who probably included freed and 'housed' ex-slaves – who generally had no land other than their *cotagium* or cottage plot. These small plots needed only small forces: analysing the plough team figures for bordars and cottars together, Lennard found that nearly 40 per cent had no plough beasts at all, and 23 per cent had a share in a team. In most Domesday counties bordars had two or more plough beasts.[62]

The close connection of the bordars with the inland explains the etymology of their name. It was the seigneurial table and its needs that gave bordars and bordland their name, from OE and Norman French *borde*, table. This, at any rate, is how the term was understood by the author of the thirteenth-century legal treatise *On the Laws and Customs of England*. In his discussion of the various categories of *dominicum*, demesne, an area which he considers included people as well as land, he states: 'That is also demesne what a person has privately for his table, as are Bordlands in English' (E*st autem dominicum quod quis habet ad mensam suam et proprie, sicut sunt bordlands Anglice).*[63] The abbot's 'hinlandes' were still known as 'land for the abbot's table' at Ramsey in the twelfth century.[64]

A.J.L. Winchester has gathered references to 'bordland' from a wide range of estates in England and lowland Scotland in the later middle ages. He found it was associated with major estate centres, and in Scotland was an import 'associated with the new pattern of lordship and lordly seats created by twelfth century feudalization'.[65] In Wales *tir byrdd*, 'table land or demesne land at the lord's court', was 'an element in the native landholding pattern' and Ireland too had its 'mensal land'.[66] The Normans were to develop their 'table lands' on their new possessions in England, Wales and Ireland, and give an anglicized Norman French term to them and their inhabitants, but Anglo-Norman bordland was essentially the same institution as Anglo-Saxon inland. It is probable that Domesday classifies as bordars a very heterogeneous

61. S. Oosthuizen, 'Isleham: a medieval inland port', *Landscape History* 15 (1993), 29–35.
62. R.V. Lennard, 'The economic position of the bordars and cottars of Domesday Book', *Economic Journal* 61 (1951), 342–71; *Rural England 1086–1135: a study of social and agrarian conditions* (1959), 338–64.
63. *Henry de Bracton, de legibus et consuetudinibus Angliae*, ed. G.E. Woodbine, reissued with translation by S.E. Thorne (4 vols, Cambridge, Mass. 1968–77), III, fo 263 at 273.
64. *Cartularium monasterii de Rameseia*, ed. W.H. Hart and P.A. Lyons, Rolls Series, (3 vols, 1884–93), II, 25.
65. A.J.L. Winchester, 'The distribution and significance of "bordland" in medieval Britain', *AgHR* 34 (1986), 129–39.
66. G.R.J. Jones, 'Post-Roman Wales' in *Ag. Hist.* I.II, 299–349 at 338.

group of inland workers, distinguishing them simply by their smallholdings near the curia, their inferior housing, their work on the inland and their dependent status. Encountering a group of people who seemed so similar to the servile smallholders they knew from Normandy, the compilers of Domesday gave them a familiar French name and Latinized it.

Bordars resident at seigneurial and royal centres often had quasi-domestic jobs. Some worked in the hall itself or, like the *cotmen territorii* on the bishop of Worcester's manor of Fladbury, Worcestershire, in the kitchen, bakehouse and brewhouse. They are the *servientes curiae* of the church at Evesham, and at Tewkesbury they live around the hall.[67] The inland tenants in Kent lived on lands that the early kings of Kent had reserved for their own use, and their duties reflect this, being largely concerned with provisioning and preparing royal residences for the king's use and that of his usual retinue of companions and servants. This domestic service may account for the number of small servile tenancies commonly found at the sites of major minsters and other centres: they are quite distinct from the concentrations of agricultural tenancies found in neighbouring vills. C. Dyer has drawn attention to the large numbers of bordars who lived in towns. In the Northgate and Westgate wards of Canterbury they far outnumbered *villani*.[68] Some were members of an urban proletariat of a notably servile kind. Forty-eight in Norwich were 'too poor to pay 'customs', 20 in Thetford paid only head-money.[69] The towns that grew up at the feet of a great minster had *quartiers* where the minster's servants lived. The 'Bondgate' at Peterborough was said to have been the home of the '*nativi* of the inner vill', probably descendants of abbey servants. They had their own tofts, later augmented by arable holdings outside the town.[70] Others worked on the agricultural lands which still formed part of the fabric of the eleventh-century town. Colchester's royal inland had 10 bordars living on it and working as labourers, and 10 bordars with no land of their own worked on the royal grange at Ipswich. Holywell, outside the walls of Oxford, had 24 'men with gardens' who may have been entrepreneurial market-gardeners exploiting the market for fresh produce, or something more akin to bordars: Oxford had its urban farmyards on which they would have found employment.[71] As town populations expanded these urban

---

67. *The Red Book of Worcester*, ed. M. Hollings, Worcestershire Historical Society (4 vols, 1934–50), IV, xi; *DB* I, 175c, 163b.
68. C.C. Dyer, 'Towns and cottages in eleventh-century England' in *Studies in Medieval History presented to R.H.C. Davis*, ed. H. Mayr-Harting and R.I. Moore (1985), 91–106; K.P. Witney, 'The economic position of husbandmen at the time of Domesday Book: a Kentish perspective', *EcHR* 2nd series 37 (1984), 23–34.
69. *DB* II, 116b, 173a, 290a.
70. E. King, *Peterborough Abbey 1086–1310: a study in the land market* (1973), 59, quoting W.T. Mellows, *The Local Government of Peterborough* [2 parts 1919–24], 195.
71. J.H. Round, 'The Domesday of Colchester', *The Antiquary* 6 (1882), 8–9, 95–100, 251–6; *DB* I, 158c; J. Blair, *Anglo-Saxon Oxfordshire* (1994), 145.

agricultural lands were developed for housing: by 1086 at Bury St Edmunds 342 houses had been built on the abbey demesne lands which had been under the plough in the time of King Edward.[72] The small tenancies which had formed part of urban inlands may have been shifted to extra-mural lands, like the tofts of the Bondgate tenants at Peterborough.

Like slaves, bordars worked as part of the labour force of the upper peasantry and small gentry, their cottages and smallholdings forming miniature inlands on large farms. Sokemen in Lincolnshire and Derbyshire had bordars 'under them' and many Domesday holdings of a hide or so had one or two.[73] But they are much more commonly found on great estates where they played an important part as general labourers. Those on Westminster Abbey's estates 'bore the brunt of demesne demands for labour' in 1086.[74] *Micel weorcrædan* would have been as appropriate a description of their obligations as it had been for the worker-tenants of the *Rectitudines*. This involvement in the economy of agrarian inlands is at the root of their existence. Post-Conquest evidence shows how important the regular labour rent of the holders of very small plots of land was in the seigneurial economy. C. Dyer records through the wide estates of the bishop of Worcester the process by which the bishop and his sub-tenants 'found it more convenient to grant a smallholding to their permanent labour force rather than to feed and clothe them directly'.[75] These people owed exceptionally heavy labour rent in the twelfth century. It is widely typical of the bordars as a class, and a mark of their servile condition, that their labour rent is very heavy in relation to the amount of land that they held. At Crondall, a Hampshire manor of St Swithun's Priory, the cottar owed the same range of services as did the holder of a standard yardland.[76] The hard terms on which they held their land must make us suppose that bordars' tenancies had evolved to meet seigneurial demands for labour from a group which was in no position to bargain. Figure 11, from C.C. Thornton's meticulous description of the evolution of the demesne of one of the bishop of Winchester's manors, Rimpton in Somerset, shows in detail how bordars' holdings evolved from what might well have been a common piece of estate management. A core of freedpeople were first provided with a cottage and toft, then given small service holdings on the inland.[77]

72. *VCH Suffolk*, I (1911), 509. For urban bartons, see pp. 37–8 above.
73. F.M. Stenton, *Types of Manorial Structure in the Northern Danelaw* in Oxford Studies in Social and Legal History 2 (1910), 19.
74. B.F. Harvey, *Westminster Abbey and its Estates in the Middle Ages* (1977), 102.
75. C.C. Dyer, *Lords and Peasants in a Changing Society: the estates of the bishopric of Worcester 680–1540* (1980), 97.
76. A.E. Levett, *Studies in Manorial History* (1938), 52–3.
77. C.C. Thornton, 'The demesne of Rimpton 938 to 1412: a study in economic development' (Ph.D. thesis, University of Leicester, 1988), 60–3.

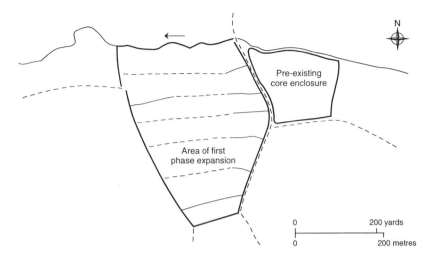

Figure 11 Rimpton, Somerset. In the first settlement phase as suggested by C.C. Thornton, seven small plots were provided for estate workers just outside a previously existing core area, later the site of the manor house and church. *Source*: after M. Aston, 'Medieval settlement sites in Somerset' in *The Medieval Landscape of Wessex*, ed. M. Aston and C. Lewis (1994), 219–37, fig. 11.6.

Wage workers

M.M. Postan showed how the medieval estate worker, the *famulus*, came to be replaced by wage workers on many thirteenth-century estates, and when extra labour was needed at critical times in the farming year it was bought in.[78] There may have been a pool of available wage labourers in Anglo-Saxon England but the size, even the existence, of this group is a matter of guesswork. It may be anachronistic to make too much of the difference between slaves and wage labourers. Slaves could earn money: the laws refer to their earnings, and the slave's property (the *peculium* of Roman law) was given the translation *ceorles æhte* (*ceorl*'s property) in one vocabulary list.[79] *Hyringmanna*, hired labourers, were put to work on Ely's new lands in the tenth century and in the *Gerefa* treatise the reeve is in charge of *hyrmen*, whom he directs to work where they are needed. He is to see that they are clothed and paid their correct wages and the writer recommends that, for better discipline, they should not be drawn from within the lord's own household, his *folgðe*.[80] The word

---

78. Postan, *The Famulus*.
79. *Anglo-Saxon and Old English Vocabularies*, ed. T. Wright and R.P. Wullcker (2 vols 1884), IV.115.19.
80. Robertson, *Charters*, app. 2, IX at 252–7; Liebermann, I, 453–5 (*Gerefa*).

hyrman is not a common one and perhaps the *Gerefa*, a literary exercise, is not secure evidence of Anglo-Saxon practice. However, the amount of low denomination currency in circulation from the eighth century on suggests that there were many small-scale transactions in the economy. If there were small spenders, there may well have been small earners too.

Geburs

A law of Ine refers to a man who 'takes a yard of land or more at a fixed money rent (*rœdegafole*) and cultivates it'. If the lord wishes to increase the rent to include labour as well as money rent he need not accept the new terms unless the lord gives him a house, but in that case he has no option. Had he not been housed, he could have left, forfeiting the tenancy and that year's crop. In this important text, for T.M. Charles-Edwards, 'the roots of villeinage' can be seen and T.H. Aston drew on it as evidence for the existence of the manorial system, with its division into demesne and tenant land, in seventh-century Wessex. Here it is considered as vital and early evidence of the status of the inland population, but it is not extrapolated to apply to the peasantry at large, still less to explain phenomena which were essentially part of the post-Conquest world.

Charles-Edwards's lucid analysis of this law begins by showing what the most readily available printed texts do not: that it is one of a group of laws relating to people who give up their tenancies, and the conditions relating to their departure. It is the fact of being housed that prevents the yardlander from leaving. Charles-Edwards shows how crucially this undermined his independence: 'By living in a home provided by the lord the tenant renounces the right to depart from land or lord, and gives the lord the power to choose whether to demand only rent or both labour or rent.'[81] Ine's law does not assign this yardlander to any particular social category, but the peasant with a yardland who is housed and tied to the estate corresponds in several respects to the *gebur*, and about the *gebur* we know a fair amount. He appears in the *Rectitudines* as an 'outfitted' farmer, granted seven sown acres on his yard of land, two oxen, six sheep and a cow, and 'tools for his work and utensils for his house', in return for which 'outfit' he does certain work and makes certain payments. His labour rent was 'in some places heavy, in some places light' and varied not according to the custom of the region, *folces geriht*, which would have made it in some sense subject to the law, but from estate to estate according to the rights of the lord of the estate, *hlafordes landriht* and estate custom, *landlaga*. P.D.A. Harvey has detected in the language of

---

81.   T.M. Charles-Edwards, 'The distinction between land and moveable wealth in Anglo-Saxon England' in *English Medieval Settlement*, ed. Sawyer, 97–104 at 103; Aston, 'Origins of the manor'.

the *Rectitudines* references to how 'we' do things on a particular estate, and we have in the circumstances of the *gebur* signs of the formation of the local manorial custom which was to govern the lives of the inland population and their successors.[82]

The *gebur* had his land rent-free for a year, after which he owed regular week-work of two days a week as directed during most of the year, rising to three days at harvest and from the feast of the Purification (2 February) to Easter. During the winter ploughing season he ploughed an acre a week. He owed as 'boon works' three acres more ploughing and ploughed and sowed with his own seed three acres as ploughing rent, *gafolyrðe*. He maintained a hound at his own expense for the lord – perhaps the equivalent of 'walking' a puppy for a hunt pack today – and took a turn as shepherd for the lord's flock. He owed ten pence *gafol* and food rents in barley and hens.

A very similar package or regular week-work, ploughing, boon works and renders in cash and kind was owed by the *geburs* on the abbey of Bath's manor of Tidenham, Gloucestershire, whose holdings were also probably a yardland.[83] A charter of about 900, conveying land at Stoke next to Hurstbourne Priors, Hampshire, to the Old Minster at Winchester, lists 'the dues (*rihta*) that the *ceorls* must do at Hurstbourne'.[84] Week-work, ploughing rent, payments in cash and kind very similar to those at Tidenham were due 'from each *hiwisc*'. This word means both 'hide' and 'household' and we do not know whether they were due from each hide of the 60 that comprised the property or from each household or tenant, as was the case with the Tidenham *geburs*. Finberg pointed out that the 40 pence due from each hide would have amounted to the same 10 pence from each yardland due from the *gebur* of the *Rectitudines*. C. Thornton's analysis of the development of tenancies at Rimpton shows that yardlands were let to the bishop of Winchester's tenants on very similar terms.[85]

It is plain, then, that at least a century and a half before the Conquest major minsters like Winchester and Bath were able to draw on the well-organized labour of a class of *geburs* in return for the grant of yardlands which they may have stocked with the essential capital equipment and which very likely reverted to the landlord at the tenant's death. The role of the *geburs* on the estate was as ploughmen and general labourers, not as skilled stockmen or specialist workers. Their weekly ploughing rent was very heavy by the standards of post-Conquest customary tenancies. It would probably have taken at least

---

82. Liebermann, I, 444–52; *EHD* II, 813–16; Harvey, '*Rectitudines*'.
83. See note 6.
84. See note 5. BCS 594 (S 359) records the donation of ten hides at Stoke to the Old Minster, Winchester, adjacent to land it already had at Hurstbourne. The list of obligations follows the witness list and is headed 'Here are written the dues (*rihta*) that the *ceorls* must render at (*to*) Hurstbourne'. Both Hurstbourne and Stoke were exempt from all royal dues. Finberg, 'Anglo-Saxon England to 1042', 452–3.
85. Thornton, 'Demesne of Rimpton', 60–3.

three days a week, and while we cannot calculate the exact acreage involved it must have been a large amount, as the ploughing season extended over several months – demesne cultivation may already have been the 'very long-winded affair', involving repeated ploughings, that J. Langdon describes for the post-Conquest demesne.[86] The *geburs* may on some estates have been responsible for the regular ploughing that elsewhere was the responsibility of permanent professional ploughmen, often slaves. No ploughman is named among the estate servants in the *Rectitudines* (although he may appear there as the *folgere*), and no demesne plough teams appear in the Domesday entry for Tidenham.[87]

The *gebur*'s economy was very closely involved with the lord's. The *Rectitudines* shows that on that estate he was lent stock from seigneurial flocks and herds, and pastured his pigs with the lord's. What kind of people would be willing, or forced by necessity, to take on land on such terms? Not every family could support all its members, and it is possible that free but poor people looking for land and work fell outside the protection of the kin. Any peasant society will produce some unmarried and landless people, even if they remain in this state only for part of their lives. *Anilepimen* (from OE *anlepig*, solitary), unmarried people, are found looking for work on the post-Conquest manor. Many became servants in husbandry in prosperous peasant families. Before the Conquest, when the supply of land was greater, their counterparts may well have been prepared to take on holdings on terms which could easily slip into servitude.[88] Although burdened and dependent, the *gebur* was not an estate worker with a 'wage in land' but a self-sufficient small peasant. He produced a surplus from which the lord could command dues in kind: 'from land sown with their own seed' the *gebur* at Tidenham and the *ceorls* at Hurstbourne paid rent in grain, ale and malt. He had no responsibilities on the estate which would demand his continual residence at the curia, and although his labour rent made heavy demands on his strength and time it did not demand all of it and nothing is said of the labour of his children.

The close connection of *geburs* with the inland may have meant that their holdings were contiguous to, or intermingled with, the lord's arable. The 'yard of land' granted to the tenant in Ine's law was measured by a linear measure, the rod. Later examples of measuring land in this way strongly suggests that what was involved was a strip of arable about a rod (4.65 or 5.03 m) wide along its top edge and a furlong in length.[89] Because the 'yardland' later came to be a standard term for a holding in common field arable, the 'yard' of land rented out

86. J. Langdon, *Horses, Oxen and Technological Innovation: the use of draught animals in English farming from 1066 to 1500* (1986), 73.
87. Faith, 'Tidenham, Gloucestershire', 47.
88. G.C. Homans, *English Villagers of the Thirteenth Century* (Cambridge, Mass. 1941), 136–7, 210–11.
89. P.J. Huggins, 'Anglo-Saxon timber building measurements: results', *Medieval Archaeology* 35 (1991), 1–28.

to a tenant in Ine's law and the seven sown acres allotted to the *gebur* in the *Rectitudines* have been taken as evidence of open field systems, within which, it is assumed, the tenant would have had a scatter of strips amounting to a holding of about 30 acres, among the strips of the other farmers of the community.[90] There are other possibilities. One is that in the early phases of settlement formation there was an intensively cultivated discrete field system at the centre of the inland, adjacent to the manorial curia. This 'infield' comprised the land of the lord and his inland tenants, whose holdings may have been quite small. The histories of the fields in several of the Northamptonshire villages studied by D.N. Hall may have included a phase of inland field systems as 'core systems' which were later extended. In these the demesne arable was originally concentrated close to the settlement, only later was it dispersed among the open fields which by then comprised all the township's arable. (This had happened by 1086 at Garsington, Oxfordshire, when a hide of inland consisted of scattered strips.[91])

Gebur holdings associated with the inland of the curia may be the forerunners of some later customary tenancies (although, as Chapters 8 and 9 will argue, post-Conquest developments added many more customary tenancies from quite another source). The lands of a distinct group of peasants associated with a seigneurial centre, widely noted as an element in the post-Conquest village, may sometimes stem from these early inlands (although in many places they can be identified as post-Conquest settlements). At Tidenham the geburs' yardlands before the Conquest lay in the field systems that developed at the individual vills of the estate. They seem to have been part of an inland field system in which they were adjacent to or intermixed with the lord's arable. By the thirteenth century these holdings, each split into two, were customary half-yardlands.[92] A 'husbandland nucleus' lay next to the area of the great hall at Aylcliffe, Co. Durham.[93] Vills in the Vale of York had groups of bovated holdings associated with manorial demesnes.[94] What looks like planning on a much larger scale in Dorset gave rise to plots or 'regular closes' laid out on a standard module in

---

90. Ine: A.R.H. Baker and R.A. Butlin, 'Introduction: materials and methods', *Studies of Field Systems in the British Isles*, ed. A.R.H. Baker and R.A. Butlin (1973), 1–40 at 25; *Rectitudines*: Finberg, 'Anglo-Saxon England to 1042', 513 and n. 1.
91. D.N. Hall, 'Late Saxon topography and early medieval estates' in *Medieval Villages: a review of current work*, ed. D. Hooke, Oxford University Committee for Archaeology Monograph 5, (1985), 61–9; 'The late Saxon countryside: villages and their fields' in *Anglo-Saxon Settlements*, ed. D. Hooke (1988), 99–122 at 115. Garsington: *DB* I, 156d; H.C. Darby, *Domesday England* (1986 edn), 95.
92. Faith, 'Tidenham, Gloucestershire', 47–8.
93. L.H. Campey, 'Medieval village plans in County Durham: an analysis of reconstructed plans based on medieval documentary sources', *Northern History* 25 (1989), 60–87 at 81.
94. T.A.M. Bishop, 'Assarting and the growth of the open fields', *EcHR* 1st series 6 (1935–6), 13–29 at 15.

several vills where C.C. Taylor found them in 'a repetitive pattern over
... more than ten kilometres'.[95]

Elsewhere the *geburs'* land was apart. A category of place-name,
little investigated as yet, is the *gebur-tun* or *gebur-land*. The *geburland*
of Abingdon Abbey is described in a charter of the tenth century, and
when copied into the abbey's cartulary-chronicle appears as its
geburatunas, Latinized as *appenditia*, berewicks. I have interpreted it
earlier as the abbey's inland. In the tenth century it appears to have
been an area of dispersed settlement, but the abbey established a
grange with a substantial curia there by the twelfth century. Ridge and
furrow shows its adjacent arable, possibly the site of *geburs'* holdings
which had become part of an organized inland field system.[96]

Burton and Bourton place-names have several different explanations. The land devoted to feeding the monks of Christchurch,
Hampshire, included a Burton and the minster at Bampton, Oxfordshire, has Black Bourton nearby. These may once have been their
gebur-tuns.[97] Hardwich Barton, Devon, was interpreted by H.P.R.
Finberg as the 'enclosed manor farm' or *burh-tun* of Tavistock Abbey.
It became part of the abbey demesne and its inhabitants were notably
servile. At the 'heart and centre' of what Finberg called the bondland
of Tavistock is Bowrish, taking its name from *bur-hiwisc*, the *geburs'*
hide. Finberg considered it to be a hamlet deliberately settled with
dependent workers.[98]

The social and legal status of the *gebur*

Gebur is one of a group of cognate words, German *bauer* and Dutch *boer*
among them, meaning peasant, countryman. Its root, *buan*, means
simply to dwell, inhabit. Yet in England it seems to have denoted a
peasant of low status, and survived in spoken English as 'boor'. When,
after the Conquest, Anglo-Saxon legal works were being translated into
Latin the *gebur* was evidently considered to be much the same kind of
person as the Roman *colonus*, the peasant who was tied but free.[99]
Colonus was one of the Roman law terms which seem already to have

95. C.C. Taylor, 'The regular village plan: Dorset revisited and revised' in *The Medieval Landscape of Wessex* (1994), ed. M. Aston and C. Lewis, 213–18 at 217.
96. BCS 1002 (S 663); bounds: M. Gelling, *The Place-Names of Berkshire*, EPNS 51 (3 vols 1974), 729–31, and p. 44 above.
97. P. Hase, 'The mother churches of Hampshire' in *Minsters and Parish Churches: the local church in transition*, ed. J. Blair, Oxford University Committee for Archaeology. Monograph 17 (1988), 45–66 at 52; Ekwall, *English Place-Names*, s.v. *Bourton*; M. Gelling, *The West Midlands in the Early Middle Ages* (1992), 119–22 for Burtons with the element *burh*, fort.
98. H.P.R. Finberg, *Tavistock Abbey: a study in the social and economic history of Devon* (1969), 48.
99. For example, Aldhelm, *De laude virginitatis*, Brussels, Royal Library, MS 1650; W.M. Lindsay, ed., *An Eighth Century Latin-Anglo-Saxon Glossary (Cambridge, Corpus Christi College m.s. 144)* (1921); Aston, 'Origins of the manor', 72.

found a certain circulation in Anglo-Saxon England. While from the tenth century Frankish scholars were able to study Roman law at a much more advanced level, and from better texts, in the somewhat isolated cultural milieu of English monasteries the only available text on Roman law – and it was a very inferior one – was probably the *Ten Books of Etymologies* of Isidore of Seville. Isidore had written in an era when slavery was being overtaken by a mass of semi-free peasant tenures: in the pages of his ninth book his clerical Anglo-Saxon readers encountered the *servus, colonus, inquilinus* and *advena* and tried to find equivalent Anglo-Saxon terms. They chose *gebur* for *colonus*. To be a *colonus* was to be in some way unfree, although not a slave. Between 959 and 967 five people, Wurcon, Æthan, Iudnerth, Wurfothu and Guraret thought it worth having drawn up, and no doubt paying for, a document which proclaimed their free status 'since their fathers were said by evil men to be *coloni* of the king'.[100] *Gebur* was not part of the normal vocabulary of Domesday Book, although there are some *buri* there who seemed to the compilers to be very like *col(l)iberti*, found mostly on royal and ecclesiastical estates.[101] Although not a slave, the *gebur* was tied to the estate, with consequent legal restrictions and disabilities. It cost two people at Great Bedwyn, Wiltshire, 300 pence 'to be done out of the geburland' and 'given freedom to go wherever they please'. A Wessex lady was able to bequeath 'the geburs that are tenants of the rented land' to the nuns of Shaftesbury in 950 because 'she owns the stock and the people', and this is typical of lay wills which routinely grant land *mid mete und mid mannum*, 'with provisions and with people'.[102]

The owners of great estates needed to be able to move their dependent workforce to where it was most needed. This meant that they expected to have information available about the human stock at their disposal and over whom they had rights. A small handful of texts which illustrate this survive. D.A.E. Pelteret has edited two of these documents, whose very existence shows the close supervision a landowner could have over his *geburs* and their whereabouts. A list from the end of the tenth century gives the names of some 45 people with connections with the abbey of Ely's land at Hatfield.[103] Some are 'geburs belonging to Hatfield', some are native-born, *gebyrde*, of Hatfield, and Pelteret believes that these too are *geburs*. The names of children and grandchildren are given, and in all thirteen family groups can be identified. Some of the *geburs* had left Hatfield, all going to other places in Hertfordshire or the nearest part of Essex, and none more than seventeen miles off. Some women had moved to other places to marry, for others who had moved no reason is given but one

---

100. *Councils and Ecclesiastical Documents*, I, 682.
101. Pelteret, 'The *coliberti* of Domesday Book', 43–54.
102. Finberg, 'Anglo-Saxon England to 1042', 509–10.
103. D.A.E. Pelteret, 'Two Old English lists of serfs', *Mediaeval Studies* 48 (1986), 470–513.

is described as being 'under' another, perhaps working for them. Some *geburs* were specialist workers: Wœrlaf, described as *riht æhte*, legally owned, by Hatfield (in other words a slave) was a swineherd in charge of the 'grey pigs', one was a beekeeper, one an archer. Despite their mobility their semi-free status dogged their footsteps and those of their children. Pelteret shows how important it was for the abbey to 'keep tabs on' its *geburs* and their families even when they had moved off the estate. A man called Æflweald had been persuaded to sell Ely a hide of land at a price very favourable to the abbey in return for the grant of freedom to his wife and children, all 'natives' of Hatfield. It was their unfree status that gave the abbey this commanding bargaining position, and the care taken in recording the names of *geburs*, their children and their spouses emphasizes that their status was hereditary. None who had left Hatfield had gone to another Ely property, and Pelteret speculates that they may have emigrated to set up holdings of their own: this was a heavily forested area which offered opportunities for the colonist. Alternatively – and there is no means of knowing what really happened – they may have been 'poached' by rival landlords: several went to vills where a formidable religious house, St Albans, held land. Competition for servile labour became acute after the Conquest and transfers, loans and sales are likely to have been common in the circumstances of estate development on the larger church landholdings.

The tenth-century foundations in eastern England such as Ely were newcomers competing for land in a society thronged with minor landowners. Perhaps as a result of Scandinavian influence, this area already had the vibrant land market which was to be so characteristic of it in later centuries. They did not step into the inheritance of a royal house, as the early minsters had done, their lands were accumulated piecemeal, in large part by Æthelwold's energetic forays into the land market. A list of sureties summoned to guarantee to Peterborough Abbey the lands it bought between 963 and 992 shows well over twenty separate properties, including individual farms, bundles of acres and patches of woodland.[104] Part of its endowment income came from tithes from the neighbouring hundreds, part from berewicks which already 'belonged to Medeshamsted' (Peterborough's old name). When Æthelwold refounded Ely in 970 he not only endowed it with the core of land later known as 'the Isle', he 'bought many villages from the king and made it rich'.[105] Some of these transactions involved strong-arm tactics which made him unpopular locally: his agents put pressure on local inhabitants to sell, as the story of Ælfweald and his family shows. There seems to have followed a period of vigorous reorganization, which involved stocking or re-stocking some of the properties and setting them up as inlands. The monastic estates in the Danelaw

---

104. Robertson, *Charters*, XL at 75–83.
105. *Liber eliensis*, ed. E.O. Blake, Camden 3rd series, 92 (1962), 75–117.

consequently stand out in Domesday as islands of a much more 'manorialized' peasantry than was typical of the region as a whole. On the Lincolnshire lands of Peterborough Abbey only the people of the inland vills were of dependent status, while the rest were sokemen owing the abbey only typical soke services and attendance at its courts.[106] One member of the tiny corpus of surviving working records from Anglo-Saxon estates is a list of stock supplied by Ely for the minster at Thorney, Huntingdonshire, probably on its refoundation in 972.[107] This shows that it was a mixed farm with herds of swine and horses and a flock of sheep. Ely put in capital equipment in the shape of fishing nets and the boats essential for transport in this watery region, as well as the equipment and stock for an ox-powered mill, swine and seed corn. A considerable workforce was also brought in: thirteen 'work-worthy' men, five women, eight 'young men' (perhaps boys not yet 'work-worthy'). It included skilled workers, a swineherd, smith, dairymaid, shepherd, as well as an unspecified number of hired labourers, *hyringmanna*. A woman worker was bought in.[108]

Similar transfers of tied labour may explain the circumstances of a list in Old English of over eighteen adults and eleven children found in the twelfth-century cartulary of Rochester Cathedral, and also edited and analysed by Pelteret.[109] It is headed 'these were the *æhtemen* at Wouldham and their offspring'. Old English has a variety of terms for people incorporating the element *æhte*, property. They indicate slave status, or something very akin to it, and are often related to inland occupations, like the *æhteswon* who is in charge of the *inherd*, the inland herd.[110] Eight family groups are given and we are told that some had come from Aylesford, some from Chalk. There follows what Pelteret describes as a 'quittance-document' which records that 'Æthelsige at Wouldham has lent for bishop Sigeweard's lifetime his daughter and her daughter from Tottel's kin [Tottel was one of the Wouldham *æhtemen*] and has placed other persons there.' Sigeweard was bishop of Rochester from 1058 to 1075 and Pelteret provides a context for both documents: Wouldham had been leased several times to members of the same family and one of these lessees had attempted to block its return to Rochester, which the original owner, Ælfheah had intended and had arranged by his will. That will lies behind this document, which records his right to the land and its *æhtemen*. Firm

---

106. King, *Peterborough Abbey*; E. Miller, *The Abbey and Bishopric of Ely: the social history of an ecclesiastical estate from the tenth to the early fourteenth century* (1951); S. Raban, *The Estates of Thorney and Crowland: a study in medieval monastic land tenure* (1977).
107. Robertson, *Charters*, XXXIX.
108. *Ibid.*, app. 2, IX at 252–7. There is an illustration of this manuscript, its three sundered parts reunited, in *The Golden Age of Anglo-Saxon Art*, ed. J. Backhouse, D.H. Turner and L. Webster (1984), no. 150.
109. Pelteret, 'Lists of serfs', 492–503.
110. Bosworth and Toller, s.v. *aehte swan*.

title to both was important to Rochester, then in a parlous state financially.

The ability to transfer bound tenants must have made records of their ownership, and the names of their children who were included in the transaction, particularly important. A charter of 887, granting land in Oxfordshire to the minster at Pyrton in that county, transferred with it six people, Alhmund, Tidulf, Tidheh, Lull, another Lull and Eadwulf and their descendants *mid heara team und mid ƀy tudre*, with their descendants and their progeny, from the royal estate at Bensington 'in eternal possession'. The wording of the charter shows that the whole transaction was a solemn and public act, carried out in front of witnesses and that writing down their transfer and recording their names would ensure the perpetual possession of these families by Pyrton 'without gainsaying by anyone, noble or commoner'. These *gebur* families are truly serfs, or *nativi* as they would be called after the Conquest, their tie to a particular estate recorded in writing and maintained over the generations.[111]

The role and status of inland tenants

Inland was a necessity in the conditions of the early formation of minster properties, and the inland population remained a vital source of labour on the increasingly intensively exploited estates, lay and ecclesiastical, that came into being in Anglo-Saxon England. There is no doubt that they formed a class of workers who were tied to their holdings and were considered part of the capital assets of the estate on which they lived and worked. There is a very real sense in which even those who were not slaves came to be regarded as the personal property of their lord: the corollary of this is that they were his personal responsibility also. Taxation illuminates this way of thinking. As we saw in the previous chapter, inland was geld-free in many counties. This seems to have meant not only that the *holder* of the manor in question was not charged geld for the inland. It also meant either that its *inhabitants* were commonly exempt or that the lord paid on their behalf. Ownership of the land is the root of the matter here, for the principle was becoming established that to pay the geld for land established a legal claim to it.[112] Inland tenants had not such a claim. Paternalistic responsibility for the most servile people is also implied by the arrangements for the taxation paid to the church. The twelfth-century *Leis Willelme* records that in the Danelaw the lord pays Peter's Pence on behalf of those *qui in dominico suo manent*, 'who dwell on his demesne', and in other regions for his bordars, oxherds and servants.

---

111. BCS 547 (S 217); Blair, *Anglo-Saxon Oxfordshire*, 112; BCS 559 (S 1415) also refers to people transferred with an estate, but their names do not survive.
112. M.K. Lawson, *Cnut: the Danes in England in the early eleventh century* (1993), 191.

The ploughmen's land on the bishop of Rochester's estates was tithe-free. By contrast, to pay one's own church dues was the duty of 'every free hearth'. As to the other regular payment due to the church, church scot, it was possibly only the slave who was completely exempt: the Tidenham *gebur* certainly owed it, though he paid in labour.[113]

The bias inherent in our sources has meant that the workers and tenants of the inland are very obscure to us. What written information we have about *geburs*, bordars, cottars defines them solely in terms of their obligations and disabilities. Nevertheless, they were a substantial proportion of the rural population of Anglo-Saxon England, as analysis of their numbers in Domesday will show. And, in so far as consciousness of belonging to a class can be said to constitute class itself, farm workers can well be regarded as a distinct social class, distinct from the peasantry. One sign of this is the fact that they had their own patron saint. He is St Walstan, born of aristocratic parents in Bawburgh, Norfolk, in 975. Very pious as a child, at the age of 13 he dedicated himself to a life of humility and abstinence and instead of entering a religious community went to work as a farm labourer for a childless couple on their farm in nearby Taverham. He worked there for 30 years, gaining a reputation locally for hard work and charity. He refused the couple's offer to make him their heir and would accept only two bull calves which, when his death drew near, pulled him on a cart back to his birthplace. He died at haymaking in 1016, having secured heavenly assurance of the promise of healing for any farm labourer afflicted by infirmity, or by disease in his cattle, who called on him for intercession. 'He became the god of their fields in Norfolk, and guide of their harvests, all mowers and scythe followers seeking him once a year.' He is commemorated in many Norfolk churches and remains the patron saint of farmers and farm workers.[114]

The inland population in Domesday Book[115]

Ultimately it was not regional but tenurial geography, the particular circumstances on particular estates, which had the greater impact on the status of the peasantry, and analysis of Domesday Book has not progressed to the point that we can describe social structure in the local detail which would get nearer to reality than do the county statistics. Using these to attempt an estimate of the inland population and its distribution has its own difficulties. Domesday uses very broad categories, of which cottars (*cotarii*) are the most important, who could have been found in various places and circumstances: living in remote

---

113. *Leis Willelme*: Liebermann, I, 505; Rochester: *Custumale roffensis*, ed. J. Thorpe (1788), 15, 33; Tidenham: Robertson, *Charters*, CIX.
114. C. Twinch, *In Search of Walstan: East Anglia's enduring legend* (1995); F. Arnold-Forster, *Studies in Church Dedications* (3 vols, 1899), II, 424–5 at 425.
115. Appendix 2.

woodland, or working on a manorial inland, possibly engaged in industrial work. There are some we do not really understand, like *bovarii*. There must have been widely varied degrees of accuracy between counting people, say, in a remote and inaccessible region and those in areas of nucleated settlement. Nevertheless, it is a useful exercise to count as a proportion of each county's recorded Domesday population the total numbers in the categories that have been counted here as related to the inland. These are slaves and freedpeople (*colliberti*), cottars, bordars and the minute number of *geburs*.

This will be an underestimate, for it will leave out the people classed as *villani*. These are the largest category in Domesday, and it may seem perverse to omit them. But the *villani* of Domesday Book were a miscellaneous group. We do not know on what basis the commissioners counted a person as a *villanus*. Bordars, it has been argued, were immediately recognizable by virtue of their smallholdings, the services they owed and their inferior housing. Sokemen and free men were evidently of such distinctively free status, and had such a loose relationship to the manor, that they were well known locally, perhaps the members of the county court could list them individually by name. *Villani* may well have included all the other peasants. The status of some must in fact have been no different from that of *geburs*, owing heavy labour rent on inlands. But we do not know what proportion of the peasant population such people were, nor where they were to be found. *Geburs* are only noted in six counties, and only 65 are recorded altogether: the eleventh-century counterparts of the *geburs* at Tidenham appear in Domesday as *villani*, as do those of the Hurstbourne *ceorls*. A Domesday entry tells us nothing about the labour rent typical of the *gebur*. Although it records some agricultural services, these are of a particular sort, and were owed from the peasantry of the warland.[116] The much heavier services which we know to have been owed by *geburs* and others like them are not recorded, being essentially a matter of manorial custom, not ancient *scir* obligations. This should make us very wary of using Domesday as the basis of any kind of assumption about the extent of labour rent in Anglo-Saxon England and the number of people who owed it. Lennard's cautious conclusion was that 'Of predial services ... nothing definite can be learnt from Domesday.'[117] For all these reasons *villani* are not included in the following figures, which are an attempt to obtain some idea of the proportion of the total population recorded for each county represented by the people that, it has been argued, were most characteristically associated with the inland.

Overall, the people recorded in the categories of bordar, cottar,

---

116. See pp. 107–14 below.
117. Lennard, *Rural England*, 368–71 at 370; *per contra* A.R. Bridbury, 'Domesday Book: a re-assessment', *EHR* 105 (1990), 284–309 at 306–9. This question is discussed at length in R.J. Faith, 'Demesne resources and labour rent on the manors of St Paul's Cathedral 1066–1222', *EcHR* 47 (1994), 657–78.

collibertus, slave and *gebur* formed 44 per cent of the total recorded population, and in most counties they were over 30 per cent. The counties with the highest proportion, between 60 and 69 per cent, were Cornwall, Dorset, the Welsh portion of Gloucestershire, Wiltshire and Essex. It is the bordars who make up the bulk of the inland population. In only four counties were they less than 20 per cent of the population, and in most they were between 20 and 40 per cent.

Slaves are not recorded in every county, and in the belief that this is very unlikely to represent the real situation J.S. Moore has recently attempted to reconstruct some possible figures for the absentees.[118] His calculations are based on the assumption that slaves are likely to have comprised about the same proportion of the population of those counties where none are recorded as of those where they are: about 10 per cent. Broadly speaking, slaves were the lowest proportion of the recorded population in the eastern counties, with the addition of Sussex and Worcestershire, and for these a particular circumstance may have been involved. Essex may provide the explanation. It was in the middle rank as far as slaves are concerned, but had a high proportion of bordars: this may be the effect of the numerous conversion of slaves into bordars since the Conquest, a process which Little Domesday, with its greatly superior detail, records. Other counties which had few slaves but large numbers of bordars may have experienced a very similar process: these are Cheshire and Lancashire, Middlesex, Norfolk and Suffolk, Sussex and Worcestershire. The western counties in this group were also the counties where exempt inland was most prominent, or best recorded. The counties with the lowest proportion of inland people in any category were Rutland, Huntingdonshire and Lincolnshire, Leicestershire and Nottinghamshire with between 20 and 30 per cent.

Rough though they are, these figures show some kind of inverse correlation between inland populations and the more heavily Scandinavian-settled areas, and raise a question which recurs in any consideration of the social structure of early England: were the peasantry of Scandinavian-settled regions 'freer'? The numbers of people recorded as 'free men' or 'sokemen' there are generally called in evidence to answer this question. This is unsafe ground, for the figures can be questioned on the grounds that there was much in the way that life and settlement were organized in Scandinavian England that made the free peasant there much more 'visible' to the Domesday commissioners – a question which will be discussed further. The inland population figures are a more independent witness. They indicate that Scandinavian England was a society where there were pockets of extreme dependence – between a fifth and a third of all the population is no small total after all. But the lives of fewer people overall were dominated by the needs of the seigneurial economy than

---

118. Moore, 'Domesday slavery', n. 16.

in the rest of the country. Discussing the numbers of slaves in Sussex, Moore makes a point which is of wider significance and will be demonstrably true when we come to examine local social structure in detail: 'the determining factor ... was landlord policy'.[119]

---

119. *Ibid.*, 205.

4 Warland

The evolution of the state in Anglo-Saxon England, in the broad sense of the accumulation in the hands of the king of public functions such as defence, 'law and order' and taxation, also gave power to the landowner. In a process familiar throughout medieval Europe, the king's greatly increased need for service had to be paid for by ceding land. But the developing Anglo-Saxon state was strongly centralized, and although great landowners held administrative and judicial powers, it held them by delegation, and they were revocable.[1] Moreover, in contrast to their Carolingian counterparts the late Anglo-Saxon kings were successful in holding on to, and enriching, their own economic foundation. Thus the English magnate class, powerful and well-landed though it was, did not establish the local autonomous power bases that supported the counts and dukes of France. Again in contrast with France, a large proportion of the peasantry and smaller landowners played an essential role in the state which preserved for them a large measure of freedom and independence. Vinogradoff described them as 'small statesmen ... small freemen charged with public duties'.[2] This chapter examines the peasantry from the point of view of these 'public' obligations.

From the time of our earliest written references we can see a system in place which assessed service, in the sense of public obligations, on units of land. This is not to say that there was not a time, nor a sense, in which membership of a community or of a particular rank in itself entailed such obligations on individuals: there was, and it continued to be a potent force. But it is essentially the connection of obligation with land which has put its stamp on the records. A variety of terms is used for land from which service was due to the king. One in particular, the archaic term *folcland*, folkland, has received a variety of interpretations and we may never know exactly what was meant by it. From the sparse uses of the term, we learn that folkland was the counterpart or antithesis of bookland, that cases

1. J. Campbell, 'Some agents and agencies of the late Anglo-Saxon state' in *Domesday Studies*, ed. J. Holt (1987), 201–18; J. Campbell, E. John and P. Wormald, eds, *The Anglo-Saxons* (1982), 58–61, 168–81; F.M. Stenton, *Anglo-Saxon England* (1947), 302.
2. P. Vinogradoff, *English Society in the Eleventh Century: essays in English mediaeval history* (1908), 194–5.

concerning it should come before the royal reeve, that only the king could grant it, and that he could convert land into folkland. So it seems to be land with some close association with the king. *Folcrihte*, 'Folk-right' or 'folk-law' as it appears in the law codes, shows the nature of that close association: it is the public law which it is the king's special duty to maintain. As it appears in the charters it stands for *feorm*, or the king's dues in some wider sense. If folkland is land which owed *feorm*, and it is the whole 'folk' that pays it, this is a terminology which brought into the eleventh century, when we find it in a Yorkshire charter, an echo of the remotest Anglo-Saxon past.[3]

Feorm was only part of what was owed to king: service of many kinds was owed too. The most convenient term for this package of service and *feorm* is soke. Soke has often been given a strongly jurisdictional flavour. It derives from *socn*, seeking, and its frequent coupling with *sac*, 'cause' in the legal sense, in the tag 'sake and soke' to mean rights of jurisdiction, shows how important this aspect was. However, soke also has a wider, perhaps earlier connotation of 'service due to the king' and sokeland is land from which these services were due. There is no commonly accepted term for land which owed public obligations. *Folcland* appears to have become obsolete. The term 'sokeland' came to be restricted to eastern England, because the unit known as the soke, its inhabitants, their tenures, status and obligations became much more readily identifiable there.

The division between the inland and other land has already been shown to have been important. Inland tenants and workers had a particular status and particular kinds of obligations, and inland was recognized, although not consistently, by the tax and tithing systems. The obligations summed up above as *feorm* or soke were quite different. The language employed to express this dichotomy in Anglo-Saxon England used the noun *waru* and the verb *werian*. *Waru* is an Old English word for 'defence'.[4] To 'defend' land, in the phrase *werian land*, meant to perform the services due from it. Latinized as *defendere pro* it appears in Domesday Book with the meaning 'to perform the service due from' or 'to pay the geld due from' a number of hides. Hence services performed *to utware* were owed in respect of the 'outland', and services performed *to inware*, in respect of the inland. Anglo-Saxon practice seems to have been to lump together all 'public' obligation, whether military, judicial or administrative, as *ut-waru*. Strictly speaking, there should have been a term 'outwarland', but in fact 'warland' came to be the term for land which owed these. Inland and warland were still recognized as distinct entities on the estates of Burton Abbey, and *waracres* are found on the lands of Ely and Bury St

---

3. C.A. Joy, 'Sokeright' (Ph.D. thesis, University of Leeds, 1972), 223ff.; Robertson, *Charters*, LXXXIV at 164–9.
4. Bosworth and Toller (1898), s.v. *werian* IIIc and (1921), s.v. *ut-waru*; Liebermann, I, 446 (*Rectitudines* 3.4). I am grateful to J. Jenkyns for assistance here.

Edmunds in the twelfth century, and of Westminster Abbey into the thirteenth.[5] The essential characteristics of land which owed *waru* were common to England, and I shall use the word 'warland' to refer to it. In terms of estate structure the warland was an area related only loosely to the centre of the estate and could be of any size. When William I established his abbey at Battle, Sussex, as a thank-offering for his victory there, he established as its inland a geld-free central core or banlieu and settled taxpaying tenants to colonize an outer area of countryside: this latter was Battle's warland.[6] A little estate leased by Evesham Abbey around 1023 had three hides *to inware* and one and a half *to utware*.[7]

There was a crucial difference between the status of the peasants of the warland and those of the inland, although it was a difference much eroded over time and by the end of our period was little more than a memory. It lay less in the greater personal freedom of the warland peasantry than in the character of their obligations, which derived from the social relationships of the earliest days of kingship and extensive lordship. Inland was land organized for a particular purpose, which however fragmentarily its documentation and sometimes its archaeology reflect. To live and work on the inland has already been seen to be crucial to the status of one section of the peasantry. To live and work on the warland was of equal importance to the rest. Warland did not originate in the needs of the estate owner but in a much earlier organization of society. We should expect to find a great diversity of people there, and so we do, from peasants through royal officials and retainers to substantial lords with inlands of their own.

The assessment of public service was intimately connected with the hide, the essential unit in assessing, administering and financing service to the king. It would not be true to say that exempt land was always unhidated, but the reverse is true: service-owing land was always hidated. Figures 12 and 13 show these destinations preserved in two post-Conquest manorial surveys. The link between the hide and public obligations of those who held hidated land is to do with something of more significance than fiscal assessment. The idea of the hide was an essential part of the way that the Anglo-Saxons thought about society. Because it expressed not size but *assessment of value* it was an essential way of estimating resources in an age without maps

---

5. C.G.O. Bridgeman, 'The Burton Abbey twelfth century surveys', *Collections for a History of Staffordshire* (William Salt Archaeological Society, 1918 for 1916), 209–300, *passim*; *The Kalendar of Abbot Samson of Bury St. Edmunds and Related Documents*, ed. R.H.C. Davis, Camden 3rd series 84 (1954), 50 and n. 2; P. Vinogradoff, *Villainage in England: essays in English mediaeval history* (1892), 242; P.R. Schofield, 'Land, family and inheritance in a later medieval community: Birdbrook, 1292–1412' (D.Phil. thesis, University of Oxford, 1992), 95.
6. E. Searle, 'Hides, virgates and tenant settlement at Battle Abbey', *EcHR* 2nd series 16 (1963–4), 290–300.
7. Robertson, *Charters*, LXXXI at 156–7 (S 1423).

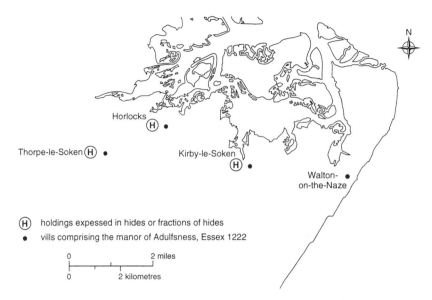

Horlocks
(H) •

Thorpe-le-Soken (H) •

Kirby-le-Soken
(H) •

Walton- •
on-the-Naze

(H)   holdings expessed in hides or fractions of hides

•   vills comprising the manor of Adulfsness, Essex 1222

0 —————————— 2 miles

0   2 kilometres

Figure 12   The manor of Adulfsness, Essex in 1222, showing hidated and unhidated land. In the thirteenth century the coastline extended considerably further east. *Source*: W.H. Hale, ed., *The Domesday of St Paul's of the year MCCXXII or registrum de visitatione maneriorum per Robertus decanum*, Camden Society 69 (1858), 38–52.

and surveyors. On the largest scale, the very existence, whatever its date, of the document known as the 'Tribal Hidage' shows how a rough idea of the capacity, or perhaps the population, of very large areas of land could be estimated and expressed as hundreds of hides. On the smallest scale, the hide could be used to 'measure' tiny landholdings.

There is more to it than measurement. The fact that it was a unit of assessment to public obligations gave the hide an association with freedom. T.M. Charles-Edwards has argued that the hide had always been the property qualification of the freeman. He traces in Welsh and Irish as well as in early Germanic society the freeman as someone with 'full legal rights ... entitled to participate fully in the life of the community'. Freemen were farmers with hides.[8] The link between hides, public obligations and freedom will be a constantly recurring theme throughout this chapter.

---

8. T.M. Charles-Edwards, 'Kinship, status and the origins of the hide', *Past and Present* 56 (August 1972), 3–33 at 9.

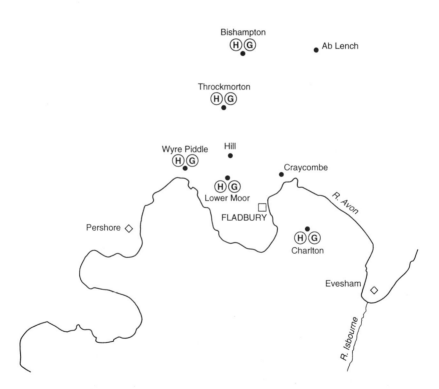

Figure 13 Hidated and unhidated land on the manor of Fladbury, Worcestershire, *c.* 1170. *Source: The Red Book of Worcester*, ed. M. Hollings, Worcestershire Historical Society (4 vols, 1934–50), II, 145.

Public service

Rectitudines singularum personarum describes 'the law relating to thegns'.[9] It describes first a superior thegn. He is a landowner who is expected to have his own estate held by charter. It is within this class that the prospects of social mobility were best, and the route to the top was through service to the great. A thegn who rose in the world so that he served the king would expect to have thegns under him who in turn derived their status from their master's success. We know from literary sources that the thegn was in origin a 'companion' or subaltern, from the OE word for servant or follower. He was a member of that large class of ministerial nobility common in northern Europe: people whose status was determined by the men they served and the nature of the service. Rather than their status deriving from their economic position, land rewarded their career. Their public service was an essential part of their status. They held their land by charter (*bocriht*) and had been granted with it exemption from all dues save the three obligations of military service, bridge and fortification repair, universal since the eighth century on all landholders. Inseparable from what we would nowadays recognize as 'public service' were their more personal duties to the king, and it seems from the wording of this passage that these were not universal but were due from particular landholdings. 'On many estates (*landum*) more estate duties (*land riht*) arise on the king's command, that is deer hedge [making] at the king's lodge (*hame*)', equipping a guard ship, coastguard duty and acting as bodyguard. 'Almsgiving and church scot and many other things' were also due.

Then the obligations of the *geneat* are described. Again, these are described not as if they were the generic obligations of an entire class, but 'varied according to what is fixed on the estate'. The *geneat* must pay *gafol*, ride and perform carrying service and provide transport, reap and mow, make deer hedges, work and provide *feorm* for the lord, build and fence the lord's fortified enclosure (*burh*), escort strangers to the *tun*, pay church scot and alms, act as guard to his lord and take care of the horses, and carry messages far and near, wherever he is ordered.

Geneats, and the lesser thegns who seem to have been similar to them, were a widespread and important class. *Geneat* does not seem to have had wide currency as a term, although a law of Edgar on tithe distinguishes between inland and *neatland*.[10] The twelfth-century translator of the *Rectitudines* seems to have been at a loss as to how to translate it, making a guess with *villanus*. But Maitland and Jolliffe both drew attention to the class of people known as 'drengs' and 'thanes' or 'thegns' in Northumbria, and G.W.S. Barrow found that thanes played an important role in the small *scirs* of medieval Scotland.

---

9. Liebermann, I, 444–5; *EHD* II, no. 172 at 813; see also *EHD* I, 432 (A).
10. Liebermann, I, 196: II Edgar 1.1.

They survived after the Conquest as a distinct group but with a much reduced status, and 'thanage' was a distinctive tenure in the northern counties well into the later middle ages.[11]

It is in the nature of the available sources that what we principally know about people is not what kind of economy or society they moved in but what their duties and obligations were. The very distinctive and personal nature of some of the services of drengs and thegns, 'riding-men' and people like them, especially those connected with military and semi-military service, conveyed honourable status. (Many thegnage services may have become the serjeanties of the later middle ages.) This ensured that they continued to be recorded in the documentation of medieval society and attracted the attention of Maitland, Jolliffe and Barrow. Yet these were only the upper and more visible range of a larger class of free landholders owing a wide variety of public or royal services. In the language of the charters it is the *land* which expressly owes the threefold obligations of bridge work, army service and fortification work. Yet when we come to examine the range of people who actually performed the service it is so wide that it suggests that these were services which the entire free population had once owed. In investigating them, we will constantly come across the hide and its obligations. Warfare, and the service connected with it, must head the list.

Fyrdworthiness

Freedom and arms-bearing virtually defined each other in much of early medieval Europe. For this reason we cannot separate the question of the status of the Anglo-Saxon peasantry from the question of the extent to which they were involved in warfare. It is not simply a matter of who bore arms. Such was the sophistication of the late Anglo-Saxon state that responsibility for what in our own times was known as 'the war effort' became widely disseminated, through taxation and forms of representative service, among a great many people who did not themselves fight. The military and defensive policies of Alfred and Edward the Elder in the sphere of military and defence organization were all based on the basic unit of the hide and thus on the resources in people, wealth and land of the warland population. Service to the king or any other leader had always involved loyalty in battle as one of the duties of the aristocratic life. But with the granting out of land to

---

11. Vinogradoff, *English Society in the Eleventh Century*, 60–89; F.W. Maitland, 'Northumbrian tenures', *EHR* 5 (1890), 625–32; G.W.S. Barrow, *The Kingdom of the Scots: government, church and society from the eleventh to the thirteenth century* (1973), ch. 1; J. Jolliffe, 'Northumbrian institutions', *EHR* 41 (1926), 1–42; F.M. Stenton, *Types of Manorial Structure in the Northern Danelaw* in Oxford Studies in Social and Legal History 2 (1910); R. Reid, 'Barony and thanage', *EHR* 35 (1920), 161–99; E. Miller, 'Social structure: northern England' in *Ag. Hist.* II, 685–98.

followers, who may in turn have granted it out to theirs, or passed it on to their children, there was a danger that kings might begin to lose their grip on this essential *quid pro quo*. From the eighth century on, grants of land had begun to specify that the grantee, though exempt from other dues, could not escape the obligation to provide soldiers for the *fyrd* and to contribute to the upkeep of bridges and fortifications. The threat and reality of invasion from across the North Sea was the factor which brought large changes in Anglo-Saxon society.[12] Arrangements which had sufficed to provide for the needs of royal courts, to ensure a reasonable amount of law and order and to give each kingdom the military force to secure temporary advantage over its neighbours, were inadequate to organize effective defence against the raiders who began to harry the north-east coast in the 790s and the succession of Danish 'great armies' from the 830s. In response to the disastrous Danish inroads into Wessex of the 870s King Alfred put the military organization of his kingdom on a more organized footing, reorganizing the 'call-up' to the *fyrd*, part of which was kept as a standing army. Famously, Alfred thought that *weorcmen* and *fyrdmen*, labourers and warriors, were two of society's three 'orders', and this is often taken as evidence that *fyrd* service was not the responsibility of the peasantry. Alfred was surely concerned to make the general point that society must be fed as well as fought for, rather than to define mutually exclusive social categories. Some of the peasantry at least were among the *fyrdmen*. A national 'peasant army' is much less likely than a two-tier system, one with a distinction between higher status commanders and soldiers in the field, who were perhaps people not unlike the 'rustic knights' that S.P.J. Harvey has found in Anglo-Norman England.[13] A passage in the Worcestershire section of Domesday Book explains the system: 'when the king goes against his enemy' each man 'so free that he has his sake and soke and can go with his land wherever he wishes' was summoned by the king and served personally. He forfeited his lands for failure to attend.[14] R.P. Abels has argued that the people summoned to fight were holders of bookland, responsible for service with the king in person, the king's thegns who 'rode in his household band on expeditions'. Another interpretation views them as independent allodial landholders who could commend themselves to and fight for any lord they pleased: such people may well have included

---

12. N.P. Brooks, 'Ninth century England: the crucible of defeat', *TRHS* 5th series 29 (1979), 1–20; 'The development of military obligations in eighth and ninth century England' in *England before the Conquest: studies in primary sources presented to Dorothy Whitelock*, ed. P. Clemoes and K. Hughes (1971), 69–84; R.P. Abels, *Lordship and Military Obligation in Anglo-Saxon England* (1988), 52–7.

13. Abels, *Lordship and Military Obligation*, ch. 5; S.P.J. Harvey, 'The knight and the knight's fee in England', *Past and Present* 49 (November 1970), 3–43, reprinted in *Peasants, Knights and Heretics*, ed. R.H. Hilton (1976), 133–73.

14. *DB* I, 172a.

prosperous peasants.[15] Those summoned were also liable for providing troops, who are described in the customs of Berkshire recorded in Domesday. Hidated land provided this supply of auxiliaries and a levy for their support: 'one soldier went from every five hides, and four shillings were given for his wages or support for two months from each hide'. He could send a substitute, but if the substitute defaulted a fine of fifty shillings was incurred.[16] These soldiers from the hides were 'fyrd-worthy' free people, but Abels doubts that many were peasants. True, the few known individual examples of fighting men of this rank – two were Hampshire men who died at Hastings – were *liberi homines*, whose land is described as *alodium*, and when it is possible to discover how much land they had it is a small 'gentry' holding with a little inland and a few tenants, rather than a peasant family farm that is found.[17] A warland tenant of Burton Abbey in the early twelfth century, for instance, who owed military service as well as attendance at courts, had seven sub-tenants of his own on the eight bovates which he held from the abbey.[18] He is an example of the way that service could become attached to a particular person or holding. Soldiers who were paid to serve may more often have been professionals, some with no land at all and were resident men-at-arms kicking their heels in monastic or episcopal households. But what it is particularly appropriate in this context to call a yeomanry surely provided a large number of fighting men. 'Tenant right' in the north, one aspect of which was the obligation to do military service on the border, survived into the seventeenth century as a particular kind of leasehold.[19] A Peterborough Abbey document of between 1100 and 1116, known as the *Descriptio militum*, the 'assessment of knights', refers to tenants who 'serve with' the knights owed by the abbey: some are sokemen, and they serve 'as much as by right they should' (*quantum illis iure contigit*). 'Franklins' (*franchelani*) from Peterborough's land also served, of whom 'some have a hide, some more some less': 'we do not know their service, unless it is that according to their hides they help the other knights to do the service of the king'.[20] A. Williams's work on the cartulary of Shaftesbury Abbey has revealed the *knystemetehom*, the holding or farm which provides the *mete-hom* or living for one knight. These 'knight tenements' owed boon works (occasional agricultural services) and ploughshares, as well as guard duty and suit, alongside their military service. ('Hyde Farm' in

---

15. Abels, *Lordship and Military Obligation*, 56–7; Joy, 'Sokeright', 382.
16. *DB* I, 56c.
17. Abels, *Lordship and Military Obligation*, 135–7, 142–5.
18. *EHD* II, 823.
19. E. Kerridge, *Agrarian Problems in the Sixteenth Century and After* (1968), 42–59; for another view of its origins: R. Hoyle, 'Tenant right in north-western England in the sixteenth century', *Past and Present* 116 (August 1987), 24–55.
20. E. King, 'The Peterborough *Descriptio militum* (Henry I)', *EHR* 84 (1969), 84–101.

Pimperne, Dorset, is one of these knightly farms.)[21] Possibly many Anglo-Saxon 'rustic knights' of this sort went under names that make it difficult for us to recognize them. When Lanfranc took over the archbishopric of Canterbury, for instance, he is said to have turned the 'threngs' he found there into knights.[22]

All these examples date from after the Conquest, which had brought in a tendency to regularize military service and tie it more strictly to the individual landholding, the 'knight's fee'. It is possible that the social composition of the *fyrd* before the Conquest was very different, and varied between regions. Drengs and thanes and *radcnihts* are all pre-Conquest categories of people about whom we do not know very much except that they had horses and owed services connected with that fact: military service of some kind would be an obvious extension. Wherever they were found, 'riding men' are likely to have been liable to turn out when called on or at least to have provided substitutes. This is R.P. Abels's interpretation of the 'faithful men subjected to me' to whom Bishop Oswald of Worcester leased land and whom, as Oswald said in a letter to King Edgar, he expected to help him fulfil the military obligations which all holders of 'bookland' owed. They did all the things that *geneats* and riding men did, erecting deer hedges, lending their horses and so on, as well as fighting under the command of the chief commander (*archiductor*).[23] The military element is but one part of a whole bundle of service: it may have declined in importance as a real contribution to the army but it remained an important, even defining, characteristic of certain free tenures. It is particularly well articulated in the case of sokeland. There was a tradition among socage tenants in thirteenth-century Oxfordshire that 'their forefathers had been soke-men who had fought in the king's wars'.[24]

Bridge and fortification work

Bridge and fortification work were, like *fyrd* service, expressed obligations on owners of bookland which ultimately devolved on the hides of the warland. The most dramatic example of fortification work in Anglo-Saxon England is undoubtedly Offa's Dyke, but the actual organization, assessment and provision of the labour it required remains unknown territory. The best documented example of public works in Anglo-Saxon England shows the warland and its population at

---

21. A. Williams, 'The knights of Shaftesbury Abbey', *Anglo-Norman Studies* 8 (1985–6), 214–37. A.K.G. Kristensen, 'Danelaw institutions and Danelaw society in the Viking Age: *sochemanni, liberi homines* and *königsfrei*', *Medieval Scandinavia* 8 (1975), 27–85 interprets *all* soke landholding as having originated in land-grants to 'soldier-colonists'.
22. F.R.H. du Boulay, *The Lordship of Canterbury: an essay on medieval society* (1966), 79; Vinogradoff, *English Society*, 65, 71, 83–7.
23. Abels, *Lordship and Military Obligation*, 152–7.
24. Joy, 'Sokeright', 253–4.

the centre of the arrangements. N.P. Brooks has been able to show how the responsibility for providing the timber and keeping in repair the Roman bridge at Rochester was assigned to a territory – the lathe of Aylesford – and within that territory to land-units each of which had a royal centre (Fig. 14). The work itself was assessed on the sulung – the Kentish equivalent of the hide. Felling, dressing and hauling the 50-foot oaks to Rochester and cutting planking for the roadway of the bridge were jobs for skilled woodsmen and huge haulage teams, probably of oxen which were best fitted for this kind of work. Here we see two of the hallmarks of the warland farmer: skilled work with valuable stock.[25] Work with stone and the provision of heavy waggons were also needed. Oswald, bishop of Worcester, describing what was owed from his tenants as 'the riding law ... which applies to radmen' insisted that they should 'be ready to build bridges and do all that is necessary in burning lime for the work of the church'.[26] When Alfred established a network of fortified towns, *burhs*, he gave local inhabitants the responsibility of maintaining their defensive walls: skilled building work and shifting heavy materials must have been involved. The responsibility was reckoned on the hide, each hide to be represented by one man. Maintenance and guard duty were linked: four men were to patrol each pole of wall, 80 men to maintain 20 poles of wall. The shires – the modern word now becomes appropriate, rather than *scir*, for many of the modern shires originated in these arrangements – which were to provide this support for the burhs had their hidage assessed in round numbers. With Æthelflæd and Edward the Elder's conquest of the land previously under Scandinavian control, burhs and their shires were extended to the midlands. These innovative policies would, if they were consistently carried out, have given the hides of the warland a much more precisely defined 'public' role: they became the armature of the shire.

Public administration

It is not certain how effectively Alfred's scheme operated, but old warland dues still occur in the thirteenth century among the wide variety of obligations owed to the shire and organized by the sheriffs' officers. They were commonly commuted into money payments, and were due only from geldable land. Among them were 'wardpenny', which preserved the ancient obligation of guard duty recorded by the *Rectitudines*. 'Pontage' and 'murage' were commutations of two of the

---

25. N.P. Brooks, 'Rochester Bridge', AD 43–1381' in *Traffic and Politics: the construction and management of Rochester Bridge AD 43–1993*, ed. N. Yates and J.M. Gibson (1994), 1–40.
26. F.W. Maitland, *Domesday Book and Beyond: three essays in the early history of England* (1960 edn), 358–63; S 1368.

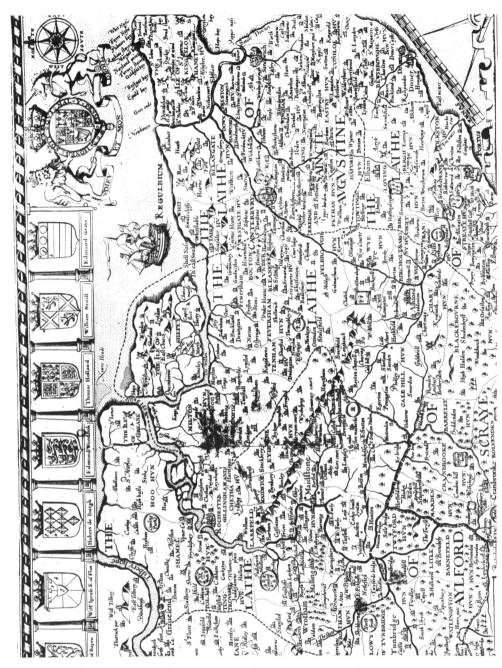

Figure 14 The lathes of Kent. The responsibility for the upkeep of Rochester Bridge lay with the lathe of Aylesford. *Source*: John Speed (1611), Oxford, Bodleian Library, Gough Maps 10 (reproduced with the permission of the Bodleian Library, University of Oxford).

old threefold national obligations, bridge and fortification duty.[27] The zealous Abbot Samson of Bury St Edmunds in the late twelfth century compiled a list of 'regalian' or royal services owed by free sokemen to the abbey. They had mostly become commuted into cash payments, and some were probably largely symbolic, but they show the important part that the warland had played in the running of the Anglo-Saxon state.[28] The tendency over time was for these payments to be diverted to the lords of the greater estates who were also lords of franchises. They came to look like rents, but they were not in origin rents, but the commutation of public obligations.[29] A whole range of payments owed to the sheriff or to the bailiff of the hundred was all that was left of these duties in many places, surviving under such names as 'sheriffsilver' and 'hundred aid' or lumped together as 'forinsec service'. Military and semi-military duties like escort and guarding prisoners, which long pre-dated knight service, survived as ward-pennies and the duty of 'street-ward', the obligation to keep up public highways in payments such as the annual shilling which the township of Chimney had to pay the lord of Bampton for 'the road called the New Way' at Chimney.[30] These public duties retained an association with freedom. Glastonbury Abbey tenants of the late twelfth century, seemingly of lesser status than those who held by knight service but who hold their land 'freely except for service to the king from ancient times', were a distinct category.[31]

It is a characteristic of these ancient public dues that they are frequently owed and administered by a community as a whole, and that they retained some vestigial association with free status, particularly in East Anglia. The manors into which the large estate of Wymondham, Norfolk was broken down after the Conquest were laid over the system of 'shifts', which were local divisions of vills, presided over by elected 'wickeners'. Their job was to collect the dues and rents, but their name may take us back to a link with the *vicus*, the smallest unit of Roman administration.[32]

The process of 'shiring' – the defining of territories, expressed in hundreds of hides, to provide for the defence and upkeep of the burhs – may have been an important stage in the definition and fixing of specific burdens on specific land. The proliferation of public obligations in late Anglo-Saxon England was the occasion for a greater precision in defining the borderline between warland, subject to these burdens, and exempt inland.

---

27. Abels, *Lordship and Military Obligation*, 68–78; N. Neilson, *Customary Rents* in Oxford Studies in Social and Legal History 2 (1910), chs 6–7.
28. *Kalendar of Abbot Samson*, xv, xxii–xlvii.
29. Neilson, *Customary Rents*, chs 6, 7.
30. Extent of Bampton deanery manor 1317: Exeter dean and chapter MS 2931. I am grateful to Dr J. Blair for lending me his transcript of this ms.
31. *Liber Henrici de Soliaco*, ed. J.E. Jackson (1882), e.g. 73 (East Brent).
32. T. Williamson, *The Origins of Norfolk* (1993), 95.

Public service connected with royal circuits

The tribute system which supported early kings was in essence a purveyance network on a very large scale, an expression of a king's capacity to exact regular supplies of *feorm*, provisions, and labour from his own subjects. Chapter 2 described the effect this had in establishing royal inlands dedicated to supplying the king. Traditionally, *feorm* was to serve the needs of a travelling court. Given the importance of the personal presence of the king, the royal vill where his *feorm* was assembled and consumed was an essential element in the early state. These royal residences were important political centres, places where assemblies were held. The earliest courts fused both meanings of the term 'court': entourage and place of judgement. Here the king could be approached informally to settle a dispute or judge a crime considered beyond the competence of other courts, such as a thief caught red-handed three times who 'shall be brought to the royal vill'; here an important marriage could be arranged.[33] Consequently, kings tended generally to retain royal residences even when they granted away the surrounding land, and kept the rights to the services which maintained them. They were especially liable to retain, as something particularly royal, services related to attendance at court and personal services in household and hunting field.

Hunting was part of the royal and noble way of life in the later Anglo-Saxon period at least and services connected with hunting such as building temporary lodges, feeding hounds and horses and driving game, feeding the king's servants and repairing royal halls were an essential part of royal tribute. It is likely that the royal circuit may, in peacetime, have been partly a matter of going from chase to chase. Many Anglo-Saxon royal halls were in good hunting country like Cheddar in Somerset and Hartland ('Stag island') in Devon. 'The West Saxon kings showed an early preference for the four shires of Hampshire, Wiltshire, Dorset and Somerset, a preference which continued into the tenth century when all England was theirs to choose from.' Was this in part because there they had the Mendips and the Quantocks and the forests of Selwood and Savernake to hunt in? Ceolwulf, King of Mercia, was careful to mention the fisheries, fowling grounds and hunting grounds on land in Kent that he granted in 822, and the people there had been obliged to entertain his keepers of dogs,

33. T.M. Charles-Edwards, 'Early medieval kingships in the British Isles' in *The Origins of Anglo-Saxon Kingdoms*, ed. S. Bassett (1989), 28–39 at 28–33; P.H. Sawyer, 'The royal *tun* in pre-Conquest England' in *Ideal and Reality in Frankish and Anglo-Saxon Society*, ed. P. Wormald, D. Bullough and R. Collins (1983), 273–99, describes the institution of the Anglo-Saxon royal centre and lists those known, including 'Kingston' place-names under this head. J. Campbell, 'Bede's words for places' in *Names, Words and Graves*, ed. P.H. Sawyer (1979), 34–53 at 45; thief: BCS 357 (S 180).

horses and hawks.[34] The late twelfth-century collection of surveys of the lands of the bishop of Durham known as Boldon Book shows that certain of his tenants had still to turn out for the bishop's 'great chase' (*magnam cazam*).[35] We can well imagine that their predecessors had done the same for his predecessors, the Northumbrian earls.

Feorm also means 'entertainment' and the circuit system was in part sustained by the very strong feelings that were invested in the notion of hospitality. It was more likely to be expensive hospitality than simply provisions that nobles owed to the king, as Lear's daughters experienced to their cost. Costly though it was it conveyed and expressed status: entertaining the king in person as T.M. Charles-Edwards has pointed out, gave noble families access to his patronage.[36] It is probable that, unless they explicitly released a donee from the obligation, kings continued to be able to expect hospitality for themselves and their entourage from all their subjects. *Dovræth servientium*, in a charter to the church at Worcester, incorporates the Welsh term for the purveyance rights of the king's officers.[37]

Kings, indeed anyone in a position of power, could probably once command – or commandeer – whatever they needed in food and drink and service. With Ine we saw the beginnings of bureaucratization and systemization, stipulating the amount of *feorm* due from ten hides.[38] To ensure that these supplies were actually produced it was necessary for the responsibility to be more minutely distributed. By another law Ine enjoined that a nobleman leaving an estate must prove (*taecnian*) that a certain proportion of the land there is *gesett land*.[39] There has been much debate about the meaning of the term *gesett land*. *Gesett* is the past participle of the verb *gesettan*. It has variously been interpreted as 'cultivated', 'tenanted' or 'settled'.[40] However, it is more likely that another sense of *gesettan* is more revealing here: 'to fix, appoint'. There is a cognate abstract noun, *gesetnes, gesettnys*, a decree or statute. In post-Conquest England we will encounter the 'assizing' of land, the fixing of the rents and services due from it, and the 'assize' as the name for this process, as it was also the name for a royal decree or

---

34. D. Hill, ed., *An Atlas of Anglo-Saxon England* (1981), 82 and maps 145–6; S 186, translated *EHD* I, no. 83 at 474–5.
35. *Boldon Book: Northumberland and Durham*, ed. D. Austin (1982), 67.
36. Charles-Edwards, 'Early medieval kingships', 28–39.
37. Neilson, *Customary Rents*, 1–20; Worcester: *ibid.*, 20.
38. Liebermann, I, 119–20: Ine 70.1.
39. Liebermann, I, 118: Ine 64.6.
40. F.L. Attenborough, *The Laws of the Earliest English Kings* (1922), 57–9; T.H. Aston, 'The origins of the manor in England', *TRHS* 5th series 8 (1958), 59–83, reprinted with 'The origins of the manor in England: a postscript', in *Social Relations and Ideas: essays in honour of R.H. Hilton*, ed. T.H. Aston, P.R. Coss, C. Dyer and J. Thirsk (1983), 1–43 at 7–11; J.F. McGovern, 'The meaning of "gesette land" in Anglo-Saxon land tenure', *Speculum* 46 (1971), 589–96; N. Higham, *An English Empire: Bede and the early Anglo-Saxon kings* (1995), 241 and note 57 proposes 'hides of the house', those which provided 'renders which go directly to the focal settlement of the estate'.

statute.[41] It seems likely that to *gesettan* land was to make some kind of formal establishment of this kind: perhaps to allot the overall tax liability of an estate among individual hides or groups of hides. We have seen this was a process which had already taken place at Farnham when Cædwalla gave 60 hides there 'already assigned to their own places and names'. 'Assigning the hides to their own places and names' may have been to *gesettan* or 'assize' them, and Ine's concern may have been to make sure that a landholder giving up an estate should leave its tax burden properly provided for.[42]

Kings commonly reserved certain food renders to themselves when they granted land away: the clergy of the minster at Berkeley, Gloucestershire, still owed ale, honey, bullocks, swine and sheep in 883 and were willing to pay heavily for exemption from these dues.[43] But, in the main, to grant land was to grant rights to the *feorm* due from it. Some of the earliest reliable charters explicitly conveyed the right to collect from an area of land the food renders which would otherwise have come to the king. The right to take it was an effective endowment. When Offa granted land in Islingham, Kent (Kent being then under Mercian control) to the bishop of Rochester in 764 what he granted was 20 ploughlands near the Medway, with all its proper bounds and appurtenances, 'and all the tribute which by law belongs to the kings' (of Kent). Another transfer, again by a Mercian king of land in Kent, included 'all the tribute formerly given to kings which as long as you live in this life shall be subject to your power'.[44]

This 'privatization' of *feorm* resulted in the very considerable transfer of produce from the warland producers to the owners of land in bookright. Yet although this undoubtedly began a process which ultimately made *feorm* into a kind of rent, there seems to have been a sense in which the obligation to provide it should be distinguished from rent. *Feorm* originated in the obligations of the warland, and retained something of this fact. It is widely recorded in Domesday as 'custom'. It would be a mistake to think that geld was the only tax with which the commissioners concerned themselves. Under the blanket term 'custom' a tremendous amount of transferred surplus is concealed.[45] 'Customs' of cheese, sheep and lambs, honey, wheat, and so on are sometimes recorded in detail, and when they are they look very like the components of ancient food rents – sometimes the 'custom' is explicitly the 'custom belonging to the farm of one night' and is still rendered to the king, but much custom has been diverted

---

41. See p. 40 above.
42. R.J. Faith, 'Tidenham, Gloucestershire and the origins of the manor in England', *Landscape History* 16 (1994), 39–51; G.B. Grundy, *Saxon Charters and Field Names of Gloucestershire*, Bristol and Gloucestershire Archaeological Society, (2 parts, 1935–6), 237–252 at 247–51.
43. H.P.R. Finberg, *The Early Charters of the West Midlands* (1961), no. 83 at 49–50.
44. E. John, ed. *Land Tenure in Early England: a discussion of some problems* (1960), ch. 2; BCS 195 (S 105); BCS 254 (S 128).
45. Maitland, *Domesday Book*, 106–9, 208–10.

into private hands. Very often custom has been commuted into a cash sum. But for a great monastic house able to organize its lands to provide it, *feorm* remained an attractive option. The system of food farms which supported the greater monasteries from highly organized weekly supplies from their estates was in essence an elaborated form of the regular *feorm* deliveries which supported Anglo-Saxon kings and aristocrats.[46]

Gafol

Early kings had the right to a payment in cash known as *gafol*. *Gafol* became a widely used term for various kinds of rent, but it was in origin not a rent but a payment made to the king or other superior and in that sense was a form of tribute. Money payments known as *gafol*, and the people who owed them, *gafolgeldas*, appear as early as the Kentish and West Saxon laws of the seventh century, and in literary works *gafol* comfortably and consistently translates words for tribute or tax: Wihtred of Kent freed the church from *gafol* in this sense, and the classical terminology of tribute and the royal fisc went into Old English as *gafol* and its derivatives. It regularly appears among the obligations owed at royal centres.[47] In 1086 the thegns of the manor of West Derby owed to the king as lord of the manor of West Derby a cash payment of two *orae* (36 pence) for each carucate.[48] Kings initially retained their rights to *gafol* on land they had granted out. This remained the case on the manors of Gloucester Abbey and some of the land of Rochester Cathedral, where *gafol* was explicitly reserved to the crown. In an agreement between Harold Harefoot, son of King Cnut, and the cathedral priory of Christ Church, Canterbury the king assured the community that they should hold the port of Sandwich 'as ... they had done in any king's day, with *gafol*, water and shore'.[49]

Like *feorm*, *gafol* became more precisely assigned as time went on. It seems from the Bexhill charter already quoted that the various settlements of 'the *gavolland* of the *utland*' or outland had had their hidages allotted to particular places: 'at Barnhorn three hides, at

---

46. R.V. Lennard, *Rural England 1086-1135: a study of social and agrarian conditions* (1959), 128-39.
47. *Tributum* translated as *gaval* and *fiscale* as *gafollice*: Abels, *Lordship and Military Obligation*, 19 and n. 35. The source for this is probably Isidore of Seville, *Etymologies: Isidori hispalensis episcopi etymologiarum sive originum libri XX*, ed. W.D.Lindsay (2 vols, 1911), II, Bk II. XVI.18, Bk XX.9. *Gafol* paid at royal centres: Barrow, *The Kingdom of the Scots*, 12; as rent, tribute or tax: Aston, 'Origins of the manor', 10-11; Neilson, *Customary Rents*, 49-55; Abels, *Lordship and Military Obligation*, 19 and n. 34. Alfred and Guthrum's treaty: Liebermann, I, 126-8; Stenton, *Anglo-Saxon England*, 259 and n. 1.
48. E.B. Demarest, '*Inter Ripam et Mersham*', *EHR* 38 (1923), 161-70, treats these payments as commuted royal food rents; for a contrary view see C. Stephenson, '*Firma unius noctis* and the customs of the hundred', *EHR* 39 (1924), 161-74.
49. Robertson, *Charters*, XCI at 174-9 (S 1467).

Worsham one, at *Ibbanhurst* one, at Crowhurst eight, at Ridge one, at *Gyllingan* two, at *Fuccerham* and *Blacanbrocan* one'.[50] Figure 6 shows some of these scattered outliers. *Gafol*-paying land was evidently a particular type of land, perhaps land which owed money payments rather than *feorm*. The late tenth- or eleventh-century survey of Tidenham, Gloucestershire, shows the hidages of *gafolland* similarly assigned to various places on the estate.[51] When King Alfred negotiated with Guthrum of Denmark the terms on which disputes between the English and the Danes should be settled, slain English *ceorls* 'who live on *gafolland*', it was agreed, were to be rated for compensation at the same sum, 200 shillings, as the Danish *liesingar* or freedman.[52]

As land which owed *gafol* increasingly came into private hands *gafol* lost its association with kings and became indistinguishable from rent. *Gafelian*, to rent, is found as a verb in the tenth century, when it is clear from the laws that a lord would expect to have under him *geneatmanna* who owe him *gafol*, as the *geneat* in the *Rectitudines* did. *Gafol* was very widely charged at 32 pence a hide and could be apportioned among divisions of the hide such as the yardland, as at Tidenham where 'throughout the whole estate twelve pence is due from every yardland'. *Gafol*, sometimes *landgable*, was typically owed by sokemen at these or similar rates.[53]

Yet it was not only the *geneat* who paid *gafol*: it was due from the *gebur* as well at Tidenham and in the *Rectitudines*, and from the *ceorls* at Hurstbourne. There is a contradiction here. If *gafol* was in origin a public or royal due laid on the hides of the warland, how is this compatible with the fact that not only the population of the warland but also the *geburs*, so closely dependent on the inland, paid it too? One explanation is that it was originally a universal burden, which remained due from free people who had fallen into dependence. Stenton considered that even the *ceorls* at Hurstbourne, who owed heavy labour rent as well as *gafol*, included families who had once been free taxpayers holding taxable land. Despite their servile status the ambiguous term *ceorl* still, in Aston's view, indicated 'legal worth and recognition in the public courts'.[54]

---

50. BCS 208 (S 108); see p. 30 above; M. Gardiner, 'Some lost Anglo-Saxon charters and the endowment of Hastings College', *Sussex Archaeological Collections* 127 (1989), 39–48, discusses the outland at Bexhill at 39–43.
51. Faith, 'Tidenham, Gloucestershire', 44–5.
52. Liebermann, I, 126 (Alfred and Guthrum's treaty).
53. W.H. Hale, ed., *The Domesday of St Paul's of the year MCCXXII or registrum de visitatione maneriorum per Robertum decanum*, Camden Society 69 (1858), lxix; Barrow, *Kingdom of the Scots*, 12.
54. Stenton, *Anglo-Saxon England*, 469; Aston, 'Origins of the manor', 13.

Service at centres: building and repair work

Warland agricultural services are notable for their intense conservatism: some very powerful imperatives prevented them being either increased or abolished, and tenants can be found in fourteenth-century England claiming to hold their land by services which may date back to the era of extensive lordship.[55] Set amounts of work to be performed at centres were one of the common duties owed by the people of Scottish and Northumbrian *scirs* and southern sokes alike, among the drengs of Northumbria as among the free tenants on the lands of the abbey of Bury St Edmunds. Building work figures strongly among them. A defensive enclosure – palisade or fence and ditch and bank – was vital to any prestigious or seigneurial site. All the more detailed accounts of service, both sides of the Conquest, include work on this. The *geneat* of the *Rectitudines* must build and fence the lord's enclosure, *bytlian und burh hegegian*. It was very likely an ongoing job, which needed all the resources available. The excavated seigneurial site at Goltho, Lincolnshire, shows that it had an impressive rampart and palisade throughout its ninth-, tenth- and eleventh-century phases.[56] The work of digging and fencing, cutting and carrying fencing materials (virtually never stone for walling) was laid on the hides of the small manor just as the large-scale construction work for bridges and fortresses were laid on the hides of the great estate. It may even have been laid on individual hides to do a specified section: at Littlebourne and Stodmarsh, two Kentish manors of St Augustine's, Canterbury, two tenants of a particular sulung owed, along with cheese, the obligation to *claudere ubi antecessores sui soliti claudere fuerunt*, to do fencing work where their ancestors used to do.[57] These ancient obligations remained in force even when much more elaborate building services were also demanded. In the twelfth century the tenants of hides on one vill of St Paul's Essex manor of Adulfsness as well as fencing the curia were responsible for repairing the barn, oxhouse and *bateria* and those at another were obliged to fell and prepare the timber to repair the barns, and construct an oxhouse.[58]

Horse work: escort, messages, supervision

Medievalists are accustomed to stressing the importance of the horse to the social position of the knight, but horses were equally vital to the

55. See pp. 206–7 below.
56. G. Beresford, *Goltho: the development of an early medieval manor c 850–1150*, English Heritage Archaeological Report no. 4, Historical Buildings and Monuments Commission for England (1987), 30–2, 67, 72.
57. *The Register of St Augustine's Abbey, Canterbury, Commonly Called the Black Book*, ed. G.J. Turner and H.E. Salter, British Academy Records of Social and Economic History (2 parts 1915, 1924).
58. *Domesday of St Paul's*, 43, 48.

economy and social position of the upper ranks of the peasantry. Horses crop up in every context in which we meet the people of the warland: part of the *geneat*'s duties is simply 'horse-ward' (*horswearde*). The superior form of services connected with horses was 'riding', which probably included messenger work, escort, and administrative duties which involved riding long distances. All this was responsible work. In their role on the great estate, and perhaps before that in the governing of the *scir*, men with horses had much in common with the thegns of the northern counties.[59] *Radmen, radchenistres* or riding men were fairly common in Lancashire and the border counties (119 in Lancashire, 174 in Shropshire, 126 in Gloucestershire, 53 in Herefordshire), and the cumulation of these figures indicates a social class of some significance. Riding horses were unlikely to have been part of the stock of the average peasant holding before the Conquest, so it is clear that riding men and their like were evidently a superior group economically.[60] They must have been people of widely differing wealth, although it is only from Domesday Book that we have any information about individuals. Three radknights in Tewkesbury, Gloucestershire, in the reign of Edward the Confessor had six, three and two hides respectively. These were not large peasant holdings but small estates and were almost certainly worked by slaves or sub-tenants.[61]

The riding men's distinct status was more than simply a matter of wealth, it had also to do with personal service of a responsible kind that brought them closely in touch with the great figures they served. A supply of trusted people like this was essential to the running of a large estate: 'As with a king and his shires, so with a lord and his vills: he must have needed men to ride to and fro'.[62] The Tidenham *geneats* owed services which, although agricultural in the sense that they were connected with the estate, did not specifically include any ploughing or harvest work. This work depended on them owning their own riding horses, and the dues they owed allowed the landlord access to this costly resource and to their time. Their duties – droving stock and 'riding', perhaps with messages or on escort – involved care of important assets, and were responsible jobs.[63] Riding men were among the lessees of the bishop of Worcester and Bishop Oswald's leases show that the bishop expected from them 'the whole law of riding as riding men should'.[64] They had to lend their horses and do service at the hunt.

---

59. Maitland, 'Northumbrian tenures', 639.
60. *Radmanni* as minor officials or councillors: G.L. Gomme, *Primitive Folk-Moots or Open-Air Assemblies in Britain* (1880), 300; H.C. Darby, *Domesday England* (1986 edn), app. 3.
61. *DB* I, 163b.
62. S.P.J. Harvey, 'Domesday England' in *Ag. Hist.* II, 45–136 at 82–4; Campbell, 'Some agents', 212–14.
63. Robertson, *Charters*, CIX at 205–6.
64. BCS 1136 (S 1368).

Horse work: droves, carting and packhorses

The warland population was the backbone of the long-haul transport system of Anglo-Saxon England. The Tidenham *geneat* 'must work whether on or off the estate, whichever he is bidden, ride and supply transport, lead loads and drive droves and do many other things' – the phrase 'drive droves and lead loads' seems to have been a common tag for this kind of work. The need for driving large numbers of stock over long distances is virtually built into the structure of the early land-unit: whether swine from Kentish arable lands to their Wealden dens, or from the Hwiccan lands to their peripheral woodlands. The importance of long-distance sheep and cattle transhumance to upland pastures is harder to trace, and it may well have declined over time, but there is no doubt of the early importance of seasonal grazing which was enough to influence place-name formation in the shape of Somertons and Wintertons. The hill grazing for cattle in the Forest of Bowland, the summer grazing of Bodmin Moor of early Cornwall, the 'pasture common to all men of the hundred' are examples of the communally exploited resources of early communities.[65] The 'privatization' of land which the emergence of estates represented gave landlords access to what had been communally organized resources. D. Hooke's mapping of the discrete assets of eighth- and ninth-century estates in the west midlands shows how the fragmentation of early-land units into estates preserved and was influenced by these ancient links.[66] Lords of estates gained access to the skilled work of droving which became an obligation on the warland tenant.

Droving and carrying were important not only in the internal economy of an estate but in the long-distance trade which has given the eighth century the name 'the age of *emporia*'. Salt, lead, cattle, hides, and wool are all bulk commodities on which international ports like Hamwih and London thrived in the eighth century. *Geneats* and the like 'leading loads' on packhorse and wagons were the long-distance hauliers of this essential traffic. Driving droves and leading loads also furnished the short-distance traffic to local markets, the conveying of food rents to centres and minsters. One interpretation of the dreng's duties was that he was responsible for collecting and delivering the renders in kind owed by the township and delivering them to the centre.

These were services devoted to the lord's own stock. A vital and related obligation of the warland tenant was carting and lending his own carts and draught stock. The Tidenham *geneat* must *averian* as one of his duties.[67] *Averian*, to supply transport, was a widespread warland obligation and its usefulness to the seigneurial economy can be judged

65. Ekwall, *English Place-Names*, xxxii; Darby, *Domesday England*, 153.
66. D. Hooke, *Anglo-Saxon Settlements of the West Midlands: the charter evidence*, BAR British Series 95 (1981), part II.
67. Robertson, *Charters*, CIX at 205–6.

by the fact that it remained a valuable asset to lords throughout the middle ages. It was particulary important where large amounts of food rent went up from manors for consumption or sale at some distant central place, as was the case with the 'country manors' of St Paul's Cathedral. The hides of one of the Essex manors in the early thirteenth century lent carts and horses at harvest and a harrowing horse at Lent and carted four and a half loads 'from the barn to the boat', possibly to a small inland port.[68] In Fulbourne, Cambridgeshire, 26 sokemen 'only owe the sheriff carrying and guard service'.[69] *Avermanni* on the Canterbury estate owed services connected with providing hospitality to a travelling household, providing stabling, fodder and food, although by the time that these were recorded in the thirteenth century they had become not far removed from the much more demeaning carting service owed by the serfs.[70]

Agricultural work: haymaking and harvesting

Farmers of every kind needed large inputs of labour in a comparatively short time at the crucial points in the agricultural year: harvest and haymaking. Depending on their status, we see traces of customs which enabled them to call on the labour of neighbours, tenants, or subjects. We do not know what kind of arrangements peasants made in the era before the development of common field farming, but Ine's laws refer to the lending of ox-teams and to common 'share lands' which needed co-operation. Early land-units had common resources which would have needed a pooling of labour to exploit.[71] Studies of the small *scirs* have noted that their inhabitants, apparently regardless of status, were obliged to do regular set amounts of agricultural service at their centres. One of the duties of the Lancashire thegns was to send their men to reap the lord's corn at harvest time. Each sent his men one day at harvest to reap the king's crops (or paid for exemption). If he wished to 'withdraw' he paid 40 shillings.[72] Scanty though it is, this information is full of resonances, for the dues it records are widely found. At first sight it seems anomalous to find people of the rank of thegn owing labour dues: labour is the form of obligation which we associate with the most unfree tenants of the post-Conquest manor. However, service like this was very commonly owed by people of independent status and with sizeable lands of their own – sokemen, *geneats* and lesser thegns – who were obliged to plough a certain number of acres, to make hay and to harvest for a set number of days at an estate centre. The *geneat* of the *Rectitudines* 'must ... reap and

---

68. *Domesday of St Paul's*, 42–3, 47.
69. *DB* I, 190a.
70. Du Boulay, *The Lordship of Canterbury*, 166–7, 189.
71. H.P.R. Finberg, 'Anglo-Saxon England to 1042', in *Ag. Hist.* II.II, 385–525 at 416–17. For the development of common field agriculture, see pp. 143–7 below.
72. *DB* I, 269d.

mow' and for the three hides at Thorne, Worcestershire, that he leased from the bishop a thegn 'works with all his might' twice a year, once at haymaking, once at harvest'.[73] Harvesting and haymaking on a set number of days, always less than the entire harvest period, is occasionally recorded in Domesday and may be included within the variety of *consuetudines*, customs, or unspecified 'rustic works' or 'work such as the *villani* do'. One of the bishop of Worcester's tenants in 1086 was Aluric, who held land from him at Kempsey. He paid the same rent as his ancestors but had to do 'rustic labour' when the bishop's reeve 'requested' him to do so.[74] W.E. Kapelle has used the records of the Templars' estates in Yorkshire to show that in the twelfth century their peasant tenants in the West Riding ploughed and harrowed the Templars' lands in just this episodic way: they ploughed and harrowed for four days, mowed and made hay for one day. As well they did four 'boon days' work at harvest time.[75] This service was entirely honourable (the more so as it was very likely performed by the thegn's own tenants or servants). 'He must reap and mow and entertain his lord' was not seen to be a contradiction in terms. One prime reason why this is so is because such service was initially owed not on private estates but at royal vills and centres of *scirs*. That is to say it was part of attendance on the person of a king or great man: the haymaking was for the king's horses, as was the 'foddercorn' of East Anglia. Major ecclesiastical houses inherited the rights to these dues along with their endowment. The burgesses of Bury St Edmunds owed 'reapsilver' in the late thirteenth century, which they knew to be a relic of the days when 'everyone used to do the reaping'. From the perspective of the free burgesses of the thirteenth century this manual work seemed demeaning, 'like serfs'.[76]

It is often difficult, and sometimes no doubt misleading, to detect ancient *scir* dues in medieval rents. Yet the large category of food rents which incorporate the element *scat*, from OE *sceatt*, such as the 'wheat *scat*' and 'malt *scat*' paid by the bishop of Durham's tenants in the twelfth and thirteenth centuries, may preserve its early sense of 'tribute' or 'tax'.[77]

Hunting and harvest duties sometimes went together, and much must have depended on whether the centre being serviced was primarily agricultural or was a residence in hunting country. Even the superior thegn of the *Rectitudines* owed the service of repairing the deer hedge at the king's *hame*. 'By custom' the West Derby thegns constructed 'houses' for the king – these were likely to have been temporary hunting lodges – and kept up his fisheries and deer

73. Liebermann, I, 445; BCS 1110 (S 1305), Robertson, *Charters*, XXXVI at 66–7.
74. *DB* I, 172d.
75. W.E. Kapelle, *The Norman Conquest of the North: a region and its transformation 1000–1135* (1979), 66–7.
76. *Kalendar of Abbot Samson; Jocelin of Brakelond, Chronicle of the Abbey of Bury St Edmunds*, ed. D. Greenaway and J. Sayers (1989), 88–9.
77. Neilson, *Customary Rents*, 28–9.

hedges.[78] Denewulf, bishop of Winchester, leasing 40 hides of land at Alresford, Hampshire, late in the ninth century, enjoined on the tenant that 'when the need arises, his men shall be ready for harvesting and hunting.' The see of Winchester had originally received Alresford from King Cenwalh of Wessex (d. 672), and it is likely that these hunting and harvesting services had passed with it.[79] At Kingstone, Herefordshire: 'the wood called Triveline renders no custom except game (*venatio*). The *villani* there at the time of King Edward used to carry the game to Hereford and did no other service.' Significantly, it is the shire that provided this information about what had surely anciently been a *scir* custom.[80]

The agricultural services owed at the centres of the *scir*, and the less formal communal obligations of the farmers of an area, were the roots of the common obligations known on the post-Conquest manor, and probably earlier too, as 'boon works'.[81] These were communal workdays principally at ploughing time, haymaking and harvest, at which the whole tenantry were obliged to turn out, or send workers in their stead. The American sociologist G.C. Homans described the nature of 'boons' and their role in peasant life in the thirteenth century. Perhaps influenced by the mores of New England country life which he knew so well, he stressed their neighbourly aspect. By contrast, Vinogradoff, who came from a country which still remembered serfdom, emphasized their compulsory nature.[82] Both may be right, for boons evolved over time and may have retained something of an earlier, more voluntary, element into the age when they had become simply a form of labour rent. The post-Conquest Latin term for boons is *precaria*, 'that which is given as a favour or in response to prayer', and the conventional derivation of the ME term 'boon' is from OE *ben*, 'prayer'. 'Bidreap' may signify reaping which is 'bidden' or may derive from *bede*, prayer. While boons seem to have originated in the circumstances of 'extensive lordship' they were evidently very greatly developed and extended over time. We will see in Chapter 6 the important part they played in the economy of the small estate in late Anglo-Saxon England, and on the post-Conquest manor they were an important obligation on tenants.

Agricultural work: ploughing

The importance of ploughing rent is that it gives lords access to valuable draught stock which they do not need to maintain all through

---

78. *DB* I, 269v.
79. BCS 617 (S 1287); Robertson, *Charters*, XV at 28–9, 288.
80. *DB* I, 178b.
81. The *gebur* of the *Rectitudines* owed three ploughings *to bene*: Liebermann, I, 447.
82. G.C. Homans, *English Villagers of the Thirteenth Century* (Cambridge, Mass. 1941), 260–8; Vinogradoff, *Villainage*, 281–4, 308.

the year. S.P.J. Harvey has shown that the home farms of many lords in 1086 are likely to have had three plough teams or fewer, and this meant that they had to have recourse to the teams of the peasantry to plough their inland arables.[83] Where there was a large population of dependent tenants on the inland with their own ploughs, like the *geburs* at Tidenham or the *ceorls* at Hurstbourne, their heavy ploughing service would have more than compensated for the shortfall in seigneurial teams. But there must have been very wide variations before the Conquest in the extent to which the cultivation of the inland arable could depend on labour from inland plough teams.[84]

Very few ploughing obligations are recorded in Domesday Book and those that are are measured in acres, generally between one and three per tenant. These works were often the responsibility of the entire vill. This is significant because services owed by the vill were considered by Jolliffe and others to be typical of *scir* service.[85] The people who are noted as owing labour rent in Domesday are comparatively free people and the comparatively light fixed ploughing services recorded in Domesday resemble the occasional ploughing services on some northern *scirs*. Radknights at Deerhurst, Gloucestershire, in King Edward's day 'all used to plough for the lord's use'. On the royal manor of Leominster (Herefordshire) 238 *villani* used to plough 140 acres when Queen Edith held it, 224 ploughed 125 in 1086, a rate of little more than a half an acre per team. This seems to have been the general order of magnitude of other Domesday ploughing obligations. At Eckington six *colliberti* ploughed and sowed twelve acres and 40 *villani* ploughed 151 acres at Much Marcle, both also in Herefordshire. Similar work obligations are occasionally included in pre-Conquest leases and wills. A thegn leasing a hide at Cotheridge from the bishop of Worcester was obliged to cultivate two acres for church dues.[86]

Although Domesday records these ancient dues of ploughing, haymaking and reaping, which appear to have been relics of ancient *scir* obligations, it says nothing about routine week-work. The agricultural services recorded appear to be owed from the warland peasantry and it is possible that they were recorded because they were considered to be the custom of the *scir*, not of the manor. The services due from warland were particularly appropriate to the centre-plus-dependencies type of estate: they serviced the centre on a periodic basis, provided transport, help in the hunting field, and extra labour at peak times. They were a supplement to the labour supply on central inlands where the day-to-day work was carried out by slaves, *geburs* and

83. S.P.J. Harvey, 'The extent and profitability of demesne agriculture in England in the later eleventh century' in *Social Relations and Ideas: essays in honour of R.H. Hilton*, ed. T.H. Aston, P.R. Coss, C. Dyer and J. Thirsk (1983), 45–72 at 53–4.
84. R.J. Faith, 'Demesne resources and labour rent on the manors of St Paul's Cathedral 1066–1222', *EcHR* 47 (1994), 657–78.
85. Jolliffe, 'Northumbrian institutions'; Barrow, *Kingdom of the Scots*, 23–4.
86. Lennard, *Rural England*, 368–71 (Leominster, Eckington and Marcle); Robertson, *Charters*, xxxv, xxxvi (Cotheridge, Thorne).

bordars. However, most estates in late Anglo-Saxon England are likely to have had a similarly mixed labour force. The ploughs of the freer *geneats* and hide tenants prepared the lord's arable alongside the joint teams of the tied *geburs* and bordars. At the major labour-hungry times of the year, haymaking and harvest, warland and inland tenants would have worked side by side. Tenants of every kind owed the vital work of keeping the curial defences in repair. What distinguishes the service of the warland tenants from those of the inland is their strictly defined nature, for they are on occasion recorded in Domesday, that book named from the Day of Judgement whose decisions, like those of the Last Judgement, 'are unalterable'.[87] They derive from service once owed to the king and are 'the custom of the country', not 'the custom of the manor'.

The warland population and the state: tax

The counterpart of the fact that inland is detectable by virtue of its tax-exempt status, although this was not originally its most important characteristic, is that one of the distinguishing obligations of warland came to be its liability to taxation. The connection of geld liability with the warland is integral to the language of taxation. Geld was levied on the hide and its fractions the yardland or virgate (and in the Danelaw the carucate and its fractions the bovate or oxgang). The simplest description of the distribution of individual liability to geld is that the occupants of the warland were the geld-payers and their land was assessed accordingly, in fractions of the hide. An entry in Domesday for Hurstingbourne Hundred, Huntingdonshire, makes this abundantly clear: while the inland was geld-free the '*villani* and sokemen pay geld according to the hides recorded in the schedule'.[88] Only for Middlesex does Domesday give us information about individual peasant holdings in any detail. There, it reveals two broad categories: on the one hand bordars and cottars with smallholdings reckoned in acres or with no land at all, on the other *villani* with holdings which are almost invariably reckoned in units of hides and their fractions – in other words fractions of geld assessment units.[89] Some scholars have taken this argument further, interpreting the manorial populations recorded in Domesday as the actual taxpayers, and the common Domesday phrase *terra villanorum* has itself been interpreted as indicating 'geld-carrying liability'.[90] Peasant geld-payers seem to have been more likely to have been recorded individually in the eastern counties, but D. Roffe surmises that geld liability in some northern counties may have been

---

87. *Dialogus de scaccario*, ed. and trans. C. Johnson (1950), 64.
88. Harvey, 'Domesday England', 56-7.
89. P.D.A., Harvey, 'Introduction' to *The Peasant Land Market in Medieval England*, ed. P.D.A. Harvey (1984), at 9–10; Joy, 'Sokeright', 322.
90. Harvey, 'Domesday England', 56.

assessed on the basis of the number of peasant holdings and that 'it is likely that only the peasants who were responsible for the payment of the geld are recorded'.[91] In some Domesday entries it is specifically stated that holdings are 'to the geld' and we know that in East Anglia geld liability was arrived at by dividing the total owed by the hundred, reckoned for the purpose at 100 hides, and then subdividing this among divisions known as 'letes'. Within the lete each vill paid its share and it seems that within the vill the liability to taxation was laid on the *ware* acre. These *ware* acres were real holdings as well as units of assessment. Most were very small – five acres or less – for this was an area where partible inheritance and a brisk market in land had combined to bring into being a mass of peasant smallholdings.[92]

Long after the geld lapsed and taxation assessed on the hide was superseded by taxation on moveable property, the specific character of tax-assessed land survived. It is explicit in the term *virgatae terrae geldabiles de antiqua tenura*, 'geldable yardlands of ancient tenure', in an early fourteenth-century extent of Bampton manor in Oxfordshire.[93] Tenants on land assessed in hides, as the *hidarii* at Thorpe and Kirby in Essex, of whom the latter held land 'geldable to the king's geld', the tenant of a hide at Navestock in the same county who 'used to defend it against the king', were still remembered as taxpayers, as well as rent-payers, in 1222.[94] There are connections between taxation, personal freedom and ownership. In the confusion of the post-Conquest land settlement, paying tax for one's land came to confer a claim which would defeat all others. This placed the taxpaying warland inhabitant, however small his holding, in a different world from that of the worker on the exempt inland.[95] We might not nowadays be inclined to see taxation in quite this light, but it was expressly associated with freedom: 'in the old days (*antiquitus*) his father held this geldable yardland freely by the king's taxation': this was said of a Worcester holding in 1170 which was also described as 'of the villeinage' (*de villenagio*).[96] By the thirteenth century, however, the hide and its fraction the yardland, or the carucate and its fraction the bovate, were losing their link with taxation and had become simply units for assessing area and rent. The last recension of the land tax was

---

91. D. Roffe, 'Domesday Book and northern society: a reassessment', *EHR* 105 (1990), 310–36 at 333 (n.2); Stenton, *Types of Manorial Structure*, 87; D.C. Douglas, *The Social Structure of Medieval East Anglia*, Oxford Studies in Social and Legal History 9 (1927), 99; Vinogradoff, *Villainage*, 242; *Kalendar of Abbot Samson*, 105, n. 3.
92. *Kalendar of Abbot Samson*, xv–xxii.
93. Extent of Bampton deanery manor.
94. *Domesday of St Paul's*, 46, 75.
95. M.K. Lawson, *Cnut: the Danes in England in the early eleventh century* (1993), 191–4.
96. *The Red Book of Worcester*, ed. M. Hollings, Worcestershire Historical Society (4 vols, 1934–50), I, 82.

probably the 'hidage' which continued in some areas into the fourteenth century.

The warland population and the state: justice

The early Anglo-Saxon laws concerned themselves with the rights and wrongs of a large undifferentiated class of *ceorls*, non-noble freemen, with a *wergeld* of 200 shillings, and it is clear that among them were substantial peasant farmers whose enclosed farmsteads and personal property rights the laws protected. That royal law-makers dealt with independent farmers and their disputes shows that they were regarded as part of the body politic; that they and their families had *wergeld* values shows that they were 'law-worthy' people. *Wergeld* ratings continued to be part of the way in which people were regarded long after they ceased to be part of the legal process. There was a strong popular attachment to the *wergeld* system as a method of dispute settlement, which kept compensation in being as an unofficial 'alternative' legal method well into the period when the notions of tort and crime had become part of officially sanctioned legal mentality.[97]

There is little doubt that the later history of the large land-unit was to be intimately bound up with jurisdiction, and no doubt at all that English landlords from the tenth century became closely involved in the administration of justice. But we should be careful not to antedate this development. Under the early Anglo-Saxon kings private individuals certainly had a financial interest in justice. A *gesithcund-man*, someone of the appropriate rank to be a royal companion, could normally profit from fines imposed on members of his household; only if they got out of hand and came before the king or his ealdorman did he lose this right.[98] Ealdormen, in charge of *scirs*, are key figures in the era of extensive lordship. It is anachronistic to separate the various strands in the ealdorman's office and authority, but, as the laws are more explicit on his judicial and executive roles, we will consider them first. He was expected to make sure that anyone in his *scir* who demanded justice should receive it. He was responsible for making sure that thieves did not escape, for supervising cattle sales, and his permission had to be sought by migrant workers to move elsewhere. He was undoubtedly a powerful figure, his 'peace' protected by high tariffs, as was the king's.[99] Yet the ealdorman's role in court seems to have been more presidential and executive than judicial. The nature of Anglo-Saxon justice – in fact of justice throughout early medieval northern Europe – has something to do with this. A recent synoptic

97. N. Hurnard, *The King's Pardon for Homicide Before A.D. 1307* (1969), xi–xiii, 9–10; *Leges Henrici Primi*, ed. L.J. Downer (1972), ch. 76.
98. Liebermann, I, 110–12: Ine 50.
99. Liebermann, I, 92, 104, 70, 50, 72: Ine 8, 36, Alfred 37, 3, 40.

survey of dispute settlement in early modern Europe has summed up some of its most important common characteristics:

> courts were ... organized around judicial tribunals rather than dominated by single judges. Generally courts had presidents ... who certainly took a direct part in proceedings, but who shared judgement with others. The type of person to be president of a court was, most often, the local representative of a wider authority, be it the king's, emperor's, prince's ... [and] provided the link between local justice and higher authority.

Appeal was not to written law, in the main, but to 'collective judgement in an atmosphere of public witness ... local standing was the major qualification for membership'. Sworn testimony and written documents both played a part in establishing right.[100]

This is not to say that there were no judges in early Anglo-Saxon England. We know of the 'judges of the Kentish people', the *Cantwara deman,* and a place called Damerham in Hampshire gets its name from being the judges' residence or estate.[101] But these judges may have been less like impartial dispensers of judgement and punishment than the presidents of tribunals at which both parties, each backed up by supporters who are prepared to stand surety for them, seek an equitable solution. This solution will take the form of some kind of compensation, according to the rank of the aggrieved and the nature of the injury. Early medieval dispute settlement was informed at every level with the idea of reinforcement by oath: the oaths of witnesses to the truth of a statement, the oaths of the parties' 'oath-helpers' who together reinforced their credibility, the oaths of those who would ensure that the decision arrived at was carried out, or who swore to the authenticity of customs and boundaries. Publicity is an important matter: disputes were settled in early Kent and perhaps in other regions too in a *medle* or a *thing,* an assembly or meeting, with witnesses and sureties ensuring that the agreement is a matter of public knowledge. This made the early court a crowded place, and one in which custom and collective memory were important. It was perhaps not the 'folk-moot' in the idealized democratic sense that early writers on English history would like to have seen. But neither does it look to have been an institution in a landlord's pocket.

The importance of membership of a court, of procedure by oath and compurgation, and of collective judgement, meant that the idea of 'law-worthiness', of entitlement to participate in the system, was of paramount importance to personal status. Law-worthiness is intimately connected with the status of the warland population. Tenth-century

100. P.J. Wormald, 'Conclusion' in *The Settlement of Disputes in Medieval Europe,* ed. W. Davies and P. Fouracre (1986), 215–19.
101. Liebermann, I, 10: Hlothere and Eadric 8; Ekwall, *English Place-Names,* s.v. *Damerham.*

legislation put a very greatly increased emphasis on law and order. The shires and hundreds which were administrative units, in some ways the successors to the *scir*, came to be administrative and judicial districts as well, and the business that arose in them came to be settled in a court at each of these levels. The shire court was soon seen as a much handier place than the full meeting of the king's council in which to carry out land transactions and to settle disputes. Edgar gave the hundred more policing and judicial powers: the men of the hundred were to pursue thieves and supervise compensation, and the hundred was to have its own court, meeting every four weeks. The emergence of presenting juries, which came to be responsible for bringing crime to the attention of the courts, gave more legal identity to the freemen who served on them. Within the hundred all males of 12 years and over were to be in a 'tithing' or group of ten, presided over by one of their number who collectively would ensure the conformity of individual members to the law.[102] These new, or re-invigorated legal structures made possible a far-reaching degree of social control. The laws recognized no boundary between Christian observance and secular good behaviour, nor did the machinery of tithing and hundred: the tithing was made responsible for the collection of alms and the observance of fasts as well as for ensuring the good behaviour of its members.[103] Yet the courts conferred real benefits on their users too. The court of the hundred, as it evolved, administered the imposition of standard weights and prices and the buying and selling of cattle. It provided a forum for settling local disputes and settling boundaries – matters of importance to farmers.

The evolution of local courts and peace-keeping arrangements was in itself instrumental in drawing a line between different sections of the rural population. To be a member of a tithing and a hundred was a duty and a right open only to freemen, to 'every person who wishes to be held worthy of his *wergeld*'. It is not certain where the inland tenants and workers stood in this respect before the Conquest, but by the twelfth century 'vile and poor persons' were not to act as doomsmen and suit of court came to be attached to landholdings of a certain minimum size.[104] Most interpretations of 'sokeland' and 'sokeright', which in their wider sense meant the warland and its obligations, have treated them as purely jurisdictional terms, and it was in respect of courts and attendance at them that personal status increasingly became defined. In eastern England, what it meant to be a 'sokeman' became particularly well defined. Stenton saw the soke as a Danish institution, and although there are good reasons for discarding that view he was surely right to emphasize the fact that the most important and primary feature of a soke was that its sokemen had an

---

102. Liebermann, I, 193–4: I Edgar; 322: II Cnut 20. A. Harding, *The Law Courts of Medieval England* (1973), 17–20.
103. Liebermann, I, 265: VIII Æthelred 8.
104. *Leges Henrici Primi*, ch. 8; see p. 258 below.

obligation to attend its court, and in a very real sense *were* its court.[105]
E. Miller has shown how the obligations of free tenants in the Isle of
Ely in the thirteenth century were related to the duties to the hundred
and its court of their pre-Conquest predecessors.[106] After the Conquest
the characteristic tenure of the warland population became known as
socage, the 'great residual free tenure' distinct from military tenure
and tenure by serjeanty. To hold land in the way that sokemen held it,
'in socage', was the freest kind of tenure; in the later middle ages
socage was the nearest that English law came to freehold.[107] Holders of
land in socage evidently retained a strong belief in their right to attend
the public courts: when the legal reforms of Henry II were increasingly
putting these beyond the reach of the mass of the peasantry, now
defined as 'unfree', it was the sokeman who was the typical peasant
litigant.[108]

Lordship over men was part of Anglo-Saxon society from its earliest
beginnings. From slave to nobleman, each had a lord, and for the
highest born their lord was the king. Yet it is striking that although the
law codes, of which the earliest come from sixth-century Kent, are full
of references to the authority of lords, *hlafordas* and *dryhten*, many of
whom must have been holders of land, there is very little evidence that
their authority expressly derived from such ownership. Almost all the
references in the laws which relate to superiority over people are
concerned either with the social superiority of those of higher rank, or
with the personal responsibility of the head of a household over his
dependants. From the relationship of a slave owner or employer to his
domestic or agricultural slaves or servants, to the judicial responsibility of the ealdorman over his *scir*, it is responsibility for disciplining
people under personal control that is the law's concern. Punishment in
the early Anglo-Saxon laws is harsh, but, apart from the punishment of
thieves, it is mostly a matter of the discipline of the slave or the
servant by the master. With one important exception, the king's
written laws – and they may represent only a fraction of what
effectively law was – were concerned with keeping the peace, not
governing the relations of landlord and tenant. Unlike his Frankish
counterparts, on only one occasion did Ine lay down rules about such
matters. The exception – and it is an important one – is his law about a
yardlander who, having been housed by the landowner, cannot give up
his tenancy: the previous chapter argued that such a person would
have been the tied tenant known as the *gebur*. While there is no doubt
that the intended effect of this law was very oppressive of the inland

---

105. F.M. Stenton, ed., *Documents Illustrative of the Social and Economic History of the
    Danelaw from Various Collections,* British Academy Records of the Social and
    Economic History of England and Wales 5 (1920), cix–cx; *Types of Manorial
    Structure,* 21.
106. E. Miller, *The Abbey and Bishopric of Ely: the social history of an ecclesiastical
    estate from the tenth to the early fourteenth century* (1951), 116–19.
107. Joy, 'Sokeright', 229–45.
108. See Chapter 10 below.

tenant, it seems to have had some wider purpose than that of governing relations between landlord and tenant. Charles-Edwards puts this in its context: it is one of a group of laws which are about people with various amounts of property leaving their land and the conditions which govern their departure. Probably tax is the issue here.[109]

Ine did make rules for farmers and sometimes we can guess that they had approached him for an authoritative decision on things that concerned them and which they had not been able to settle among themselves: what to do if neighbours have not kept up their fences and there has been damage to crops and hay in consequence? how should damage to stock and woodland be assessed? how to settle disputes over hiring neighbours' plough oxen? But that such matters come into the purview of the king itself suggests local communities are as yet not consolidated enough to have their own decision-making forum, or not seigneurialized enough for the landlord to be settling disputes.

Many disputes which in the early days of Anglo-Saxon England would have been settled by force and feud by the tenth century came through the courts, and this meant that public legal process mattered more. There were certain advantages to be gained, and dangers to be avoided, by personal attachment to a powerful neighbour, and many free people 'commended' themselves to a powerful landlord to secure his advocacy in disputes both in and out of court: a personal subordination by what were called in medieval Scotland 'bonds of manrent'. Commendation was a personal bond in origin, an example of the many kinds of swearing of loyalty which bound the lower to the higher. Although it undoubtedly worked towards subordination of the commended person and the erosion of his personal freedom, it reflected the political strength of important landlords rather than lord and tenant relationships.[110]

It was in the right to preside over public courts on their own lands, rather than to hold private courts from which the public law was excluded, that landlord power made itself felt. In the eighth century one of the most powerful of estate owners, the bishop of Worcester, began to reserve to himself the profits of justice (fines for all except the most serious offences and penalties for non-attendance) which would otherwise have gone to the king, and the bishops were careful to retain these jurisdictional profits from land granted away. By the eve of the Conquest the bishop was only one among many holders of large 'franchises' who administered the law of the land in their own courts. Receiving the profits of justice, however, is not necessarily a sign of

109. T. Charles-Edwards, 'The distinction between land and moveable wealth in Anglo-Saxon England' in *English Medieval Settlement*, ed. P.H. Sawyer (1979), 97–104 at 102–3.
110. Joy, 'Sokeright', ch. 7; J.M. Wormald, *Lords and Men in Scotland: bonds of manrent 1442–1603* (1985); Maitland, *Domesday Book*, 66–79; R. Fleming, *Kings and Lords in Conquest England* (1991), 126–8.

having the power to dispense it. (And Worcester's most extreme claims are now thought to be a fabrication.)[111] Pre-Conquest lords were quite evidently people with important policing powers over people on their land. But it was not for a long time that landlords could explicitly exercise jurisdictional rights in private courts over their tenants as tenants, settling the disputes which arose from their economic relationship. Of course, it is more than likely that they, or their officials, did this in an *ad hoc* way: one of Edgar's laws draws an analogy between God's wrath with those who do not pay their tithe and that of the landlord who will eventually and rightly evict *and kill* a tenant who does not pay his rent.[112] But until the evolution of courts which the lord held explicitly for his own tenants, in his own hall, from which they had no appeal, and to which they had to bring all landlord and tenant business, we are not yet in the era of truly seigneurialized justice. Such courts were not to make their appearance in England until the twelfth century.

The representation of the warland population in Domesday Book

Peasants on warland were a much more socially diverse class than peasants on inland, but they had one important characteristic in common: they were notably freer. 'Free men' and the 'sokemen' who seem to be equivalent or similar to them, amount to 36 per cent of the recorded Domesday population. The Domesday commissioners asked for them to be listed as two of the standard categories of people, but they appear almost exclusively in the eastern and north-eastern counties and form over 20 per cent of the population in Norfolk and Suffolk, Lincolnshire, Leicestershire, and Nottinghamshire (taking sokemen and free men together), and nearly half in Essex. They were an important category in Northamptonshire and appear, though in smaller numbers, in Yorkshire and Kent.[113]

This raises the same question that was prompted by the Domesday figures for inland populations: were the peasants of Scandinavian England as a whole freer than those of the rest of the country? The Domesday figures just quoted certainly suggest that they were, yet what seems to be emerging as crucial to the status of the peasantry is

111. Vinogradoff, *English Society in the Eleventh Century*, section II, ch. 2; Maitland, *Domesday Book*, 118, 122; Stenton, *Anglo-Saxon England*, 485–95; C.C. Dyer, *Lords and Peasants in a Changing Society: the estates of the bishopric of Worcester 680–1540* (1980), 35–6; Joy, 'Sokeright', introduction; J. Goebel, *Felony and Misdemeanor: a study in the history of English criminal procedure* (New York 1937), 339–61. Worcester: P.J. Wormald, 'Lordship and justice in the early English kingdom: Oswaldslaw revisited', in *Property and Power in Early Medieval Europe*, ed. Davies and Fouracre, 114–36.
112. Liebermann, I, 206: IV Edgar 1.2.
113. Darby, *Domesday England*, 61–5 and appendix 3.

not a simple question of geography. What matters is the extent to which individual lords on individual estates had succeeded in bringing the local peasantry into dependence. It has been just as possible to quote examples of a heavily dependent peasantry from the inlands of eastern England as from Wessex.

None the less, there are real differences between northern and eastern England and the rest of the country. Here, as elsewhere, it is not racial origin but the structure of the estate, and the relationship of the peasantry to its different components, that determines their status. Nevertheless the nature of the Danish settlements of the ninth century, and the subsequent separate political identity of the Danelaw, may explain some important characteristics of its social structure. The terms on which Scandinavian landholders took over land seems, in some way not yet understood, to have preserved many aspects of a comparatively free peasantry and an institutional form, the soke, which the Domesday commissioners recognized. As to what exactly the character of that settlement had been, what the *Anglo-Saxon Chronicle* meant when it said that the Danes 'shared out the land', the evidence is mostly from place-names. Place-names with a Scandinavian element are found thick on the ground in the east midlands, particularly in Lincolnshire and Leicestershire; in south Yorkshire, Nottinghamshire, Derbyshire, they are present, but are fewer in East Anglia and occasional in Essex. That many vills came into the hands of new landlords is deduced from the widespread occurrence of hybrids like Grimston, Grim's -*tun*: what had been an English lord's *tun* had become a Scandinavian's. The newcomers, if not numerous, had the same relationship to their eponymous *tuns* as did the owners of *tons* and *burhs* elsewhere in England to theirs.[114] (But because the local population probably spoke a Scandinavian dialect, vills which did not change hands may also have found new names.)

Other names were formed by adding to a Scandinavian personal name the term -*by*, settlement. The relationship of -*by* settlements to *thorp*, the other most common Scandinavian place-name element, also has a parallel with estate structure elsewhere in England. A *thorp* is an outlying farm, often a farm dependent on a more important settlement.[115] This suggests the existence, albeit on a small scale, of the kind of estate which consisted of a centre with its dependencies: the 'complex' or 'multiple' estate. While elsewhere the multiple estate broke down into its component fragments, in the Danelaw it seems to have remained in being. Stenton's analysis showed that in much of Scandinavian England the warland of estates consisted of scattered outlying areas – whole swarms of smaller settlements (which were

---

114. M. Gelling, *Signposts to the Past* (1978), 215–36; P. Stafford, *The East Midlands in the Early Middle Ages* (1985), 118–21. For *tuns* and *burhs* see pp. 173–5 below.
115. Gelling, *Signposts*, 226–7; Ekwall, *English Place-Names*, s.v. *thorp*; D. Hadley, *Early Medieval Social Structure: the Danelaw* (forthcoming).

their sokes) in Derbyshire, Nottinghamshire and Hertfordshire.[116] It is the peasant population of these scattered warland vills which contributes to the large number of free peasants recognized by Domesday Book. It must be a related fact that the vill rather than the manor remained the principal administrative unit and taxation unit in much of northern and eastern England: in Wessex and the south the reverse is true. When the Domesday commissioners recorded the information from Suffolk, for instance, there were a great many people who could not be fitted under the heading of any single manor: they are listed separately, and it is likely that they were quite independent of the manorial structure. In areas of dispersed settlement the independent peasant holding, paying its own tax, was more likely to be recorded separately.[117]

Domesday's portrayal of the Danelaw was also partly a question of perception. Inland was more recognizable in Kent, Wessex and Mercia where kings had established a strong network of well-founded centres, both royal and ecclesiastical. Here landlords who took over so much land and power from the old established state also took over many estates with inlands and inland populations fully and early organized to serve the seigneurial needs. These inlands early on won tax-exempt status and therefore make a clear mark in Domesday.

Warland or sokeland is more easily detectable in the Scandinavian counties. The complex estates with their networks of small dispersed berewicks imposed their own pattern on the text, which recognized their different components under the headings 'manor, soke, berewick'. Similar estate structures elsewhere, although they existed, were not treated like this.

Outside the Danelaw many free people went unrecorded. There are free landholders who preserved the traditions of honourable personal service at royal and lordly centres which date from the very earliest days of Anglo-Saxon and perhaps British kingship and who hardly show up in Domesday at all. It is in the nature of the evidence that we only encounter members of this heterogeneous group of people in the context of the large post-Conquest estate, when they are defined in terms of what they owe on the estate in the way of services. Only occasionally is their status so distinctive that it is recognized in Domesday as free. The *geneats* at Tidenham who work on and off the estate, 'ride and carry and lead loads, and drive droves' are not in its Domesday entry, where we find only *villani* and *bordarii*.[118] There were 'riding servants', radknights, on the bishop of Worcester's estates with much the same obligations as the *geneat* in the *Rectitudines*, who must also 'bring strangers to the village … and carry messages near and

---

116. Stenton, *Types of Manorial Structure*; Stafford, *East Midlands*, ch. 7. Sokemen: Lennard, *Rural England*, 218–19; Harvey, 'Domesday England', 69–78; Vinogradoff, *English Society in the Eleventh Century*, section III, 'Social classes'.
117. Joy, 'Sokeright', 357–8.
118. *DB* I, 164a.

far', and they were probably common, but the only respectable numbers of radmen were those on the Welsh border as far as Domesday is concerned. Thegns do not make much of a showing, being confined to the area of south Lancashire recorded as 'between the Ribble and the Mersey', besides one in Staffordshire and five in Warwickshire; drengs are even thinner on the ground: six between Ribble and Mersey. The inhabitants of jurisdictional areas granted out by the tenth-century kings of Wessex did not call themselves 'sokemen'. But there were free men in Worcestershire in 1086 who had at least a hide each: the churches of Evesham, Westminster and Pershore and 'all other landlords' have jurisdictional rights alone over people such as these, who would have counted as 'sokemen' in the Danelaw. But none is mentioned in the appropriate Domesday entries.[119] There was no villeinage in Kent, or so most Kentishmen believed in the middle ages, yet Domesday did not record many free men there (44 sokemen is the meagre total).

What was known on the continent as *allod*, the landholding notionally held only from the king himself, was 'the fullest ownership that there can be'. The scheme on which Domesday was composed had very little room for this concept, being framed around the idea of tenure, of holding *from* a superior lord. There were few people in England in 1086 who were so independent of any such tenurial chain that they recognized no lord at all, for they are recorded as owing service to one, or not being allowed to 'withdraw' their land from another. Nevertheless there is a class of *allodarii*, or some version of this, in Domesday, as if the clerks recognized a few people who were in some way akin to the Norman allodialist. They are rather mysterious, a result perhaps of trying to fit an English phenomenon into Norman phraseology; nevertheless, they seemed to Maitland to be free men who held their estates hereditably. There were large numbers of them in Surrey, Sussex and Hampshire, and they were long recognized as a distinct class in Kent, where the king took reliefs from the allodialists of the whole county. It may be that the term *allodarius* was used here where elsewhere 'sokeman' or 'free man' would have been, and if this is so – and Maitland thought that it might have been – they extend to those counties a significant number of unmanorialized independent small landowners.[120]

It has already been argued that the catch-all Domesday term *villanus* must have included a very wide range of people of low status, but it must be equally true that many free peasants were also entered as *villani*. The Devonshire *villani* were probably independent farmers.

---

119. Vinogradoff, *English Society in the Eleventh Century*, 418–20.
120. Kent: *DB* I, 1. L. Mussuet, 'Réflexions sur *alodium* et sa significance dans les textes normands', *Revue historique de droit français et étranger* 4th series 47 (1969), 606; F. Pollock and F.M. Maitland, *The History of English Law before the Time of Edward I* (1968 edn), I, 68–72, quotation at 68; Maitland, *Domesday Book*, 191–2. The calculations of their numbers in Darby, *Domesday England*, 343 are misleading, as Darby did not take into account the variety of spellings.

Peasants who rented holdings may well be counted as *villani*: 'how many otherwise free tenants hired yardlands without becoming *geburs* ... we do not know except in the Danish district ... they have left ... no trace in the Domesday Survey'.[121] The rent-payers (*censarii*) on the Burton Abbey estates, who owed typical warland services of suit of court, attendance at the hunt and messenger service as well as rent, and who resemble sokemen, may not be counted there under any heading.[122]

There is no way of knowing how many of the Domesday *villani* outside Scandinavian England were very similar free men under no manorial lordship but obliged to attend the hundred courts – there may have been thousands. We do not know what term was translated by *villanus*, but if it was a Norman-French term it must have been *vilein*, which simply meant rustic. Maitland thought that it may have translated OE *tunsmen* with no particular connotations of status.[123] Both terms relate the *villanus* to the vill or *tun* to which he is thought to belong, but that relationship may have taken widely varying forms. All men by 1086 were to be in a tithing, after all, without that necessarily implying dependent status. Domesday records many aspects of pre-Conquest society that resembled the manorial regime of the twelfth and thirteenth centuries. It may well conceal others. But we must not let it beguile us into thinking of eleventh-century England as more seigneurialized than in fact it was.

121. F. Seebohm, *The English Village Community* (1896), 146.
122. Darby, *Domesday England*, 85–6; Bridgeman, 'Burton Abbey', 209–300; F. Baring, 'Domesday Book and the Burton cartulary', *EHR* 11 (1896), 98–102; J.F.R. Walmesley, 'The *censarii* of Burton Abbey and the Domesday population', *North Staffordshire Journal of Field Studies* 8 (1968), 72–80 at 75–7.
123. D. Bates, *Normandy before 1066* (1982), 95; Maitland, *Domesday Book*, 86ff.

5 Warland farms and families

The three previous chapters have proposed an important dichotomy between inland and warland and have seen it principally from the point of view of estate management. But even from this rather restricted viewpoint, profound differences between life on the inland and life on the warland have become apparent. While the demands of the estate shaped the inland and dominated the lives of the inland peasantry, other influences shaped those of people on the warland. This chapter looks at the warland peasantry essentially as farmers, examining in turn their family organization and inheritance customs, the changing relationship of people to agrarian resources and the impact of this on the landscape.

It is with the farmers of the warland that the use of the catch-all term 'peasant' is most open to criticism. One obstacle to our better understanding of early rural society is that we are limited to working with an inappropriate vocabulary. The very word 'peasant', particularly in countries like England which have long lost their peasantries, has taken on connotations of poverty and subordination. Many of the status terms we are accustomed to using to denote social class – 'yeoman', 'husbandman', 'gentry' – come from the later middle ages, a period of acute class consciousness, when it was thought very important to distinguish between peasants and those of 'gentle' birth or pretensions. Earlier, Anglo-Norman England had seen an increased emphasis on birth and status at every level. Yet it is not at all certain that the borderline between peasant and gentry was drawn with the same emphasis in Anglo-Saxon England. True, this was a society utterly dominated by royal and aristocratic families and their connections. True, well before the Conquest smaller landowners with bookland (as Chapter 6 will illustrate) came to be a self-conscious class, whom there is no reason not to regard as gentry, however anachronistic the term. Yet the fact that their status was based entirely on the possession of land may have seemed to be something new. A famous text from the early eleventh century associated with Archbishop Wulfstan II of York is devoted to the question of status or rank.[1] In Wulfstan's characteristically gloomy tone it looks back with regret to an earlier age, when it had been service, not land alone, which had bestowed

---

1. Liebermann, I, 456–8; *EHD* I, 432.

social rank. 'Once it was that' it had been possible for any *ceorl*, provided he had acquired a sufficient estate of five hides, to rise by service to his lord from the rank of *ceorl* to that of thegn. This text, *GeÞyncðo*, is sometimes cited as an illustration of 'accelerating social mobility' in late Anglo-Saxon England.[2] It could equally well be read in quite another way, as a lament for the fact that the thegnage was becoming more of a closed and landed elite, less of a ministerial class, and that upward mobility by means of service was no longer possible. A Northumbrian text, also in Wulfstan's collection, emphasizes how essential to thegnly status was not only the possession of the requisite five hides but inheritance of the land over three generations.[3] Here we may be seeing evidence of the emergence of a self-consciously gentry class, rooted in their estates, not in service to the powerful.

Yet it must be equally significant that there continued to be such a large and loosely defined social category as *ceorl*, which included all those who were neither unfree nor of aristocratic birth. And it must also be significant that there continued to be a category of *twi-hynde* people, those with a wergeld of 200 shillings, irrespective of the amount of land they had, who corresponded to the rank of *ceorl*, and that this category of people was to be found in Wessex, Mercia and Northumbria alike.[4] Categories of this type, enshrined in laws and texts, are of course likely to have become out of step with the realities of a developing, and increasingly socially stratified, society. Yet they were still respected in the twelfth century, when the texts which record them were drawn on by the compilers of legal works.[5]

Ceorls may preserve vestiges of a social class of a type which escapes our modern typologies, a class in which both peasant farmers and lesser landowners were to be found. They were not by any means equal economically, and this makes all the more significant that they owed the similar 'public' obligations which the previous chapter outlined. Chapter 10 will show that long after the Conquest, when the economic status of the warland peasantry had declined drastically from what it had been in Anglo-Saxon England, many peasants retained a strongly held notion of their free and independent legal and social status. The warland peasantry, like the 'gentry' landowners, of Anglo-Saxon England considered that they owned their own land and, like them, expected to pass it on in some way to their descendants. They paid their geld and attended the public courts, served in the *fyrd*, or helped pay for a soldier to go from their area, and contributed their draught stock to bridge and fortification work. All this was compatible

---

2. W.G. Runciman, 'Accelerating social mobility: the case of Anglo-Saxon England', *Past and Present* 104 (August 1984), 3–30, n. 16.
3. D. Whitelock, *The Beginnings of English Society* (1952), 85–6; Liebermann, I, 458–61 (*Norðleoda laga*); *EHD* I, 433.
4. Besworth and Toller, s.v. *twi-hynde*; Liebermann, I, 456–63 ('GeÞyncðo', 'Norðleoda laga', 'Mircna laga'); *EHD* I, nos 52 a, b, c at 431–3; F.M. Stenton, *Anglo-Saxon England* (1947), 300–1. The *wergeld* of the Kentish *ceorl* was 100 gold shillings.
5. *EHD* I, 431.

with the fact that they were obliged to turn up at estate centres to do the occasional ploughing and harvesting boons that were evidently considered unservile work. As is often the case, Kentish historians have written vividly about the particular characteristics of their county, singling out the particularly well-defined and well-preserved identity of the independent farmers of yokelands, 'the land of the Kentish peasantry *par excellence*, where the lord has no right of property, and tenure is by gavelkind, the ancient custom of Kent'. Their farms were mostly in 'minor, outlying places', very often on the Downs and away from the important settlements where inlands developed. The yokeland farmers, 'hardy, well-found and with a good conceit of themselves', survived to become a 'class of obscure "yokeland" gentry' in the later middle ages. This can stand very well as a description of the upper ranks of the warland peasantry.[6]

The importance of the hide as the basic unit of assessment of so many of the obligations due from warland means that our understanding of hides, and of the kinds of people associated with hides, is crucial to the way we view rural society. It is also crucial to our view of the nature of the Anglo-Saxon polity. T.M. Charles-Edwards has put the link between land and status at the centre of his discussion of this topic: possession of a hide was the qualification for free status and membership of the community.[7] Like the *mansus* in Frankish documents, the hide was at once a real unit and a fiscal one, and like the *mansus*, the way the word was used changed over time and according to context. Bede took for granted that what the English meant by the word 'hide' was 'the land of one *familia*'.[8] He was equally familiar with the hide as a fiscal fiction, useful, when reckoned in hundreds, as a rough indication of the extent of very large areas of land, such as a whole territory or *regio* – the kind of thinking about land which, whatever its purpose, the Tribal Hidage uses. He was familiar too with the way that it was used in a more precise sense to describe the endowments of individual minsters in the language of charters.[9] What it seems *not* to have meant to him was a fixed acreage of land, and it was only well after the Conquest that the hide was given even a nominal areal measurement, generally around 120 acres (there were local variations), and even then this must in the nature of things have been very approximate. We have to make what we can of these facts.

---

6. K.P. Witney, *The Kingdom of Kent* (1982), 175; A. Everitt, *Continuity and Colonization: the evolution of Kentish settlement* (1986), 178–9; J. Jolliffe, *Pre-Feudal England: the Jutes* (1933), 324.
7. T.M. Charles-Edwards, 'Kinship, status and the origins of the hide', *Past and Present* 56 (August 1972), 3–33; F.W. Maitland, *Domesday Book and Beyond: three essays in the early history of England* (1960 edn), 416–596.
8. *HE* I, 25; II, 9; III, 4, 24; IV, 3, 13.
9. N. Higham has recently interpreted the hide as the amount of land which would produce a *surplus* which, when paid in tribute or rent, could support a 'gentry' family. In his view the 'family' of Bede's remark is the consumer, not the primary producer. N. Higham, *Rome, Britain and the Anglo-Saxons* (1992), 144–52.

Bede's 'land of one family' has meant that questions about the nature of the family unit and questions of agricultural organization are involved together. Although arguments about the hide have often been at best hard to follow and at worst, in Maitland's word, 'dreary', it would be difficult to think of two more important topics in peasant history than the family and the farm. The family farm, a holding worked principally, though not exclusively, by the labour of one family and producing enough to support it in normal years, is the universal basis of peasant agriculture, but in spite of its economic importance it is not an easy matter to trace its development. If we try to consider family farms as agrarian enterprises we would ideally like to know something about their main elements: the farming family, the capital assets in the shape of land and other physical resources, and the labour supply. Such farms have always been run without written records, and by definition passed through inheritance within the family, again without recourse to writing. Even when Domesday Book reveals so much detail about eleventh-century landholders it is not easy to extract from its figures any information about holdings below the level of the manor. We have to turn to the landscape itself, and the terms people used to describe it, settlement forms and their development, and the small amount of information we can glean about families and their arrangements.

Houses, farms and settlements

It will help to start with a model in mind. A kin-based group living in a nucleated settlement surrounded by its own land has long been identified as a primary type of northern European settlement.[10] Such a model needs to be tested by more fieldwork than has yet been done before we accept it as widespread in early England. Yet it proves invaluable in understanding and co-ordinating the very disparate types of evidence that we have about Anglo-Saxon farmers. The small settlements of the migration generation could have housed three or four families, and even the larger cemeteries of the period served a dozen at most. The most thoroughly investigated settlement has been Mucking, on the south Essex coast.[11] Excavation there has revealed loosely associated groups of houses of two distinct types, timber buildings and dugouts, and these two types of building have been found associated with each other on other sites. It has become customary to call the larger timber buildings on such sites 'halls', but this reflects a particular set of ideas about Anglo-Saxon social structure which we are under no obligation to accept without question.[12] They are of a size

10. H. Uhlig, 'Old hamlets with infield and outfield systems in western and central Europe', *Geografiska Annaler* 43 (1961), 285–307.
11. H. Hamerow, *Excavations at Mucking*, II, *The Anglo-Saxon Settlement*, English Heritage Archaeological Report 21 (1991).

similar to a timber medieval farmhouse of the 'Wealden' type, and there seems no good reason not to regard them as farmhouses. Figure 15 shows a Hampshire example of a group of such 'halls' or substantial farmhouses, and conjectural reconstructions.

These groups of farmhouses will have housed 'broadly-equal, internally ranked, patrilineal descent groups farming their own territory' if we follow C. Scull's account of the development of political power in Anglo-Saxon society, which includes an analysis of the social structure of settlements in the migration period. Similar – sometimes strikingly identical – houses grouped closely together might suggest that close neighbours were frequently close relatives.[13] Over time, marriage and the birth of new generations, particularly if it was virilocal marriage at which the woman moved to the man's territory, would expand the settlement.[14] Marriage with British women and their cultural assimilation may have been an important factor in the archaeological 'disappearance' of the British population. Early Anglo-Saxon settlements could thus well be the separate dwellings of a family farming group with rights in the surrounding land.

The study of village morphology as it changed over time can be helpful here. There is a form of settlement, which was evidently socially and economically viable for examples are still found today, which seems to have developed by a farm or group of farms being joined by others in a piecemeal fashion as population grew. Irregular, seemingly random, hamlets formed which were composed of aggregations of farms and cottages, with equally irregular fields surrounding them. C.C. Taylor has linked these 'polyfocal' plans with the working of inheritance on landholding. Partitioning land and farming it co-operatively among siblings are both processes which might house co-heirs in groups of neighbouring farmsteads, which the growth of population might eventually cause to coalesce.[15] Many such kin-based hamlets or groups of farms may be concealed by the standardizing schemata of Domesday entries. M. Aston describes the reality behind the Domesday entry of a vill at Bagley, Somerset. It comprised two complexes of farmsteads at Bagley and Sweetworthy in Luccombe of a

---

12. P.V. Addyman, 'The Anglo-Saxon house', *Anglo-Saxon England* 1 (1972), 273–307; S. James, A. Marshall and M. Millett, 'An early medieval building tradition', *Archaeological Journal* 141 (1984), 182–215.
13. C. Scull, 'Archaeology, early Anglo-Saxon society and the origins of Anglo-Saxon kingdoms', *ASSAH* 6 (1993), 1–18 at 8–11, quotation at 9.
14. For patrilocal marriage see the text known as 'On Marriage', *EHD* I, no. 51 at 431; C. Fell, *Women in Anglo-Saxon England and the Impact of 1066* (1984), 58.
15. G.R.J. Jones, 'Nucleal settlement and its tenurial relationships: some morphological implications' in *Villages, Fields and Frontiers: studies in rural settlement in the medieval and early modern periods*, ed. B.K. Roberts and R.E. Glasscock, BAR International Series 85 (1985), 153–70; B.K. Roberts, *The Making of the English Village* (1987), ch. 4; C.C. Taylor, *Village and Farmstead: a history of rural settlement in England* (1983), 130–3.

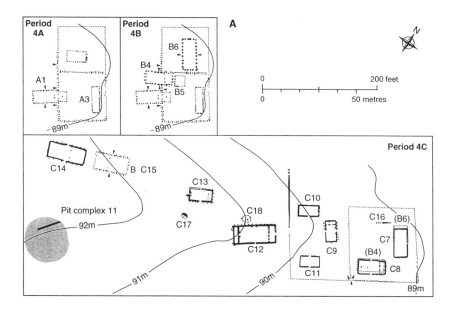

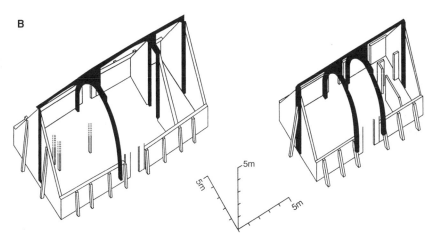

Figure 15 A. Early Anglo-Saxon farmsteads of the sixth and seventh centuries: three successive building phases at Cowdery's Down, Hampshire. The first two phases consisted of a pair of fenced farm units (4A and 4B). In phase 4C they were rebuilt on the same site and a series of larger timber-framed buildings, and two sunken featured buildings, were constructed to the west.
B. Reconstructions of two of the Phase C timber buildings (C8 and C9) at Cowdery's Down.
Source: after M. Millett and S. James, 'Excavation at Cowdery's Down, Basingstoke, 1978–81', *Archaeological Journal* (1983), fig. 27 and 141 (1984) fig. 7.

type which may well be prehistoric.[16] Detailed analysis of the fields of Clanfield in Oxfordshire shows that the 'settlement groups' which preceded the nucleated village created and worked their own arable systems.[17] In Wessex, isolated farmsteads or small clusters of farms seem to have been associated with a pair of fields, sometimes a single field, perhaps worked on an infield–outfield system. The Erdeland or ploughland at Wedmore, Somerset was its early, single, field.[18]

It may be that the size, shape and building techniques of the substantial timber houses of the early settlements can also reveal something about questions of kin. Frederic Seebohm must have been one of the earliest medievalists to have had an interest in anthropology. He was struck by the account given by Gerald of Wales in the twelfth century of the way that the Welsh built their houses and by the fact that the physical components of the house had their counterpart in the terminology of kinship in the tenth-century Welsh laws. The *gafael*, or share of land, drew its name from the word for the timber 'forks' or crucks which were the timber frames or crucks which formed the structure of the shared family homestead.[19] This building tradition was common in parts of medieval England, and it is interesting to compare Seebohm's account with later descriptions of raising a 'cruck' building.[20] Unfortunately, we have no evidence as to whether the larger Anglo-Saxon 'hall-houses', constructed in much the same way, can be 'read' like this.

Families

What Bede meant by *familia* is still not certain, in spite of much debate. Was it a nuclear family of parents and offspring, or some more extended family group? The Old English word used for 'the place of one family' in the Old English translation of Bede's *History* is *stowe hiwscypes*, and *hiwscipe* is a word widely used to mean family or household in a wide sense, extending even to the 'family' of

---

16. M. Aston, 'The development of medieval rural settlement in Somerset' in *Landscape and Townscape in the South West*, ed. R. Higham (1989), 19–40 at 24–6; S. Everett, 'The Domesday geography of three Exmoor parishes', *Proc. Somerset Archaeological and Natural History Society* 112 (1968), 54–60.
17. H.S.A. Fox, 'Approaches to the adoption of the midland system' in *The Origins of Open-Field Agriculture*, ed. T. Rowley (1981), 64–111 at 88.
18. M. Aston, 'Medieval settlement sites in Somerset' in *The Medieval Landscape of Wessex*, ed. M. Aston and C. Lewis (1994), 219–37 at 228.
19. F. Seebohm, *The English Village Community* (1896), 239–42; *The Law of Hywel Dda: law texts from medieval Wales*, trans. and ed. D Jenkins (1986), 190, 121 and notes.
20. S. Wrathmell, 'Peasant houses, farmsteads and villages in north–east England' in *The Rural Settlements of Medieval England*, ed. M. Aston, D. Austin and C. Dyer (1989), 247–67. The social significance of architectural forms is explored in E. Guidoni, *Primitive Architecture*, trans. E. Wolf (1975).

mankind.[21] Our earliest evidence from before the age of Bede is of larger groups than the family and their relationship to larger units of land than the hide.

There is no sign in Germanic law of 'clans' owning land and no sign of such a phenomenon having developed in Anglo-Saxon settled England.[22] But there are many signs of groups of descendants with strong links with particular areas, and the sense of an area being the territory of a people was very tenacious. The earliest land-units we are able to identify from prehistoric times had a cultural as well as an economic identity; they were marked by the burials of ancestors. Farmers established on regularly and long-exploited land gained continuity enough from generation to generation to build up strong ideas of belonging and established boundaries 'known to the locals' in early charters. Law codes from the seventh century onwards expect a person to have local roots, through which he may be controlled, 'a *tun* to which he belongs' and where he is known, and in Kentish law he must get permission from the ealdorman if he is to leave one *boldgetæl*, settlement, for another.[23] People in neighbouring settlements came to arrangements over grazing rights and commoning which can only have worked through the recognition of the rights of certain groups to certain places. They also retained long-distance transhumance routes to distant woodland and pasture which are a strikingly enduring feature of early land-units.

Place- and people-names show links between particular groups of kinspeople and particular areas of land. It has been conjectured that some of the larger land areas of the sixth and seventh centuries were named from individuals and their descendants, such as the 'Stoppa' who may have given his name to the land of the Stoppingas.[24] There are also examples of much smaller settlements with place-names formed in a similar way by combining a personal name with the element *-ingas*. They are not associated with the earliest phase of settlement but with a slightly later colonizing process. That is to say, they were the product of people who had in some way chosen to act as a group. Some were in existence before 800.[25] The decision as to which translation of names in *-ingas* is favoured as between 'belonging to the descendants of' X or 'belonging to the people of' X is to some extent dependent on of which analysis of Anglo-Saxon society it forms a part. One tendency has been to identify the eponymous individuals

---

21. Bosworth and Toller, s.v. *hiw scipe.*
22. A.C. Murray, *Germanic Kinship Structure: studies in law and society in antiquity and the early middle ages* (1983).
23. Liebermann, I, 9–10: Hlothere and Eadric 5.
24. S. Bassett, 'In search of the origins of Anglo-Saxon kingdoms' in *The Origins of Anglo-Saxon Kingdoms*, ed. S. Bassett (1989), 3–27 at 18.
25. M. Gelling, *Signposts to the Past* (1978), 106–22; J.M. Dodgson, 'The significance of the distribution of English place-names in *-ingas, -inga-* in south-east England', *Medieval Archaeology* 10 (1966), 1–29. Such names were also formed with a topographical feature as the first element.

with 'manorial estate owners', or as the leaders of 'followers'.[26] An opposite one has identified these place-names with the peasant family living in 'small family or hamlet-sized groups'.[27] Jolliffe detected in some Kentish holdings the lands of groups of heirs. He saw the *Kenewoldinges*, a group who held land in Wye in the thirteenth century as the descendants of one named ancestor.[28] A Kentish sulung – a large peasant holding equivalent to two hides – called *Dunwalinglond* may have been the property of Dunwalh or of 'a group of people of whom he was chief'.[29] Such names would be very appropriate for the land of small communities of kinspeople.

Nevertheless, a walker who follows an Anglo-Saxon charter boundary today – and it will necessarily record the landscape as it was from the ninth or tenth century, when such detailed boundaries begin – will often have the impression of walking through a landscape of small-scale private property. Many of the landmarks will be valleys, woods, hills, and substantial cleared areas of arable belonging to, or at least named from, individuals, not families: farmers with their own arable and pasture and woodland in a well-worked landscape. The boundaries of 30 hides at Witney, Oxfordshire, given by King Eadwig to his *minister* in 969, skirted Ofling's ploughed land, Ecgerde's hill, and Cytel's well, and a second charter of 1044 includes Leofstan's bridge and Ketel's acres as landmarks. The archaeological record shows that west Oxfordshire had long been an area of small discrete settlements, or farms.[30] The lands leased by the bishops of Worcester were in densely settled and intensively farmed regions, where farming families had been living and working for generations. Ploughland, copse and wood, weir and mill and river crossing all have owners, jealous of their rights. They are not necessarily the current owners when the charter was drawn up: Cunda of 'Cunda's acres' in Beoley, Worcestershire, may have been long dead and forgotten by the time that his name appeared in a tenth-century charter.[31]

Does this individual landholding mean that the group with a claim over family land became smaller over time? The relationship between families and land is perpetuated through inheritance. From a large group of descendants, such as may have given rise to the *-ingas* names, did the farming group become a group of siblings, even a single heir? In some places this may well have happened. T.M. Charles-Edwards has given an important anthropological explanation of the origins of the hide and its relation to the family. He takes as his starting-point the

26. Gelling, *Signposts*, 111–12, 177–85.
27. W. Davies and H. Vierck, 'The contents of the Tribal Hidage: social aggregates and settlement patterns', *Frühmittelalterliche Studien* 8 (1974), 223–93 at 239.
28. Jolliffe, *Pre–Feudal England*, 27–30; Charles–Edwards, 'Kinship, status and the origins of the hide', 30.
29. Stenton, *Anglo-Saxon England*, 278–9.
30. BCS 1230 (S 771); J. Blair, *Anglo-Saxon Oxfordshire* (1994), 18–27.
31. D. Hooke, *Anglo-Saxon Landscapes of the West Midlands: the charter evidence*, BAR British Series 95 (1981), 187.

fact that the Old English word for hide, *hiwisc*, was related to an Indo-European root meaning 'to lie down', and by extension to a married couple. Thus, in his view, the typical farming family in Anglo-Saxon England was the nuclear family of parents and children. Charles-Edwards argues that family land was physically divided as it passed from generation to generation, with each son setting up house independently, on the hide which ensured his standing in the community.[32]

Inheritance

Such evidence as we have about Anglo-Saxon and medieval inheritance practice supports this view. Kent in many ways preserved Anglo-Saxon arrangements into the later middle ages, and for this reason Kentish evidence is particularly interesting. One of the most important aspects of 'gavelkind, the ancient custom of Kent' which made the Kentish yokeland peasantry seem so notably freer and more independent than their counterparts in other parts of medieval England, was the fact that land in gavelkind was partible among the sons of a family, and between daughters if there was no son. The 'custom of Kent' as we now know it, is likely to have been essentially a post-Conquest formalization of practices which had never had the status of law. Nevertheless, taken with other evidence, medieval inheritance custom is an important clue to how families and land were related in Anglo-Saxon England. The question of inheritance brings us back to what Bede may have meant by 'the land of one family'. We need to bear in mind that shared rights in land do not necessarily lead to its physical division, and local conditions and individual choice determined whether the practice was for heirs to farm land jointly or physically partition it among themselves.

Early settlement forms suggested a group of kin with rights in all the surrounding land, and giving their name to the entire area. Such a group can be found in Irish and possibly in Welsh law including four generations: great-grandfather, grandfather, sons and grandsons sharing rights to the holding: only on the death of the great-grandfather did a new generation step into the position of heir.[33] But over time this Celtic agnatic lineage inheritance group, which had given so many people rights over the land, lost its sway and it became the practice for the land to be shared on the father's death only among his sons.

The Anglo-Saxon vocabulary relating to kinship does not give support to the notion of a wide inheritance group, which would have included fourth cousins and might have numbered a great crowd of

---

32. Charles-Edwards, 'Kinship, status and the origins of the hide'.
33. Jones, 'Nucleal settlement', 153–70; 'Post–Roman Wales' in *Ag. Hist.* I.II, 299–349.

prospective heirs.[34] Peasant inheritance practice in post-Conquest England may have been a development from Anglo-Saxon practice.[35] It is not easy to separate what was peasant custom from what was imposed by the demands of seigneurial administration, but it seems that one important principle was that which gave each son, and each daughter if there was no son, a right in the family land. Partible inheritance was the custom in many parts of East Anglia, Sussex, Essex and in a very wide area of northern England from Furness to the Yorkshire Dales. It links the peasants of Kent with parts of England as distant as Devon and the Welsh border. Elsewhere, primogeniture was the preponderant rule on peasant holdings.[36]

Ethnic origins have sometimes been put forward as an explanation of this important regional difference. The settlement of Frisian immigrants in East Anglia has been said to have been responsible for partible inheritance customs there.[37] Partibility was particularly characteristic of the Danelaw, and of upland and pastoral districts, but neither geography nor geology alone can explain its distribution. A more likely explanation of these regional differences is one that looks to the different circumstances in the development of estates. It was where seigneurialization was weakest that an older peasant culture survived which arranged matters so that all the able-bodied males in a family, and failing males the females, had rights in the family land. P.D.A. Harvey has detected a movement still in progress in the twelfth century which was beginning to efface the joint claims of a group of kin and replace them with the tenure of a single man, but this was a landlord's device, not a peasant strategy.[38]

The inheritance customs of the warland peasantry stood a better chance of survival unmodified by seigneurial interference than did inheritance either among the aristocracy or among the more dependent peasantry. The tenure which represented in Anglo-Norman England the way in which the warland tenant had once held his land was socage.[39] Socage differed significantly from villeinage and tenure by knight service – the new post-Conquest tenures. One of the most important of these differences lay in the role of the family with regard to land. Socage land was partible between sons and between daughters if there was no son. A boy came of age, and could inherit socage land, at 15 not 21. And until heirs came of age they were in the wardship of

34. L. Lancaster, 'Kinship in Anglo-Saxon society', *British Journal of Sociology* 9 (1958), 230–50, 359–77.
35. R.J. Faith, 'Peasant families and inheritance customs in medieval England', *AgHR* 14 (1966), 77–95 at 78–86.
36. F. Pollock and F.W. Maitland, *The History of English Law before the time of Edward I* (1968 edn), II, 240–83; Faith, 'Peasant families and inheritance customs', 81–2, appendix I at 92–5.
37. G.C. Homans, 'The Frisians in East Anglia' *EcHR*, 2nd series 10 (1957–8), 189–206.
38. P.D.A. Harvey, ed., *The Peasant Land Market in Medieval England* (1984), 354–6.
39. C.A. Joy, 'Sokeright' (Ph.D. thesis, University of Leeds, 1972), 375–8; Pollock and Maitland, *History of English Law*, I, 291–6, II, 269–70.

their family, not the manorial lord. It took a long time for Norman notions of primogeniture to thoroughly permeate people's thinking about land and families. This was true even at the level of the landholders of sufficient rank to be recorded individually in Domesday. Two brothers can be found living alongside each other but in separate households: 'each had his house (*domus*) though they dwelt in one court (*curia*)'. Domesday holdings *in paragio* preserved an arrangement by which an older heir was responsible for the rent from a partitioned holding and his younger siblings held the holding as his tenants.[40]

It would be pressing the evidence too far to suggest any direct links between settlement form and inheritance practice: cultural and ethnic values, as well as the pressures of lordship, come into the picture. But all these factors may have been working in much the same direction, narrowing down the group which had rights over land and simultaneously narrowing down the area over which those rights could be exercised. It seems likely that the landholding kin had been the primary social group in the early settlement period. Over time this wider kin group narrowed down to a group of collateral heirs. In some areas this led to the physical division of the land into farms owned by individuals. Yet in other areas, and particularly where the warland peasantry had retained more autonomy, perhaps too where pressure on land was lightest, an older regime of shared rights in land persisted, becoming associated with the other 'free' characteristics of the warland, and eventually becoming itself a sign of free tenure.

Hide farms

If the hide had once been in some sense 'the land of one family' it is of particular interest when we can see examples of hides which were real farms, some surviving today. Anglo-Saxon hides have given their names to many modern place-names. In Somerset 21 settlements of various sizes with names including the element 'huish' have taken their name from *hiwisc*, a hide, and M. Costen takes some of them to be the oldest type of independent Anglo-Saxon farm, pre-dating the open field system. They were large farms of up to 586 hectares (almost 1450 acres) according to the type of land, 'agricultural unit(s) ... self-contained if not self-sufficient'.[41] Figure 16 shows one of Costen's 'huish' farms. The larger hides were in the west of the county and included large tracts of rough grazing. This reminds us that hide farms, if they were in any way self-sufficient, must have had their own supply of mixed resources or access to a common supply: woodland for fuel and timber, water, grazing and arable land. A charter of 977 granting a

---

40. Joy, 'Sokeright', 382.
41. M. Costen, *The Origins of Somerset* (1992), 93–5; 'Huish and worth: Old English survivals in a later landscape', *ASSAH* 5 (1992), 65–83 at 72.

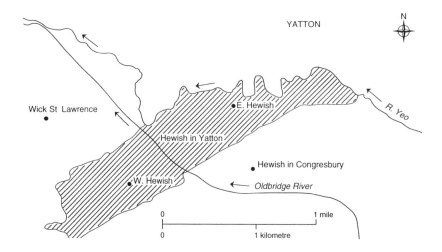

Figure 16   Hide farm at Yatton, Somerset. Hewish Manor, which survived into the eighteenth century, may have covered the area of the original *hiwisc*, Hewish Farm and the East and West Hewish shown here. *Source*: after M. Costen, 'Huish and worth: Old English survivals in a later landscape', *ASSAH* v (1992), 65–83, fig. 14 at 72.

hide in Himbleton in Worcestershire shows that it was a discrete piece of land with recognized boundaries. Part of the farm lay among the enclosed arable fields of the township and ownership brought with it rights to a defined share 'which belongs to the hide' of the township's woodland and meadow.[42] The hide had to produce a surplus as well as supporting a family and would have needed a labour supply in addition to the labour resources of the farming family, particularly, as with any family farm, before the children were 'work-worthy'. Boys over 12 were considered responsible adults in the eyes of the law and were probably at work at that age. At 15, they could inherit the family land.[43] If an analogy from later pre-industrial England is allowed, we might guess that the farming couple, particularly if they took over the farm when their own children were too young to work, would have employed and housed young men and women from other farms as part of their *hired* or household, like St Walstan, whom we have already encountered working for a childless couple in a Norfolk village.[44] *Ceorls* in seventh-century Kent included substantial husbandmen who were employers of

42.   Hooke, *Anglo-Saxon Landscapes of the West Midlands*, 161; Robertson, *Charters*, LVI.
43.   Harvey, 'Introduction' to *The Peasant Land Market*; P. Vinogradoff, *English Society in the Eleventh Century: essays in English mediaeval history* (1908), 418, 409.
44.   See p. 85 above.

slaves and agricultural workers whom they fed and perhaps housed.[45] They may have had much the same size labour force as the hide tenants in post-Conquest surveys who were expected to send their own agricultural workers to the lord's haymaking and harvesting 'boons'.[46]

Outside the dispersed settlements of the west country, the hide had less chance of surviving as an agrarian unit through the centuries, although vestiges of it and its services may be preserved in the terminology of tenures: the 'hydars' on some Devon manors were sharply distinguished from the 'bartoners' or villeins in the fourteenth century.[47] The transformations of the rural landscape brought about by the formation and then the dissolution of common field systems meant that such hide farms as did survive do so only as relics of a vanished type. Nevertheless, farms and small place-names containing the element 'Hide', or more commonly 'Hyde', can still be found. They are often at the edge of the parishes in which they lie, and seem quite unrelated to any nucleated settlement.[48] A typical example of the type in this respect, although untypical in its fine surviving thirteenth-century hall house, is Hyde Farm, Marcham, Berkshire (see Fig. 17). This appears in Domesday Book as a discrete holding of a single hide. It became the property of the sacrist of Abingdon Abbey, and later of a succession of prosperous yeoman farmers.[49]

Peasant holdings of an entire hide are rare by the twelfth century, when in a typical midland village the tenant of such an amount of land would be an outstandingly well-provided farmer, the English equivalent of the Russian *kulak*, and almost always a free man in contrast to his servile neighbours. Well before Domesday there are signs of the 'gentrification' of the hide. In many districts hides had developed into small manors, although we have to bear in mind that the conceptual framework of Domesday imposed the term 'manor' on a wide range of holdings, some of which were little more than farms. The farmer of a hide might well have tenants of his own. That of Tuesley in Godalming, for instance, had one plough in demesne, one slave, one *villanus* and six cottagers. A hide in Dorking comprised one demesne plough, a mill at the hall and one bordar or estate worker.[50] Often the line between independent farm and small manor must be too fine to draw. The settlements at three Exmoor parishes described in Domesday and analysed by S. Everett can still be recognized today as individual farms, probably, given the limitations of the terrain, with much the same

45. *Ag.Hist.* I.II, 432; Liebermann, I, 4: Æthelbert 16, 25.
46. R.J. Faith, 'The topography and social structure of a small soke in the middle ages: The Sokens, Essex', *Essex Archaeology and History*, 27 (1997), 202–13.
47. F. Rose–Troup, 'Medieval customs and tenures in the manor of Ottery St Mary', *Report and Transactions of the Devonshire Association* 66 (1934), 211–33.
48. Work in progress by the author.
49. C.R.J. Currie, 'Larger medieval houses in the Vale of the White Horse', *Oxoniensia* 57 (1992), 81–244 at 167–71.
50. J. Blair, *Early Medieval Surrey: landholding, church and settlement before 1300* (1991), 28.

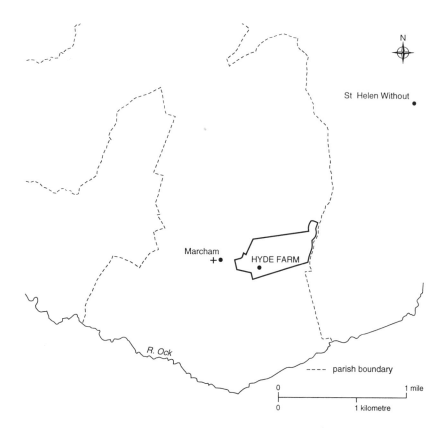

Figure 17 Hyde Farm, Marcham, Berkshire, the property of Abingdon Abbey in the twelfth century and thereafter farmed by a succession of prosperous yeoman families.

cultivated area that they have always had. Their tiny inland populations of one or two bordars and slaves and their single plough teams *in dominio* represent the workforce and capital equipment of substantial independent farmers, probably much resembling Kent's 'obscure yokeland gentry'.[51]

Smallholdings

There must surely always have been many farms much smaller than hides and even in Bede's time the peasantry must have been a very heterogeneous class. The hide came to be not the land of one family,

---

51. Everett, 'Domesday geography of three Exmoor parishes'.

but of several. On hides on the bishop of Worcester's land in the tenth century lived eight or ten peasant households.[52] Only for Middlesex are we able to see the actual size of peasant farms in 1086 and there almost half (42 per cent) of the *villani* were half-virgaters; that is to say they held only one eighth of Bede's 'land of one family'. Many smallholdings were fragments of hides and yokes: half-virgates, 'ferdlings' and 'yokelets'.[53] When the hide was divided it retained its old warland obligations in terms of the kind of services it owed, but more people now owed them.

Analysis of the place-names of very small places has not yet advanced very far, and we do not know whether or not an important social difference lies behind the fact that some places which derived their names from an enclosure – the very many place-names ending in *worth* – were often named not from a group or family but from an individual, as was Isleworth, 'Gislhere's enclosure'.[54] Costen says of the *-worth* place-names in Somerset that they 'probably bear witness to many small individual farmsteads which existed in the seventh and eighth centuries'.[55] Such a farm may still have been surrounded by a substantial area of its own land, recognizably owned and enclosed.

Domesday Book records a large number of people with small holdings of land under the names of cottars, 'coscets', and miscellaneous categories such as Oxford's 23 'men with gardens'. Among them were those whose land, it is argued, were essentially part of the inland, and who worked there, and these have already been considered. Many others, though they had a poor living, were less subordinated to seigneurial control than the holders of service tenancies on the inland. The processes that divided the hide into fractions can be observed in the known conditions of rising population in the twelfth and thirteenth centuries, but they seem to have been already at work by the time of Domesday Book. Twin pressures were at work: the need for land of a growing peasant population and the need for labour of intensive seigneurial agriculture. What had once to support a family must now support two families, or four, and rent could now be demanded from this larger group.[56] We can see from

---

52. H.P.R. Finberg, 'Anglo-Saxon England to 1042' in *Ag. Hist.* I.II, 385–525 at 411–15; C.C. Dyer, 'St Oswald and 10,000 west midland peasants' in *St Oswald of Worcester: life and influence*, ed. N. Brooks and C. Cubitt (1996), 174–93 at 181.
53. For a good example of divided standard holdings see P. Brandon and B. Short, *The South East from AD 1000* (1990), 51–3. The holdings of smallholders in Domesday Book are analysed by R.V. Lennard, *Rural England 1086–1135: a study of social and agrarian conditions* (1959), ch. XI; *idem*, 'The economic position of the bordars and cottars of Domesday Book', *Economic Journal* 61 (1951), 342–71.
54. For names in *-worth*: D. Hooke, 'Early medieval estate and settlement patterns: the documentary evidence' in *Rural Settlements of Medieval England*, ed. Aston, Austin and Dyer, 9–30 at 24–6.
55. Costen, *Origins of Somerset*, 93–4.
56. R.J. Faith, 'Demesne resources and labour rent on the manors of St Paul's Cathedral 1066–1222', *EcHR*, 657–78; H.E. Hallam, 2nd series 47 (1994), 'Some thirteenth-century censuses', *ibid.* 10 (1957–8), 340–61 at 342–9.

post-Conquest developments how this could happen. Holdings began to be morcellated, producing the tiny quarter-yardlands and fardels on which it was barely possible to make a living. At Martham, Norfolk, a sokeman's farm called 'Blakemannestoft', which in the early twelfth century had supported Blakeman and his family and descendants, had by 1292 been divided into ten parcels and absorbed into the common fields. Those fields, which had fed perhaps 107 families in 1101, were now supporting 376.[57] It can only be speculation to ask whether this pressure on land was already at work in Anglo-Saxon England, but when we look at what was happening in Anglo-Saxon farming practice, it looks more than likely.

One sign of population pressure is the important category of smallholders making a living on woodland or 'waste' – of all people the least likely to be picked up by archaeology or recorded in documents. Smallholdings of 'free men' and sokemen which were in some way not part of the regular tenemental structure of the manor are particularly characteristic of large estates south of the Humber: large numbers are found in the Isle of Ely, Cambridgeshire in 1086. The proliferation of smallholders recorded in Domesday Book in the eastern counties produces relatively high population densities there, but it is possible that if the clerks in other counties had recorded unattached peasants as assiduously as the clerks on the eastern circuit did, we should be able to detect more of these independent smallholders elsewhere. Many kinds of smallholding are indigenous to the rural economy. S.P.J. Harvey has argued that the Domesday bordars may have been such dwellers on the margin, and although a different interpretation of the term 'bordar' is adopted in this book, the category of small farmers on marginal land is a very important one.[58] Settlements in the Weald and in forest areas of the midlands were offshoots of parent villages, and grew up round the swine pastures or 'dens' belonging to them. Land at the geographical margin was not necessarily marginal in the sense of giving only meagre returns. What made the smallholding viable was a wide range of by-employment, and the opportunities for these were much greater on the margins and waste. Domesday entries only give information about industries and crafts to the extent to which they are manorial assets, and very seldom give any at all about the workers in them. Rural industries such as smithing, timber and charcoal production supported smallholders 'in the heart of the Weald' in the thirteenth century and 'men in the wood' in Domesday entries may signal similar semi-industrial or craft holdings elsewhere. Fishing and boat people, such as the Welsh boatmen who rented holdings from

57. J.B. Harley, 'Population trends and agricultural developments from the Warwickshire Hundred Rolls of 1279' *EcHR*, 2nd series 11 (1958), 8–18; B. Campbell, 'Population and the genesis of commonfields on a Norfolk manor', *EcHR* 2nd series 33 (1980), 174–92 at 181.
58. S.P.J. Harvey, 'Evidence for settlement study: Domesday Book' in *English Medieval Settlement*, ed. P.H. Sawyer (1979), 105–9; for bordars, see pp. 70–4 above.

Bath Abbey at Tidenham, may have been partly supported by smallholdings, although in Norfolk both 'fisheries' and smallholdings are common. The 30 bordars at Taynton, Oxfordshire, are likely to have worked in the important stone quarries there. The tinners of Cornwall and the lead miners of Derbyshire and the Mendips later in the middle ages had smallholdings and the fact that these industries are not mentioned in Domesday but were almost certainly active before the Conquest may mean that the workers in them were self-sufficient smallholders then too: if they had been purely wage labourers on larger enterprises it is likely that these would have been entered as seigneurial assets.[59] The variety of work, including waged work, available in wood and waste, made smallholdings there as viable, if not more viable, than smallholdings in a mainly arable/pastoral economy. Nevertheless, they must have provided a meagre living.

Common fields

Population pressure is likely to have been one of the precipitating factors behind the profound change in large parts of England, from the ninth to the twelfth century, in fields and settlements, the essential bases of peasant farming. Part of a development which was taking place in much of northern Europe, this was the shift from single fields attached to individual farms to common field systems.[60] In their most developed form the arable of several farms, sometimes all the farms in a district, was laid together and cultivated on a communally agreed rotation, generally including a fallow course and the grazing of the stubbles.[61] Its causes, chronology and effects are still very imperfectly understood. Population growth, changes in agrarian systems and technology, shifts in settlement size and shape were all linked together and we cannot separate one from the rest as the prime cause. It is

59. Wealden settlements: Everitt, *Continuity and Colonization*, 119–80; Taynton: *DB* I, 157a (the suggestion of C. Day); H.C. Darby, *The Domesday Geography of Eastern England* (1957), 114–15, 133–4; Lennard, *Rural England*, 241–3; J.R. Maddicott, 'Trade, industry and the wealth of King Alfred', *Past and Present* 123 (May 1989), 3–51 for tin and silver extraction in the west country.
60. W. Rosener, *Peasants in the Middle Ages*, trans. A. Stutzer (1992), 45–52.
61. J. Thirsk, 'The common fields', *Past and Present* 29 (December 1964), 3–25 initiated the debate. R.A. Dodgshon, *The Origin of British Field Systems: an interpretation* (1980) with an extended review of the literature in ch. 1; *idem*, 'The landholding foundations of the open-field system', *Past and Present* 67 (May 1975), 3–29; T. Rowley, ed., *The Origins of Open-Field Agriculture* (1981); Taylor, *Village and Farmstead*, ch. 8; A.R.H. Baker and R.A. Butlin, *Studies of Field Systems in the British Isles* (1973); G. Astill, 'Fields' in *The Countryside of Medieval England*, ed. G. Astill and A. Grant (1988), 62–85. A short and clear guide to the working of the 'midland system' is D. Hall, *Medieval Fields* (1982). D.Hall, 'The late Saxon countryside: villages and their fields' in *Anglo-Saxon Settlements*, ed. D. Hooke (1988), 99–122; 'Late Saxon topography and early medieval estates' in *Medieval Villages: a review of current work*, ed. D. Hooke, Oxford University Committee for Archaeology Monograph 5 (1985), 61–9.

unlikely that any firmer chronology for the process of the growth of common fields can be established than to say that there is no evidence for them in early Anglo-Saxon England, and that some such system was widely found by the twelfth century when written information in the form of extents and surveys becomes available.

The work of D. Hooke shows that many different degrees of co-operation could exist in a single area, and suggests a state of flux and change which must have been very common. What is so far lacking is pre-Conquest evidence that the entire arable of any particular settlement was divided into two or three fields and subject to agreed cropping rotations, and the stubble communally grazed. On the contrary, there is evidence of a mixture of regimes in the same place. We find some intensively cultivated enclosures, perhaps in shares, supplemented by 'outfield' occasionally cropped, a system which improved fertility while not needing a wholesale upheaval of farms and fields.[62] The impression given from the west midlands terms for land is of a mixture of farming organization with a wide range of possible co-operative practices including arrangements between a few neighbours, or between kin. There are some fields that are small and enclosed and owned by a single person or shared among some people, and there are areas of arable regularly divided into strips, owned by different people. There is common meadow and pasture, but also a great number of meadows owned by individuals. The growing number of regional studies has resulted in a flexible idea of common field systems as a range of *ad hoc* responses by farmers to their immediate circumstances, but influenced too by extraneous and non-agrarian factors. Such studies have greatly expanded the earlier model of two or three large fields, cultivated in strips and subject to common crop rotations and common grazing rights. Now we can see that in Anglo-Saxon England common rights could extend to a part only of the arable, that there could be a multiplicity of small common fields, coexisting with land in severalty. Field systems once evolved did not become set: many were to change considerably after the Conquest: for England before the Conquest Hooke speaks cautiously only of a 'degree of nucleation and a limited area of open field' being widespread in southern England.[63] To cast *all* the arable of an area into a common field system may have been only the final stage in a gradual shift that started with the kind of piecemeal co-operation just described.

Whenever it took place, reorganization into any kind of common field system, cropped, fallowed and grazed in agreed and regulated rotations, was an important change in the economy of any group of farmers. What were the causes of this considerable socioeconomic change? In purely agricultural terms, the development of various forms of common field farming can be seen as a response to the growing

---

62. Hooke, *Anglo-Saxon Landscapes of the West Midlands*, 207–8.
63. D. Hooke, 'The administrative and settlement framework of early medieval Wessex' in *The Medieval Landscape of Wessex*, ed. Aston and Lewis, 83–95 at 90.

pressure of people and their stock upon the land available to them. Hooke stresses that the areas where these sharing practices were most common were areas of early, continued and dense settlement and there is much about them that suggests pressure on land both from farmers and from their stock. Two analyses by economists propose the drive for fertility as a response to increased population pressure as a crucial factor in reorganization.[64] The arable of a primary Anglo-Saxon settlement – the 'kin-based group living in a nucleated settlement surrounded by its own land' discussed at the beginning of this chapter – may have been under permanent cultivation. Such an intensely cultivated arable core would, under pressure of an expanding population, need renewal and expansion. To reorganize the arable so that a regular amount could be fallow each year would restore productivity, which may have been under threat. The combined grazing of the community's stock on the fallow and its aftermath rewarded all who participated in the system with more grazing and the increased fertility of the land.

The second impulse towards new agricultural practices was the pressure on grazing and meadowland. One of the shaping influences in the formation of early land-units was their rights to grazing.[65] This is true at all stages in the development of such units: the primitive *regio* could not have functioned without pasture accessible to its inhabitants, and the 'multiple estate' can almost be defined as a core settlement, or settlements, with rights to grazing on distant, or not so distant, land elsewhere, rights which are recognized if not always uncontested. In late Anglo-Saxon England communal grazing lands were coming under pressure. The breaking down of large units into smaller estates, and the fragmentation of these in turn, left many farmers without access to what had once been the traditional grazing grounds and pig pasture. A growing market for cattle and sheep encouraged stock farming and there was pressure from numbers of cattle on the available grazing. Human settlement began to extend into land once used for rough and woodland pasture and there was pressure from stock on the highly valued meadows near streams and rivers – it is partly for this reason that streams so often mark the boundaries between settlements. The stubbles of arable land were the only remaining source of grazing. Grazing the arable demanded co-ordinated cropping, and it was helped by, though it did not absolutely demand, open and undivided stubbles. Strips in common arable need not have been grazed in common at all, but fenced: many open field systems had their stubble divided by temporary fencing.

Much work on the origins of common fields has stressed social causes. The apparent egalitarianism of common field agriculture, an idea that membership of a community represented an entitlement to

64. E. Boserup, *The Conditions of Agricultural Growth* (1965); Dodgshon, *British Field Systems*.
65. Fox, 'The midland system', 93ff.

rights in all its land and in shared risks and advantages, has led sociologists and economists to construct a model of common field agriculture as an effective and rational system, constructed at a single point in time to maximize profit and minimize risk among a group of participants who all had equal shares in it.[66] There are some difficulties in applying this 'communal' approach to early husbandry: the shifting settlements of Anglo-Saxon England look too small to be likely seedbeds of communality, while the communities associated with land-units such as the *scir* were too large to have given rise to individual field systems. In one way, because it created and preserved a mutual investment in maintaining and running a field and farming system, common fields can be said to *create* a community by giving a group an interest in co-operation, a process which could well have taken centuries.[67] Moreover, early common field systems appear not to have been as all-embracing as such an egalitarian interpretation demands. Not all the land of a vill was necessarily involved, for the midland and Wessex evidence discussed above suggests a mixture of farming in severalty and communal practice. Not all the people of the vill were involved, for no field system was so benevolent that it bestowed rights in land on those who were previously landless. Nor, if it is true that increased pressure from livestock led to the reorganization of field systems, was this necessarily done on the basis of equity, nor was the result beneficial for all. Midland farmers who were producing cattle and sheep for markets such as Hamwih had an interest in rationalizing their fields so as to give them access to more grazing. Apart from a small plough team of a couple of oxen the important stock on the small peasant holding was likely to be pigs, raised for subsistence. Smallholders who depended on the diminishing woods and wastes for pig pasture could only lose by developments which extended the arable.[68] In many areas, as the Domesday figures for pannage payments show, pig pasture, along with other woodland benefits, came to be a valued asset, assessed and charged for, rather than a free common resource, and peasant pig stocks may have been in competition with large-scale seigneurial pig farming. Contemporaries were shocked that the Conqueror had even the pigs counted for Domesday Book: this was not quite the case, but what *was* widely reckoned was what could be got from charging the peasants for pig pasture.

As to who provided the initiative in these important changes in farming practice, if there was one social group which valued notions of equal rights in land and resources, and which left its mark on the way that these resources were organized in late Anglo-Saxon and early

---

66. Rowley, *Origins*, outlines the main lines of the 'shared advantage, shared risk' approach, with references to the most important work.
67. S. Reynolds, *Kingdoms and Communities in Western Europe 900–1300* (1984), 110–12.
68. Lennard, *Rural England*, 254–60.

Norman England, it was more likely to have been a group of neighbouring substantial farming families such as has been suggested as the occupants of early settlements, rather than the 'village community' whose full development still lay in the future.

In general, the notion of 'rights to shares' is more helpful in understanding early peasant life than is the notion of 'community'. In co-operative farming systems, rather than any idea of 'communal ownership' it was the principle of equal entitlement or 'aliquot shares' that mattered, whether between sons within the family or between participants.[69] The principle of aliquot shares could operate within different agricultural systems. In areas where access to good pasture, rather than arable, was what mattered in the peasant economy, a share in the fields of a township brought with it an aliquot share in its pasture.[70] It was an important and persistent part of the culture of northern England, where the terminology of entitlement, 'manslot', the man's share, rather than the terminology of the hide, predominated in descriptions of peasant landholdings. Here, the *bondagium*, the farmer's holding (from ON *buendr*, farmer) was a share in a bundle of rights and obligations rather than a measure of land. The obligations were the characteristic warland ones of food rent and hospitality duties, and payments for grazing cattle. Here it was pasture that mattered, not the organization of the arable. It was the township which organized tranhumance, and the pasturing of the 'shire commons' and services were owed by the vill, not by the individual peasant landholding. (Much the same is found in Scandinavian East Anglia, where the manslot, the *wong* or the *tenementum* was the unit of peasant farming, and public obligations, including geld, were assessed on the vill and divided among its members.[71]) The importance of the vill, rather than the manor, is a characteristic of upland areas and it was no doubt partly the slow development of manorial inlands in areas of less desirable agricultural land that preserved this antique social structure and its attitudes.

Farming in severalty

Local studies have greatly enriched our awareness of the diversity of field systems, and the bold dichotomy into open field and non-open field England which H.L. Gray laid down in 1915 no longer holds. But there is still a broad division between areas where there was some kind of co-operation in the use of the arable and those where there was little or none. This is a more effective division between rural

---

69. H.M. Cam, 'The community of the vill' in *Medieval Studies presented to Rose Graham*, ed. V. Ruffer and A.J. Taylor (1950), 1–14.
70. Dodgshon, *British Field Systems*, 38ff.; T.A.M. Bishop, 'Assarting and the growth of the open fields', *EcHR* 1st series 6 (1935), 33–29 at 27–9.
71. T. Williamson, *The Origins of Norfolk* (1993), 173–4.

economies than the division between field systems themselves, but it is much harder to investigate for the pre-Conquest period. There is a rough, but not absolute, association of dispersed settlement and absence of common field farming which it is reasonable to ascribe chiefly to the ready availability of grazing land. Because they lacked the pressure on the arable that was such a strong factor in the evolution of the common fields, thinly populated highland areas with ample grazing are the natural setting for dispersed settlement: the Pennines, Dartmoor and Exmoor, the Breckland of Suffolk and Norfolk, may always have supported scattered and isolated farms, each with its own fields. Later north and north-west Wales provides good examples of undivided holdings and 'the further back in time we trace their history, the more they appear associated with a single family or settlement'.[72]

Other dispersed settlement areas seem to represent a different history: they were second-best regions not far from areas of more desirable land that was settled early. There was the same ready availability of pasture in woodland regions such as the Weald, but settlement there only seems to have come late in the Anglo-Saxon period, when the more attractive old arable lands, with their appendant wood-rights, were fully, perhaps over fully, settled.[73] Similarly, the 'high bleak country on cold clay' of the Northamptonshire and Leicestershire wolds, investigated by H.S.A. Fox, supported a poor pastoral economy which Scandinavian settlers probably established in the ninth century, the better lands being settled long before.[74] Dispersed and un-nucleated settlements are also found in areas of predominantly arable husbandry where though the easily worked arable was in short supply there was in addition an area which remained unexploited because of its inaccessibility, rough terrain or poorer soils: this gave opportunity for the expansion into waste and Weald described above. The farmers of the Kentish yokelands were very conscious of their independent status, and they survived intact into the early modern period without ever having been involved with the manorial regime of a larger estate.[75] Even in the intensely manorialized picture given by Domesday Book the independent farmstead, or group of them, is sometimes visible, the holdings of outlying farmers 'in the wood'.

72. Dodgshon, *British Field Systems*, 128.
73. Everitt, *Continuity and Colonization*, 119–40.
74. H.S.A. Fox, 'The people of the wolds in English settlement history' in *Rural Settlements of Medieval England*, ed. Aston, Austin and Dyer, 77–101.
75. Everitt, *Continuity and Colonization*, 323–5.

Nucleated settlement

The shift from scattered farms to nucleated settlement was a European-wide development, and so too was the emerging difference between nucleated and non-nucleated settlement areas.[76] Although we know that there was a 'wide street' in West Malling, Kent, and an 'east gate' and a 'north half street' at Brightwell near Wallingford, Berkshire, in the tenth century these are two of the extremely few references in pre-Conquest documentary sources to village layouts.[77] The emergence of villages seems to have been a long-drawn-out process taking place from the ninth century onwards, and the village is itself now seen as a form of social organization continually in flux. Much of the archaeological evidence is of small scattered settlements ending, rather than of new nucleated ones forming, and the early stages of nucleation are still obscure. Archaeologists have coined the term 'the middle-Saxon shuffle' for the phenomenon of settlement shift, detected by the evidence of sites deserted in the seventh and eighth centuries, but settlement 'drift' and 'shift' appear, archaeologically, to have continued into late Saxon times and to have remained a continuing though less pronounced phenomenon throughout the medieval period. In the earliest phases 'drift' could mean no more than a few houses being abandoned and replaced not far away: the assumption is that the community continued to farm the same land but from different habitation sites nearby. From the ninth century there are signs of what has been interpreted as an important change in social organization: a tendency in some areas for dispersed farms and hamlets to be replaced by nucleated settlements which survived to become the villages of medieval England. If true, this was a watershed in England's regional geography, for the nucleated settlement reached its full development in what B.K. Roberts has called 'Village England' which to this day 'runs down the middle of the country from Northumberland and Durham to Dorset and Wiltshire'. Outside this region scattered farms and hamlets remained a 'landscape which any Bronze Age, Iron Age or Roman farmer would have found familiar'.[78]

Interpretations of how, why and when villages developed have tended to group around two different positions. One group has emphasized 'organic' growth in response to stimuli such as the increase in population and the demands of a particular farming regime. Changes in peasant husbandry may well have been of great importance. Even on a small scale the process of establishing some kind of common field system must very often have made an impact on

---

76. Rosener, *Peasants*, ch. 4; J. Chapelot and R. Fossier, *The Village and House in the Middle Ages*, trans. H. Cleeve (1985), 129–44; B.K. Roberts, *Rural Settlement in Britain* (1977), ch. 6; *Making of the English Village*; 'Nucleation and dispersion: distribution maps as a research tool' in *Rural Settlements of Medieval England*, ed. Aston, Austin and Dyer, 59–75.
77. BCS 779, 810 (S 514, 517).
78. Taylor, *Village and Farmstead*, ch. 7, 124.

local settlement patterns, bringing homesteads in from the fields to a new centre. Many village layouts seem to correspond closely to the large-scale field systems which surround them, and presumably were created as part of the same operation that reorganized the fields.[79] Nevertheless, common field agriculture cannot alone account for village formation, for villages are found in areas with diverse agricultural systems.

Between those who would argue for a conscious human agency making its mark on settlement, there is disagreement whether this agency was that of lords or of peasants.[80] An account of primary nucleation 'from below', which leaves no role at all for seigneurial or other intervention 'from above', is perfectly plausible: the advantages which a change to common field farming would bring, or at the very least the hazards which it would avert, would have been known to local farmers, and nucleation was an almost inevitable concomitant of such a shift. The lordless village is a possibility that should not be ruled out. H.P.R. Finberg drew attention to the fact that modern villages called 'Charlton' and 'Carlton', from *ceorlatun, ceorls' tun,* are found all over England.[81] Finberg looked at them from the point of view of the role they may have played on the great estate. All kinds of large estates have Charltons: they are found on the lands of the bishop of Worcester, the abbot of Malmesbury, the archbishop of York and so on, as well as on the Godwinesons' lands – Earl Godwin had no fewer than five Charltons on his estate at Singleton, Sussex. Finberg pointed out that they are often near, in fact 'uncomfortably near', to royal vills and places with 'king' in their name. Many by the eleventh century were dependencies of royal manors, such as Charlton, Berkshire, less than a mile from King Alfred's birthplace at Wantage. He interpreted them as essentially berewicks, 'places where the king's own husbandmen live, tilling the soil partly on their own account, but partly also, and perhaps chiefly, for the king'. When Finberg wrote, it was assumed that 'Kingston' place-names were royal vills, but that is no longer thought to be the case, and it is the Kingstons which now look more like subordinate berewicks, rather than the Charltons.[82] It is true that some Charltons are found on inland, but it does not somehow now seem quite so likely as it once did that all Charltons were berewicks or settlements of the most dependent tenants, as Finberg thought. Finberg's work was part of a trend to see Anglo-Saxon England as

---

79. Hall, 'Late Saxon topography', 65–6.
80. C.C. Dyer, 'Power and conflict in the medieval English village' in *Medieval Villages: a review of current work,* ed. D. Hooke, Oxford University Committee for Archaeology Monograph 5 (1985), 27–32; P.D.A. Harvey, 'Initiative and authority in settlement change' in *Rural Settlements of Medieval England,* ed. Aston, Austin and Dyer, 31–43.
81. H.P.R. Finberg, 'Charltons and Carltons', in *idem, Lucerna: studies of some problems in the early history of England* (1964), 144–60.
82. Gelling, *Signposts,* 184–5; p. 32 n. 66 above.

heavily manorialized, a trend which was itself a reaction against Stenton's view of the *ceorl* as a free peasant.

It may be that to contemporaries the term *ceorls' tun* meant a settlement with a specific characteristic: a *tun* with no resident lord. Some of these were no doubt settlements – possibly deliberately planted and planned – of inland workers, 'the king's own husbandmen'. But some may have been settlements of peasants with a much more tenuous connection with an estate centre: the example Finberg quotes of the dues owed from the peasants of Charlton Marshall, Dorset, were light.[83] Ekwall's interpretation of Charlton was 'tun of the free peasants', but he too struggled to make this fit into an overall picture of Anglo-Saxon society as heavily manorialized. His conclusion, that the existence of such a term implies that there were also tuns *not* held by freemen, seems reasonable. If a nucleated settlement of farmers was known as a *ceorls' tun*, and if this was the kind of place that was readily distinguishable to contemporaries from the seigneurial *tun* of the owner of bookland, this would go some way to account for the frequent proximity of Charltons to estate centres, while signalling them as something different from the subordinated vills at those centres.[84] The Domesday Book commissioners may have been recognizing these lordless villages when they recorded manors with no inland and no hall, or where all the land seems to have been in the hands of the peasants.[85]

Villages where a seigneurial centre was absent, or a late arrival on the scene, may have their own characteristically unplanned-looking morphology. C.C. Dyer has described a common type of nucleated settlement which might well have evolved through co-operation among farmers. This is the 'interrupted row', in which farms straggle down a village street with gaps between and no sign of planning by any higher authority. He speaks of them as 'a very successful and long-lived settlement type'. The availability of woodland, the relative freedom from seigneurial control, the irregular field systems, all played a part in making it viable in his case-study, Pendock in Worcestershire, and this combination of circumstances could well have been widely found.[86]

The second interpretation of the impetus towards nucleation gives much more of a role to conscious human agency, indeed individual will, a thesis B.K. Roberts forcibly puts like this:

> the nucleated village is a product of the emergence of ... formal legalised arrangements for sharing resources, where neighbours rather than kin are involved, and where lordship implies not a remote ruler, exacting tribute, but both a real presence within

83. Finberg, 'Charltons', 160.
84. Ekwall, *English Place-Names*, s.v. *Carleton, Charlton*; Blair, *Anglo-Saxon Oxfordshire*, 80.
85. Maitland, *Domesday Book*, 142, 175–88.
86. C.C. Dyer, 'Dispersed settlements in medieval England: a case study of Pendock, Worcestershire', *Medieval Archaeology* 34 (1990), 97–121.

the settlement or the neighbourhood and the recipient of regular payments of rents, dues and indeed taxes.[87]

This sets the crucial shift towards nucleation in a particular political context: the change from the 'extensive lordship' of the *regio* or the small *scir* to the individualized lordship of the bookland estate, and the concomitant transformation of the services owed from the warland into rent. With Roberts's picture in mind, we can now look at the impact that the 'real presence' of a lord with bookland might make on the landscape.

---

87. Roberts, *Making of the English Village*, 72.

6 The growth of small estates and the beginnings of the seigneurial life

There is no doubt that the small estate – defined for convenience here as a landholding larger than was needed to support a family, and confined to a single locality – formed a class of property which must have been extremely important in early and medieval England. But small landlords are underrepresented in our written sources until Domesday reveals a host of minor gentry, lords of small manors, lessees and sub-tenants of estates of a handful of hides. Laypeople may have had their dealings in small amounts of land recorded in written deeds of the kind so common after the Conquest, but these have only survived when the estate subsequently passed to the church and they have been preserved in monastic archives. Charters and leases *to* laymen survive from the late eighth century, but they are mostly in favour of important magnates or officials. More is known about individual East Anglian landholders than about those from any other area. A corpus of laypeople's wills of the tenth and eleventh centuries survives, many of which are from East Anglia, and these provide invaluable detail about the property, personal possessions and family strategies of the testators.[1] The abbey of Ely preserved a record of the manifold negotiations and lawsuits by which its landholdings were built up after the refoundation of the abbey by Æthelwold in the mid-tenth century, and the 'Book of Ely' (*Liber eliensis*) preserves a great deal of information about landowning families associated with, and often in conflict with, the abbey.[2] But our best source of information is the landscape itself, its names and its divisions. One consequence of the growing number of small estates was the more detailed delineation of landed property. By the ninth century it was evidently no longer sufficient to say airily of a landholding that 'its bounds are well known to the natives'. Boundary clauses describing the bounds of an estate by a series of landmarks began to be attached to charters from the

---

1. D. Whitelock, *Anglo-Saxon Wills* (1930).
2. *Liber eliensis*, ed. E.O. Blake, Camden 3rd series 92 (1962).

mid-eighth century and became common in the ninth and tenth.[3] They show boundaries defined with extreme precision, recording landmarks sometimes only a few yards apart. In some regions entirely new and artificial boundaries were formed, sometimes cutting through traditional units by ploughing a furrow or making a ditch to serve as a landmark, but new units often respected older boundaries, which make frequent appearances in charter boundary clauses.

The smaller landholdings were brought about by the progressive fragmentation of the large land-units and complex estates typical of the era of extensive lordship. Large units seem often to have fragmented along natural fault lines, giving each of their component parts a rough balance of resources. The region which supported the peoples of part of the south Essex coastline from a mixture of workable soil and valuable marshland grazing fragmented into the Essex coastal parishes, each with grazing rights on the Isle of Sheppey.[4] The large area once known as Ashdown, now the Lambourn Downs, split into long thin parishes, each with upland grazing, a share of the greensand ridge suitable for settlement, and clayland in the vale.[5] Newly created estates often preserved the existing deployment of people over the land: J. Blair finds that in Surrey 'tenurial changes had respected not merely the ancient boundaries but ... township and sub-township units'.[6] Fragmentation proceeded apace in eastern England. In areas of Scandinavian settlement a lively market in land for cash hastened the process of estate fragmentation. Peasants and lords alike in eastern England seem to have been more alert to the possibilities of land as a saleable commodity than were their counterparts in Wessex and Mercia.[7] The big buyers in this market were the new monastic foundations of the tenth century, but Scandinavian settlers may also have bought their way into rural England. To some extent it was the nature of lordship that made this extreme fragmentation possible. In areas such as East Anglia warland dues played a much more important role than did services on seigneurial inlands, and these dues – suit of court, riding service and so on – were much easier to divide and re-allocate than were the rents and labour owed for inland holdings. This eased the process that T. Williamson has described as ' "fission from above", as the East Anglian kings and their West Saxon and Anglo-Danish successors granted away estates, or portions of estates, and the obligations due from their inhabitants, to aristocratic families'.[8] Peripheral farms or hamlets split off, eventually becoming separate

---

3. F.M. Stenton, *The Latin Charters of the Anglo-Saxon Period* (1955), 55–6, 66.
4. J.H. Round, 'The Domesday survey' in *VCH Essex*, I (1903), 333–425 at 369–71.
5. D. Hooke, 'Anglo-Saxon settlements in the Vale of the White Horse', *Oxoniensia* 52 (1987).
6. J. Blair, *Early Medieval Surrey: landholding, church and settlement before 1300* (1991), 33.
7. J. Williamson, 'Norfolk: thirteenth century' in *The Peasant Land Market in Medieval England*, ed. P.D.A. Harvey (1984), 31–105.
8. T. Williamson, *The Origins of Norfolk* (1993), 121–5.

manors. Vills divided between several lords in dizzying confusion. Yet even in this fluid and fissiparous society, traces of old resource territories still remained. Williamson finds that the core areas retained by major estates were ancient centres. They were better supplied with woodland than were the peripheral landholdings, not only near the centre itself but woodland rights in distant vills. These 'estate heartlands' had a much more 'manorialized' organization, with a smaller proportion of 'free men'; in other words they were islands of inland in a sea of warland. The preservation of old rights to common resources produced long tapering parishes here too, giving each access to woodland, and parochial allocations of marshland.

The dissolution of multiple estates into their component parts was an important force in creating smaller holdings. Those of Nottinghamshire were in an 'advanced state of decay' by the Conquest, and part of this decay was caused by the granting away of berewicks with some of the 'service network' of the soke still adhering to them.[9] An intermediate stage was the splitting of a multiple estate into several smaller ones: the 20 hides carved out of the huge Southwell estate and given in 956 by Eadwig to Oscytel, archbishop of York included inland with a 'servants' enclosure' and seigneurial arable intermixed with that of the peasants, outlying farms in four townships, and two thirds of an estate at Fiskerton.[10] The break-up of the large old estate of Fawsley, Northamptonshire, gave a foothold for new lay and ecclesiastical owners: between 944 and 1023 four small manors had been created and two of these were split among eight tenants by Domesday.[11]

From service to landholding

The proliferation of smaller estates was the result of many factors, some of which were very long-standing. One which came to have a much more pronounced effect in the later Anglo-Saxon period was the accompanying proliferation of service holdings of all kinds. The process was in part due to the evolution of bureaucracies to administer major private estates and their establishment as a landed class. But a very large part was played by the endowing of agents of the 'state' with permanent landholdings and provision of lesser warriors with land. To grant land was to fund a permanent salary. The creation and landed endowment of a many-layered ministerial class firmly rooted the English state in private landholding.

9. M.W. Bishop, 'Multiple estates in late Anglo-Saxon Nottinghamshire', *Trans. Thoroton Society* 85 (1981), 37–47.
10. P. Lyth, 'The Southwell charter of 956: an exploration of its boundaries', *ibid.* 49–61; F.M. Stenton, *Types of Manorial Structure in the Northern Danelaw* in Oxford Studies in Social and Legal History 2 (1910), 78–81.
11. P. Stafford, *The East Midlands in the Early Middle Ages* (1985), 34–9.

Ine's laws recognize smaller landholders, *gesithcund* men with 3–20 hides (and Welsh people with up to five), whose *wergeld* is as much as twice as high as that of their unlanded counterparts and four times that of an ordinary commoner. *Gesithcund* men were, by their name, originally the king's companions, and came up that way, receiving grants of land in reward. The class that came to replace them were thegns, whose route to power had more commonly been through service in the royal or aristocratic household. The rise of this intermediate class of landowner, a group of widely differing wealth but all between the lord of the great estate and the family farmer, was intimately connected with the growth of the late Anglo-Saxon state.[12] At every level, from the king and members of the royal family to lords of great tracts of land, the thegn became more important as the need grew for permanent reliable servants, for specialized household officers, for supervisors of royal vills, for diplomacy and simply for maintaining a reliable communication system over a large kingdom. Grants to *ministri*, officials of all ranks, become common in leases and charters of the tenth century. Thegns had thegns, who served them as they served the king and represented them in the law-courts. Service was at the root of their position even when they became landed: they still owed service at court, 'special service in the king's hall'.[13]

Some of these important ministerial families were beginning to build up one or more centres on their estates, marked by a large inland, a church and most probably – though here evidence is generally lacking – a prestigious house. A.F. Wareham has reconstructed the landholding of Wulfstan of Dalham, a Suffolk landholder who acted as an important agent of King Edgar.[14] His entire landholding of 138 hides would have put him in the top rank of landholders after the Conquest. From Domesday's description of Wulfstan's descendants' landholdings we can see that they had established some prestigious centres of power and wealth. Desning, Suffolk, appears to have been the principal manor of his family. There was in 1086 what must have been an imposing headquarters. Wulfstan had 91 bordars at work on his land – although we do not know how they were distributed around the vills of the manor – and there were five mills and two churches. Another manor of this family in 1066 was at Clare. Here in 1086 were 30 bordars and 20 slaves at work at a centre which included a market and a vineyard: both signs of an important Anglo-Norman establishment. At Hundon was much the same kind of centre, with two churches.[15]

---

12. J. Campbell, 'Some agents and agencies of the late Anglo-Saxon state' in *Domesday Studies*, ed. J Holt (1987), 201–18; H.R. Loyn, 'Gesiths and thegns in Anglo-Saxon England from the seventh to the tenth century', *EHR* 70 (1955), 529–49; L.M. Larson, 'The king's household in England before the Norman conquest: a thesis', *Bulletin of the University of Wisconsin* 100 (1904).
13. See p. 253 below.
14. *Liber eliensis*, xiii; A.F. Wareham, 'The aristocracy of East Anglia *c.* 930–1154' (Ph.D. thesis, University of Birmingham, 1992), 92, 155.
15. *DB* II, 389b, 390a.

One of the most important assets of the power base of these East Anglian lords was their following: the sub-tenants and commended men who could be relied on to support them in disputes, and who owed suit at their courts. Wihtgar had 302 men under his lordship in this way.[16]

Lesser king's thegns formed a lesser nobility, 'lords of a handful of places', who while not yet connected with a single place, yet had a much more localized area of influence like the lesser Kentish nobles, Wulfstan of Saltwood, Lyfing of Malling, Leofstan of Mersham, Leofwine of Ditton, Sidewine of Paddlesworth and Ælfnoth of Orpington who witnessed a charter around 995.[17] The members of the gentry of Scandinavian England described by P. Stafford were evidently claiming thegnly status on the basis of much smaller holdings than this. At Carlton-in-Lindrick, Nottinghamshire, each of six thegns who held only two carucates between them, claimed the status of a thegn and each had a hall. Honourable status here was connected as much with rights as with possessions: the right to carry weapons and to attend the local courts.[18]

'Thegnland' became a recognizable entity. A thegn's inland with his inland tenants, the eight 'bordars' or smallholders who lived on the thegnland, appear at Spaldwick, Huntingdonshire, in 1086.[19] At Lambourne, Berkshire, shortly before the Conquest, the *geneatland* was also a distinct and recognizable area.[20] Two Somerset studies illustrate how the growth of thegnland altered the landscape. M. Costen has mapped clusters of estates near the royal centres of Frome and Ilmington: they are over six hides each, so falling into the category of the property necessary to support a thegn in the royal service. At a later date a large category of villages emerged whose names show that they were the property of an eleventh-century Anglo-Saxon landowner – the Allertons near Wedmore, named from 'Ælfweard's *tun*', are an example. These are in much smaller units – in fact Costen reveals a whole Somerset minor gentry or thegnage, many of whom were dependants of the church, with less than five hides.[21] N.J. Corcos's analysis of the Shapwick estate in Somerset is an example of what a landscape influenced by this process might look like (see Fig. 18). Shapwick may have been a substantial Roman estate, covering the Polden Hills west of Glastonbury. In 729 it came into the hands of the abbey. Corcos suggests that its six constituent parishes resulted from dividing up the area and laying out a field system and village in each, a piece of very large-scale rural planning of the tenth to eleventh century. He argues that the establishment of villages and field systems was contemporaneous with this creation of new small estates. In

---

16. Stafford, *East Midlands*, 161–3; R. Fleming, *Kings and Lords in Conquest England* (1991), 71–9, describes the Godwineson following.
17. Robertson, *Charters*, LXIX.
18. Stafford, *East Midlands*, 156–7.
19. *EHD* II, 884.
20. Robertson, *Charters*, app. 1 no. V, at 240–1.
21. M. Costen, *The Origins of Somerset* (1992), 113–21.

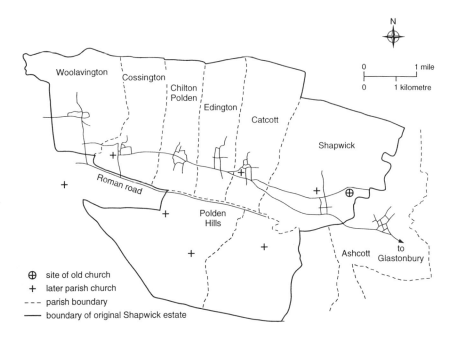

Figure 18 The Shapwick estate, Somerset, possibly once a substantial Roman landholding, divided into smaller units as a result of deliberate landscape planning in the tenth or eleventh century. *Source*: after M. Costen, *The Origins of Somerset* (1992), fig. 5.2 at 120.

Domesday it was held by fourteen thegns of the type Costen has described.[22]

Geþyncðo, the text on status associated with Wulfstan, has already been quoted as evidence of a landowning class whose status had been primarily based on service. It ascribes to the thegn five hides of land. This is the size of estate which was thought of as appropriate to support an armed warrior, and the under-thegn in this text was responsible for the public duties, the 'king's *utware* due from the land', which included military service.[23] The 'five-hide unit' used as a basis for the assessment of military obligation gave rise to a class of estates of this size, whose remnants are still visible in Domesday Book. The five-hide unit gave us the place-names Fifield and Fifehead, of which seven

---

22. N.J. Corcos, 'Early estates on the Poldens and the origins of settlement at Shapwick', *Proc. Somerset Archaeological and Natural History Society* 127 (1984), 47–54.

23. Liebermann, I, 456–8; *EHD* II, 432, and pp. 95–8 above. S.P.J. Harvey, 'The knight and the knight's fee in England', *Past and Present* 49 (1970), 3–43 at 12; P. Vinogradoff, *English Society in the Eleventh Century: essays in English mediaeval history* (1908), 63 and n. 2, 344.

are still in use, and very many more may have disappeared.[24] The typical landholding of the fighting man may be the Knighton, the *tun* of a *cniht* or retainer – Knightons are legion among English place-names.

Few great estates were able to afford the upkeep of a large household of administrators, and grants of land were made for their support. Grants to 'Godric, my reeve', to 'my steward Aelfnoth', 'to my steward Aelfwig' record the establishment of little estates for the administrators of a large one.[25] 'Reeveland' too became a recognized category, perhaps when the term *gerefa* had come to mean estate administrator rather than public official.

Bookland

Late Anglo-Saxon England knew of the Roman idea of property, although it knew very little about its workings. The notion of the absolute ownership of land or, rather, of the perpetual possession of it by an individual, which was the nearest approximation to absolute ownership that Roman law allowed to anyone other than the emperor, had to contend with another, and contrary, set of ideas about property: the claims of kin.[26] While the introduction of the charter brought something of the Roman notion of property to England, it was employed in a cultural milieu in which the claims of kin remained vital. The security of 'bookland', land granted by charter (*boc*, 'book'), made it so attractive to the lay nobility that, as Bede complained, they had formed family monasteries precisely to secure such an advantage.[27] Rather than see this process through the shocked eyes of Bede and Alcuin as a profanation of the monastic ideal, we can see it as part of family strategy: the family monastery was the forerunner of the family estate, providing a permanent inheritance, a cultivated milieu and an education for children and for aristocratic women quite unattainable in the world outside. J. Blair has proposed that the many place-names which are made up from a woman's name and the suffix *burg* were small family nunneries. Land at Bibury, Gloucestershire, was leased to Beage and her mother in the early eighth century for their two lives. Beage, having inherited the lease 'may have built a new manor house, referred to by the local people as *Beagan byrig*', or her 'house' may have been a small nunnery. Perhaps a small seigneurial house and a

---

24. F.W. Maitland, *Domesday Book and Beyond: three essays in the early history of England* (1960 edn), 194–204; J. Blair, *Anglo-Saxon Oxfordshire* (1994), 78; Ekwall, *English Place-Names*, s.v. *Fifehead Magdalen*.
25. Whitelock, *Wills*, XXIX.
26. E. John, *Land Tenure in Early England: a discussion of some problems* (1960), ch.1; R.J. Faith, 'Peasant families and inheritance customs in medieval England', *AgHR* 14 (1966), 77–95.
27. Bede, letter to Egbert: *Councils and Ecclesiastical Documents relating to Great Britain and Ireland*, ed. A.W. Haddan and W. Stubbs (3 vols, 1869–71), III, 314–25.

small domestic minster were not physically very different – the landowner Æthelgifu freed by her will some of her slave women to create a kind of chantry-household of pious women.[28] That the prevailing atmosphere in many family minsters was that of the lay aristocracy was, as P. Wormald has pointed out, because they were part of that world.[29]

Nevertheless, while the charter played an important part within the milieu of the family, it ultimately made easier the division of hereditary lands. One theory is that the charter conveyed the authority to circumvent the customary claims of certain members of the family in favour of others. To 'book' land to someone not only gave a bundle of rights, it gave them to an individual. Sometimes specifically, perhaps always by implication, it gave the recipient in turn the right to grant or sell the land on in the same unfettered way. The will too conveyed land and possessions to chosen individuals. Land held by charter was not only secure against resumption by the king and had written authority against another claimant: it was also freed from the claims of other members of the family, particularly the brothers who would expect to be co-heirs. European law sought over time to preserve customary family rights but the means by which it did so, the *retrait lignager*, only achieved a shadowy existence among the landed class in England, although it retained a vigorous hold in peasant culture.

The charter did not bring in a social revolution, but it made a number of important things possible. If the power of devolution had been used to bring about a massive shift of property away from families, there would indeed have been a social revolution, but (although the analysis of the charter material from this point of view is not well advanced) this did not happen. This may be because only *acquired*, not inherited, land could be transferred by charter.[30] But it was also because alienation from the family is not what the landholding class broadly wanted: lineage and family were becoming more, not less, important to them in their striving for 'the unchallenged possession of lands and office'.[31] What the charter did make possible was the effective family strategy: marriage portions to ensure profitable marriage alliances, the favouring of particular children at the expense of others, the support of favoured kin lines and the disadvantaging of others. Originally only used in favour of the church, the charter spread

28. M. Gelling, *Signposts to the Past* (1978), 182; J. Blair, 'Anglo-Saxon minsters: a topographical review' in *Pastoral Care Before the Parish*, ed. J. Blair and R. Sharpe (1992), 226–66 at 234.
29. P.J. Wormald, *Bede and the Conversion of the English: the charter evidence* (Jarrow 1984).
30. P.J. Wormald, 'The age of Bede and Æthelbald' in *The Anglo-Saxons*, ed. J. Campbell, E. John, P.J. Wormald (1982), 70–100 at 97; A.C. Murray, *Germanic Kinship Structure: studies in law and society in antiquity and the early middle ages* (1983), 136ff.
31. D.A. Bullough, 'Early medieval social groupings: the terminology of kinship', *Past and Present* 45 (November 1969), 3–18 at 17.

through the upper ranks of lay society and the device, if that is what it was, of the ersatz minster-foundation was no longer necessary. Estates broken up to endow selected sons and daughters produced smaller units and put land into women's hands as landowners. Thirty or more Domesday place-names have a women's name as one element, and women who can be assumed to be landholders of some rank are found in most counties for which charters survive. Women estate owners issued charters in their own name and appear to have had control over their own land and wealth.[32]

Charters alone cannot be said to have introduced the idea of property. Nor was bookland typical. M. Costen finds that estates conveyed by charter in Wiltshire and Dorset are larger than most estates in those counties as a whole.[33] A good deal of land probably descended within families without ever being conveyed by charter – which was after all a register of conveyance, drawn up for a particular purpose. Hereditable land which was not booked is *ipso facto* almost invisible in the written record, but what S. Reynolds calls 'old family land' could in fact have been *most* land. 'The ordinary hereditary property of nobles and free men' forms a continuum, in her view, with no boundary save their economic status marking off the peasantry.[34]

Leasehold

Leaseholds were an almost equally important source of land. Leasing land, by large and small tenant alike, remained a very important form of landholding throughout the Anglo-Saxon and Anglo-Norman centuries.[35] The 'resumption of manors', or adoption of 'demesne farming' in the last quarter of the twelfth century – by which is meant the taking of property in hand and managing it directly instead of leasing it out – was an expedient born of the circumstances of the time: leasing was the traditional method of estate management. Virtually all the pre-Conquest leases which have survived are of church property. It was canonically forbidden to alienate the possessions of the church, and the lease for several, generally three, lives was a device to circumvent this ban. Many of these leases were forms of *emphyteusis*, devices explicitly meant to result in the land eventually returning to the church. This was a practice the church often came to regret, because land once leased was extremely hard to regain in the face of the continuous urge among the laity towards establishing the

---

32. C. Fell, *Women in Anglo-Saxon England* (1984), 92–100.
33. M. Costen, 'Settlement in Wessex in the tenth century: the charter evidence' in *The Medieval Landscape of Wessex*, ed. M. Aston and C. Lewis (1994), 97–107.
34. S. Reynolds, 'Bookland, folkland and fiefs', *Anglo-Norman Studies* 14 (1992), 211–27 at 219.
35. T.H. Aston, 'The origins of the manor in England', *TRHS* 5th series 8 (1958), 59–83 at 22; R.V. Lennard, *Rural England 1086–1135: a study of social and agrarian conditions* (1959), chs 5–7.

heritability of their land. Long leases opened up opportunities for an emerging class of smaller landlords. Those issued by Oswald, bishop of Worcester are our best collection from a single archive, and show the dangers from the bishopric's point of view as well as the opportunities they offered the lessees.[36] C.C. Dyer, the historian of the bishopric estate, has traced the process by which these lands became to all intents and purposes alienated from it: 'most of the lands known to have been leased in the tenth century were still held by laymen in the late eleventh ... leasing meant the permanent alienation of substantial amounts of land – about 45 per cent of the hidage of the estate recorded in Domesday was held by lay tenants'.[37] Although some leases were granted *gratis* to reward retainers and support administrators, many were bought and sold and could be expensive. Leases to rich laity were an important addition to monastic finances. The large sum paid to Peterborough Abbey for Swineshead, 1000 shillings down and a day's food rent each year, looks more like a mortgage: an effective way for a religious house to raise a cash sum under the pretext of a lease.[38] Such arrangements cannot have been typical of small leaseholds.

Leases from the religious were often for renders in kind. Another Peterborough lease for two lives was for land at Sempringham: it brought in (or should have brought in) the traditional components of the *feorm*: ale, bread, cattle and firewood. When the bishop of Worcester leased Æthelmær his two hides Æthelmær paid over two pounds of silver, 30 ewes with their lambs, four oxen, two cows and a horse.[39] It is impossible to put this information in any kind of context for we are not often able to find out what was paid for a lease, even less often what was paid as rent. This must surely have been part of the agreement, but it may have been only a verbal arrangement: leases, like permanent grants, were made in the presence of witnesses.

Land was evidently leased stocked with workers, livestock and sown land, judging by a lease by Evesham Abbey of four and a half hides at Norton, three of which were inland and the rest warland (*to inware ... to utware*). After three lives the land was to revert to the monastery with one man and six oxen and 20 sheep and 20 sown acres.[40] This meant that attention had to be paid to recording what stock was present at the beginning of the lease. In 1086 local juries were able to swear – we do not know with how much accuracy – to the numbers of horses, cattle, pigs and sheep on a manor, to the value of its mills and pannage rights, to the extent of its woodland, and to its leasable value. Some of this information must surely have been provided by the lord of

---

36. V. King, 'St Oswald's tenants' in *St Oswald of Worcester: life and influence*, ed. N. Brooks and C. Cubitt (1996), 100–16.
37. C.C. Dyer, *Lords and Peasants in a Changing Society: the estates of the bishopric of Worcester 680–1540* (1980), 17.
38. BCS 271 (S 1412).
39. Robertson, *Charters*, VII, LXV.
40. *Ibid.*, LXXXI.

the manor or his bailiff, and the regular form of the entries of livestock in Little Domesday may reflect some kind of record keeping. There was an established body of law relating to leasehold or 'fee-farm' by the early twelfth century, which reveals that strict records were kept, by tally, of live and dead stock, of seed sown and grain in the granaries.[41]

Court and hall

It was a complex of processes that transformed the nobility of early Anglo-Saxon England into the seigneurial class well rooted in its estates which we recognize as a European phenomenon. But if we were to fasten on one element which was crucial to it, it must be the lord's hall and complex of buildings later known as the *curia*, the court.[42] These buildings, apart from their obvious utilitarian value, made an important statement to the world. Without his defensible seigneurial centre, with its hall large enough to house under its roof his household and his followers, we could not recognize the medieval seigneur, and he certainly would not have been able to recognize himself. In the literature of the development of European feudalism the house and the family are tightly linked. In the upper echelons of society the *domus*, house in the sense of building, became the house in the sense of family and descent group. While the full development of this seigneurial culture was still to come, we can recognize its beginning in late pre-Conquest England. The many place-names which derive from a personal name followed by *-tun* give an indication of what an Anglo-Saxon thegn's *domus* might have been like. The *tun* was coming to be a private and defensible space fortified with a palisade of some kind – hence the regular occurrence of labour rent devoted to building and keeping this in repair. It was increasingly likely to include a hall and separate 'bower' for the lord and lady's living accommodation. Although they were asked only for the name of each vill, the

---

41. *Leges Henrici Primi*, ed. L.J. Downer (1972), 56.1–3; for leases dating from a little later in the century: W.H. Hale, ed., *The Domesday of St Paul's of the year MCCXXII or registrum de visitatione maneriorum per Robertum decanum*, Camden Society 69 (1858), 122–39.
42. J. Chapelot and R. Fossier, *The Village and House in the Middle Ages*, trans. H. Cleeve (1985); A. Williams, ' "A bell-house and a *burhgeat*": lordly residence in England before the Norman Conquest' in *The Ideals and Practice of Medieval Knighthood*, ed. C. Harper–Bill and R. Harvey (1986), 221–40; J. Blair, 'Hall and chamber: English domestic planning 1000–1250' in *Manorial Domestic Buildings in England and Northern France*, ed. G. Meirion-Jones and M. Jones, Society of Antiquaries of London Occasional Paper 15 (1993), 1–21; P. Rahtz, 'Buildings and rural settlement' in *The Archaeology of Anglo-Saxon England*, ed. D.M. Wilson, (1976), 49–98. On *aula* as estate centre and taxable unit: Maitland, *Domesday Book*, 159; discussed by J.J. Palmer, 'The Domesday manor' in *Domesday Studies*, ed. Holt, 139–53.

Domesday clerks expected to find a 'hall' there. Where there was none, they made a note of the fact.[43]

Excavation is beginning to reveal some of this seigneurial home-making taking place from the ninth century. Defensibility and impressive building work seem to be their characteristics. The context for the two best-known examples is the process, discussed above, of endowing members of the service gentry or nobility. A retainer of one of the Mercian kings, granted bookland and diverted royal *feorm*, is suggested as the client behind the new building at Goltho, Lincolnshire.[44] Raunds, Northamptonshire, too had been a part, perhaps the centre, of a royal estate. At Raunds, two large timber buildings were superseded by an enclosed group of structures, soon to be joined by a church, which were the forerunners of the stone and timber manor house which succeeded them on the same site.[45] Goltho was a collection of farmsteads until midway through the ninth century. Then the site was cleared 'for the construction of the first of the sequence of fortified aristocratic homesteads which were to stand on the site until the middle of the twelfth century'. The new 'imposing Saxon houses' included a hall and the domestic living quarters or 'bower' which were to become the setting for the seigneurial life, weaving sheds and kitchens, the whole surrounded by a fence (see Fig. 19). Almost all the assets which a later era thought essential to the lordly life, 'chapel, kitchen, bell-house and castle-gate' were to be found at Goltho by the end of the ninth century.[46] 'Bury' (from OE *burh*, 'fortified place') occurs frequently in village plans as a field, street or croft name. It may indicate the former presence of a built-up seigneurial site. The Bury at Thorverton, East Devon, shown in Fig. 20, a large rectangular open space with the church at one end, was the 'original nucleus' of the village in Hoskins's view, and nearby Silverton has a Bury on a similar site.[47] There was an *up-hæme* and a *byrihæme* at Lambourn, Berkshire in the eleventh century, separate townships which became Up Lambourn and Chipping Lambourn. The *byrihæme* took its name from the seigneurial (originally royal) centre with an impressive building.[48]

43. Maitland, *Domesday Book*, 141–3; for place-names in -*tun* see pp. 173–5 below.
44. G. Beresford, *Goltho: the development of an early medieval manor c 850–1150*, English Heritage Archaeological Report no. 4, Historical Buildings and Monuments Commission for England (1987).
45. G. Cadman and G. Foard, 'Raunds, manorial and village origins' in *Studies in Late Anglo-Saxon Settlement*, ed. M.L. Faull (1984), 81–100.
46. *EHD* I, 432.
47. W.G. Hoskins, *The Making of the English Landscape* (1955), fig. 5 at 51.
48. Robertson, *Charters*, appendix 1.V and notes to ll, 13 and 14 at 492.

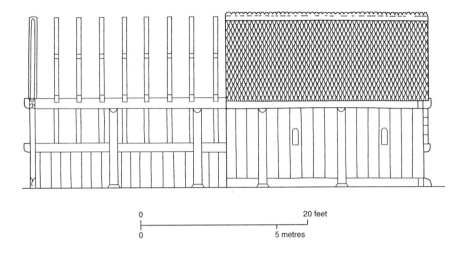

Figure 19 Reconstruction of the hall at Goltho, Lincolnshire, *c.* 950–975. *Source*: after G. Beresford, *Goltho: the development of an early medieval manor c 850–1150*, Historical Buildings and Monuments Commission for England (1987), fig. 65.

Manorial churches

The church was part of the seigneurial complex: 'church and manor kept company from the outset' and church and hall were often contiguous, as they were at Thorverton.[49] Church and defensible hall were the most solid and well-built buildings of the curia. In some cases it seems that the church tower may have had a domestic function too: the forerunner of the stone keep. The belfry may have topped this building: solid testimony to seigneurial prestige, with a bell likely to have been rung for curfews and military alarms as well as for services. The church was the lord's property, and could be bought and sold. The priest was his too: some were unfree men, and could be bequeathed by will as slaves were, and were part of the noble household. Many priests must have been inland residents, like Recelbert, priest at Burton, Staffordshire, in the early twelfth century, with four acres of inland and a dwelling on them.[50] Other seigneurial priests were well-founded. Substantial dues were to be paid to the priest at the royal chapel at Lambourn, Berkshire, which had its own hide of geld-free inland

---

49. R. Morris, *Churches in the Landscape* (1989), at 249.
50. *EHD* II, 822.

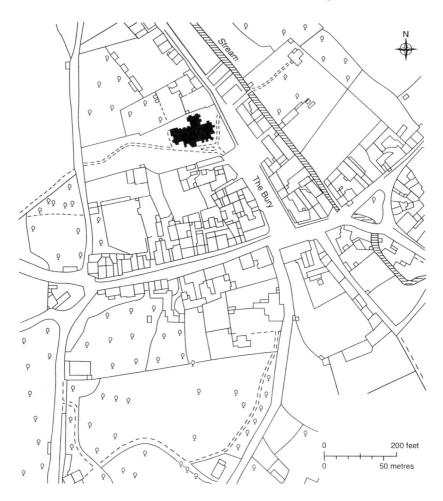

Figure 20   Thorverton, Devon. A core area, now known as the Bury, is immediately south of the church. *Source*: after W.G. Hoskins, *The Making of the English Landscape* (1955), fig. 5.

which developed into a manor in its own right. The parish church financially supported by its parishioners and physically embedded in the village was part of a wider change in settlement which is essentially part of the social history of Anglo-Norman England.[51]

However, the founders of Anglo-Saxon churches were not all major landowners. Everitt has charted the spread of 'bookland churches' in

---

51.   J. Blair, 'Introduction: from minster to parish church' in *Minsters and Parish Churches: the local church in transition 950–1200*, ed. J. Blair, Oxford University Committee for Archaeology Monograph 17 (1988), 1–19 at 7–9.

Kent, which was part of the gradual breakdown of the ancient estates and the growth to manorial status of outlying farms and settlements in the Weald. Some were so proprietary that they took their founder's name: *Ælsiescirce* and *Blacemannescirce* were held by and probably founded by Ælsi and Blaceman in the reign of Edward the Confessor.[52] The *tunkirke* in Marlingford, Norfolk, to which five acres, a toft and two wagonloads of wood were bequeathed in a tenth- or eleventh-century will may have been more of a seigneurial chapel than the parish church we know today. Siflæd, its owner, had her own priest and it is he and his descendants 'as long as they are in holy orders' who held services there and who benefited from her bequest of land and firewood.[53] This may be an example of the many churches in Norfolk which were not seigneurial foundations but built by local prosperous peasant families.[54]

The close links that were evolving in late Anglo-Saxon England between seigneurial curia and seigneurial church provided a setting in which a much closer degree of social control could be exercised by landowners over peasants who were also the congregations of 'their' churches. The sermons of Wulfstan, with their emphasis on the decline of personal morality as a matter of state, are perhaps untypical of what might be heard in a small local church – if indeed a sermon was heard there at all. But a tighter supervision of the morals and behaviour of the people of a locality became possible, particularly in relation to the payment of tithe: it is notable that the rules on church payments are included among customary rents and dues in both the *Rectitudines* and the Hurstbourne custumal. Priests would expect to be supported from tithes from their lord's estate, and many parishes evolved in the tenth century as co-terminous with the estate, parish and estate boundaries, when they stabilized, tending to coincide. Tithe was, technically speaking, due from the faithful from the period of the conversion of the English. It came to matter more as 'an expanding asset in an expanding economy' with the growth of population and the increasingly intensive exploitation of the land.[55] Edgar's laws on tithe show that the landlord (*landhlaford*) was entitled to profit from the penalties levied on tithe defaulters. Resistance to paying tithe may have become a source of conflict in the countryside: Æthelstan invoked the law of the Old Testament against non-payers on his own lands in blood-curdling terms.[56]

---

52. A. Everitt, *Continuity and Colonization: the evolution of Kentish settlement* (1986), 198–205.
53. Whitelock, *Wills*, XXXVII and XXXVIII, 93–5.
54. Williamson, *The Origins of Norfolk*, 156–61.
55. Robertson, *Charters*, appendix 1.V, pp. 240–1, 490–3; Blair, 'From minster to parish church', 8.
56. Liebermann, I, 196–8, 146–8: II Edgar 3; I Æthelstan (ordinance concerning tithes).

Hounds and hawks

Blood sports in Anglo-Saxon England had begun to take on the important role they were to retain in the life of the English gentry. Many a barrow is named after hawk or hound, and an often-quoted passage in King Alfred's translation of Augustine's *Soliloquies* extols the life of the man who has been granted bookland:

> Every man when he has built himself a home on land lent to him [i.e. leased] by his lord, likes to stay there some time, and go hunting, fowling and fishing, until the time when he shall deserve bookland and a perpetual inheritance through his lord's kindness.[57]

Or she: Æthelgifu's huntsman and her pack of hounds were among the possessions she was keen to dispose of with care.[58] Specialized stud-farms make their mark on place-names, and an enclosed private deer park or *haga*, which features in some Anglo-Saxon charters, enclosed with a 'deer hedge' whose upkeep on the king's land was among the cottar's duties, probably provided a readily accessible source of meat, rather than an opportunity for prestigious hunting in open country.[59]

The economy of small estates

Lords who wanted to support themselves from the proceeds of these smaller estates needed to adopt appropriate management policies. Here we may begin to see the impact of Roberts's 'lord ... [as] a real presence within the settlement or the neighbourhood and the recipient of regular payments of rents, dues and indeed taxes'.[60] Whether its lord or lady had obtained it by lease or by charter the creation of the small estate had implications for the peasantry: landlords who had paid good money would want to recoup the investment they had made and to create for themselves a life suitable for their position. The creation of smaller landholdings by hiving off parts of a large composite estate had implications for them too. Such an estate, with its centres and

57. S. Keynes and M. Lapidge, eds, *Alfred the Great: Asser's life of King Alfred and other contemporary sources* (1983), 138.
58. D. Whitelock, *The Will of Æthelgifu: a tenth century Anglo-Saxon manuscript* (1968), 34.
59. Stud–farms: Ekwall, *English Place-Names*, s.v. *stod*. Deer parks: D. Hooke, 'Pre-conquest woodland: its distribution and usage', *AgHR* 37 (1989), 113–29; *Anglo-Saxon Settlements of the West Midlands: the charter evidence*, BAR British Series 95 (1951), 227–9, 238–47. Deer hedge: *EHD* II, 814 (*Rectitudines singularum personarum*).
60. P.D.A. Harvey, 'Initiative and authority in settlement change', in *The Rural Settlements of Medieval England*, ed. M. Aston, D. Austin and C. Dyer (1989), 31–43 and work cited there; B.K. Roberts, *The Making of the English Village* (1987), 72.

specialized berewicks, was a large-scale enterprise whose parts were intended to work as a whole, and whose purpose was to support an important centre. When dismembered and divided it fragmented into pieces that were not independently viable.[61] The small estate was often a fragment of a much larger one, or the fragment of a fragment – perhaps a few hides hived off to reward a faithful steward, or to set up a married daughter. Owners of such modest properties did not have the option of benefiting from large-scale food renders that larger landlords did, and it is doubtful whether a thegn granted five hides split off from such a unit could have lived on the *feorm* due from it alone. Nevertheless he had to exploit his lands somehow, for he and his household had to be fed. The spread of the small estate is likely to have brought about an intensification of exploitation of inland arable and meadow, woodland and pasture, livestock and people.

The smaller the estate, the more likely its owner is to have depended entirely for his supplies on its *inland* worked by slave or hired labour. Kosminsky's study of the peasantry of the thirteenth century revealed that the typical small manor had a specific structure: it was more likely than the large estate to have a large proportion of its land 'in demesne'– that is to say, in a home farm. Looking back to the pre-Conquest period for the origins of this situation he conjectured that 'the embryo of the small manor was the large holding of the English *ceorl*, who was already to some extent exploiting slaves'.[62] Studies of Domesday Book, including Kosminsky's own, found that large demesnes and a resident servile labour force were typical elements on the small manor, where the landlord was likely to be resident himself. A detailed study by J.D. Hamshere of the manors of the bishop of Worcester, his chapter and of other major landlords in Worcester, as displayed in Domesday Book, shows that the smaller and poorer manors of the cathedral clergy had a much higher proportion of slaves and bordars working on their lands than did the rich bishop on his large prosperous manors; and so too did sub-tenants, 'men of modest means'.[63] S.P.J. Harvey's analysis of the Domesday estates found too that they were more likely to have been devoted to exploitation of a home farm than to exploiting the rents and services of

61. H.S.A. Fox, 'Approaches to the adoption of the midland system' in *The Origins of Open-Field Agriculture*, ed. T. Rowley (1981), 64–111 at 100–1.
62. E.A. Kosminsky, *Studies in the Agrarian History of England in the Thirteenth Century* trans. R. Kisch (1956), 280–1.
63. J.D. Hamshere, 'Domesday Book: estate structures in the west midlands' in *Domesday Studies*, ed. J. Holt (1987), 155–82; 'The structure and profitability of the Domesday estate of the church of Worcester', *Landscape History* 7 (1985), 41–52.
64. S.P.J.Harvey, 'The extent and profitability of demesne agriculture in England in the later eleventh century' in *Social relations and ideas: essays in honour of R.H. Hilton*, ed. T.H. Aston, P.R. Coss, C. Dyer and J. Thirsk (1983), 45–72. The workforce as recorded in Domesday is discussed more fully at pp. 85–8 above. For the higher proportions of slaves on demesne manors in Domesday see J.S. Moore, 'Domesday slavery', *Anglo–Norman Studies* 11 (1988), 191–220.

the wider peasantry.[64] We cannot assume that this was true before the eleventh century, but it seems likely enough in the tenth by which time even small estates were divided into *inland* and other land. 'The inland belonging to it which Leofinc had' was added to a small estate of three hides at Newbold on Stour, Worcestershire, leased by Bishop Oswald in 991 to his thegn Eadric.[65] Others consisted of inland alone. Two ploughlands at Rottingdean, Sussex, held *in dominio* with two bordars, the 'inland of St Martin' at Canterbury of half a ploughland and seven bordars, and the countless small berewicks of the Danelaw which were entirely classed as inland, would simply have been large farms with a resident labour force, even though for Domesday's fiscal purposes they were entered there as manors.[66] Wills which 'set up' a favoured retainer on a small estate are likely to have provided him with a nucleus of slaves or freedpeople.

The small estate could be a fragmented one none the less. The bishop of Worcester's leases in the tenth century generally conveyed quite small amounts of land, between one and six hides, and Dyer tells us that they were generally on the edge of larger land-units. Small as they were, the landholdings conveyed were not always coherent blocks of land: 'two hides in two places' granted by Oswald to Æthelmær, for instance, lay half near his homestead at Compton and half at Marsh, and he was leased in addition 'the homestead at Bryne's enclosure ... and the croft ... to the east of the highway'.[67] Larger holdings in areas of scattered settlement may have been a scaled-down version of the multiple estate: a gift of fifteen hides at Knighton on Teme and Newnham, Worcestershire, in the late eighth century consisted of land at three places 'with their hamlets' (*cum villulis earum*).[68]

The inlands of small estates may have been islands of distinct husbandry practice. Domesday provides us with a certain amount of evidence that lords may have used a larger plough team than their peasant neighbours. This is a possible interpretation of the fact that on some manors the *villani* had only half the number of plough teams per hide that the lord had on land *in dominio*. A larger team may imply that lords used a heavier plough and arranged their arable to use it to the best advantage, creating systems based on longer furrows.[69] This may have been connected with a shift – at present only barely perceptible in the evidence – of a move to more cereal production over stock farming. Specialization may have become possible on these intensively

65. Robertson, *Charters*, LXVII, 138–9.
66. *DB* I, 26c, 2b.
67. Robertson, *Charters*, LXV, 134–5.
68. BCS 1007 (S 1185).
69. E. Miller, *The Abbey and Bishopric of Ely: the social history of an ecclesiastical estate from the tenth to the early fourteenth century* (1951), 45; J. Langdon, *Horses, Oxen and Technological Innovation: the use of draught animals in English farming from 1066 to 1500* (1986), 32, 69 (n. 114), 69–74, 241–4. Lennard, *Rural England*, 349–57, assumes a demesne team of eight oxen to be the norm, and shows that the average *villanus* holding had about three plough beasts.

cultivated lands. The 'wheat land' on a manor leased by the bishop of Worcester at Kempsey was a discrete and specialized arable enterprise.[70] Stenton found that the inland furlongs of Lincolnshire lords lay separately from those of their tenants, and lords can be found deliberately consolidating their arable and separating it off from that of the bulk of their tenants.[71] Some late Saxon inlands retained their identity even when engulfed by extensive medieval common field systems. The medieval demesne lands at Higham Ferrers appear in D. Hall's study of Northamptonshire field systems as distinct elements, near to the original seigneurial sites and separate from the village's common fields (Fig. 21). The township of Buscot represents a late Saxon seigneurial field system and the area around the village of Higham itself is also a block of seigneurial land which Hall considers may be a continuation of a late Roman estate.[72] In 904 the *innlond* on a small estate of one hide leased at Aston Magna, Gloucestershire, to the bishop of Worcester's efficient and obedient reeve Wulfsige was said to be completely surrounded by a ditch and must have been cultivated separately.[73] Figure 22 shows the village of Aston Magna as it is today: the odd road pattern may reflect the old inland enclosure.

Did the holder of bookland have rights over the peasantry on his or her land which did not exist there before it was 'booked'? The answer would have important implications for rural social relations, but what bookright really meant to the relationship of landlords and peasants has remained an open question. It has always seemed significant that 'land and men' were routinely conveyed together from one owner to another, whether by charter or by will. Werfrith, Bishop of Worcester, leased two hides of land at Elmstone Hardwicke, Gloucestershire, to his kinswoman about 900. This small estate was part of five hides which the bishop had himself leased for three lives. It had formerly belonged to the minster at Cleeve. Originally Worcester was to have it at the end of the lease, but Werfrith arranged for it to be returned to Cleeve 'for the bishopric'. He made various stipulations: his tenant had the right to cut wood in 'the wood that the *ceorls* use' and leased the '*ceorls*' grove' separately as well (a reminder of the great economic importance of woodland). He made further provisions about the remaining two hides: these, with Elmstone wood *and the ceorls*, 'shall

70. Cereal production: D. Banham, 'The knowledge and use of food plants in Anglo-Saxon England' (Ph.D. thesis, University of Cambridge, 1990), ch. 2. Kempsey: Robertson, *Charters*, LV.
71. F.M. Stenton, *Documents Illustrative of the Social and Economic History of the Danelaw from Various Collections*, British Academy Records of the Social and Economic History of England and Wales (1920).
72. D. Hall, 'The late Saxon countryside: villages and their fields' in *Anglo-Saxon Settlements*, ed. D. Hooke (1988), 99–122 at 113–15.
73. Robertson, *Charters*, XVIII; *pace* H.P.R. Finberg, *Early Charters of the West Midlands* (1961), 52, who identifies the *dic* with an earth bank still visible, within which are the remains of a large motte.

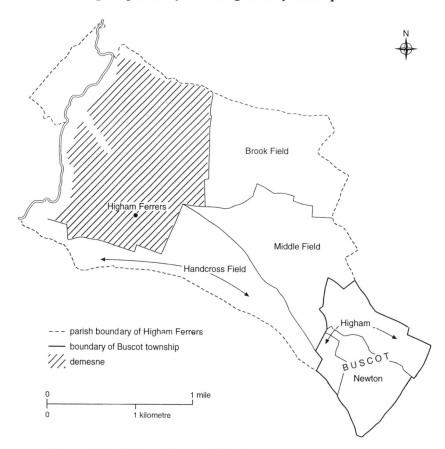

Figure 21   Higham Ferrers, Northhamptonshire in the later middle ages. Two blocks of seigneurial land are shown: the demesne surrounding the village, and Buscot, probably late Saxon in origin, held by the lessees of the demesne. *Source*: after D. Hall, 'The late Saxon countryside: villages and their fields', in *Anglo-Saxon Settlements*, ed. D. Hooke (1988), 99–122, fig. 5.8 at 114.

belong to Prestbury'.[74] These rather long-winded arrangements about two fairly small pieces of land certainly show that *ceorls*, like woods and hides, could be assigned to one landholding or another. Lords undoubtedly had the power to shift their inland tenants and workers about their estates, as we have seen with the *geburs* of Hatfield and Wouldham.[75] But it would not be sensible to assume that to make provisions about the peasantry on an estate in itself implied their

74.   BCS 559 (S 1415); BCS 560 (S 1283); Robertson, *Charters*, XVI at 28–9; Dyer, *Lords and Peasants*, 34.
75.   See pp. 81–4 above.

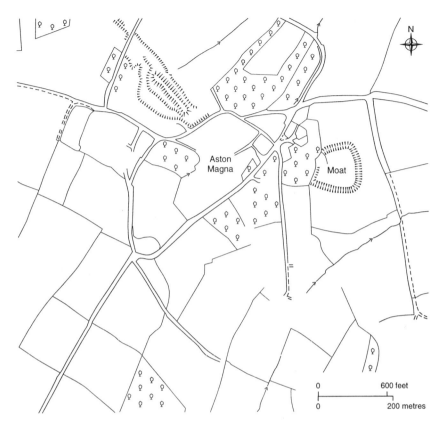

Figure 22   Seigneurial site and possible inland: Aston Magna, Gloucestershire. The odd road pattern may enclose the inland, said in a lease of 904 to be 'surrounded by a ditch'. The moat probably enclosed a post-Conquest seigneurial building.

subjection, any more than does a modern landlord's ability to convey property with sitting tenants. Peasants' relationship with landlords was subject to a spectrum of dependence and independence.

Bibury, Gloucestershire ('Beaga's *burh*') bears the name of its eighth-century owner; Woolstone, Berkshire ('Wulfric's *tun*') was named from the Wulfric who in 960 put together a handsome estate of seventeen vills in Berkshire, Hampshire and Sussex.[76] Place-names of this sort, formed by adding the ending *-tun* or *burh* to a personal name in the genitive case, have been widely interpreted as evidence of 'manorialization'. They are so obviously proprietorial, it has been argued, that they must imply 'manorial overlordship' over a whole estate and all the people on it. Stenton believed that they had only

---

76. Gelling, *Signposts*, 178, 181.

gradually taken on this meaning, having evolved from the farm and homestead of the 'great man and leading settler' after whom they were named. This led him to argue that 'the seignorial idea [was] a primitive force in the organization of rural society' – a conclusion at odds with his belief in the existence of a largely free peasantry. Since Stenton wrote this it has been shown that very many examples of this kind of place-name date not from the early settlement period but from grants to identifiable individuals from the eighth to eleventh century, and that these people were people of the thegnly class, very often servants of the king receiving their reward in bookland.[77] But were they 'manorial lords'? Certainly Beaga and Wulfric *owned*, respectively, the land they held at Bibury and Woolstone and were its lady and lord. Wulfric may indeed have been in some sense the 'founder' of Woolstone: the village, as B. Yorke has pointed out, straddles the former boundary between the two parts of his estate and so was probably created after he came into possession of both parts.[78] It is one of a string of similar (*-tun*) villages along the foot of the Berkshire Downs. Certainly in time the *tun* came to stand for the manor which bore its name: Woolstone would be known in the middle ages as 'the manor of Woolstone' and its inhabitants as tenants of that manor, just as many of its companion villages are probably named from their late Anglo-Saxon owners. Yet we need to be careful not to import back into the ninth and tenth centuries the fully fledged manorialism of a later era. It is more useful to try to envisage what ownership of a *tun* would have meant at the time.

A cautious interpretation of this important category of place-names, which does not depend on any pre-existing notion of 'the manor', is to treat them as topographic and descriptive. It is important to bear in mind that the *tun* and *burh* element in these place-names is not by itself indicative of rights over land and people: we have already noted the many Charltons or *ceorls' tuns*. The word *tun* had quite a wide variety of uses, but they nearly all involve nothing more than the enclosure of a fairly small area with a building or buildings inside it, and they occur in various contexts, by no means all of them seigneurial. The cognate Germanic and Scandinavian words have this connotation too, as does the common use of 'town' in rural Devon to mean a farmstead or a small collection of houses, a 'tunstall'. OE *burg*, *burh* seems generally to indicate a more impressively built place: Ekwall gives 'fort', 'town', and it is often attached to sites with stone buildings or their remains.[79] From this perspective we can regard the *tuns* and *burhs* which gave their names to so many English villages as in origin just what their names suggest: a building or buildings within an area of enclosed land or space. With the development of nucleated settlement as the dominant form in large parts of England they came to

---

77. *Ibid.*, 180–4; Aston, 'Origins of the manor', 38–40.
78. B. Yorke, *Wessex in the Early Middle Ages* (1996), 272.
79. Ekwall, *English Place-Names* and Bosworth and Toller, s.v. *tun, burg*.

be villages. The early *tuns* of the seigneurial class with which this chapter is concerned were the embryos of villages: the manorial curias and inlands of their eponymous owners. They must have been a dominant feature in the landscape, with their substantial domestic and farm buildings, their inland workers' and tenants' housing, and in many cases their church. A later chapter will explore how these seigneurial core areas became overtaken by later developments in village morphology.[80]

Anglo-Saxon charters convey land, not manors, and the extent to which, and the processes by which, this land was 'manorialized', in the sense that all its peasant inhabitants were subjected to the will of the owner and involved in the cultivation of his land for his profit, needs to be discussed in the light of a much wider range of evidence than that of place-names alone. Grants in bookright might well alter rural social relations, for the growth of the private estate brought new demands on land and people. These demands affected the inland and the warland peasantry in different ways. An earlier chapter has investigated the position of the inland peasantry. The bundle of rights over the warland peasantry which had belonged to the era of extensive lordship, suitable for the provisioning and maintenance of royal centres and the hunting and feeding of kings, was inappropriate for the owner of a small bookland estate, living at his manorial centre and supported from the produce of his inland. They were even increasingly inappropriate for the needs of the large lay landowner, with a scattered estate in many counties but a single principal dwelling, his *heafod-botl*.

Probably by the Conquest the system of *feorm*, which needed a large bureaucracy to administer it and a well-organized transport system to deliver it, was only really viable as a way of provisioning the major religious houses and the courts of king and earls. *Feorm* survived in the form of regular food farms to the great monasteries, and people late in the twelfth century could still remember the king's supplies being brought to court, but many payments of *feorm* due on lesser estates were given a money value, and recorded and priced in Domesday as 'customary payments', *consuetudines*.[81] We have already seen how the more 'public' services of the warland, those connected with court attendance and military service, remained in the public domain so to speak, performed through the agencies of the county or the franchise-holder.[82] Many more were commuted into cash payments (also recorded as 'custom' in Domesday), and as money payments in the manorial accounts of the thirteenth-century estate, hunting service appearing as *hunteneselver* and so on.[83]

---

80. See chapter 9 below.
81. For *consuetudines* as an important component of manorial revenues in Domesday: D. Roffe, 'From thegnage to barony: sake and soke, title and tenants-in-chief', *Anglo–Norman Studies* 12 (1989), 157–76.
82. See chapter 4 above.
83. N. Neilson, *Customary Rents* in Oxford Studies in Social and Legal History 2 (1910).

These commuted warland services provided a cash income, but to the small landowner it was agricultural services that mattered more. The process is entirely impossible to date, but there seems to have been over time a move to systematize and extend them. Boon works, it has been argued, were relics of the era of extensive lordship, evolving to meet the needs of royal vills and the central places of small *scirs*. With the proliferation of small landholdings they came to be reorganized and more fully exploited. The smaller his inland population, the more a landowner depended on this vital supply of labour which could be summoned up when needed. The need for labour at the crucial operations of the agricultural year, harvest, haymaking, and spring and winter ploughing could not be met by the inland workforce alone unless it was an exceptionally large one. Nor were there often enough peasant plough teams on the inland for the demands of heavy demesne ploughing. The ploughing, haulage and carrying service owed from the warland peasants, giving the lord access to their valuable draught stock, was particularly valuable. The arables of a small *tun* such as Woolstone could well have relied largely on the ploughs of its warland farmers, who were working huge fields on the slopes of the Downs when Wulfric got the land.[84] Boon works seem to have been extended in circumstances in which lords had had to bargain for labour. The very detailed provisions in post-Conquest records about the circumstances in which boons are to be performed – when the work should begin and end, how many men should be sent, how much food should be provided – may well have evolved over a long period of time and as a result of a long series of bargains.[85]

We have seen that the proliferation of small estates brought into being a distinct kind of place, the seigneurial *tun* or *burh*, and a class of landowner supported by inlands and their distinctively dependent inhabitants. The warland farmers of the locality were becoming increasingly involved in the seigneurial economy. But although these smaller Anglo-Saxon estates have much in common with the small manor of the post-Conquest period, it would be a mistake to draw the parallel too closely. It is more illuminating to recognize in them a social form *sui generis*. Certainly on the firm foundations of the security of tenure given by bookland, a long lease from a local monastic house, or part of their family's hereditary land, the lesser landlords of later Anglo-Saxon England were able to build their 'magnate farmsteads' and strike the roots of the seigneurial life. They farmed their inlands using the regular labour of their inland workforce of bordars, slaves and *geburs*, and called in the boons from the warland farmers at haymaking and harvest time. The 'ploughs of the men' as

---

84. Hooke, 'Anglo-Saxon settlements in the Vale of the White Horse', 129–43.
85. A. Jones, 'Harvest customs and labourers' perquisites in southern England 1150–1350: the corn harvest', *AgHR* 35 (1977), 14–22 and 'Harvest customs and labourers' perquisites in southern England 1150–1350: the hay harvest', *ibid.* 98–107.

Domesday puts it, worked on their arable for a few days a year and the teams of the 'men' took care of many of their transport needs. Nevertheless complexes of buildings like those at Goltho and Raunds, curias with their intensively farmed inlands and tied inland labour force, may have remained for a long time seigneurialized islands in a landscape still largely occupied by the holdings of independent peasant farmers. It was to take important changes in the economy and geographical context of these farmers, and in their social and legal position, before most landlords could draw on the labour of a completely dependent and 'manorialized' local peasantry, the 'villeins' of the twelfth and thirteenth centuries (and in many parts of England they were never able to do so). It was a long-drawn-out and many-sided process that was to remodel the agrarian landscape to suit seigneurial needs, and it took the great upheaval of the post-Conquest land settlement to bring about the conditions for the final stages of that remodelling to take place.

7   Anglo-Norman landlords

> So foreigners grew wealthy with the spoils of England, whilst her own sons were either shamefully slain or driven as exiles to wander hopelessly through foreign kingdoms.[1]

So Orderic Vitalis, English-born monk of St Evroul in Normandy who wrote early in the twelfth century, perhaps with divided loyalties, described the Conqueror's disposition of his new territories. In the upheaval of the Conquest land settlement 'the king granted his land by the most profitable deals that he could make' (*swa deorlice to male*) in the words of the *Anglo-Saxon Chronicle*. This set in train a series of disputes, evictions, negotiations and lawsuits which were still reverberating 20 years later. It is not only in the view of contemporaries that what happened in England after 1066 appears 'a tenurial revolution', the prelude to the virtually total dispossession of the Anglo-Saxon landholding class in favour of new Norman lords. A computer-assisted analysis of the information Domesday gives about the changes in landownership concludes that by 1086 'Norman lords, with their retainers in tow, [had] gained the bulk of England's farms and villages – holdings which had, until the Conquest, supported an altogether different aristocracy'.[2] Over the following centuries these holdings came not only to support new lords, but to deliver that support in a new way.

Radical as William's large-scale grants were, even more land changed hands unofficially and by violence. Norman lords once granted land in a county or an area were able to consolidate their holdings by absorbing the land of lesser men. This was sometimes done legitimately, by strategic marriage and perhaps by purchase, but the many examples of 'taking' land show that outright seizure was common.[3] People were taken as well as land, simply annexed to new lords. Others found it prudent to transfer their allegiance. Many East Anglian sokemen once commended to an Anglo-Saxon lord or monastery, not only those who had been his *antecessor*'s men, became

---

1. *The Ecclesiastical History of Orderic Vitalis*, ed. and trans. M. Chibnall (1969), IV, ii. at 267.
2. R. Fleming, *Kings and Lords in Conquest England* (1991), 107-8.
3. M. Chibnall, *Anglo-Norman England* (1986), 23-34; Fleming, *Kings and Lords*, ch. 6.

the commended men of a powerful newcomer. The splitting up of old estates and the transfer of commended men is particularly visible in the eastern counties. In the vill of Abington Pigotts, Cambridgeshire, the land of four pre-Conquest lords went to five new ones, and the men who had commended themselves to Archbishop Stigand all went to different lords.

It was by this building up of estates and power bases at the local level that the Norman landowners dispossessed, piecemeal, the English thegnage, while William broke up the great English aristocratic estates wholesale. Domesday Book records the almost total dispossession of the Anglo-Saxon landholding class of the first rank, and the virtual dispossession of the thegnage. It also records a drastically changed balance of power between the king and the aristocracy: there was no Norman landowner who had anything like the largest Anglo-Saxon estates. Nine of the wealthiest together, it has been estimated, had only 80 per cent of what the Godwinesons had held. None held a really commanding advantage, in land, over his rivals in any county. Even the richest received a much lower income from their lands than had their predecessors. By contrast, the royal demesne was now huge. The king had twothirds of all the land held by royal and aristocratic families combined, and was to get still more when the land of rebel lords was forfeited.[4]

The year 1066 brought not only defeat but a purveyance problem on a nationwide scale. Over time a quota of knights came to be demanded from tenants-in-chief, including the religious houses. A great aristocratic household could afford to house its crowd of knights, but the eventual solution – and one which offered the knightly class a chance to put down roots and establish families in England, and thus to become more politically reliable – was to provide them with land. Five hides was the notional holding reckoned to supply a knight, but the actual military service was performed by much lowlier figures than this: they too needed land. This 'landing' of the army brought a category of knights into the landholding class who were more self-consciously an 'order' but were not perhaps far removed in status and culture from the thegns they widely replaced.[5]

Where it did not result in eviction, the creation of landholdings for Norman barons and knights resulted in a widespread diminution of personal status for the English landowning class. The fate of the English landowner varied very much from county to county: in Middlesex the lay landlords of 1066 had all been dispossessed by 1086, but their counterparts in Gloucestershire and Worcestershire survived. Seventy Warwickshire sub-tenants in 1086 had English

---

4. Fleming, *Kings and Lords*, 120-1 (Abington Pigotts) and ch. 7.
5. Chibnall, *Anglo-Norman England*, 28–35; S.P.J. Harvey, 'The knight and the knight's fee in England', *Past and Present* 49 (November 1970), 3–43, reprinted in *Peasants, Knights and Heretics*, ed. R.H. Hilton (1976), 133–73.

names and may have retained their lands on terms.[6] Inter-marriage between the two races brought an Anglo-Norman gentry into being. It included on its fringes the many English lesser thegns of whom Domesday records that 'they had a hall' before the Conquest in a vill now part of a Norman fee, and who hung on as tenants of the land they had formerly owned.

A powerful incentive to take part in the campaign in England was the hope of profit, and William's companions expected to see it. It may be that the first generation thought of their Norman lands as their patrimony, their English as an opportunity for quick gains. There was pressure from above to maximize returns. The *Chronicle* talks of lessees of royal manors (often their previous owners) who, charged a high rent themselves, recouped the cost from their tenants: the king 'recked not how very sinfully the reeves got it from poor men'. Agricultural returns are unlikely to have been the first resort of lords seeking to profit from their new estates.[7] They could make more immediate returns from their lands from swingeing tallages. These forced payments appear in Domesday in addition to the regular 'value' of a manor. *Taille* was well known and well hated in Normandy, principally as a forced payment from towns. We do not know exactly how it was raised in England from places like Spalding in Lincolnshire which gave £30, or Folkingham and Bolingbroke in the same county, giving £50 and £80 respectively.[8]

Many Norman incomers, though they were granted wide estates, must have found that their most valuable rewards for supporting their duke in his enterprise were the profits of office and justice. Public office in a locality, as sheriff, custodian of royal castles, or forest officer may have been the quickest route to an immediate fortune. Valued servants like goldsmiths and huntsmen too had their reward. S.P.J. Harvey has described the managerial policies of many smaller landowners among the first generation of Norman incomers: the most immediate routes to improved manorial profits were probably to levy swingeing tallages, to rent out assets such as mills and meadowland, perhaps to increase flocks and herds for the market.[9]

Leasing and lessees

For the larger landlords to lease out their manors was unquestionably the favoured option. Leasing parts of large estates for a fixed rent or

---

6. R.W. Finn, *The Norman Conquest and its Effects on the Economy* (1970), 126–39.
7. Chibnall, *Anglo-Norman England*, 142-3; R.V. Lennard, *Rural England 1086–1135; a study of social and agrarian conditions* (1959), 155, 157 and n. 1.
8. Lennard, *Rural England*, 216.
9. S.P.J. Harvey, 'The extent and profitability of demesne agriculture in England in the later eleventh century' in *Social Relations and Ideas: essays in honour of R.H. Hilton*, ed. T.H. Aston, P.R. Coss, C. Dyer and J. Thirsk (1983), 45–72; 'Domesday England' in *Ag. Hist.* II, 45–136 at 85–95.

'farm' had, as we have seen, been an accepted management strategy since the eighth century.[10] Domesday Book shows that leasing was widespread and routine in the eleventh century: the 'values' that are recorded for each manor are probably an estimate of the sum for which it could be let.[11] The lessees of the eleventh and twelfth centuries, who took whole manors 'at farm', included some substantial people who controlled substantial collections of property, built up by a mixed strategy in which leasing, inheriting and marrying property all played a part. They shared the lifestyle and attitudes of the landholding class of which they were a part. What these people did with their estates would affect many lives.

Hereditary tenure for a fixed rent 'in fee farm' was a widespread form of leasing used by members of this class, and a body of law was beginning to evolve to deal with the mass of disputes and problems to which widespread leasing gave rise.[12] Tenants who took land on lease did all they could to hold on to it, and though landlords did all they could to get it back, a *de facto* title often came to be established. This striving for permanent tenure was probably felt at all levels of society, by the great landlord as well as the small farmer. The struggle for permanent possession came up against a shift in attitudes to leasing on the part of landowners. The first thing to change was the length of leases. It was a comparatively new arrangement in the twelfth century to lease land for a fixed rent to a *firmarius* (lessee) for a term of years, and many landlords kept up the time-honoured practice of leases for lives, but where it did come in, it was an influence for change. There was competition for land, bringing an upward pressure on rents. If they could get them, landlords charged substantial entry fines or *gersumae* and higher rents than the Domesday 'values'. This was the policy of Odo, bishop of Bayeux, who had received a large tract of Kent and rented out his manors for rents well over their 'values'; these practices seem to be routine. In order to make a profit, Odo's *firmarii*, like Robert Latimer who farmed several of his Kentish manors for a great deal more than they were 'worth' and whose total rent amounted to at least £114, had to extract at least that large sum each year from his lands.[13] Pressing lessees for higher rents could be an effective spur to a more effective exploitation of manorial assets. Although it is sometimes seen as a sign of economic stagnation, under conditions of growing population and increased demand the leasing system could be a potent force for economic change and growth.[14] Estates in both England and northern France experienced sometimes startling growth

10. Lennard, *Rural England*, chs 5 and 6.
11. E. Miller and J. Hatcher, *Medieval England: rural society and economic change 1086-1348* (1978), 204–13; Lennard, *Rural England*, 105–212.
12. *Leges Henrici Primi*, ed. L.J. Downer (1972), 56.1–3.
13. Lennard, *Rural England*, 113–14.
14. M.M. Postan, 'A note on the farming out of manors', *EcHR*, 2nd series 31 (1978), 521–5 at 524; R.J. Faith, 'Demesne resources and labour rent on the manors of St Paul's Cathedral 1066-1222', *EcHR* 47 (1994), 657–78 .

when managed in this way, and seasoned administrators like Abbot Suger of St Denis recommended leases as advantageous, provided they were short and the rent could be adjusted regularly to take account of rising values.[15] Traditions of aggressive and efficient estate management were being developed at Winchester and Bury St Edmunds. At Bury before 1200 Abbot Samson brought in a much more businesslike regime towards the abbey's lessees. He was careful to specify the live and dead stock and farm buildings on the manors he leased. It was good twelfth-century practice to do this and, when the lease came to an end, to make another thorough check on the stock and revenues, based on enquiries from the herdsmen and other farm servants, who would have been expected to produce tallies recording their sales and receipts and the numbers of different kinds of animals.[16] Keeping accurate records of what was leased was an important part of good management. When ecclesiastical properties were let, as were the manors of St Paul's throughout most of the twelfth century, their ready supply of literate men made it possible to keep accurate records of leases, of the stock and crops and the state of repair of the buildings on the various properties. The careful supervision by the canons of St Paul's, who monitored their assets, shows that the manors at lease throughout the twelfth century experienced in some cases a rise in leasable value and in most an expansion and improvement in their demesnes.[17] In fact, it was greatly to the advantage of any lessee to maximize his output over and above his fixed rent or farm. In many cases the *firmarius* of a church estate may have been nearer to a bailiff than a lessee, responsible for seeing that the 'farms' or rents were paid and for carrying out the landlord's instructions. It became easier to monitor receipts when they began to be paid in money. Food farms began to be commuted for money rents before the Conquest on royal lands – the huge sums that the sheriffs paid for these 'farms' are a sign of their value – and Canterbury, Ely and Bury had all begun to take their farms in cash by the 1170s.[18] A common way of administering a monastic estate came to be to assign the revenues from particular manors to individual officers of the community or to the department of the house which they administered. And there was a growing tendency to assign a separate collection of properties to the cathedral chapter on the one hand, and the bishop on the other. In non-monastic cathedrals the members of the chapter were often assigned individual properties as prebends, from which they drew rents for their support. Obedientiaries, prebendaries and members of cathedral chapters were recruits to the Anglo-Norman landlord class, increasing the number of people who had an active interest in maximizing returns.

---

15. G. Duby, *The Early Growth of the European Economy: warriors and peasants from the seventh to the twelfth century*, trans. H.B. Clarke (1974), 215.
16. Miller and Hatcher, *Medieval England*, 206; *Leges Henrici Primi*, 56.3.
17. Faith, 'Demesne resources'.
18. Miller and Hatcher, *Medieval England*, 207.

The Anglo-Norman economy and landlord policies

There was evidently room for growth in the late eleventh-century countryside. Looking at estates with an eye for what the king could extract from his tenants-in-chief, the Domesday commissioners came to them with a new perspective. S.P.J. Harvey has proposed that the Conqueror may well have had a new tax in mind, based on a much more accurate assessment of the cultivated ploughland.[19] The commissioners were asked to enquire 'whether more could be had than was accustomed to be had'. It is probably in response to this query that in reply they gave figures, in some circuits, for both the amount of arable in a manor, measured in the number of ploughlands (the amount of land that one team could plough in a year's cycle of husbandry) and the number of plough teams actually at work there.[20] In many manors they reported that there was spare arable capacity: there is land for so many ploughs but only so many are at work. On some Ely manors the actual plough-team strength was between 25 and 40 per cent of the potential.[21] Undercultivation, measured by this criterion, is very marked in the midlands and Yorkshire. There could be many different circumstances behind such a bald statement, not all related to real agrarian conditions. Thus apparent underexploitation was most marked in Devon and Cornwall, but this may simply be a result of the way that the commissioners recorded particular cultivation practices.

Historians have been inclined to take the Domesday assessments of plough-team capacity seriously as evidence of the underexploitation that was evidently a feature of many eleventh-century estates. What were its causes? We know almost nothing about how large lay estates were run before the Conquest but a telling analysis by S.P.J. Harvey of their structure as it appears in Domesday Book shows that by 1086 some were strikingly 'demesne oriented'. Some magnates' estates, particularly the lands of the Godwin family, had large inlands. In Domesday terminology these appear as home farms detectable by the comparatively high ratio of ploughs at work there *in dominio*, 'in lordship', to ploughs owned by the peasants, *villanorum*. These supported impressive centres, at which a large household and resident soldiers could be fed and all the expensive business of the aristocratic life kept up. The Norman lords who took over such properties thus acquired agricultural enterprises which had been geared up primarily for direct production, and the castles which they built on estates such

---

19. S.P.J. Harvey, 'Domesday Book and Anglo-Norman governance', *TRHS*, 5th series 25 (1975), 175–93; 'Taxation and the ploughland in Domesday Book' in *Domesday Book: a reassessment*, ed. P.H. Sawyer (1985), 86–103.
20. H.C. Darby, *Domesday England* (1986 edn), ch. 8; Harvey, 'Extent and profitability of demesne agriculture', 64–5.
21. Darby, *Domesday England*, fig. 38 at 102; E. Miller, *The Abbey and Bishopric of Ely: the social history of an ecclesiastical estate from the tenth to the early fourteenth century* (1951), 40.

as these were merely the continental expression and expansion of a way of life already well established in the upper reaches of Anglo-Saxon society.

By contrast many estates in 1086 were poorly supplied with demesne assets. Some had actually lost land overall in the last centuries of Anglo-Saxon England. Many monasteries, for example, had seen the great estates they had built up in the tenth century whittled away. All tenants-in-chief had now to provide for quotas of knights and had lost, or were about to lose, the land they granted them as fees. The huge estate of the bishop of Lincoln in Oxfordshire, for instance, was diminished by the 30 hides his *milites* had in Dorchester, the 9 in Great Milton and 25 in Cropredy.[22] As we have seen, long before the Conquest very many multiple estates had fragmented into smaller holdings supporting a mass of lesser landlords. In the England of 1086 landlords with large agricultural resources kept in hand were a minority. Many were under-equipped, with no more seigneurial plough teams than a handful of substantial peasant families could have commanded. Manors with only two or three ploughs at work on the home farm seem to have been very common, there were many with no home farm at all, and others where a group of peasants had taken over the inland for a fixed rent and ran it themselves. Although there were a few landlords renowned for their efficiency and knowledge of agriculture, it was not until the twelfth century that improvements such as better stock production became widespread.[23]

Into this somewhat underdeveloped countryside there burst a greatly increased consumer demand and a pressure for improved revenues from land. Its impact was felt at many levels.[24] That this demand was met is suggested by the physical evidence of an expanding population, a very considerable amount of new building, the ability of the economy to sustain an unproductive ruling elite and to export money abroad. The most compelling need in the nearly three hundred years between the Conquest and the Black Death was to feed more people. There are a great many problems attached to the exercise of turning the information given in Domesday Book into any credible figure of national population. Estimates have ranged between 1.1 and 2.5 millions, but historians have been broadly in agreement that the period between 1086 and the early fourteenth century saw a steep rise in England's population, possibly a threefold increase. This population growth had many causes, perhaps first among them the apparent absence of serious epidemic disease in England before the plagues

---

22. Harvey, 'The knight and the knight's fee', 14–23; *DB* I, 155a–c.
23. Harvey, 'Domesday England', 118-21; Lennard, *Rural England*, 81; R.S. Hoyt, 'Farm of the manor and community of the vill in Domesday Book', *Speculum* 30 (1955), 147–69.
24. E. Miller, 'England in the twelfth and thirteenth centuries: an economic contrast?', *EcHR* 2nd series 24 (1971), 1–14.

that hit it in the fourteenth and fifteenth centuries.[25] Although there is evidence of mounting pressure on the land which may well have resulted in malnutrition, it is not until the second decade of the fourteenth century that England experienced a significant agrarian crisis. Though under strain, the agrarian economy was evidently able to sustain the demands put upon it, in other words to feed the people.

We cannot measure the 'size' of the twelfth-century economy in terms of its Gross National Product. Yet in producing a surplus which supported seigneurial revenues with expensive tastes and the demands of rulers inclined to expensive wars abroad, while at the same time supporting a growing peasant population, agriculture in the eleventh and twelfth centuries must surely have been by and large productive, efficient and expanding. This is easier to state than to prove, and such an optimistic view runs contrary to the view of M.M. Postan: that medieval agriculture suffered drastically from diminishing returns during this period.[26] But what is at issue here is the relationship of lords and peasants, and what can be demonstrated is how pressures to increase returns from land in the twelfth century urged much more ambitious policies on landlords of all kinds, leading many to extend cultivation and exploit their resources, including their tenants, more efficiently. It was the combined needs of the seigneurial economy to produce higher returns and of the peasant economy to feed more people that together created the dynamic growth of the twelfth century. Here some seigneurial policies will be explored before we turn to examine their interaction with the changing peasant economy.

Current views of twelfth-century landlord policy are very much influenced by a series of important articles by the late M.M. Postan. J. Hatcher and E. Miller have incorporated the basic theses of Postan in their overall view of the twelfth- and thirteenth-century economy, and the 'Postanian' view has received wide support.[27] Postan looked at the agrarian scene from the point of view of the management strategies adopted by the great ecclesiastical estates, and his argument centres on a supposed retreat by these landlords from the direct exploitation of their demesnes. The actual area of demesnes, he proposed, was 'contracting or even dissolving' as lords leased their demesne land either piecemeal to manorial tenants or *en bloc* to more substantial lessees who took on the entire manor as a going concern.

---

25. J.L. Bolton, *The Medieval English Economy 1150–1500* (1980), 47–58; H.E. Hallam, 'Population movements in England 1086-1350' in *Ag. Hist.* II, 508–93; Darby, *Domesday England*, ch. 3; Miller and Hatcher, *Medieval England*, 28–33; R.M. Smith, 'Human resources' in *The Countryside of Medieval England*, ed. G. Astill and A. Grant (1988), 188–212 at 189–90.
26. M.M. Postan, *The Medieval Economy and Society* (1972), ch. 4.
27. M.M. Postan, 'The chronology of labour services', *TRHS* 4th series 20 (1937), 169–93; 'Glastonbury estates in the twelfth century', *EcHR* 2nd series 5 (1953), 358-67; 'Glastonbury estates in the twelfth century: a reply', *ibid.* 9 (1956), 106–18, reprinted in M.M. Postan, *Essays on Medieval Agriculture and General Problems of the Medieval Economy* (1973), at 89–106, 249–61 and 261–77; Miller and Hatcher, *Medieval England*, 204–10.

There were many reasons why ecclesiastical estates in particular were lagging in the efficient cultivation of the arable of their inlands and bartons, the land classed in Domesday as *in dominio*. We should not rule out a culture of inherent conservatism as one reason why although few landlords were ultimately unaffected by the quickening economic climate, large ecclesiastical estates remained for a long time apparently immune from these pressures. There is a culture of monasticism which is relevant here. On the old-established monastic estates consumption, not efficient agriculture, had long dictated supply and many of the stable monastic communities had been content to receive food farms that had not changed for generations. In fact some old-fashioned ecclesiastics may have retained a tradition that a sufficiency, not a profit, was all that their lands and tenants should provide for a community of Christian ascetics: at Ely 'the Old English abbots seem to have had scarcely any of the economic virtues', even though the abbey sold surplus stock locally later in the middle ages. The monks of Peterborough Abbey ran their lands throughout the middle ages primarily to feed themselves, not for profit.[28]

Another cause of delay in implementing change in estate management was the existence of a free food supply. Food rents brought in tenants' carts to the abbey kitchen door were an easy option. Abingdon Abbey was able to collect substantial supplies of cheese, hens and eggs and meat from tenants on its doorstep in the manor of Cumnor with the minimum of trouble.[29] Conservative lay landlords too in many parts of the country, such as Northumbria, preserved virtually intact the ancient supply systems which had supplied their ancestors. Nevertheless, even the archaic food farm system, under pressure, could lead to change. It was suggested long ago by the American historian Neilson, who studied the wide variety of manorial rents, that the demands of providing heavy food farms were 'of great influence in creating the rudiments of the demesne ... the distinction between land used to produce the lord's food and lord's land being easily lost.'[30]

That large ecclesiastical landowners were capable of pursuing effective exploitation of their demesne resources is shown on the bishop of Worcester's wide estates. Here a much more deliberate investment in direct exploitation of the land is found. On the bishopric manors kept in demesne (that is to say, not rented to sub-tenants or enfeoffed to military tenants) the average number of demesne plough teams was high – there were three or more on most, and seven at

---

28. Miller, *The Abbey and Bishopric of Ely*, 42; K. Biddick, *The Other Economy: pastoral husbandry on a medieval estate* (Berkeley 1989), 133.
29. *Chronicon monasterii de Abingdon*, ed. J. Stevenson, Rolls Series (2 vols, 1858), II, 322–44.
30. N. Neilson, *Customary Rents* in Oxford Studies in Social and Legal History 2 (1910), 18–19.

Fladbury and nine at Blockley. Here the best land on the entire estate was to be found, and in the largest concentrations.[31]

Postan's thesis that the twelfth century saw a widespread running down of demesnes was to a very considerable degree based on the evidence of the estates of Glastonbury Abbey and of the canons of St Paul's Cathedral, both of which have exceptionally full documentation for the period. They had very different histories. To take Glastonbury first. Certainly the abbey lost land overall soon after the Conquest as a result of enfeoffments, the creation of sub-tenancies and simple thieving. However, all its manors went up in value between the 1070s and 1086 and it had an exceptional commitment to demesne agriculture, measured by the high proportion of ploughs at work on the demesne to those of the peasantry. S.P.J. Harvey characterizes Glastonbury as 'the most widely interested in demesne agriculture in 1086' and the wealthiest of all the great abbeys.[32] This is not to say that it did not change course during the century that followed, but the evidence is of expansion rather than of decline. A survey of 1189 shows that the abbey was an active colonizer of new land, especially in the Somerset Levels. Much of the new land was leased rather than kept in hand, but within the area of the 'Twelve Hides' however, that is to say within the abbey's core of ancient inland, extensive assarts were being made, much of which was kept in hand by the abbey.[33] The size of the arable *in dominio* on almost all St Paul's manors was increased before 1222 by taking in land from the waste, mostly at the expense of woodland. Much assart was leased to manorial tenants but the demesne arable showed a significant growth on seven manors.[34] Peterborough Abbey seems to have been expanding its demesnes in the twelfth century. Despite half its properties being lost by sub-infeudation 'the abbey managed to maintain the value of its demesne propert[ies] after the conquest', increasing their value from £167 in 1086 to £284 in 1125, whereafter they remained stable for the next century. This was simply because their arable area increased: careful management and investment contributed to this result. But the abbey was a great colonizer, adding to its lands from the fens and from what King calls the 'colonisation of Northamptonshire', notably from Rockingham Forest.[35] C.C. Dyer's study of the bishop of Worcester's estates shows that there was loss of demesne through enfeoffments and the granting out of lands to tenants for cash rents. But there was also expansion, the result of assarting in Malvern and Feckenham

---

31. Harvey, 'Domesday England', 106; J.D. Hamshere, 'Domesday Book: estate structures in the west midlands' in *Domesday Studies*, ed. J. Holt (1987), 155–82.
32. Harvey, 'Domesday England', 107–8, quotation at 107.
33. H.E. Hallam, 'New settlement: southern England' in *Ag. Hist.* II, 203–24 at 219–22.
34. Faith, 'Demesne resources', 661–2.
35. E. King, *Peterborough Abbey 1086–1310: a study in the land market* (1973), 70–87.

forests.[36] Du Boulay has not found from his study of the archbishop of Canterbury's estate that the archiepiscopal demesnes were suffering any decline in the twelfth century, though they may have been stable rather than increasing.[37] On Ramsey Abbey's demesne manors Raftis found that 'there is a frequent picture of increase in productive capacity both as regards ploughs and villein labour ... increases of twenty to thirty per cent in ploughing potential on at least nine manors in the two generations after Domesday' and 'rapidly increasing values from the majority of ... manors' kept in hand, although Raftis was tentative about 'whether or no the actual demesne production was increased to a corresponding degree'.[38] There is 'no very clear evidence for a contraction of any magnitude in the size of the demesne' during the twelfth century on the bishop of Ely's estates: 'there is considerable evidence for an expansion of the demesne in the later part of that century'.[39] Episcopal demesnes also show a modest increase between 1066 and 1086 on some Oxfordshire manors, where Domesday notes that land has been added to the inland. At Banbury the bishop of Lincoln had land for ten ploughs and three hides *in dominio* besides the inland, at Eynsham land for three ploughs had been added to the two ploughlands of inland. Some of this new demesne may have been created out of what had been peasant farms. The bishop of Bayeux enlarged his demesnes in Oxfordshire at the expense of his warland tenants. At Stanton Harcourt he had taken a hide and a yardland of geldable land into his *dominium* by 1086. The bishop of Lincoln had ten hides in Banbury 'in addition to the inland': this looks very much like ten hides of land newly brought into demesne.[40]

The Conqueror himself provides the most dramatic example of inland created at a stroke. As a thank-offering for his victory he founded his abbey and created its inland, the *leuga* of surrounding land, and set it up with tenants. The use of the term *leuga* is a Norman innovation: it corresponds to the *banlieu* or area of special jurisdiction which surrounded the castle, and it is an interesting sidelight on the Anglo-Norman mentality that it was thought appropriate for a monastic house. The *leuga* was not geld-free as early monastic inlands had been, but it was rated more leniently than the surrounding countryside. Its tenants were directed to the supply of the abbey and were to all intents and purposes a tied dependent workforce settled for this purpose on new holdings. Of the other religious houses founded after the Conquest only the Cistercians, whose rule virtually imposed it, managed such a policy of totally reshaping the countryside, by

36. C.C. Dyer, *Lords and Peasants in a Changing Society: the estates of the bishopric of Worcester 680–1540* (1980), 61–3.
37. F.R.H. du Boulay, *The Lordship of Canterbury: an essay on medieval society* (1966), 203 and n. 8.
38. J.A. Raftis, *The Estates of Ramsey Abbey* (1957), 65, 58.
39. Miller, *Abbey and Bishopric of Ely*, 101.
40. *DB* I, 155b, 155c.

establishing in effect large blocks of demesne land close to their granges or farms worked by a permanent labour force under the supervision of lay brothers. This labour force was in part composed of servile peasant families who had been 'given' to them as pious gifts, much as land was, and who were housed in what C. Platt has called 'a diminutive *kraal* of peasant families'. Traces of this workers' housing can be found near the sites of several Yorkshire granges: unfortunately these late examples of settled inlands have not yet been investigated archaeologically.[41]

Most religious orders who founded English houses after the Conquest had to assemble estates piecemeal. The new orders, like the Hospitallers and Templars, had to buy their way into an already crowded land market and piece together an estate as best they could, building up estates composed of a patchwork of rents and small freeholds, a process in which small donors played an important part. Typically, they were initially more likely to depend on rent income than on working their own lands with tenant labour. None the less, the knights of St John set out to build up an agricultural demesne for themselves even from their fragmented holdings in north and central Essex.[42]

The numerous pious foundations by Norman lords reshaped local society, albeit often on a small scale. In 1088 Roger de Busli founded a Cluniac priory in Blyth, Nottinghamshire. At the time of Roger's foundation it had only four *villani* and four bordars, and was classed as sokeland of an adjoining manor. Roger created a little 'scrudland' or designated inland for the new foundation, giving them 'to build the church and feed and clothe the monks', the ploughing, reaping and carrying services owed on his small demesne there by the people of the neighbourhood. The more substantial endowments must have been the tithes he transferred to them from a widespread collection of places scattered over three counties and the licence he granted them to have a market at Blyth. The foundation charter of a Cistercian house at Revesby in 1142 shows the process of demesne formation in action. In 1086 Revesby had been a large manor with a population of sokemen and *villani*. Its demesne was tiny and consisted mostly of pasture. On the foundation of the abbey in 1142 William de Roumare, earl of Lincoln, gave the peasant inhabitants a choice when their land was needed for its grange: they could leave, or stay and receive land in return for their old holdings on the terms that William laid down. In the case of six who accepted new holdings, three agreed to do regular week-work, one to do a week's harvest work. Most preferred to leave.[43]

41. D. Knowles, *The Monastic Order in England* (2nd edn, 1962), chs 13, 14; C. Platt, *The Monastic Grange in Medieval England* (1969), 83–91, at 87; Battle: p. 91 above.
42. *The Cartulary of the Knights of St John of Jerusalem in England. Secunda Camera, Essex*, ed. M. Gervers (1982), lxxx.
43. F.M. Stenton, *Types of Manorial Structure in the Northern Danelaw* in Oxford Studies in Social and Legal History 2 (1910), 24–6, 92–3; E.A. Kosminsky, *Studies in the Agrarian History of England in the Thirteenth Century*, trans. R. Kisch (1956), 284.

Such developments are often impossible to date, but Norwich Cathedral provides a datable example of the creation of a central demesne and the effect this might have on the local social structure. When a community of monks was established at Norwich Cathedral around 1100 one of the properties given for its support was the vill of Martham, Norfolk. Martham has been intensively studied by W.H. Hudson, who has shown how the bishop created a demesne there, adding land from the nearby berewick of Hemsby, and turning the 36 freemen of Martham into villeins, working on his land.[44]

A similarly vigorous and determined new broom was wielded by the bishops of Durham. During the reign of William II they came into a great inheritance: the land which had been the territory of the Anglo-Saxon earls of Bamburgh and before them of the kings of Northumbria.[45] This had been the territory of Jolliffe's 'Northumbrian institutions' *par excellence*, where it was the *scir* and its customs, not the manor and the 'custom of the manor', that dictated relations between inhabitants and lords. By 1183 when the collection of surveys of the bishop's lands and the rents and services due from them which we now call Boldon Book was drawn up, a totally different picture appears. W.E. Kapelle has brought out the distinction on the Durham estates between those vills which had no demesne, and where by and large payments and services of the old Northumbrian type still generally prevailed, and those with demesnes. On the latter he finds that alongside the *scir* customs a 'tradition, which was an integral part of extensive demesne cultivation and had no discernible roots in Northumbrian custom, was in force'. It is the coincidence of *scir* custom with demesne-oriented labour services in the bishop's demesne vills that convinced Kapelle that these 'villages with big demesnes had once been typical Northumbrian villages'. Domesday Book does not cover Northumberland and Durham, and there is no secure way of dating the emergence of these large demesnes. Inlands at central places and berewicks had long been part of the *scir* economy, and the bishop's demesnes may have simply perpetuated and developed them.[46]

Probably the greatest opportunity was to create demesne from new land. Under the pressure of a growing population the area of cultivated land in England expanded dramatically after the Conquest, an expansion which was only to be checked in the early fourteenth

---

44. W.H. Hudson, 'Traces of primitive agricultural organisation as suggested by a survey of the manor of Martham, Norfolk (1101-1292)', *TRHS* 4th series 1 (1918), 28-58; 'The status of *villani* and other tenants in Danish East Anglia in pre-Conquest times', *ibid.* 4 (1921), 23-48.

45. P. Vinogradoff, *Villainage in England: essays in English mediaeval history* (1892), 354-6; J.E.A. Jolliffe, 'Northumbrian institutions', *EHR* 41 (1926), 1-42; G.H. Lapsley, 'Boldon Book', *VCH Durham*, I (1905), 259-321.

46. W.E. Kapelle, *The Norman Conquest of the North: a region and its transformation 1000-1135* (1979), 182-90 at 183, 185. For the influence of the new demesnes on settlement see chapter 9 below.

century. Peasant farmers like Wealden families had long been making piecemeal encroachments on the waste, and a slow and steady growth in woodland holdings may always have been part of the forest farming economy, but the twelfth and thirteenth centuries saw an extension of cultivation that was new in scope and nature. Land was won from the forest by felling and burning; from the uplands by turning summer 'shielings', where fields had not been seen since the Iron Age, into permanent farms.[47] Population did not increase to the same extent in all regions and new land fit for cultivation was not available everywhere, but where these conditions were present there was startling growth. In some parts of the Lincolnshire Fenland recorded households increased sixfold in the hundred years after 1086 and clearance in the Arden region of Warwickshire led to a fourfold increase in one hundred, Stoneleigh, between Domesday and 1279. Villages named from 'leahs' or woodland clearances, 'ends' and 'dens', field names with words for 'stump' and 'stock' witness the 'long process of attrition' which established farms in old woodland. The common-edge settlements of East Anglia, the drained marshlands of Kent, Sussex and Somerset, the boundary walls built to delimit the grazing rights of different communities on the Yorkshire moors are all testimony to this new frontier of cultivation. The 'journey to the frontier' was very largely the work of peasants and small landlords, but some very large-scale enterprises were undertaken by religious houses. By 'colonisation ... pushed to the limits of medieval technology' the abbeys of Crowland and Thorney took in and drained from the Fenland land which substantially increased the value of their manors.[48] The bishops of Ely 'were winning new land in all their manors' in Norfolk and Cambridgeshire from the fens and made large incursions into the forest in the soke of Somersham, and although most of it went into the hands of their peasant tenants the bishops' demesnes profited as well, as had those of Peterborough and Worcester, from forest clearance.[49] If the creation, expansion and exploitation of demesnes is taken as a criterion of growth, then the ecclesiastical estates and their lessees deserve a better reputation for economic dynamism than has often been allowed them.

To turn to lay landlords. If we were to single out principal physical impacts of the Norman Conquest on the English countryside, the appearance of the stone-built castle, manor house, and parish church would immediately come to mind: they are there today as witness. In the present context, the significance of the appearance and proliferation of

47. The chapters on 'New Settlement' in *Ag. Hist.* II give a great deal of detail, Miller and Hatcher, *Medieval England*, 26–45, a good summary. Regional studies include P. Brandon and B. Short, *The South East from AD 1000* (1990), 49–56; A. Everitt, *Continuity and Colonization: the evolution of Kentish settlement* (1986), part 3.
48. S. Raban, *The Estates of Thorney and Crowland: a study in medieval monastic land tenure* (1977), ch. 5 at 89.
49. Miller, *Abbey and Bishopric of Ely*, 96–9.

the stone-built church and manor house in the twelfth-century economy is the investment they represented in non-agricultural materials and specialist labour. To put it simply, a tenth-century timber hall could probably have been built from materials and by skills available locally – indeed we know that peasants could be summoned to do just such work. To build in stone in the new Norman styles required cash and expertise. As the parish church represents an investment by both landlords and parishioners, it may be taken as some kind of a measure of their joint capacity to invest whether in money or in land. The glebe at Stonham, Suffolk, had been 'given by nine free men for the good of their souls', and the local people gave 30 acres for their church at Stifford in Essex. The 'great rebuilding' of a multitude of parish churches, albeit in a rather old-fashioned style at first, is a witness to a corporate investment no less impressive for being as yet unquantified. It is significant that it is largely an achievement which dates, not to the first two generations of Anglo-Norman England, but from the mid-twelfth century.[50]

The buildings whose influence was to displace and reorganize the settlement pattern of the immediately surrounding area with the most dramatic impact were castles and bishops' palaces. Our archaeological knowledge of bishops' palaces hardly begins before the thirteenth century, but the long-standing importance of episcopal and monastic establishments which had long been surrounded and supported by their 'table-lands' or inlands has been a recurrent theme. In England as in France the castle became the centre of noble life, often replacing the central places of leading Anglo-Saxon families. Many Norman lords reproduced on their English lands the fashionable French 'mottes' or mounds topped by a seigneurial house or more ambitiously a castle, and laid out the village anew at its feet. Many Anglo-Norman centres of power were on sites which had a long history of dominance. The 'bordlands' which A.J.L. Winchester has described surrounding the headquarters of the large baronies of the north and the Scottish border, like the 70 acres at Egremont, *caput* of the honour of Copeland, may represent inlands at the centres of ancient *scirs* remodelled to meet the demands of new masters. Clare, Suffolk, has already been mentioned as an important centre for the family of the tenth-century nobleman Wulfstan of Dalham, and, with its market and vineyards and extensive sheep flocks distributed around its manors, was already a noble 'seat' before its new owner, Richard FitzGilbert, took it over.[51] Nevertheless his building of the

---

50. J. Blair, 'Local churches in Domesday Book and before' in *Domesday Studies*, ed. Holt, 265–78; R. Gem, 'The English parish church in the eleventh and early twelfth centuries: a great rebuilding?' in *Minsters and Parish Churches: the local church in transition 950–1200*, ed. J. Blair, Oxford University Committee for Archaeology Monograph 17 (1988), 21–30; R. Morris, *Churches in the Landscape* (1989), ch. 6.
51. See p. 156 above.

castle brought about a total reorganization of the immediate settlement pattern.[52]

Seigneurial centres

At the level of the lesser aristocracy and gentry the seigneurial house and curia were themselves changing. What R. Fossier has called the 'seigneurial cell' was developing a more substantial presence. His work has done much to show how important were the social and even psychological impacts of the castle and the seigneurial centre on rural social structure.[53] This had important spatial implications. What has been remarked of the Welsh nobility is true of the Anglo-Norman: 'the higher the status of the owner, the greater was his ability to keep distinct the domestic and agrarian functions of the manor'.[54] A similar wish to express status through the creation of a space devoted purely to domestic use, sport and display lies behind the development of the manorial house and curia in the twelfth and thirteenth centuries. Important Anglo-Norman signals of status were the defensive work, the gatehouse, the park, and the moat. Not all of this was new: enclosure had always marked important and high-status dwellings. The *burh*-gate had been part of the thegn's establishment in the tenth century, and many, perhaps most, Anglo-Saxon seigneurial sites were surrounded by some kind of fence or palisade. Nevertheless, these characteristics became particularly important in the culture of the twelfth-century aristocracy and gentry, and the 'great rebuilding' in stone on many seigneurial sites was not simply a change in materials but part of a major new emphasis on an imposing, separate, luxurious and defensible seigneurial centre. William of Malmesbury summed up a crucial cultural divide between the English and their conquerors: 'They [the English] consumed their whole substance in mean and despicable houses, unlike the Normans and French who, in noble and splendid mansions, lived with frugality.'[55]

Frugal they may have been, but the Normans brought in new kinds of consumption which made their impact just as did new buildings. The creation of deer parks and gardens, vineyards, dovecotes and moats

---

52. France: J.-P. Poly and E. Bournazel, *The Feudal Transformation 900-1200*, trans. C. Higgitt (New York, 1991); Italy: P. Toubert, *Les structures de Latium* (2 vols, Rome, 1973). Bordlands: A.J.L. Winchester, 'The distribution and significance of "bordland" in medieval Britain', *AgHR* 34 (1986), 129–39. Clare: Harvey, 'Domesday England', 119–20; Chibnall, *Anglo-Norman England*, 27, 38, 51.
53. J.G. Hurst, 'Rural building in England and Wales', *Ag. Hist.* II, 854-98; R. Fossier, 'Land, castle, money and family in the formation of the seigneuries' in *Medieval Settlement: continuity and change*, ed. P.H. Sawyer (1976), 159–68; J. Chapelot and R. Fossier, *The Village and House in the Middle Ages*, trans. H. Cleeve (1985), 144–50.
54. Hurst, 'Rural building in England and Wales', 944.
55. *William of Malmesbury's Chronicle of the Kings of England*, ed. and trans. J.A. Giles (1847), 279. I am grateful to Dr H. Mayr-Harting for this reference.

and fishponds to provide the ingredients of a high-status diet for the Anglo-Norman aristocracy and gentry made itself felt. These adjuncts to the seigneurial life occasionally appear in the twelfth-century documents and when they do it is clear that a major reorganization has been made to make room for them. The history of medieval deer husbandry and hunting is the domain of J. Birrell. She has demonstrated how much expertise and investment went into the production of venison, and how it was carefully signified as a high-status meat. There were enclosures for deer in late Anglo-Saxon England, and a handful of deer parks appear in Domesday Book but many more were created throughout the twelfth century and more still in the thirteenth.[56] While the Norman creation of royal forests was to a great extent a matter of defining an already existing area as subject to forest law, the deer park was a deliberate reshaping of the landscape, in which peasant holdings and houses could be swept away. Many old inlands may lie beneath medieval parks.

The same disruption occurred when manor houses were rebuilt in a more prestigious setting. A larger curia, a moat and fishponds all demanded a much larger core area near the curia, cleared of the peasant houses, yards and crofts of the early inland. What the process of establishing the Norman seigneurial lifestyle could mean in physical terms is dramatically illustrated by the manor house at Goltho, Lincolnshire. We have already seen it develop in a series of seigneurial rebuilds, albeit on a fairly modest scale, from the ninth century (Fig. 19). In Norman hands in the second half of the eleventh century Goltho was again radically reshaped: a ringwork was built and within this defended space up went a motte, hall and tower. Then the weaving sheds and kitchens which had surrounded the seigneurial halls and bowers were cleared away and their occupants with them, the ringwork was levelled and an 'imposing fortified house for a man of considerable status' was built; later still the manorial site was moved to a new site with the latest status symbol, a moat (Fig. 23). On a more modest scale were the stone hall and accompanying chamber which J. Blair identifies as typical of early post-Conquest seigneurial building (Fig. 24).[57]

---

56. D. Hooke, 'Pre-conquest woodland: its distribution and usage', *AgHR* 37 (1989), 113–29; O. Rackham, *The History of the Countryside* (1986), 122–8; J.R. Birrell, 'Deer and deer farming in medieval England', *AgHR* 40 (1992), 112–26.
57. G. Beresford, *Goltho: the development on an early medieval manor c. 850–1150*, Historical Buildings and Monuments Commission for England (1987), 23, 41, 24; S. Bassett, 'Beyond the edge of excavation: the topographical context of Goltho' in *Studies in Medieval History presented to R.H.C. Davis*, ed. H. Mayr-Harting and R.I. Moore (1985), 21–39; J. Blair, 'Hall and chamber: English domestic planning 1000–1250' in *Manorial Domestic Buildings in England and Northern France*, ed. G. Meiron-Jones and M. Jones, Society of Antiquaries of London Occasional Paper 15 (1993), 1–21.

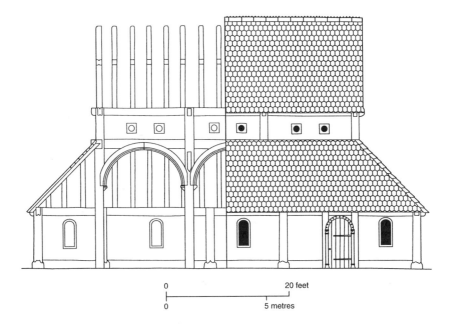

0   20 feet

0   5 metres

Figure 23 Goltho, Lincolnshire. 'Suitable domestic accommodation for a family of considerable prosperity' was provided by this newly built aisled timber hall *c.* 1150, replacing the building shown in Fig. 19. *Source*: after G. Beresford, *Goltho: the development of an early medieval manor c. 850–1150*, Historical Buildings and Monuments Commission for England (1987), fig. 127.

Consumption may have influenced Anglo-Norman settlement on a large scale. A very bold thesis along these lines has been proposed by Kapelle. What he calls the 'oat bread line', the line which divided the areas of predominantly winter-sown cereals, wheat and rye, from those of predominantly spring-sown cereals, oats and barley, divides northern counties. Climatic conditions made the southern part of the east coast plain suitable for growing wheat. Here wheat was the bread grain, the higher colder ground of the Pennines, Cumbria and north of the Vale of York was the land of oat and barley bread. When medieval people could choose, they chose wheat bread, and for the Normans the consumption of wheat bread was not simply a dietary preference, it was an essential part of the lordly image. Kapelle argues that 'William

Figure 24 Boothby Pagnell, Lincolnshire. This chamber-block providing domestic accommodation is likely to have been accompanied by a timber hall. *Source*: after T.H. Turner, *Some Account of Domestic Architecture in England from the Conquest to the End of the Thirteenth Century* (1851).

the Conqueror's followers hoped to be rewarded with land, but land that did not grow wheat, and particularly land where wheat could not be grown, was of little use to them.' He associates the overall pattern of Norman settlement in the north very closely with the availability of wheat-bearing land.[58]

The policies of the Lacy family show how the demands of high-status living could deeply influence rural social structure. The estate of Ilbert de Lacy of Pontefract in the West Riding of Yorkshire was part of an enormous landholding in several northern and midland counties. The honour of Pontefract was composed from a combination of several ancient multiple estates and reached from the fens west of the Ouse up into the Pennines. When he took over his lands, de Lacy had put in hand a thoroughgoing reorganization, concentrating the administration at four centres, including Pontefract which was to become the *caput* of the honour. Here, where there had been nothing worth noting in 1066

58. Kapelle, *Norman Conquest*, 209–230 at 220.

he established a geld-free inland and built a castle. Domesday's description (entered under Tanshelf, the actual site of what later came to be called Pontefract) shows a local semi-urban semi-rural population typical of the inland at the feet of an important establishment. Alongside 60 'petty burgesses' who are likely to have been engaged in the emerging urban economy there were sixteen cottagers, sixteen *villani* and eight bordars, who were subject to exceptionally heavy labour rent, probably imposed since the Conquest.[59] De Lacy reorganized the inlands that had previously been scattered among widespread vills. This on occasion entailed physically moving peasants and their plough teams, and presumably their houses and families too. Information from Domesday about de Lacy's English under-tenants, combined with thirteenth-century information about the crops grown on his Yorkshire estate, enabled Kapelle to conclude that he reserved the wheat lands for the demesnes of himself and his Norman under-tenants, while he left the oat lands to the 'natives'.[60]

In the many cases where the demesne assets were inadequate for the increased demands on them the new owner was powerful enough to be able to create new demesnes out of entire villages. Kapelle has argued that powerful lay landowners in Yorkshire were able to create large demesnes in the chaos left by the 'harrying of the north' by William after the northern rising of 1069. He uses the examples of manors which the Domesday commissioners found to be 'overstocked'; that is to say with more plough teams *in dominio* than there was ploughland for them. He reads this as evidence that 'what occurred in the overstocked vills during the 1070s was ... in most cases a direct expansion or creation of demesne land for the benefit of the lord of the village'. Here too, the newly demesne-oriented vills had been transformed from 'old bondage vills' (that is, vills of independent peasants).[61] Kapelle links the virtual disappearance of the sokemen in Yorkshire with this creation of demesnes. Yorkshire Domesday shows this happening. On the archbishop of York's land at Ripon, Otley and Sherburn, there had been dependencies with both inland and sokeland in 1030. Sokeland had disappeared entirely in Otley's dependent vills by 1086. It has been argued above that the multiple estate had probably from a very early date contained elements of inland with its characteristically dependent peasantry, and what seems to Kapelle as a total innovation may simply be the extension of existing arrangements; nevertheless, his argument for a widespread extension and creation of demesnes in the north is a striking one.

It receives support from other areas. A detailed description of the way in which the succeeding generations of the Montgomery family managed their lands at High Ercall, Shropshire, shows the potential for

---

59. *DB* I, 316c; Kapelle, *Norman Conquest*, 179.
60. Kapelle, *Norman Conquest*, 221–2; W.E. Wightman, *The Lacy Family in England and Normandy 1066–1196* (1966), 23–5, 54, 43–50.
61. Kapelle, *Norman Conquest*, 175.

growth there was in the old kind of multiple estate when it came into the hands of determined Norman lords. The demesne at the central settlement had already been considerably developed under the Mercian earl and countess Leofric and Godiva. By the 1180s William Peverel, whose family succeeded the first Norman lord Roger of Montgomery, had first extended the demesne around the court and then laid out a whole new township with its own demesne for his son. By opening up new blocks of arable from the waste succeeding generations of the family managed to maintain their demesne while at the same time leasing demesne to tenants. The author emphasizes that new land added to the demesnes compensated for the amounts lost by leasing. Her very detailed study of a lay estate effectively questions the supposed decline in demesne cultivation of the twelfth century.[62]

The needs of the knightly class for land could often only be satisfied at the expense of the local peasantry. At Nuneham Courtenay, Oxfordshire, Richard of Courcy had added two hides and a yardland of the *terra villanorum* to his inland.[63] *Terra villanorum*, the land of the *villani*, must have included the land of independent warland peasants.[64] Richard's establishment on what had been peasant farmland may be typical of the eleventh-century knight. Domesday shows that the *terra villanorum* was a reservoir of land from which to endow knights with small demesnes – the overwhelming majority had less than two hides.[65] The policy continued into the twelfth century. Abingdon Abbey charitably provided for a party of knights who had come off the worse in an encounter with pirates. Their right hands had been cut off and they were unable to fend for themselves. The abbey, at the king's request, provided them with small estates from land which had been in the hands of its peasant tenants. A late twelfth-century survey of Abingdon's manors shows that many supported the demesne land of a modest knightly establishment or larger freeholding alongside the land of the peasants.[66] The enfeoffment of a plethora of 'rustic knights' such as these, while it created no large concentrations of land in demesne to compare with those of the great estates, nevertheless on aggregate brought a great deal of land out of the sphere of peasant family farming and into the sphere of seigneurial husbandry. This meant that it had to meet the demands of a new kind of consumer, one whose priorities, in their modest way, were those of the Norman ruling class: building, piety, conspicuous consumption, the expenses of the courtly and military life. These 'new settlers of knightly status who helped to speed up the process of manorialization' were a potent force

---

62. M.C. Hill, *The Demesne and the Waste: a study of medieval enclosure on the manor of High Ercall 1086–1399* (1984).
63. *DB* I, 159a.
64. See pp. 121–5 above.
65. Harvey, 'The knight and the knight's fee'; F.M. Stenton, 'Domesday survey: introduction', *VCH Oxfordshire*, I (1939), 373–95 at 394.
66. *Chronicon monasterii de Abingdon*, 99, 7; D.C. Douglas, 'Some early surveys from the abbey of Abingdon', *EHR* 44 (1929), 618–25.

in the creation of new demesnes, just as the Anglo-Saxon bookland thegnage had been.[67]

The owner of a small estate faced quite different pressures from those of the large landlord, and met them in a different way. The pressure to increase the size and profitability of demesnes on small estates was even greater than on large, for their owners can have had few peasant tenancies from which to draw rent in any form. Much as the lesser thegn before the Conquest had needed to get the maximum returns from his inland, so too did the post-Conquest knight from the knight's fee, the sub-tenant from his holding.[68]

The difference between large and small landlords shows up in the contrast between the way that the sub-tenants of the important Oxfordshire landholder Robert d'Oilly ran their manors and the way that Robert ran the manors that he kept in hand. D'Oilly had between three and four plough teams at work on his demesnes: on their much smaller properties his sub-tenants had not far off as many teams at work – on average two. But while he was able to draw on 'customs' and rents from his considerable tenantry, on their small manors his sub-tenants needed to rely on their inlands. They kept a workforce of an average of seven agricultural labourers: despite their much greater size, d'Oilly had not many more on his large demesne manors. In short, allowing for the different size of their landholdings, his sub-tenants on their small manors were relatively much more 'demesne-oriented' than he was himself.[69]

The dismemberment of so many small Anglo-Saxon estates meant that many new lords had virtually to create a demesne from scratch. Grantees of small five-hide manors, 'housecarls' and 'rustic knights' established on 'manors' that were not much more than peasant farms, had no land to spare from which to create tenancies and tended to run their small estates on slave or bordar labour. B. Dodwell has described the creation of a demesne after 1066 at Welnetham, Suffolk. In Edward the Confessor's time there had been 41 freemen and a dozen cottagers there: signs of a tiny inland, if there was one at all. By the reign of Edward I there was a substantial demesne of 260 acres.[70] Stenton demonstrated the creation of demesnes as portions of sokes were broken off to form discrete holdings as at Norton Disney, Lincolnshire.[71]

It appears that to study the fortunes of the great estate alone is not the most illuminating point of view from which to look at the important changes in the agrarian economy in the century after the Conquest. We

---

67. Chibnall, *Anglo-Norman England*, 141.
68. See pp. 168–77 above.
69. *DB* I, 158a–c; Harvey, 'Domesday England', 79.
70. B. Dodwell, 'Holdings and inheritance in medieval East Anglia', *EcHR*, 2nd series 20 (1967), 53–66 at 55; for demesnes created on small Gloucestershire manors after the conquest: R.J. Faith, 'Tidenham, Gloucestershire, and the origins of the manor in England', *Landscape History* 16 (1994), 39–51 at 47 and n. 15.
71. Stenton, *Types of Manorial Structure*, lxxxi.

can consider instead the overall balance between peasant farming on the one hand and, on the other, inland or demesne farming for the benefit of a landlord, whether large estate owner or small lord or lessee. What Maitland called 'the making of manors' and the creation of demesnes at a stroke, the leasing of valuable properties to men well intent on exploiting them to the full, may well have tipped the balance in favour of the inland sector, devoted to producing for the consumption needs of a class of new lords who can be well described as consumers *par excellence*.

8 The Conquest and the peasantry

The previous chapter sketched in the expansive policies of the new landowning class; the effect of these and of the demands of the 'consumers *par excellence*' on the local peasantry will be the main theme here. The growing needs of the twelfth-century seigneurial economy came up against the limits imposed by the restricted labour supply and undercapitalization of many manors. Extra general labour and more plough teams were needed for expanding and improving demesnes. Ultimately, the problem was solved by the expansion of peasant tenancies, which provided lords with increased labour, plough-team capacity, and cash income. Lords' need for more labour met peasants' need for more land. Population pressure provides a convincing rationale for the fact that tenants were apparently willing to take on holdings on distinctly less advantageous terms than they had been held in the past, to accept smaller holdings and to agree to new and harsher terms of tenancy.

Most of the available information about estate management comes from the archives of the great ecclesiastical landlords (and generally speaking from the southern counties). Quite different arrangements may have characterized the small manor. But by the end of the twelfth-century lords of all kinds were evidently beginning to prefer to replace the huddle of cottages and smallholdings clustered around the curia typical of the pre-Conquest cottagers and *geburs* with holdings permanently hived off from the inland, at some distance from it – sometimes in a separate settlement altogether. It is likely that this was particularly the course that the resident landlord on a small manor would be inclined to follow. The new emphasis on a discrete seigneurial space, clearly differentiated from the workaday activities which supported it, led to the emergence of the 'demesne' in the sense of a home farm, a purely agricultural unit, with only a core staff of permanent estate workers or *famuli* resident on it.

This is the physical reality behind a conceptual shift. Even to think about their assets in this way was something new for landlords: B.F. Harvey describes the attitudes of the twelfth-century monks of Westminster like this:

> The earlier the period, the more blurred this distinction between demesne and tenant land become ... demesne and tenant land might be together on lease or together in hand ... the notion that these two parts of the manorial estate were readily separable, or that the one rather than the other should supply them with this or that kind of income lay in the future.

By the end of the thirteenth century the demesne and tenant land were sharply differentiated and subject to different kinds of policy.[1] The Anglo-Norman period was in this, as in so many other ways, a period of change. While the ancient form of inland with its tenants and resident workforce was still a reality in the twelfth century, it becomes increasingly possible for us to follow the Westminster monks and speak of the 'demesne' as an untenanted home farm. The concept of 'tenant land', as Harvey's observation points out, was also a novelty, and one which came to supplant the old notion of warland. In the high-pressure economy of Anglo-Norman England inland and warland alike were transformed. It is with tenancies that this chapter will chiefly be concerned.

Peasant holdings and tenancies

The major problem in understanding peasant tenancies and their obligations is not one of evidence: they are superbly documented – Boldon Book, covering the bishop of Durham's lands in 1183, is just one among a dozen or so similarly impressive estate surveys, all from major ecclesiastical estates, listing tenants, their tenancies and their rents in cash, kind and labour, which survive from the twelfth and thirteenth centuries.[2] Rather, the problem is one of dating. How long had the peasant holdings we can see in the surveys been in existence? Do they record an ancient unchanged tenemental pattern, one that had recently come into being, or one that had gradually evolved? To look 'beyond Domesday' into the Anglo-Saxon past, as earlier chapters have attempted to do, has shown that while we know a good deal about the different *kinds* of obligations owed before the Conquest from both inland and warland peasants, it is difficult to calculate the *extent* to which they had developed by 1066. But if we look forward from Domesday to the position described in the earliest surveys we learn something about peasant holdings which, although its implications are at present little understood, may prove to be important. This can be summed up as the difference between 'closed' and 'open' tenemental systems.

---

1. B.F. Harvey, *Westminster Abbey and its Estates in the Middle Ages* (1977), 129–30.
2. H.B. Clarke, 'The early surveys of Evesham Abbey: an investigation into the problem of continuity in Anglo-Norman England' (Ph.D. thesis, University of Birmingham, 1978), part IV.

First it is important to be clear about two other terms we are using. All our documentation about the post-Conquest peasantry is imbued with the language of *tenure*: from high to low, people 'held', rather than 'had', land.[3] To speak of the peasant 'tenancy' is to speak of the land held by a particular peasant from a lord and the terms on which he held it. To speak of a peasant 'holding' or 'landholding' (or, occasionally, 'tenement') is to speak of an agrarian unit, which might consist of strips in a common field system, or a farm with its own fields, and appointment rights.

Manors with 'closed' systems give an impression of tremendous conservatism. They have a fixed number of tenements (although these could be split or amalgamated), which remains the same over long periods of time, and the aggregated area of these tenements corresponds to the hidage of the manor. This can be shown to be true of about half the manors in Middlesex Domesday and of many of Ramsey Abbey's manors in 1100, and may well be true of many more.[4] These have the same number of *villani* in Domesday Book as they have customary tenants with regular tenancies in the twelfth and thirteenth centuries. A good example is Gressenhall in Norfolk, held by the Warenne family, where the ten *villani* of Domesday Book seem very likely to have been the forerunners of the holders of ten standard *tenementa* there which persisted as units of assessment until the fifteenth century. The 'common services' each holding owed in 1282 – three days' mowing, an acre's ploughing, small food rents and so on – are typical *warland* obligations, and might well have been owed in 1086, and long before.[5] On some of Peterborough Abbey's manors the numbers of Domesday *villani* correspond to the yardlanders owing week-work in the 1120s. The hundredal manor at Oundle, for instance, an ancient estate centre which had been part of Æthelwold's endowment of the abbey, had 23 *villani* and ten bordars in 1086 with nine plough teams between them: in the 1120s 25 yardlanders and ten bordars provided week-work and their nine teams ploughed very large areas of the demesne.[6]

An even greater conservatism can be demonstrated in some midland common field manors. When it is possible to identify individual peasant holdings with collections of strips in the common fields, as D. Hall has been able to do for the champion county of

3. S. Reynolds, *Fiefs and Vassals: the medieval evidence reinterpreted* (1994) has undermined this statement as far as the upper ranks of society are concerned, but it remains true at the level of the peasantry.
4. P.D.A. Harvey, ed., *The Peasand Land Market in Medieval England* (1984), introduction, 9–10 where his calculations for the Middlesex Domesday entries involve allowing a hidage assessment for land *in dominio*: it is likely that this on some manors was not assessed in hides (above, chapter 2); J.A. Raftis, *The Estates of Ramsey Abbey* (1957), 70.
5. J. Williams, 'Norfolk, the thirteenth century' in *Peasant Land Market* ed. Harvey, 31–105 at 36–7.
6. *Chronicon petroburgense*, ed. T. Stapledon, Camden Society 47 (1849), 157–83.

Northamptonshire, a striking stability over time can be seen. Domesday hidages, twelfth-century yardlands, and common field systems which were still operating in the eighteenth century, can all be seen to relate to one another.[7] Hall believes that the Domesday hidages in Northamptonshire represent not the traditional fiscal rating of a manor but the actual area of peasant holdings in the common fields. In his view, the hidage was primary: 'At some time, presumably at the inception of the open-field system ... a village was assessed at so many yardlands and the fields made to fit.' Given the fact that common field systems in this area may well have come into existence in the ninth or tenth century, the peasant holdings there must be as old. (It should be noted that Northamptonshire hidage assessments were not necessarily typical. In other counties some hidages are of conventionally round figures such as 10 or 30, and many of these are identical with those in charters of the eighth to the eleventh century. Some were manipulated to benefit a landowner. Possibly Northamptonshire hides had already undergone a reorganization. A scheme for a more efficient taxation assessment, based on measurement of hides 'by the rope' was credited to William II's minister Ranulf Flambard.)[8]

The fact that some peasant holdings can be traced back well before the Conquest as physical units is sometimes interpreted as evidence that the terms on which they were held, in other words the *tenancies*, were equally long-standing. From such an interpretation it is sometimes deduced that the very servile tenure of the thirteenth century, which can be roughly summed up as tenure in villeinage, can also be traced back well before the Conquest. In some places this can be seen to be true. In the case of Tidenham, Gloucestershire, which has already given us so much important information about the tenurial conditions of the pre-Conquest peasantry, we can see how these set a pattern which lasted for possibly 300 years. Tidenham's *gebur* tenants holding a yardland before the Conquest – perhaps 36 in number – lived and worked under much the same conditions as the 38 *villani* who had followed them by 1086, whose tenements (by now all split into half-yardlands) were held by the customary tenants who followed *them* in the thirteenth century.[9] But on many other manors while peasant holdings, field systems and hidage were physically related and of equal antiquity, the terms on which the peasants held their land changed

---

7. D. Hall, 'The late Saxon countryside: villages and their fields' in *Anglo-Saxon Settlements*, ed. D. Hooke (1988), 99–122 at 116–22; 'Late Saxon topography and early medieval estates' in *Medieval Villages: a review of current work*, ed. D. Hooke, Oxford University Committee for Archaeology Monograph 5 (1985), 61-9.
8. D. Hall, 'An introduction to Northamptonshire Domesday' in *The Northamptonshire and Rutland Domesday* (1987), 1–17 at 16; p. 51 above; S.P.J. Harvey, 'Taxation and the ploughland in Domesday Book' in *Domesday Book: a reassessment*, ed. P.H. Sawyer (1985), 86–103.
9. R.J. Faith, 'Tidenham, Gloucestershire, and the origins of the manor in England', *Landscape History* 16 (1994), 39–51 at 47.

radically after the Conquest: this was an important development which will be discussed later in this chapter.

There are other manors where the situation was not like this at all. They are open, not closed, systems. They had many more customary tenants in the twelfth and thirteenth centuries than they had *villani* and bordars in 1086. The area covered by tenancies, as revealed in the surveys, does not add up to the hidage of the manor in Domesday Book. They provide evidence not for stability over centuries but for an increase in peasant tenants. H.E. Hallam has accumulated evidence for a widespread increase in peasant tenancies on a very large number of estates between 1086 and the thirteenth century. His calculations are based on a comparison between recorded manorial populations in Domesday, and the numbers of tenants recorded in surveys of the twelfth and thirteenth centuries. As such, they have to be treated with caution, for in some areas we cannot be sure that all Domesday slaves are included, and nowhere can we be sure that *villani* are tenants of the same kind that are recorded in the surveys.[10] Nevertheless, the cumulative impression of growth is undeniable, and one example will illustrate it here. A comparison between the total manorial population on each manor of the canons of St Paul's and their lessees in 1086 – that is to say the sum of the *servi*, *bordarii* and *villani* – and the total number of tenancies in 1222 shows an increase on virtually all their manors. By this means the canons achieved an input of labour rent per acre by 1222 which compares quite favourably with rates from the thirteenth-century period of so-called 'high farming' recorded elsewhere.[11]

The experience of St Paul's illustrates a point which a recent statistical study of Essex Domesday has established. This is that, from the point of view of manorial lords, the key factor in increasing the value of a manor was to increase its population. Analysis of the variables in manorial values in 1086 has concluded that the group whose increase can be shown to have had the greatest effect on manorial values was the *villani*. Whether these were comparatively free tenants who paid only money rent or comparatively unfree tenants who rendered large amounts of labour service, to increase their numbers was to increase the value of the manor.[12]

Many manors themselves physically grew after the Conquest, taking in more land and involving new peasant populations. This is how the apparent increase in the number of tenancies on some of the bishop of Worcester's manors may be explained.[13] On these manors it seems

---

10. H.E. Hallam, 'Population movements in England 1086–1350' in *Ag. Hist.* II, 508–93.
11. R.J. Faith, 'Demesne resources and labour rent on the manors of St Paul's Cathedral 1066–1222', *EcHR* 47 (1994), 657–78.
12. J. McDonald and G.D. Snooks, *Domesday Economy: a new approach to Anglo-Norman history* (1986), 110.
13. Faith, 'Demesne resources', table 6, 668 (e.g. Adulfsness, Caddington); Raftis, *Ramsey Abbey*, 71; C.C. Dyer, *Lords and Peasants in a Changing Society: the estates of the bishopric of Worcester 680–1540* (1980), table 6, 85.

likely that while there was a core of regular tenancies before the Conquest, probably arranged around the seigneurial *tun*, they represented only a part of the available cultivable land. Much was still in the hands of warland farmers. Over the eleventh and twelfth centuries manors like this experienced startling growth and reorganization, in the course of which their peasant populations experienced important changes in their status.

Free tenants

On open and enclosed manors the demands of the seigneurial inland had already made themselves felt to a greater or lesser degree before the Conquest. In others, it was the arrangements of peasant farming, not the needs of the curia, which had set the pattern. Here field systems and pasture arrangements survive which are much earlier than manorial boundaries and ignore them. The curia may have its own field system, and a particularly dependent inland workforce, but it hardly involves the mass of the local peasantry at all. Warland dues, rather than inland services, express the relationship between the bulk of the peasantry and the curia. Systems like this are more common in the counties where sokemen and free men make such a showing in Domesday: Lincolnshire, Norfolk and Suffolk, Leicestershire, Bedfordshire, Nottinghamshire, Essex and Kent.[14] T. Williamson's study of Norfolk shows how the numbers of 'free men' recorded in Domesday for that county included peasants who owned their own land and whose relationships with lords were personal and negotiated, rather than tenurial. The sokemen, while more closely involved with estates, owed their lords the services typical of the warland, not the rents of customary tenants.[15] Although they form one of the categories that the commissioners expected to find, Domesday does not consistently record 'free men' and we have no means of calculating the numbers of the people who came to be called 'free tenants'. They were an important category. The Hundred Rolls of 1279 provide information for parts of six southern English counties some way comparable with that of Domesday Book. Kosminsky found that free holdings probably occupied about 30 per cent of the arable in the areas covered by the Hundred Rolls: Bedfordshire, Buckinghamshire, Oxfordshire, Huntingdonshire, Warwickshire and Cambridgeshire.[16]

Free tenants were marked by their great diversity: from many substantial peasant freeholders paying only token or very light rents who were substantially the owners of their own lands, to smallholders

---

14. See pp. 121–5 above.
15. T. Williamson, *The Origins of Norfolk* (1993), 15–21.
16. E.A. Kosminsky, *Studies in the Agrarian History of England in the Thirteenth Century*, trans. R. Kisch (1956), 198–206; P. Vinogradoff, *Villainage in England: essays in English mediaeval history* (1892), 325–53.

who were poor but personally free. The nature of their services links their 'freedom' with that of the independent peasant farmers we have encountered on the Anglo-Saxon warland. They were like them in the kind of services they performed: the independent 'radmen' of the pre-Conquest *scirs* and sokes had their counterparts in the west midlands in the 'rodknyts' on the Prior of Kenilworth's manor of Loxley, Warwickshire, in 1296 and the many free tenants with large holdings – of 90 to nearly 200 acres – who owed only money rent and hunting service to the abbot of Gloucester in the thirteenth century.[17] Vinogradoff and Kosminsky were united in pin-pointing a fundamental difference in the obligations of free tenants to a manorial lord: free tenants paid lighter cash rents than customary tenants, they seldom owed week-work. Their obligations to a manorial lord were often expressed only by token and courtesy payments, such as the gilt spurs and barbed arrows owed as part of their rent by free tenants in the thirteenth century at Tidenham – perhaps a gesture towards the part that hunting services played in the relationship of the *geneat* to his lord.[18]

Other characteristics of free tenants have less to do with their part in the manorial economy, more to do with the kind of peasant farms they were. These may be the most important distinguishing characteristic of all, for they suggest that some free holdings – what Vinogradoff called 'ancient freeholds' – represent the unmanorialized peasant economy of the warland farmer. In Kent free holdings were distinguished by their distinctive inheritance customs: tenure in gavelkind implied freedom. The discussion of the characteristics of warland farmers has shown how this Kentish custom of joint inheritance preserves an early form of a kindred's relationship to its land.[19] Scattered as opposed to nucleated settlement had implications for peasant freedom. The isolated farmers of Devon and Cornwall, holding by free tenure, preserved the scattered settlement pattern of earlier centuries substantially intact. In upland pastoral areas, outside the demesnes of great estates like those of the bishop of Durham or the Percies, the bonds of lordship over dispersed hillside farmers were comparatively weak.[20]

Many free holdings, by contrast, were 'new' land. The winning of new land from forest and fenland sometimes brought a relatively independent peasantry into being on the edges of, or far from, existing settlements. 'Assart' or newly cleared land was nearly always rented on a money rent per acre basis and tenants who owed only money rent were notably freer than those owing labour rent. Assart holdings are

17. F.W. Maitland, *Domesday Book and Beyond: three essays in the early history of England* (1960 edn), 362–3; P. Vinogradoff, *English Society in the Eleventh Century: essays in English mediaeval history* (1908), 69–72.
18. Tidenham: *VCH Gloucestershire*, X, 68.
19. See pp. 134–7 above.
20. E. Miller, 'Social structure: northern England' in *Ag. Hist.* II, 685–98.

detectable as a fringe of much freer tenures, often at the margins of settlements, but marginal also in the sense that peasants could add odd acres of this new land to their basic arable holding: 'twelfth-century peasants spilling over into new lands' brought about a 'veritable boom' in new, small rented holdings that took place on some of Ramsey Abbey's colonizing manors in the twelfth century, especially in the fens.[21] Colonizing smallholders were less likely to become economically dependent because they could supplement their income from by-employment; the fen smallholders may have been part-time fishermen and fowlers as well and the expansion of the Cornish tin industry in the late twelfth century and again in the fourteenth century helped to sustain the colonizers who established themselves on farms on the wild moorlands during the same period.[22]

This winning of new land has been called the 'journey to the margin', and some families established themselves on land which would never yield them adequate returns: however 'free', the tenants on marginal land could well experience greater poverty than the manorial tenants who held larger holdings of anciently cultivated land. The villages established on the bleak Northamptonshire uplands had a weak hold on life, and seem not to have established the corporate strength of the lowland villages.[23] In more propitious areas large free holdings, the basis of substantial peasant farms, could also be built up on newly cultivated land and this may be particularly true of forest areas such as the Weald where clearance and settlement represented a considerable investment of time and labour. 'Free' villages and hamlets with individualistic field systems are a feature of the Weald and the Chilterns in southern England. Lords did not always find it possible or appropriate to charge tenants of the new lands the regular labour rents that were demanded from tenants of the growing arable core, and it was probably very difficult to get rent at all from farmers who had opened up inaccessible forest clearings by their own enterprise. The king's tenants on his manor of Havering, Essex, were able to carve substantial individual farms out of his forest and farmed the land they had created in separate fields. High rents could be charged, and tenants were able to afford them, for this desirable new land and the crown began actively to encourage assarting.[24]

Colonization of the waste left many communities dangerously short of grazing land and rough woodland. Waste was becoming a limited resource and peasants found themselves in competition for it with their lords on two fronts. Common waste – which could cover a wide variety of uncultivated land from moorland to woodlands to pastures

21. Raftis, *Ramsey Abbey*, 75, 71.
22. J. Hatcher, 'New settlement: south western England' in *Ag.Hist.* II, 234–45.
23. H.S.A. Fox, 'The people of the wolds in English settlement history' in *The Rural Settlements of Medieval England*, ed. M. Aston, D. Austin and C.C. Dyer (1989), 77–101.
24. M. McIntosh, *Autonomy and Community: the royal manor of Havering 1200–1500* (1986), 90–103.

near the village – was increasingly tightly defined as manorial, not communal, property. Timber was becoming valued and preserved and peasant tenants came to be very much restricted in what timber they were allowed to cut. All kinds of fuel may have been coming to be in short supply: payments for digging peat, gathering brushwood, as well as the manorial monopoly of ovens sometimes found, are evidence of serious shortage.

Labour supply and organization

While the demands of the expanding economy brought great changes, it is evident that there was also much continuity between the pre- and post-Conquest world. On most manors, however small, there were still likely to be specialists for skilled tasks: ploughmen and stockmen and dairymaids employed all the year round, and paid in a mixture of cash and kind. Many estates continued to house their workers 'near the hall' as they had done before the Conquest, and on remote Northumbrian farms in the eighteenth and nineteenth centuries, for instance, it was still common for the farmer to house his estate workers in cottages around the farmyard and supply them with food and coals. These workers were living much as the inland workers of the *Rectitudines* had done before the Conquest.[25] But the slave and ex-slave farm servants with their cottages huddled on the inland round the curia, supported by regular customary doles of food, were being replaced by a mixed workforce on more substantial holdings from which they were able to support themselves. There was a significant decline in the number of recorded slaves between 1066 and 1086. The most likely explanation is that they were being given smallholdings for which they owed labour rent. Ramsey Abbey's cottars, who work every Monday and two days a week at harvest time, 'dwell on the demesne' at Stukely, Huntingdonshire. Cottage holdings in Cuxham, Oxfordshire, were grouped near the curia in the thirteenth century, and South Malling's oxherds had their tenements 'in the middle of the demesne'. Smallholders on the manors of the canons of St Paul's 'who hold from the demesne' land near the curia owed regular week-work; *operarii* had holdings of 5–20 acres.[26] This created a penumbra of small labour tenancies around the home farm: a pattern of inland smallholdings familiar from before the Conquest. 'Service-bearing holdings cluster about the demesne in a fairly regular pattern' in many eastern counties

25. A. Howkins, *Reshaping Rural England: a social history 1850–1925* (1991), 19–20.
26. Stukely: *Cartularium monasterii de Rameseia*, ed. W.H. Hart and P.A. Lyons, 3 vols, Rolls Series (1884–93), III, 274; Cuxham: P.D.A. Harvey, *A Medieval Oxfordshire Village: Cuxham 1240 to 1400* (1965), 121–3 and map 5 at 122; Malling: J. Blair, *Early Medieval Surrey: landholding, church and settlement before 1300* (1991), 75; St Paul's: Faith, 'Demesne resources', 669–72.

in the thirteenth century.[27] Though small, these tenancies provided substantial amounts of labour. At Crondall, a manor of St Swithun's Priory in Hampshire, the cottars owed the same range of services as did the holder of a standard yardland. What had been slave ploughmen's tenancies on the bishop of Worcester's estates before the Conquest were by 1170 small tenancies owing a very heavy labour rent of five days a week, whose tenants still benefited from vestiges of the food allowances of earlier days in the shape of corn doles and, like many demesne ploughmen, they had the use of the lord's team on Saturdays.[28]

Such labour tenancies were often known as 'worklands', and under the names *terrae operariae* and *terrae operariorum* can be found on several twelfth-century ecclesiastical estates. The cartulary known as the Red Book of Worcester distinguishes *terra operaria* from inland, and 'workland' was a distinct part of the inland at Sherburn in Elmet in the eleventh century. This may be a sign that it was becoming physically hived off, a part of the process which was eventually to result in the inland being reduced to an untenanted home farm.[29] As the primary purpose of the creation of these labour tenancies was to provide labour they were generally let on very precarious tenure, and could be taken in hand again by the lord at will.[30]

M.M. Postan drew attention to the importance of these labour tenancies and emphasized the vital role this tied labour force came to play in the manorial economy as 'an important tributary, sometimes the mainstream of the total labour supply ...' Postan argued that the leasing of demesne land must have reflected the decline of seigneurial agricultural production.[31] When Postan wrote, the term 'land *in dominio*' was widely interpreted as meaning the lord's home farm: he did not envisage that it could include a supply of land which could be let to tenants, as the pre-Conquest inland had. The evidence quoted above from several estates points to the fact that tenancies established

27. J.A. Raftis, 'Social structure: the east midlands', in *Ag. Hist.* II, 634–50 at 637. For the size of cottage holdings and their close association with the demesne: R.V. Lennard, 'The economic position of the bordars and cottars of Domesday Book', *Economic Journal* 61 (1951), 342–71. For other examples of worklands on the inland see F.R.H. du Boulay, *The Lordship of Canterbury: an essay on medieval society* (1966), 132 (oxherds' lands), 142 (*avermanni* and *werkmanni*).
28. Vinogradoff, *Villainage*, 456–60; *The Growth of the Manor* (2nd edn, 1911), 352ff.; Kosminsky, *Studies*, 294–300; Harvey, *Westminster Abbey*, 101–3; Worcester: Dyer, *Lords and Peasants*, 97–8; Crondall: E.A. Levett, 'The financial organization of the manor', *EcHR* 1st series 1 (1927), 65–86 at 73.
29. *The Red Book of Worcester*, ed. M. Hollings, Worcestershire Historical Society (4 vols 1934–50); W. Farrer, ed., *Early Yorkshire Charters* (3 vols, 1914–16), I, no. 6 at 18–21, no. 2 at 5–10.
30. Faith, 'Demesne resources', 671–2.
31. M.M. Postan, *The Famulus: the estate labourer in the twelfth and thirteenth centuries*, *EcHR* Supp. 2 (1954); 'The chronology of labour services' and 'Glastonbury estates in the twelfth century' in M.M. Postan, *Essays on Medieval Agriculture and General Problems of the Medieval Economy* (1973), 89–106, 249–77.

to increase the labour supply were created out of the inland.

This process was part of the general increase in tenancies held for labour rent by landlords who were expanding their demesnes or attempting to increase production and found themselves with a labour shortfall. However, not all demesne lettings were for labour rent: many were rented for cash, and this is particularly the case with the meadow and grazing land which was as much part of the inland as was its arable. Disposing of small parcels of inland in this way to a rising rural population eager for land was an easy way for a manorial lessee to add to his income, though it was not always in the best interest of the owner of the estate. On one of the manors of the dean and chapter of St Paul's, Belchamp St Paul's in north Essex, it was reported in 1240 that 'tenants of the demesne lands which they call *inlandes* have added to the assized rents without the chapter's authority'. On the Glastonbury Abbey estates in the south-west portions of demesne land were rented out in small parcels of regular size.[32]

Week-work had already made its appearance as an important part of the labour rent of the inland peasantry well before the Conquest, and the tenor of the references to it in pre-Conquest sources is to associate it with the most dependent and least well provided-for sections of the peasantry. This servile connotation continued after the Conquest when the obligation to do a set number of days of regular unspecified work on the lord's home farm came to be a badge of unfreedom. In Bracton's famous remark, the serf is one 'who does not know in the evening what work he will do in the morning', and the conditions under which week-work was done, probably in gangs under the direction of a manorial official, made it particularly demeaning. From the managerial point of view week-work was the most convenient form in which to take labour rent. It was flexible, the rate being adjustable to the season, and was generally linked with specified tasks and could easily be increased by stepping up the rate. Perhaps most important of all, week-work was an adaptable labour resource which under the reeve or bailiff's direction could be directed to whatever job was in hand, notably those which were conspicuously dirtier and more labour intensive than the jobs done by boon work. While ploughing, harrowing, haymaking, reaping and carting are typical boon works, weeding, sowing, clearing land, ditching, fencing, marling and spreading muck were typically performed by week-work.

Large, organized supplies of labour rent are only well documented

32. Harvey, *The Peasant Land Market*, 10; W.H. Hale, ed., *The Domesday of St Paul's of the year MCCXXII or registrum de visitatione maneriorum per Robertum decanum*, Camden Society 69 (1858), 118; M.M. Postan, 'Glastonbury estates in the twelfth century' *EcHR* 2nd series 5 (1953), 358–67; R.V. Lennard, 'The demesnes of Glastonbury Abbey in the eleventh and twelfth centuries', *EcHR*, 2nd series 8 (1956), 355–63; N.E. Stacy, 'The estates of Glastonbury Abbey c. 1050–1200' (D.Phil. thesis, University of Oxford, 1971), 127ff. E. Miller, *The Abbey and Bishopric of Ely: the social history of an ecclesiastical estate from the tenth to the early fourteenth century* (1951), 99–101.

in the twelfth century for the larger ecclesiastical estates, and as soon as their surveys and rentals are available from the first and second decades of that century they show it as an essential part of the manorial economy. Labour services heavy and well organized enough to provide the labour for the cultivation of substantial demesnes are found in the twelfth century on the lands of the nuns of Caen, the canons of St Paul's, the abbots of Glastonbury, Ramsey, Peterborough and the bishop of Worcester, among others.[33] Broadly speaking, labour rent tended to be heavy on the large ecclesiastical estates, on their larger manors and on those near the house itself, but we must not forget that these are by far the best documented. The headquarters of a large lay honour may well have needed very much the same labour supply as a monastic house.

The major contributors of week-work that we encounter in the surveys of the twelfth century were peasants with substantial tenancies, yardlands and half-yardlands. It was from this source that the major post-Conquest expansion in the labour supply was to come. Many of these tenancies had originated as hides and fractions of hides; that is to say, as warland. Customary tenants who owed week-work on the abbey of Westminster's lands at Birdbrook, Essex, held 'ware acres', which must once have been liable for warland services and were geldable.[34] The surveys of Burton Abbey dated between 1114 and 1118 provide some of our earliest post-Conquest examples of hidated land that owed week-work. Eight *villani* each with two bovates of 'the land of the men', in contrast to the inland, owed week-work at Burton. Eighteen *villani* at Stretton on 'the land of the men ... assessed to the geld' did the same.[35] On the bishop of Worcester's manor of Kempsey in 1170 the yardlands which 'geld' owed four days' week-work each 'and one of them from a half-hide owes two furlongs' ploughing' as well as the boons and renders with which we have become familiar as typical warland dues.[36]

Lords had the option of commuting labour rent for cash. In the cash-hungry years of the twelfth century this came to seem an attractive alternative The option system meant that the supply of labour could be tailored to the needs of the demesne and it became common on large twelfth-century estates. On the manors of Ramsey

33. R.V. Lennard, *Rural England 1086-1135: a study of social and agrarian conditions* (1959), 375–87, is a clear summary of the information given by the twelfth-century survey on the various forms of labour rent. Kosminsky, *Studies*, chs 3, 6; E. Miller and J. Hatcher, *Medieval England: rural society and economic change 1086–1348* (1978), 121–8. Caen: M. Chibnall, ed., *Charters and Custumals of the Abbey of Holy Trinity Caen*, British Academy Records of Social and Economic History, new series 5 1982; St Paul's: Faith, 'Demesne resources'; Glastonbury: *Liber Henrici de Soliaco*, ed. J.E. Jackson (1882), 21–142; Worcester: Dyer, *Lords and Peasants*, 97–103.
34. P.R. Schofield, 'Land, family and inheritance in a later medieval community: Birdbrook, 1292–1412' (D.Phil. thesis, University of Oxford, 1992), 95.
35. *EHD* II, no. 176, 821–8.
36. Faith, 'Demesne resources', 669–71; *Red Book*, I, 84.

and Burton abbeys tenants were sometimes *ad opus*, sometimes *ad malam*, paying work or rent for their land as the needs of the estate demanded. Many of the heavy labour rents of the surveys may in fact have been taken in their cash equivalents, like *averpennies* paid in lieu of carting. Lords who had created blocks of tenancies for labour rent often found that they had more labour available than the home farm needed. Commutations of labour for rent aimed at correcting this imbalance and improving cash incomes, are not necessarily signs of diminishing home farm cultivation, which may well have been carried out by a regular workforce of *famuli*: the salaried specialist workers who were the successors of the pre-Conquest inland worker-tenants.[37]

Plough teams were, next to land, the most valuable capital asset in the medieval agricultural economy. It has already become apparent that many lords were poorly supplied with plough teams in 1086; still less were they equipped to cope with the expanding arables of the twelfth and thirteenth century. A handful of demesne plough teams would not have sufficed to break new land: it took the combined effort of demesne and peasant teams. An increase in the number of demesne plough teams would seem an obvious solution, but it was not widely followed. The values of the manors which Peterborough Abbey kept in hand, for instance, increased from £167 in 1086 to £284 in 1125, and manorial values doubled between 1176 and 1211, but although some at least of these improved returns were due to greater arable production the numbers of demesne plough teams remained much the same.[38] On the manors of St Paul's the expansion of demesne arable was not generally accompanied by any significant increase in demesne plough teams, and the same rather inflexible provision of plough teams is found on the Ramsey Abbey demesnes.[39]

Pre-Conquest lords, as we have seen, could count on ploughing rent from two sources: from their warland tenants on hidated land, and, if they had such, on the much heavier ploughing rent of their inland tenants. This situation substantially continued after the Conquest, but demand came up against the inflexibilities inherent in the traditional labour supply. It is sometimes assumed that the ploughing services or boons occasionally recorded for the Domesday *villani* adequately compensated for the poor plough-team provision of many demesnes. We have seen that these ploughing obligations were strictly defined before the Conquest, and they remained a very inflexible resource after it, fixed by custom and hard to alter. Obligations almost identical with those in Domesday are found owed by various categories of tenants in the twelfth-century surveys, and when the acreage of ploughing that they owed can be ascertained, it is small in relation to the amount of land from which it was owed. The 40 *villani* who hold

37. Postan, *The Famulus*.
38. E. King, *Peterborough Abbey 1086-1310: a study in the land market* (1973), 143, 145.
39. Faith, 'Demesne resources', 662-4; Raftis, *Ramsey Abbey*, 66.

between them 40 yardlands 'to the king's geld' at Kettering 'find' ploughs for the abbey of Peterborough seven times a year, the 20 'men' at Tinwell owe only 34 acres between them.[40] Around 1170 on the bishop of Worcester's manor of Kempsey, Worcestershire, the bishop charged very heavy labour rent on tenancies which paid geld, but their ploughing service was only reckoned as two furlongs (*saylonae*) from each half-hide a year.[41] The bishops of Durham were not slow to exploit their tenants but on some of their manors in 1183 the *villani* typically still only 'plough and harrow three acres as *averere* and ... each *villanus*' plough team ploughs and harrows two acres'. As W.E. Kapelle has pointed out, these services are a relic of the old *scir* customs, and their very antiquity may have conferred immutability on them.[42]

This fixed traditional ploughing service faced lords with expanding demesnes with a problem of labour supply. Even where the teams of the *villani* in 1086 were enough to make up for the demesne's deficiency, given the low acreage of ploughing which appears to have been due from each tenant, they were insufficient to meet the needs of the expanding twelfth-century demesne economy. While tenants of small labour holdings could provide amounts of ploughing service out of all proportion to the amount of land they held, they typically had few plough beasts of their own.[43] Only an increase in the obligations of the peasants substantial enough to own full teams would provide an adequate increase in ploughing rent.

What is true of ploughing is true of other labour too: in order to increase the total amount of general labour owed to meet expanding demesne needs many lords adopted a policy during the late eleventh and twelfth century of increasing the number of yardlands and half-yardlands that owed labour rent. The growing pressure on the land must go a long way to explain why this was possible.[44] Peasants, many of whom had previously been of independent status, were prepared to accept tenancies on terms that, as we shall see, led eventually to their enserfment. As time went on, and pressure increased, lords were able to strike a harder bargain and found takers for smaller tenancies – the half-yardland and even smaller parcels became more common than the yardland. There must have been many willing to take on a holding on any terms.

---

40. Lennard, *Rural England*, 378–9; *Chronicon petroburgense*, 157–8.
41. For pre-Conquest ploughing obligations, see pp. 77–8, 112–13 above; Worcester: *Red Book*, I, 84; Dyer, *Lords and Peasants*, 102.
42. W.E. Kapelle, *The Norman Conquest of the North: a region and its transformation 1000–1135* (1979), 182–3; Faith, 'Demesne resources', 664–7.
43. Faith, 'Demesne resources', 666; Lennard, *Rural England*, 353–4.
44. Hallam, 'Population movements'; Miller and Hatcher, *Medieval England*, 28–33.

Changes in peasant status

To understand how the increase in tenancies came about we need to look beyond simple economic explanations to the political situation. It has for a long time been accepted that one casualty of the Conquest was the independent peasant, who lost status and became classified as a *villanus*. A thirteenth-century account of the fate of the English after the Conquest puts it like this:

> free men who held their holdings by free services or free customs ... when they were thrown out by more powerful people, on returning afterwards took the same holdings up again to hold in villeinage, doing work for them which was servile, but set and specified (*certa et nominata*).[45]

The kind of people referred to can only be documented for those counties where Domesday recognizes distinct categories of 'free men' and sokemen, as distinct from the *villani*. (Elsewhere, it has been argued, many equivalent people of comparably independent status will have been classified as *villani*.) Their decline is striking. The numbers of sokemen and 'free men' of the eastern and northern counties fell dramatically. The numbers of sokemen in Cambridgeshire fell from nearly 900 in 1066 to 177 in 1086, in Bedfordshire from about 700 to 90, in Hertfordshire from around 240 to 43. They had gone entirely from Buckinghamshire, Middlesex and Surrey. In Yorkshire there was an 'almost complete disappearance' of the sokemen who 'had almost vanished as a significant class' except in the West Riding. By contrast there were still very large numbers of sokemen in 1086 in Lincolnshire, Norfolk, Nottinghamshire and Leicestershire, Suffolk, and Essex.[46] Where sokemen survived in large numbers, we may suspect that they had been transformed from people who were tied, or had tied themselves, to a powerful local figure by warland dues and were subject to the jurisdiction of the soke, into tenants holding their land from him for rent.

We know the personal history of some individuals. Of many a previously free sokeman Domesday tells us 'he is now a *villanus*'. It was evidently a real loss of status for a sokeman to be reduced to a *villanus*, or to be obliged to do 'work such as the *villani* do'. Simon de Lisle, tenant of the manor of Wilburton on the estate of the church of Ely in 1222, held the 'ware acres' and owed the ploughing and harvest works and suit at the hundred court typical of the warland peasantry. But he was liable to the customary marriage payments which had become by his time a mark of the unfree. Simon's ancestors 'had

45. *Henry de Bracton, de legibus et consuetudinibus angliae*, ed. G.E. Woodbine, reissued with translation by S.E. Thorne (4 vols, Cambridge, Mass. 1968-77), II, fo 7 at 37.
46. H.C. Darby, *Domesday England* (1986 edn), 62–3 and appendix 3; Maitland, *Domesday Book*, 95–6; Kapelle, *Norman Conquest*, 176.

become dependent upon the manor as well as the hundred, and that probably before *Domesday Book* was made'.[47] A great many individual histories lie behind the statistical decline of the sokeman: Maitland has vividly told some of them. One of his examples is Meldreth in Cambridgeshire. Before the Conquest it was held by fifteen sokemen, ten were under the jurisdiction of the abbot of Ely, five of Earl Ælfgar. They had only three and a quarter hides between them, so they were small but free peasants – though they may well have had land in other villages too. By 1086 Meldreth had acquired a demesne of half a hide and a typical inland tenant population of fifteen bordars, three cottagers and a slave. In Maitland's view the fifteen sokemen had been transformed into the fifteen bordars: there is absolutely no way of proving or disproving this, though the figures are strikingly the same. Whether or not the same individuals, or their children, had suffered this decline in status, the whole social structure of Meldreth had been transformed from a group of free smallholders into the typical small manor with its inland serviced by a dependent workforce.[48]

The experience of the sokemen of Meldreth highlights the fact that the change in social structure after the Conquest was not simply a matter of the general economic 'depression' of particular social classes but of a significant reorganization of rural society in relation to the manorial demesne. Even on a small scale, the making or expanding of a home farm and staffing it with a team of demesne worker-tenants in the midst of a community of free farmers was not achieved without hardship, and its effects are particularly noticeable in the Danelaw counties. At Whaddon, Cambridgeshire, fifteen sokemen had held three hides between them in 1066 and one hide was held from Ely by one Turbert. Their land was given to Hardwin de Scalers and by 1086 Hardwin had established a demesne of two hides with 20 cottars. Turbert had apparently disappeared and some of the sokemen may have been among the nine *villani* who were there. Similar stories are told widely in Domesday for Cambridgeshire. Before the Conquest vills with a social structure of gentry and free peasants were common. By 1086 there had been a change. The sokemen had disappeared. 'The Norman lords had made demesne lands where their English *antecessores* possessed none.'[49]

R. Fleming's recent computer-aided analysis of the post-Conquest land settlement is in general focused on a higher social level than that of the peasantry, but she has pointed out a significant correlation between places where there was a real upheaval in the pre-Conquest landholding pattern and a fall in manorial values. She puts this down to 'the economic strains caused by a massive manorial reorganization' and concludes that 'William's tampering with ancient tenurial patterns,

---

47. Miller, *Abbey and Bishopric of Ely*, 118–19.
48. Maitland, *Domesday Book*, 90–1.
49. *Ibid.*, 172–5 at 172; R. Fleming, *Kings and Lords in Conquest England* (1991), 122–6.

not only on the level of the fee, but on the level of the vill, had huge repercussions for the kingdom'.[50] It is in the context of this 'massive manorial reorganization', in particular the creation and expansion of manorial demesnes, that many a sokeman became a customary tenant.

Kapelle has proposed that week-work was imposed on the *villani* on the bishop of Durham's demesne manors on top of the ancient *scir* customs common to the whole estate. Only those of his manors with demesne land owed regular week-work. Kapelle attributes the imposition of week-work not to a gradual evolution but to a deliberate settlement of tenants on holdings: week-work was superimposed on the *scir* customs to meet the labour demands of the demesnes newly created by Bishop Walcher. He quotes Simeon of Durham: 'many men sold themselves into perpetual servitude, provided that they could maintain a certain miserable life'.[51]

Less extreme and sudden change was probably more general. To create new permanent tenancies held for a fixed money sum and a variety of other services, arranged by agreement between lord and tenant, was apparently known as 'assizing' land. A St Paul's survey of 1181 shows the process at work. It records how many hides of land were *in dominio* and how many were *terra assisa* both 'at the time of Henry I' and in the current year. In the case of the canons' Middlesex and Hertfordshire manors the ratio of assized land to land *in dominio* in 1181 can be compared with the situation in Domesday. An increase in the proportion of assized land appears to have taken place at three of its manors, West Drayton, Ardeley and at Sandon (where four hides had changed from demesne to assized land). Odo, the farmer of Luffenhall, a sub-manor of Sandon, was responsible for assizing a further hide there between 1181 and 1222.[52] The division of hides and half-hides among tenants may have been the occasion of the 'assizing' of their obligations and the imposition of new ones such as week-work.

Establishing tenancies and fixing their rents, whether piecemeal or *en bloc*, was a process apparently fixed in the collective memory and it is possible that the whole process was widely known as the 'assize', as it was at St Paul's. The rather high-flown term 'assize' may convey something of their quality of having been part of a solemn and permanent arrangement.[53] 'Assize' was the term used for the most important of judicial and governmental decisions like the legal reforms of Henry II, and, at a less exalted level, for a new arrangement of food rents on the Ramsey estates. 'The settlement', 'the establishment' or 'the great fixing' are as good terms as any for the process by which lords fixed the obligations of their customary tenants.

---

50. Fleming, *Kings and Lords*, 125.
51. *Boldon Book: Northumberland and Durham*, ed. D. Austin (1982), 12; Kapelle, *Norman Conquest*, 182–90 at 188.
52. *Domesday of St Paul's*, 140, 141, 20, 175; Faith, 'Demesne resources', 671–2.
53. *Pace* P.D.A. Harvey, 'The Pipe Rolls and the adoption of demesne farming in England', *EcHR* 2nd series 27 (1974), 345–59 at 348. Levett, 'Financial organization', 70.

'Rents of the assize' like the 'rents of the new assize' at Wells, Norfolk, in 1206–7 were extraordinarily unalterable, remaining recorded at officially the same level for centuries. This was something of a fiction as lords could in fact increase the rent by creating a new 'increment' alongside the old sum, but there must have been some strongly held inhibition against tampering with the assized rent. It has been argued that when land came to be in short supply, the very immutability of all the conditions of tenure on what came to be known as 'customary' tenancies came to provide the peasants who held them with a valued security and protected them against rising prices for land.[54]

Customary tenancies

Assizing land involved fixing new terms of tenancy on regular holdings based on fractions of the hide or carucate. Thus these units of land that had been the basis for assessing tax now came to be used as the basis for assessing rent. The yardland was a quarter, the half-yardland an eighth of a hide, the bovate was an eighth of the carucate. This may well be how, in the 'closed' manors mentioned earlier, the existing peasant holdings which together made up the total hidage of a manor were reassessed for a standard rent in cash, kind and labour. On many this process had taken place by the Conquest, perhaps long before. On the Westminster Abbey estates 'the hides and half-hides ... had become traditional units for the assessment of rents and services by 1086 ...'[55] But on other manors the creation of customary tenancies brought about considerable topographical reorganization: this important episode in the evolution of the English village will be outlined in the next chapter.

Some kind of systematic settlement must underlie one of the most striking characteristics of the peasant tenancy as it appears in the manorial surveys of the twelfth century: its regularity. Groups of apparently identically sized yardlands or local variations, and their fractions, are held for a uniform rent and by people of similar status. These 'customary tenancies' tend to occur in groups of equally sized holdings, held for a rent so uniform that a manorial clerk drawing up a rental or survey will take one tenant as representative of all the others. Although in some cases they can be measured and found to be genuinely equal in area, the very regularity of these standard holdings

<hr/>

54. Wells: Raftis, *Ramsey Abbey*, 318. The Kentish *mal* was a fixed money rent: N. Neilson, *Customary Rents* in Oxford Studies in Social and Legal History 2 (1910), 24–3; du Boulay, *Lordship of Canterbury*, 176. The word may derive from OE *mala*, an agreement or treaty. The king sold his lands, *to male*, by auction, after 1066: *Anglo-Saxon Chronicle*, E *sub anno* 1086. J. Hatcher, 'English serfdom and villeinage: towards a reassessment', *Past and Present* 90 (February 1981), 3–39.
55. Harvey, *Westminster Abbey*, 219.

invites suspicion. A probable explanation, suggested by P.D.A. Harvey, is that the yardland and bovate, even the acres which made them up, were originally units for the assignment of obligation, rather than actual measured acreages.[56]

While new tenancies could undoubtedly be added, and old ones divided, the regularity of customary holdings has persuaded several historians that some kind of once and for all settlement had taken place. As J. Blair puts it: 'At some point the structure must have been imposed comprehensively, and thereafter extended to new holdings on an *ad hoc* basis.' It seemed to Vinogradoff that the 'the villain system of every manor is mapped out at one stroke'; to B.F. Harvey that 'on most of their manors the monks of Westminster had made a collective bargain with the whole body of their tenants'. P.D.A. Harvey has noted a 'reallocation of holdings in equal units' in the twelfth century. He has put forward the hypothesis that the creation of regular tenancies occurred as a consequence of the 'territorialization' of the peasant holding: what had been a 'right to a share' in the resources of a community was transformed into a fixed area of land on which regular dues were owed.[57]

The notion of a formal agreement or 'collective bargain' does not necessarily imply that the parties were on an equal footing. Agreements can be made under duress. From the perspective of a hundred years later the post-Conquest settlement was seen as very much a matter of bargains and agreements, in which one party was at a disadvantage. We have three accounts, all of which stress the political context in which English people were compelled to take on lands on newly specified terms. Two describe this as a matter of their taking back their own lands on new terms. Late in the twelfth century Richard Fitzneal,the author of the *Dialogue of the Exchequer*, wrote about the period after the post-Conquest land settlement, when those who had fought against William had forfeited their land:

> Those ... who had been summoned to battle but did not turn up or being occupied with domestic or other pressing business were not present ... when with the passage of time they had gained their lords' grace by devoted services, they began to gain possession at the will of their lords, for themselves alone without hope of succession. However, as time went on, when they were everywhere being expelled from their holdings, and there was no-one to restore what had been taken away, a general complaint by the native population reached the king ... at last it was decreed whatever they had been able to obtain from their lords for due demands, should be granted to them in inviolable right, a lawful agreement having meanwhile been made. From this point on an

56. Harvey, introduction to *Peasant Land Market*, 12–14.
57. Blair, *Early Medieval Surrey*, 74; Vinogradoff, *Villainage*, 335; Harvey, *Westminster Abbey*, 21; Harvey, introduction to *Peasant Land Market*, 12–14.

Englishman who holds property only does so not as of hereditary right but by dint of paying due services or by some kind of agreement (*pactio*) having been drawn up.[58]

Fitzneal's account is echoed in the passage already quoted from the *De legibus* concerning the fate of 'free men who held their holdings by free services or free customs' who 'took the same holdings up again to hold in villeinage, doing work for them which was servile, but set and specified (*certa et nominata*)'.[59] A thirteenth-century Londoner, Andrew Horn, was the author of an eccentric tirade against the legal abuses, as he saw them, of his day. His *Mirror of Justices* incorporates wholesale passages from *De legibus* 'concealed by romance', but neither that work nor pure invention seems to be its sole source. Horn also refers to formal agreements:

> contracts were made by our first conquerors, when the counts were enfeoffed of counties ... the knights of knights' fees, the villeins of villeinages ... some received fees ... to hold by villein custom to plough, lead loads, drive droves, weed, reap, mow, stack and thresh ... and sometimes without receiving food for this and whereof various fines have been levied which may be found in the treasury which make mention of such services and vile customs, as well as of more courteous services.[60]

These accounts could be interpreted as a fictitious 'social memory', perhaps first concocted in the late twelfth century to account for the multiplicity of changes since the Conquest with a single historical explanation. C. Wickham has shown how important such constructions can be to a community's idea of itself and its past.[61] Other explanations can also be called on. Fitzneal was interested in the relationship between the Normans and the English people, and he may have wanted to present some kind of justification of the depressed status of the latter. This was also a legalistic age, to which the idea that a series of legal settlements underlay familiar social relations may have had a powerful appeal. It was an age of feudal tenure, and feudal law provided the model of enfeoffment for the establishment of tenancies. There may have been a conscious effort to use the language of the fee.[62]

---

58. *De necessariis observantiis scaccarii dialogus*, ed. A. Hughes, C.G. Crump and C. Johnson (1902), 194–5. Raftis, *Ramsey Abbey*, 44–7, takes this passage to refer to thegns and sokemen. It is possible that it refers to people liable to military service of some kind who had failed to assist in putting down the rebellions against William. E.A. Freeman, *The Norman Conquest: its causes and its results* (6 vols, 1867–79), IV, 20–4 discusses the background.
59. *Bracton, de legibus*, II, fo 7 at 37. See p. 261 n. 53 below for the question of whether these were tenants on royal manors only.
60. *The Mirror of Justices*, ed. W.J. Whittaker, Selden Society 7 (1893), 80.
61. J. Fentress and C. Wickham, *Social Memory* (1992), chs 3 and 4.
62. I am grateful to Dr J. Hudson for his advice here.

Horn's phrase 'the enfeoffment of ... villeins with villeinages' is matched by references to peasant tenures rather quaintly in the occasional use in manorial surveys of terms more suitable to the knightly class: the 'cottars of the old enfeoffment' and the 'freely enfeoffed' tenants at Ramsey, who were well below knightly status.[63]

Dominium and servitium

The discourse of 'contract', 'grant' and 'enfeoffment' embodies a conceptual dichotomy fundamental to Anglo-Norman feudalism: that between what is held *in dominio* (or *in dominico*) and what is held *in servitio*. What a lord holds *in dominio* is what is in his direct power. We can see from the way that Domesday Book is arranged how basic the idea of *dominium* is: the commissioners knew that it would be possible to go round England and find out how many plough teams, how many hides, in some counties how many horses and pigs and so on were *in dominio* on every manor. We have become used in England to thinking of land held *in dominio* as land which a lord had as a 'home farm' or 'demesne land' not let to tenants, what the French call *la réserve*. But this is a very specialized usage deriving from the manorial documents of the thirteenth and fourteenth centuries: earlier *dominium* was a much wider thing. While his *dominium* can be a lord's home farm, it can include his tenants' holdings as well. In other words, *dominium* was inland. In the *Dialogue* Fitzneal says that *dominium* 'is the land held by any man and cultivated at his own expense or by his own labour, and likewise those lands held by his own villeins in his name ... the lands they till for the benefit of the lord are rightly reckoned part of the *dominium*'. The *De legibus* says about *dominium* that 'it can be taken in many ways'. *Dominium* 'is what one has for supplying his table, such as are called in English "bordlands". Villenage given to villeins, which one may recall and revoke at will, in fair weather and foul, is also called *dominium*.'[64] By contrast, what is held *in servitio* is what is held in return for a specified service. This is what Horn had in mind when he talked of the 'enfeoffment' of villeins. From this perspective, just as a knight's fee is a piece of land held for the *servitium* of providing a knight, or his cash equivalent, so the land held by a villein is held for the *servitium* of providing the services due for it. The notion of *servitium* underlies the account given by these authors of land being granted in return for set services.

Fashionable concept it may have been, but the idea that the establishment of customary tenancies had taken place by means of a series of 'pacts', 'agreements' or 'enfeoffments' nevertheless finds echoes in our evidence. Andrew Horn claimed to have seen many examples of written agreements between lords and peasants: none of

---

63. Raftis, *Ramsey Abbey*, 48 n. 103.
64. *Bracton, de legibus*, III, fo 263 at 273.

this mysterious class of documents appears to have survived, but they are not entirely implausible.[65] Written agreements by individuals to hold in villeinage became a feature on the St Albans estates in the thirteenth century. They resulted from the fact that demand for land was so great that otherwise free people were prepared to take land on servile terms without prejudice to their personal legal status.[66] The 'neiatmen' at one of the bishop of Rochester's manors must work on St Martin's Day, there is no question about that, but on the following day only 'by agreement'.[67] Indeed, binding agreements over services may well have been the occasion on which some of the major estate surveys were drawn up: many were explicitly made by sworn juries drawn from the tenants themselves. On at least three estates the elaborate collections of surveys were known as 'Domesday' and if medieval people shared one idea about Domesday Book it was that its judgements were unalterable. In the Maconnais region of France, where a mass of small tenancies was created in this way, peasants took on tenancies by some kind of formal agreement in the late twelfth century by contracts of *amasement* or *hébergement*. To hold land like this implied subjection *ratione mansi*, by reason of the tenement, not personal loss of freedom.[68]

Collective agreements are equally plausible, indeed the evidence of the surveys implies that groups of tenants were established on holdings together, and accepted similar terms. Certainly by the twelfth century villagers were used to acting as a group in a great variety of ways: maintaining the tithing system, organizing and regulating common husbandry, in some parts of England assessing, and perhaps collecting, the geld. Bargaining and negotiating were part of their lives. It may have been as a result of such bargaining that surveys record in great detail matters such as the amount of food harvest workers should receive, and for how long each day they should work. Possibly for week-work to be limited by 'custom' to a certain number of days itself represents an advance for those who owed it: their predecessors may once have to work on demand, 'as they are bidden'. Possibly, too, some of these agreements resulted from legal action. Peasants went to the royal courts in large numbers in the twelfth century and they may have sought a legal accommodation there with their lords. A reference to a 'pact' between the yardlanders of Kempsey, Worcestershire, and the bishop of Worcester's steward 'lest they be unjustly harassed' (*ne iniuste vexentur*) uses the same words as the name of royal writ *ne vexes* which could remove into the county court cases brought by tenants – not specifically peasant tenants – in dispute with their lords about services. This particular 'pact' may have followed on the heels of a

---

65. *Mirror of Justices*, 2.
66. A.E. Levett, *Studies in Manorial History* (1938), 191–2.
67. *Custumale roffensis*, ed. J. Thorpe (1788), 10.
68. G. Duby, *La sociéte aux XI* et XII* siècles dans la région maconnaise* (Paris 1953), 585ff.

successful peasant lawsuit: Horn hints that peasants used to employ *ne vexes* before they lost their freedom.[69]

The origins of peasant tenancy are sometimes explained in terms of a supposed 'social contract' by which peasants were granted land and in return for protection agreed to supply labour rent. This explanatory model has a much better foundation in fact in France where dependent peasants on the demesnes of the great abbeys had originated as *sanctuarii* who had explicitly given up their independence in return for food and protection.[70] At the level of the slave it has some foundation of fact in Anglo-Saxon England, as those Yorkshire people witness who sold their heads for food 'in the evil days' in the tenth century.[71] It has some foundation in early modern Scotland, where it was a wise course for the weak to pledge their loyalty to powerful men by 'bonds of manrent' in return for protection, and the 'free men' of East Anglia may have taken this course too.[72] At a social level above the mass of the peasantry 'commendation' created mutual ties by which loyalty was rewarded with protection. But the notion of some kind of formal exchange of service in return for protection does little to explain the origins, still less the growth, of customary tenancies in England. More relevant here, it seems, were the labour and cash requirements of a new landholding ruling class and the need of a peasant population for land. If peasants entered into 'contracts' it was not to obtain 'protection' but to gain a livelihood on terms which they were in no position to refuse.

---

69. *Red Book*, I, 84. *Mirror of Justices*, 80. *Ne vexes*: S.F.C. Milsom, *The Legal Framework of English Feudalism* (1976), 31–2; P.R. Hyams, *King, Lords and Peasants in Medieval England: the common law of villeinage in the twelfth and thirteenth centuries* (1980), 165.
70. M. Bloch 'Personal liberty and servitude in the middle ages, particularly in France: contribution to a class study' in *Slavery and Serfdom in the Middle Ages: selected essays by Marc Bloch*, trans. and ed. W.R. Beer (Berkeley 1975), 33–91 at 78ff.
71. *EHD* I, 563–4; pp. 61–2 above.
72. J.M. Wormald, *Lords and Men in Scotland: bonds of manrent 1442–1603* (1985).

9 Tenure, status and settlement

Tracing the long trajectory of lord–peasant relationships which has been proposed throughout this book has constantly involved discovering links between settlement forms and peasant status. These links suggest a model of settlement development which is explored here with reference to some examples 'on the ground'. It would be foolish to try to suggest any overall chronology into which this model might be fitted, or even to propose it as valid throughout England. Essentially what is proposed is a series of associations between settlement morphology and the nature and degree of seigneurial exploitation of land and peasants. Its main narrative can be summarized as follows: the social structure associated with the early inland resulted in a seigneurial nucleus, an Anglo-Saxon manorial centre or *tun* of some kind, perhaps a hall and its farm buildings, very often with a chapel which might even have been part of the lord's house, surrounded by, or built among, an area of intensively cultivated lands and the plots and cottages of the inland tenants. Earlier chapters have described these inland nuclei and their distinctively dependent inhabitants.

The growing emphasis on the separation of the seigneurial curia and the proliferating small tenancies held in return for heavy labour rent gave rise to a secondary type of settlement. This consisted predominantly of agricultural workers who supported themselves on smallholdings sometimes near the curia, sometimes in a discrete settlement, even a distinct 'servile village'.

A third impulse came from the establishment of standard 'customary' tenancies, often created in 'blocks'. In the cases of the 'closed' tenurial systems described earlier, this process will not have affected the overall pattern of landholding or settlement. Elsewhere it gave rise to a drastic reorganization of the local landholding pattern. This can be associated with the seemingly deliberately 'planned' elements apparent in many villages.

In this chapter a discussion of the servile village is followed by an outline of the results of seigneurial planning and reordering of the landscape. Finally, some examples of the varied kinds of settlement that could be found within a single manor covering a limited area suggest that if we are to understand settlement morphology and its development, the 'close up' will serve us better than the broad landscape picture.

Planned settlement

The twelfth century was an era of planned development, with the most interventionist and enterprising examples of seigneurial street planning being market places. The twelfth century saw a quickening of the market economy. Lords' budgets benefited from the exaction of market tolls and the ready supply of buyers for seigneurial produce. The commutation of surplus labour rent into money rent stimulated the peasant economy to raise cash through the sale of surplus produce. Shortage of land left a growing section of the population short of food. Officially sanctioned and controlled markets shaped villages around a central trading area and stimulated many to grow to urban status, but few can be firmly dated before the thirteenth century. What large-scale development was possible is shown by the enterprise of the monks of Peterborough who built Market Deeping, 'a large vill, marking out gardens and cultivated fields and building numerous tenements and cottages'.[1]

The fact that many villages seem to have been deliberately planned, or replanned, in the twelfth century is now firmly part of our understanding of medieval topography. What appears to be a very common plan is the combination of a 'curial' end of the village, church, manor house and manor farm, with peasant houses laid out along a village street on house plots of uniform or near-uniform size. Where its date can be established, the curial area of the village is associated with the Anglo-Saxon phase of the settlement, the street-plan with the post-Conquest expansion. Some Oxfordshire villages experienced quite radical replanning along these lines in the twelfth and thirteenth centuries, with peasant houses built on a regular pattern outside the walls of a castle (which in that county could be quite an unambitious structure), along a street or around a green. The appearance of a stone-built parish church of Anglo-Norman type, replacing an earlier Anglo-Saxon structure, can be thought of as part of this phase of rebuilding.[2] A striking number of villages in south-east Somerset seem, as far as can be inferred from a fairly cursory survey of their topography and archaeological record, to have followed this pattern of development.[3] Figure 25 shows as an example South Petherton, where the Anglo-Saxon nucleus, including the churchyard and thus probably

1. R.H. Hilton, *English and French Towns in Feudal Society: a comparative study* (1992), 40–52; R.H. Britnell, *The Commercialisation of English Society 1000–1500* (1993), ch. 1; Market Deeping: M.W. Beresford and J.K.S. St Joseph, *Medieval England: an aerial survey* (1958), 99.
2. C.J. Bond, 'Medieval Oxfordshire villages and their topography' in *Medieval Villages: a review of current work*, ed. D. Hooke, Oxford University Committee for Archaeology Monograph 5 (1985), 101–23 at 111, 115, 117–21; C.R.J. Currie, 'Larger medieval houses in the Vale of the White Horse', *Oxoniensia* 57 (1992), 167–71; R. Morris, *Churches in the Landscape* (1989), ch. 6.
3. A. Ellison, *Medieval Villages in South-East Somerset*, Western Archaeological Trust Survey 6 (1983), e.g. Aller 13, Ashill 16, Barrington 18, Curry Rivel 28, Low Ham 59–60.

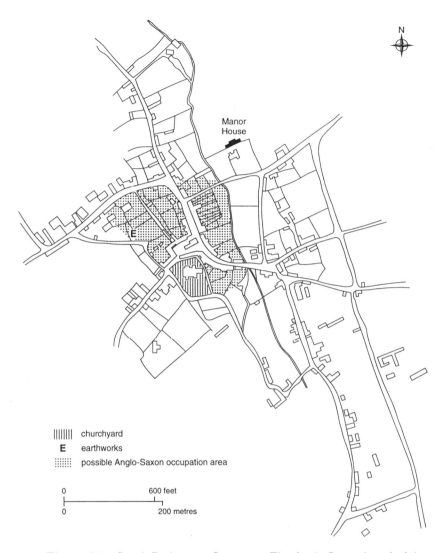

Figure 25   South Petherton, Somerset. The Anglo-Saxon 'core' of the village clusters around the site of an early minster, while the regular street pattern represents medieval and late medieval development. *Source*: after A. Ellison, *Medieval Villages in South-East Somerset*, Western Archaeological Trust Survey 6 (1983), fig. 37.

the site of the early church, can be distinguished from the medieval street pattern.

The dramatic reconstruction of settlement in the north has already been cited as an example of the results of Anglo-Norman expansion of the demesne and demesne production. Kapelle and Roberts have argued that the regular-plan villages of Yorkshire were established as completely new seigneurial plantations in which peasants were brought in, housed and provided with holdings to repopulate areas devastated by William's 'harrying of the north' in 1069. Similar plantations in Pembrokeshire and Ireland show the same kind of structure, often overlying earlier 'native' forms. Professional planters or *locatores* may have set out settlements and attracted colonists to Cumberland and Westmorland. Regular layouts in the west country show that planning is not confined to underpopulated regions.[4] A survey of north-west Lincolnshire has shown how important an agent for change in rural settlement could be the establishment of monastic houses and the granges or farms associated with them – often a product of twelfth-century lay piety. Here villages were laid out in the twelfth century and land allotments made, as was done at North Kelsey, where two furlongs 'which lie to the north of their court' were laid out associated with the monks' new grange . At Stainfield the entire village was moved.[5]

The layout of villages raises some questions about how they developed which local studies are only just beginning to answer, but some evidence suggests that their 'planned' elements might be in some cases connected with the establishment of new tenancies or the 'assizing' of already cultivated land on new terms: the process described in the preceding chapter. A general argument in favour of this view lies in the strong association between important manorial demesne manors (that is to say, manors kept in hand and exploited directly, not leased out) and villages with substantial planned elements or completely planned settlements. Planned villages seem to have been most common on large estates. Boldon Book has made it possible to explore the association of tenure and plan more deeply than has as yet been possible elsewhere on such a large scale. The bishop's demesnes (*dominium* in the text) were only found in some vills. Other vills look more like collecting points for rent and services than home farms in the conventional sense. Work from one vill could be transferred to the demesne of another. The bishop's land at Bishops Auckland in the old *scir* of Auklandshire had two great home farms, one at Coundon with Bishops Auckland, one at Wolsingham in Weardale. Kapelle's interpretation is that these were the product of Bishop Walcher's reorganization of the estate.[6]

4. C.C. Taylor, *Village and Farmstead: a history of rural settlement in England* (1983), 133ff.; *idem*, 'The regular village plan: Dorset revisited and revised' in *The Medieval Landscape of Wessex*, ed. M. Aston and C. Lewis (1994), 213–18; M. Aston, 'Medieval settlement sites in Somerset', *ibid.*, 219–37 at 226; B.K. Roberts, *The Making of the English Village* (1987), 196–201; *idem*, 'Nucleation and dispersion: distribution maps as a research tool' in *The Rural Settlements of Medieval England*, ed. M. Aston, D. Austin and C. Dyer (1989), 59–75 at 69–71.

5. P.L. Everson, C.C. Taylor and C.J. Dunn, *Change and Continuity: rural settlement in north-west Lincolnshire* (1991), 13–17.

6. W.E. Kapelle, *The Norman Conquest of the North: a region and its transformation 1000–1135* (1979), 183–6.

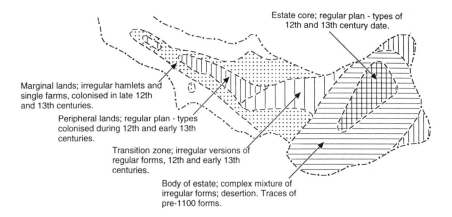

Figure 26   Episcopal demesnes and nucleated settlements: Aukland-shire, Co. Durham. B.K. Roberts's schematic map of the lands of the bishop of Durham shows regular village plans of the twelfth and thirteenth centuries in the 'estate core' and in two other areas, contrasting with areas of irregular hamlets and single farms. *Source*: after B.K. Roberts, *The Making of the English Village* (1987), fig. 9.5a.

Kapelle's evidence of planned tenancies intermeshes with the work of B.K. Roberts on the physical evidence of planned settlement. Roberts has mapped the varied village forms over the whole of Auklandshire. Figure 26 shows in a schematic form his finding that the areas of regular-plan villages coincide with the estate core. In other words what would elsewhere be called the bishop's inland was marked by planned settlement.[7] Roberts's study of County Durham revealed the association of bond holdings and elements in individual villages. Sixteen bovates of bondland, held by identical services, had eight tofts and crofts in the vill of Shelam; at Carlton street frontage and fiscal assessment were linked.[8]

More recently L.H. Campey has analysed in extreme detail the topography of some of the manors of Durham Cathedral Priory in the same county. The presence or absence of demesne land was again an important shaping factor: traces of typical inland holdings can be found in the groups of cottages and holdings of *bovatarii*, tenants with small customary holdings owing labour and money rent. Figure 27 shows the *bovatarii* tenements at Westoe. The priory had its lands in sixteen vills set out in regular tenements: 'bondlands' and cottage holdings providing labour and money rent, 'husbandlands' providing cash rent

---

7.   Roberts, *Making of the English Village*, 178–81, figs 9.5a and b.
8.   B.K. Roberts, 'Village plans in Co. Durham: a preliminary statement', *Medieval Archaeology* 16 (1972), 33–56 at 44, 52 (n. 33).

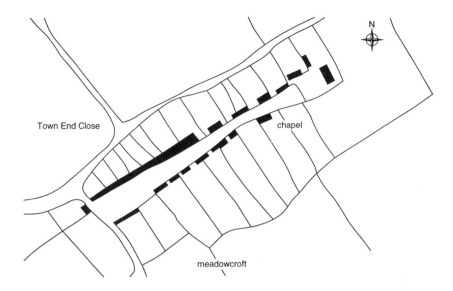

Figure 27 Village plan showing areas of customary tenancies: Westoe, Co. Durham. A planned group of twelve-acre tofts of nineteen *bovatarii* were situated in the north row of this two-row village. *Source*: after L.H. Campey, 'Medieval village plans in County Durham: an analysis of reconstructed plans based on medieval documentary sources', *Northern History* 25 (1989), 60–87, fig. 6.

alone. What was crucial to the topography of its villages was the presence or absence of 'ancient freeholds'– the holdings of drengs or 'villein sokemen'. These substantial farms, some carved out of the land of the curia, were 'focal points for expansion' and could dominate the evolution of a village, giving it a complex polyfocal shape. Where bond tenements were established alongside them they were in a quite distinct regular row or a group of small crofts. There were also entirely bond settlements with no 'ancient freeholds'. These had a regular plan with streets or lanes fronted by rows of identical tofts.[9]

Settlement and social structure

Campey was able to locate tenements on the ground in the Durham villages in a way which cannot often be done, but the different elements she investigates are widely found. It is not an exaggeration to speak of 'servile villages', resembling her 'bond settlements',

9. L.H. Campey, 'Medieval village plans in County Durham: an analysis of reconstructed plans based on medieval documentary sources', *Northern History* 25 (1989), 60–87.

elsewhere in medieval England. The estates of St Paul's provide an example of what a servile village might be like. Its location and social structure, and the role that it played in the economy of the manor in which it was a part, are interconnected. Walton, now Walton on the Naze, was one of five vills which made up the manor of Adulfsness, in north-east Essex. Set a little way off from the (probable) site of the medieval curia, it had a tenant population in 1222 of about 60 households, most of whom worked on the manorial demesne for at least part of the week, although they very likely had other jobs as well. Walton village consisted mostly of the cottages of smallholders and landless workers. Most of the inhabitants were smallholders on labour tenancies, though five people had larger composite tenancies. All but sixteen people held land jointly with up to four other tenants. At least ten people had holdings which were simply messuages. There was an unknown number of permanent demesne staff, certainly a shepherd, ploughmen, and dairy workers, who may have lived on the curia. Fishing and wildfowling, and work in the Essex river ports and in the cloth trade, may have provided additional employment. Medieval Walton was a working-class community in a way that the neighbouring villages, with their substantial peasant and yeoman farms, were not.[10] Cheam, Surrey, was much the same kind of place as this in the thirteenth century: its fourteen cotmen, who lived in a separate hamlet, had five-acre cotlands and were responsible for heavier services than the other tenants of their landlord, the archbishop of Canterbury.[11]

The survival of a very detailed Tudor survey of the Norfolk manor of Forncett enabled the American historian F.G. Davenport to make a pioneering study relating its topography to the various tenures of different classes of tenants from the eleventh century on. The difference between the dwellings of unfree smallholders and the free peasant smallholders had made its mark in a way which was still visible in 1565. While the unfree were grouped in villages in closely built rows, many of the freemen 'dwelt apart and scattered' in a way much more typical of Norfolk villages.[12] Crawley, Sussex, a manor of the bishop of Winchester studied by N.S.B. and E.C. Gras was sharply divided between two parts, as a custumal of 1280 reveals. South Crawley housed free tenants of large holdings owing the light and occasional rents by now so familiar, and North Crawley a mass of smallholders owing heavy regular labour rent on the bishop's demesne.[13] The holdings of inland workers were the original nucleus

---

10. R.J. Faith, 'The topography and social structure of a small soke in the middle ages: The Sokens, Essex', *Essex Archaeology and History*, 27 (1997), 202–13.
11. J. Blair, *Early Medieval Surrey: landholding, church and settlement before 1300* (1991), 75.
12. F.G. Davenport, *The Economic Development of a Norfolk Manor 1086–1565* (1906), 14–15.
13. N.S.B. and E.C. Gras, *The Economic and Social History of an English Village (Crawley, Hampshire AD 909–1928)* (Cambridge, Mass. 1930), 8, 232.

of what became an entirely new settlement at High Ercall, Shropshire, in the twelfth century: a fourteenth-century survey reveals that it had a distinct population of smallholders and cottagers.[14]

Some villages evidently had poorer *quartiers* of smallholdings. The cottages near the curia mapped by P.D.A. Harvey as part of his detailed analysis of the Oxfordshire village of Cuxham are shown in Fig. 28. The houses of cotmen, molmen and workers 'with doors opening onto the street' on one of Ramsey Abbey's villages must have been in very different areas from the larger messuages set among their tofts and farm buildings.[15] On the royal manor of Godalming, Surrey, the cotlands lay together along one street.[16]

Plantations and worker settlements are extreme examples of planning. Many medieval villages look as if they had neither been completely laid out from the start nor evolved haphazardly but had incorporated planned elements within a more 'organic' growth. The large-scale creation of new standard customary tenancies, often apparently at a stroke, or in 'blocks' of holdings created at intervals, may have been one of the factors behind seemingly planned elements in many villages untouched by such large-scale reshaping. Common are areas of regular tofts within the overall plan: places called 'Newlands' often have this shape, and may have resulted from deliberate planning on the part of the lord to attract new inhabitants. Many of Roberts's illustrations show blocks of regular holdings as one among many features of medieval plans and C.J. Bond's summing up of 40 years of fieldwork in the west midlands revealed a recurrent feature: regular blocks of crofts, some extending over earlier ridge and furrow.[17] The creation of these blocks of holdings is not an easy matter to document and thus to date. The splendid records which Merton College kept of its lands have provided such examples, reconstructed by retrospective analysis, of what two of their manorial villages may have looked like by the fourteenth century: Kibworth Harcourt, Leicestershire, and Cuxham, Oxfordshire, both contained two distinct elements: discrete blocks of customary villein holdings, and cottagers' tofts in the village street.[18]

---

14. M.C. Hill, *The Demesne and the Waste: a study of medieval enclosure on the manor of High Ercall 1086–1399* (1984), 22–3.
15. P.D.A. Harvey, *A Medieval Oxfordshire Village: Cuxham 1240 to 1400* (1965), map 5 at 122; P. Vinogradoff, *Villainage in England: essays in English mediaeval history* (1892), 284 n. 2. For the tofts of larger peasant houses in the street pattern G. Astill, 'Rural settlement: the toft and the croft' in *The Countryside of Medieval England*, ed. G. Astill and A. Grant (1988), 36–61.
16. Blair, *Early Medieval Surrey*, 75.
17. C.J. Bond, 'Grassy hummocks and stone foundations: field work and deserted medieval settlements in the south-west midlands 1945-1985' in *Rural Settlements of Medieval England*, ed. Aston, Austin and Dyer, 129–48 at 144–5; Astill, 'Rural settlement', 51–60.
18. C. Howell, *Land, Family and Inheritance in Transition: Kibworth Harcourt 1280–1700* (1983), map 9 at 116; Harvey, *Medieval Oxfordshire Village*, Map 5 at 122.

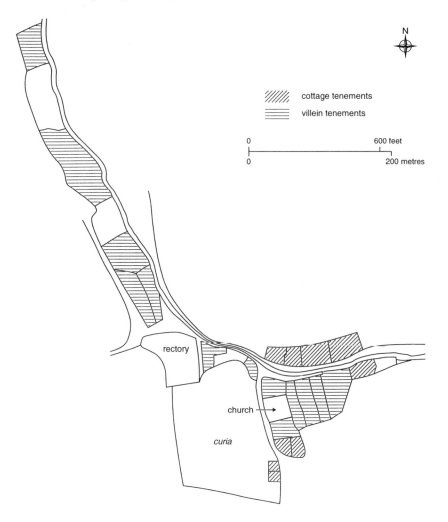

Figure 28   Cuxham, Oxfordshire, in the early fourteenth century: village plan showing distinct areas of peasant housing. *Source*: after P.D.A. Harvey, *A Medieval Oxfordshire Village: Cuxham 1240 to 1400* (1965), map 5, by permission of Oxford University Press.

C.C. Thornton's very detailed study of the tenurial morphology of Rimpton, Somerset, has already proved invaluable in illustrating the early phases of nucleation, when tenements were created round the manorial curia as the cottages and yards of housed slaves. A final phase of this long process came when the hitherto independent outlying farms were incorporated into the common arable and their owners settled on regular yardlands whose houses and tofts lay along the

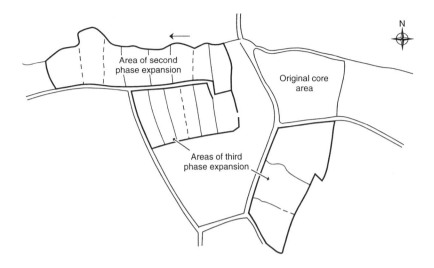

Figure 29 Rimpton, Somerset. C.C. Thornton's conjectural second and third phases of development. The smallholdings of the first phase, shown in Fig. 11, were partially replaced in the tenth century by the tofts of tenants holding land in Rimpton's newly created common-field system. *Source*: after M. Aston, 'Medieval settlement sites in Somerset' in *The Medieval Landscape of Wessex*, ed. M. Aston and C. Lewis (1994), 219–37, fig 11.6.

village street (Fig. 29). Thornton's account of Rimpton stresses the lord's need for income and a more efficient exploitation of land and labour as the driving force in settlement development, creating village and tenancies as part of the same process. A new settlement at Moortown, part of the manor of High Ercall, Shropshire, was made when seven new holdings were created out of new land, with a new township to house their tenants. These two studies have illustrated the links between the physical layout of a village and its field with the establishment of peasant tenancies, and such a process may well have put its mark on the street plans of many villages which have not yet been the subject of such painstaking local investigation.[19]

The creation of tenancies did not necessarily give rise to planned elements. The landscape imposed its own constraints on settlement. Warner's study of east Suffolk shows how the anciently settled nuclei of the region became manorial centres (with characteristic curving boundaries very reminiscent of the inlands of early minsters). Within these were what Warner sees as primary tenancies: dependent

---

19. C.C. Thornton, 'The demesne of Rimpton 938 to 1412: a study in economic development' (Ph.D. thesis, University of Leicester, 1988); Hill, *Demesne and the Waste*, 22.

holdings, whose tenants probably had land intermixed with the lord's and did his ploughing for him, while also holding peripheral grazing land. In this countryside of loose nucleation and much woodland it was natural that new settlement should take the form of straggling settlements – containing some planned-looking tenements – around large greens and commons quite far out from these old centres. They look like the setting for autonomous farmers. Nevertheless, they originated in tenements – the local equivalent of yardlands – which had been established under manorial direction. Some were older independent farms which became attached to the estate centre in the eleventh century in the post-Conquest settlement – part of the process by which free Suffolk farmers were reduced to rent payers by their new Norman lords.[20]

Agrarian change

Changes in farming practice also influenced settlement. The initiation and early development of various forms of common field farming described earlier was one response to pressure of people and their stock upon the land available to them, and it was suggested that the initial impulse to create such arrangements may have come 'from below', from the peasantry themselves, as a response to pressure on the available land from people and stock. If this was so, then it needs to be reconciled with the fact that there are some field systems which can only have been created as the result of one operation, as a system which must have been laid out *ab initio* to incorporate all the available arable. These systems are in turn often linked with the nucleated village with a regular plan. The connection is evident enough on the ground. Regular house plots in a village street seem to be a natural component of holdings which comprised regular 'packages' of strips of arable in a common field. The detailed work of M. Harvey on the long-strip cultivation of the Vale of York shows how the existence of extensive areas of land under this form of management virtually demanded settlement nucleation. Villages here had regular 'garths' or tofts abutting on to a village street and associated with fields recently laid out in regular furlongs. If regular village plans were due to seigneurial authority, then had not the fields associated with them also been planned 'from above'?[21]

20. P. Warner, *Greens, Commons and Clayland Colonization: the origins and development of green-side settlement in East Suffolk* (1987), 45.
21. M.A. Harvey, 'Planned field systems in eastern Yorkshire: some thoughts on their origin', *AgHR* 31 (1983), 91–103; J.A. Sheppard, 'Field systems of Yorkshire' in *Studies of Field Systems in the British Isles*, ed. A.R.H. Baker and R.A. Butlin (1973), 145–87 at 183–7; *idem*, 'Medieval village planning in northern England: some evidence from Yorkshire', *Journal of Historical Geography* 2 (1976), 3–20, associates village plans with fiscal assessment. Roberts, *Making of the English Village*, 46–56, 60–1.

These matters are still in dispute, but one possibility to bear in mind is that the regular patterns in village plans need not necessarily have been contemporary with the creation of the field systems of those villages. We have already seen that the process of establishing tenancies, the 'assizing' of land, may sometimes have been a matter of imposing uniform tenurial conditions on peasant yardlands and half-yardlands which were already in existence as physical units of cultivation.[22] Laying out regular tofts and house plots in a street pattern – possibly even providing houses – may have been a second stage in the process. In the early twelfth-century surveys the 'messuage' – the dwelling and its plot – does not seem to be recorded as the essential element in the peasant holding that it was to become in the thirteenth century: its appearance as an essential part of the peasant tenement may have been connected with some large-scale rehousing along these lines. Boldon Book records an example of this at Darlington where the established tenants of 48 oxgangs 'as well as of the old villeinage as of the new ... were relocated in the regular two-row village of Bondgate'.[23] Indeed the extreme regularity of plot sizes in some village plans – even to the extent of being based on a uniform unit of measurement – is itself suggestive more of planning 'from above' than the variations between house plots that might be expected in a community of farmers of varying family size and fortunes. Possibly it is in this context that we should see P.D.A. Harvey's 'territorialization' of the peasant holding: what had been a right to a share in the vill's resources was now to be not only a fixed area of arable but also its corresponding village messuage and toft.[24]

Some field systems show signs of successive expansion and reorganization as the growing population of the twelfth century came up against the limits imposed by early common field layouts. The shrinkage of the waste meant that the options for extending production were limited: one was to reorganize the fields. Some early common field systems involving immensely long strips were later subdivided. Others, which had originally been established on only part of the settlement's potential arable were reorganized to take in new land. Both of these circumstances may have been the occasion for the reorganization of holdings and housing.[25]

A common feature documented for many villages from the thirteenth century, but possibly originating much earlier, is the division into 'infield' and 'outfield'. The infield was an area of long-established holdings (the 'innox' or 'oldfield' of some west country villages was similar), each consisting of a dwelling and toft in the

---

22. See pp. 217–21 above.
23. D. Hall, 'Late Saxon topography and early medieval estates' in *Medieval Villages*, ed. Hooke, 61–9 at 65–6; Roberts, 'Village plans in Co. Durham', 52, n. 33.
24. See p. 219 above.
25. D. Hall, *Medieval Fields* (1982), 47-55; T.A.M. Bishop, 'Assarting and the growth of the open fields', *EcHR* 1st series 6 (1935), 13–29 at 19.

village nucleus and an entitlement to land in the common fields. The 'outfield', 'forland' or 'outset' consisted of an area of much freer tenure, and holdings liable to be rented by the acre for money rents. Infields are a characteristic feature of villages in the thirteenth and fourteenth centuries in areas as far apart as East Anglia, Devon, Cambridgeshire and Northumberland. Contemporaries knew them by such names as 'farmholds' or 'full lands' or 'husbandlands', and the term 'townfield' for their arable expresses the community's common interest. They are also called the 'assessed area' of the township because they owed regular rents and dues. The vocabulary of infield and outfield is late medieval but the structure itself looks earlier. It perhaps describes the nucleus of inland arable, comprising lord's and inland tenants' land, which has been suggested as a likely part of early seigneurial centres, to which new land had been added.[26]

Communal action and seigneurial interest may have at times acted in concert, and tenements laid out on land newly brought into cultivation, or newly reorganized in a common field system, may often have had something of a genuinely collective bargain about them. At Aston Blank, Gloucestershire, in the upper Windrush valley in the Cotswolds, where the earliest seigneurial complex had been worked by settled slaves, lord and peasants together enormously extended the arable after the Conquest and a separate settlement grew up, 'Cold' Aston on the high ground. C.C. Dyer, who has charted this development and the village's later decline, stresses that 'both lords and peasants were responding to the same agrarian stimuli'.[27]

A growing rural population is testimony to the essential success of twelfth-century agriculture, and peasants as consumers were themselves a stimulus to growth and commercialization. Establishing new villages or extensions to existing ones may often have been part of a communally adopted solution to an agricultural problem: the need to reorganize the fields to achieve higher productivity and feed more people. Yet it was one from which lords could profit. The more intensive seigneurial agriculture of the twelfth and thirteenth centuries brought competition for valuable resources. Peasants had long known the importance of replenishing the fertility of their land. In early field systems where land was held in severalty, or where there were small common fields, the balance of land, stock and people had probably ensured quite high fertility. The land near a settlement,

---

26. R.A. Dodgshon, *The Origins of British Field Systems: an interpretation* (1980), ch. 4. M. Aston, 'A regional study of deserted settlements in the west of England' in *Rural Settlements of Medieval England*, ed. Aston, Austin and Dyer, 105–28 at 125; S. Rippon, 'Medieval wetland reclamation in Somerset', in *Medieval Landscape of Wessex*, ed. Aston and Lewis, 239–53 at 244. Infield/outfield systems, like runrig, which combine the periodic cultivation of a shifting outland with continuous cultivation of the inland, are something different.
27. C.C. Dyer, 'The rise and fall of a medieval village: Little Aston (in Aston Blank), Gloucestershire', *Trans. Bristol and Gloucestershire Arch. Soc.* 105 (1985), 165–81 at 170.

though constantly cultivated was heavily fertilized with animal and probably human manure. Lords could benefit if their land was incorporated into common field systems for it thereafter was improved by the dung of peasant flocks and herds. This was ensured by imposing compulsory folding arrangements under which tenants had to graze their flocks and herds on the demesne acres. The extension of regular labour service and the increased access to peasant equipment in the form of plough teams and carts could be much more profitably employed in a large-scale field system. Carting and spreading marl and dung, a frequently found and extremely unpopular form of labour service, could dramatically improve fertility but required a large and well-organized workforce.[28]

In areas of traditionally dispersed settlement seigneurial agrarian interests are seen at work influencing village formation itself. M. Aston's work on Somerset has suggested a link between the nucleation of settlement and the loss of status suffered by Somerset thegns and other free people at the Conquest. He thinks that there was a physical, probably enforced, relocation of their dispersed independent farms. At Dulverton, for instance, two hides held by thirteen thegns in 1066 were 'added to' the manor.[29] (We might think of the sokemen of Meldreth, whose independent farms were replaced by inland holdings, as having been victims of a similar reorganization.)[30] As part of the same process of 'feudalization', as Aston calls it, which arranged manorial resources in a way more profitable for lords concerned to support a knightly lifestyle, places where there were evidently dispersed farmsteads in 1086 subsequently became planned settlements. The decline of the sokemen – using the term as a general indicator of the free peasantry – as a class meant that a mass of English people who had held land in some sense 'in their own right' before 1066 now held it as tenants of new lords. If Aston is right, a considerable potential seigneurial influence of settlement form has been revealed. If such a process were widespread, the implications are important. Possibly the loss of status suffered at the Conquest by many sokemen who have 'become *villani*' represented a physical disruption too: the ending of older farming patterns to create a more intensively farmed arable based on nucleated settlements. This must surely have been a considerable psychological as well as a physical upheaval.

28. C.C. Thornton, 'The determinants of land productivity on the bishop of Winchester's demesne of Rimpton, 1208 to 1403' in *Land, labour and livestock: historical studies in European agricultural productivity*, ed. B.S. Campbell and M. Overton (1991), 183–210.
29. M. Aston, 'Rural settlement in Somerset: some preliminary thoughts' in *Medieval Villages*, ed. Hooke (1985), 81–9 at 83–8. For Somerset hides as independent farming units, see pp. 137–9 above.
30. See p. 216 above.

Tenure, status and settlement

Agricultural systems, settlement form, and peasant status were interconnected, although there is no hard and fast correspondence. Looking back from the much better documented perspective of the thirteenth century we can see a rough connection between common field husbandry, nucleated settlement, and holdings held for labour rent. Labour rent was more common and heavier in midland England than in the south-west, the north and East Anglia. In areas where the terrain had encouraged small-scale independent farming, like the Arden districts of Warwickshire, tenancies for cash rent were much more common. The distinction was perhaps beginning to be felt, though it does not emerge into the recorded evidence until the end of the thirteenth century, between the comparative freedom of the peasantry outside the area of common field arable husbandry and those within it.

Nevertheless, an area of a few square miles could contain settlements of very distinct social structure, and hence of very different morphology too. The distribution of the tenant population on large manors containing several vills shows how diverse its components could be. Such a study is really only possible from the surveys of the great estates, and three such properties are discussed here. The manor of Minchinhampton, Gloucestershire, came into the hands of Holy Trinity Caen, the nunnery founded by the Conqueror's wife.[31] It is an area of some 5000 acres, comprising the entire top of one end of a long Cotswold limestone upland – what is now Minchinhampton Common – and the settlements on its steep flanks which run down to river valleys of the Frome and the Wiltshire Avon. A series of custumals survives from the early twelfth to the fourteenth century. One of these makes it possible to see how the population of the manor was distributed in 1306 (Fig. 30). There was one thing all the tenants of the manor, regardless of status, had in common. They all had to turn out for a great 'boon': haymaking on Burymore, the western part of what is now Minchinhampton Common. In every other way, different groups among them were worlds apart.

Holy Trinity did not have a cell there, but the nuns' home farm in what is now the town of Minchinhampton ('the nuns' *ham-tun*') was sizeable. Here lived a large number of regular estate workers, ploughmen, shepherds, dairywomen and so on. It must have been an impressive farm complex. Distributed mainly in three groups at Burleigh and Brimscombe on the edge of the Frome Valley and 'La Hyde' (now Hyde) were 36 customary tenancies owing week-work,

---

31. M. Chibnall, ed., *Charters and Custumals of the Abbey of Holy Trinity Caen*, British Academy Records of Social and Economic History, new series 5 (1982), 35–6, 56–62; C.E. Watson, 'The Minchinhampton custumal and its place in the story of the manor', *Transactions Bristol and Gloucestershire Arch. Soc.* 54 (1932), 203–308; N.M. Herbert, 'Longtree hundred', *VCH Gloucestershire*, XI (1976), 152–5.

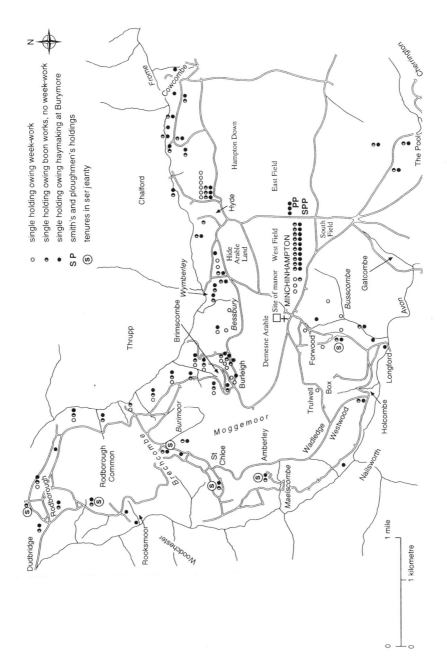

Figure 30 Minchinhampton, Gloucestershire: tenures as recorded in a custumal of 1306. *Source*: C.E. Watson, 'The Minchinhampton custumal and its place in the story of the manor', *Transactions Bristol and Gloucestershire Arch. Soc.* 54 (1932), 203–308.

some of whose tenants were *nativi*. Their arable was in the open fields adjacent to Minchinhampton town. Others were scattered in outlying parts of the manor and three were in Minchinhampton itself. There were 37 other tenants who owed no week-work, but one, two or three days' ploughing a year. A few owed suit of court, almost all owed harvest boon works, some had to supervise the reapers at harvest. Some were obliged to do the kind of specified service which became known as a serjeanty, the most responsible of which was transporting the manorial takings to Southampton for shipment back to Caen. In short they were typical warland tenants. Their holdings were in the outlying parts of the manor, and we find them mostly scattered rather than in groups, at 'The Pool', along the Avon valley sides, at St Chloe, Rodborough and 'La Hyde'. Several of these holdings, with their typical warland services, developed into small independent manors. A social gulf, as well as geographical distance, separated these various groups of tenants.

At least ten vills comprised the manor of Fladbury, Worcestershire, a manor of the bishop of Worcester (Fig. 31). A minster founded here had probably failed some time before the Conquest and the bishopric had absorbed its lands, as it had of so many others.[32] The distribution of its hidage shows that there had once been a traditional inland at Fladbury itself, the site of the minster. Around 1170 this was a typical curial centre (there was a hall there in 1299), the home of permanent estate officials like the beadle and some 'radmen', of inland workers, *famuli*, *bovarii* and cottagers, and of fifteen customary tenants with yardlands, half-yardlands and 'Mondaylands', owing week-work (and providing beer). Fladbury's arable was across the Avon, at Craycombe, and here there were also customary tenants and *famuli*. (Ungelded and with no separate demesne land, this may once have been part of the inland.) At Throckmorton was a further field system with fourteen customary yardlanders, and a small settlement at More had six. All these tenants owed boon works. The other settlements were quite different. They were small, a good way off, had gelded land, and their occupants owed the bishop only money rent. As they had none of the standard holdings it is likely that they had a much less regular layout. Their inhabitants, as far as relationship with the see of Worcester was concerned, were infinitely freer than those at Fladbury, Craycombe and Throckmorton. Some of these places too, like Minchinhampton's outliers, developed in the thirteenth century into small gentry holdings and knights' fees.

Another of the bishopric manors, Kempsey, Worcestershire, has the same division between an old minster inland, with mixed population of

---

32. S 76; Robertson, *Charters*, CXII, 208–12; D. Hooke, *Anglo-Saxon Settlements of the West Midlands: the charter evidence*, BAR British Series 95 (1981), 64; C.C. Dyer, *Lords and Peasants in a Changing Society: the estates of the bishopric of Worcester 680–1540* (1980), 30; *The Red Book of Worcester*, ed. M. Hollings, Worcestershire Historical Society (4 vols, 1934–50), II, 145.

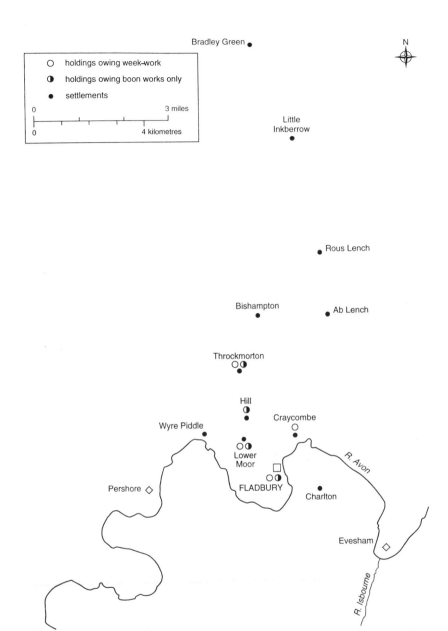

Figure 31 The manor of Fladbury, Worcestershire, *c.* 1117. The distribution of hidated and unhidated land, shown in Fig. 13, is repeated in the distribution of week-work and boon-work tenancies. *Source: The Red Book of Worcester*, ed. M. Hollings, Worcestershire Historical Society (4 vols, 1934–50), II, 145.

administrators (in this case the chamberlain), dependent cottagers and Mondaymen, and a quite separate arable centre at Broomhall with large numbers of standard customary tenancies. Here too outliers, several probably recently assarted land, had smaller, freer populations, likely to have been living in much less 'organized' surroundings. Their lands were 'anciently geldable' – the father of one tenant had 'held freely by paying geld to the king' as sokemen did. Only at the major boon works can they have really been obliged to acknowledge their link with the bishop's farm.[33]

The same pattern of an agrarian centre with customary holdings serving, but set some way apart from, the more prestigious curia can be found on the lands of Burton Abbey, Staffordshire.[34] The abbey was the foundation of the Mercian earl Wulfric Spott between 1000 and 1004 and was given additional possessions by members of his family before their eclipse under Cnut. (A possible seventh-century foundation at the same place did not survive.) It is thus out of a different stable, so to speak, than the small seventh- and eighth-century minsters with their relatively compact properties that were swallowed up by Worcester. Its endowment by 1086 included a number of small vills in Staffordshire and Worcestershire and a sizeable multi-vill property – essentially a small soke – at Mickleover in Derbyshire. None of the Staffordshire manors was individually considered very valuable in 1086, and most appear to have had very small populations. However, they shared in the startling development of the area in the twelfth and thirteenth centuries, when 'the characteristic tiny settlements of 1086 were replaced by sizeable villages'.[35] The abbey's estates were then islands of demesne husbandry in an area where small demesnes, peasant freedom and light labour rent predominated. Such week-work as had been charged was abandoned as time went on, but perhaps in compensation other customary dues and rents were increased, and the *villani* and *censarii* (rent payers) of the twelfth century were classified as *nativi* by the end of the thirteenth.[36] The surveys of the second and third decades of the twelfth century illuminate local social structure on the eve of these developments.

The town of Burton on Trent, the minster site, was a curial centre with a substantial home farm. Its geld exemption betrays an established inland. Occupations connected with the presence of the minster are well represented: cook, baker, miller, huntsman and woodward, a priest with an inn and 'the mother of Richard the monk'. The inland worker tenants are the two *bovarii*, eleven cottagers and

---

33. *Red Book*, I, 82ff.
34. C.G.O. Bridgeman, 'Staffordshire pre-Conquest charters' and 'The Burton Abbey twelfth century surveys', *Collection for a History of Staffordshire* (William Salt Archaeological Society, 1918 for 1916), 67–137 and 209–300; J.F.R. Walmesley, 'The estate of Burton Abbey from the 11th to the 14th centuries' (Ph.D. thesis, University of Birmingham, 1972); J.R. Birrell, 'Medieval agriculture', *VCH Staffordshire* VI (1979), 1–48.
35. Birrell, 'Medieval agriculture', 6–7.

eight *villani* owing week-work. There were also around 30 rent payers – probably *villani* whose labour rent had mostly been commuted for cash – some of whom owed boons, with houses or smallholdings.[37] There was a substantial home farm, with draught stock and a valuable stud farm – this last was perhaps founded on Spott's valuable gift to the newly founded abbey of a 100 unbroken and sixteen broken horses 'and all that I possess in livestock'. The stud farm, possibly all the demesne land, was probably at nearby Shobnall, where 'the demesne seems to have been a post-Domesday creation'.[38]

A minster town on the way to urbanization, Burton was a world apart from the abbey's nearby vills. Four of these, Branston, Stretton, Wetmore and Winshill, had groups of customary tenants whose services had been assessed on exactly the same basis as those at Burton, possibly at a single 'assizing'. By the late 1120s all had independent home farms of their own and two were at lease. The labour rent of the customary tenants had been very largely commuted for rent, large sub-tenancies were being carved out, and altogether the inhabitants were much less involved with the husbandry of the inland than they once had been. Nevertheless their former involvement still marked their social structure, with its bipartite division between blocks of regular customary holdings, and the curia and holdings of the curial servants. Any hypothetical reconstruction of the physical layout of these villages in the early twelfth century would surely have to include a distinct curial area and some kind of regular street plan.

At Winshill a new element had been added: 'here king William installed (*apposuit*) six sokemen belonging to Repton'.[39] Apart from owing rent and boon works, these tenants, represented in the early twelfth century by nine sokemen of whom two lived rent-free 'like a *radchenistus*'(a 'riding-knight'), owed typical warland services and suit to the shire and wapentake courts. Their holdings in Winshill were small (they may have had other land elswhere), but they passed their land on to their heirs, on payment of a heriot so substantial as to resemble the more aristocratic relief. These small freeholders must have been a distinct element in the manorial population, and a minority, but it is they and not the abbey's customary tenants who were the more typical of the region as a whole. If 'the estate of Burton Abbey may have been a reservoir of servile tenure in the Vale of Trent' it may also, and for that reason, have been a reservoir of distinctively larger and more nucleated settlements. These in turn were probably linked to common field systems, unusual for the county as a whole, in which customary tenants held arable holdings that were unusually

36. Walmesley, 'Estate of Burton Abbey', 225ff.; 'The *censarii* of Burton Abbey and the Domesday population', *North Staffordshire Journal of Field Studies* 8 (1968), 72–80.
37. Bridgeman, 'Staffordshire pre-Conquest charters', 267.
38. Birrell, 'Medieval agriculture', 15.
39. *DB* I, 273.

large for the area.[40] The existence of these 'nonconformist' field systems and settlement types shows that while peasant initiative and the demands of topography undoubtedly both played a part in shaping settlement, lordship was also able to make its considerable mark.

---

40. R.H.Hilton, 'Lord and peasant in Staffordshire in the middle ages' in his *The English Peasantry in the later Middle Ages* (1975), 215–43 at 228; B.K. Roberts, 'Field systems of the west midlands' in *Field Systems in the British Isles*, ed. Baker and Butlin, 188–231 at 212–13; C.C. Dyer, 'Social structure: the west midlands' in *Ag. Hist.* II, 660–75 at 669.

10 Villeinage

The impact of the Normans has been discussed to this point in terms of the physical realities of the agrarian economy, but an equally immediate result of the Conquest, though less tangible, was to bring England into contact with a European legal and social culture from which it had been comparatively isolated since the ninth century. The lives of many peasant families were changed by being brought within the sphere of this culture, and this final chapter outlines the principal agent of change: the evolution and application of the legal doctrine of villeinage.[1]

Legal historians of villeinage have seen it as essentially a by-product of the legal developments, generally referred to as reforms, that took place in England under Henry II, of which the most important were writs which speeded up and simplified the business of litigating over land. It had already become the rule by Henry II's reign that 'no man should have to answer for [i.e. appear in the public court with regard to] his free tenement without a royal writ'. This principle effectively limited proceedings in the royal courts to tenements which could be shown to be held 'freely'.[2] Whether a holding was a 'free tenement' or not could decide at the outset whether a case should be allowed to proceed. It was in the process of defining precise legal criteria of free and unfree tenure that the common law definitions of 'villeinage', or unfree tenure, were first evolved. Only free tenures were to receive the protection of the royal courts. (The bar on an unfree person suing there applied only when what was at issue was the tenement he held from his lord: as against the rest of the world he was free.)

What did it mean, that a piece of land was 'free', or a person was? Legal historians take this to be 'a new question', one that had only

1. S.F.C. Milsom, *The Legal Framework of English Feudalism* (1976); P.R. Hyams, *King, Lords and Peasants in Medieval England: the common law of villeinage in the twelfth and thirteenth centuries* (1980); P. Vinogradoff, *Villainage in England: essays in English mediaeval history* (1892); F. Pollock and F.W. Maitland, *The History of English Law before the time of Edward I* (1968 edn), I, 356–83, 412–32. The economic implications of villeinage tenure are discussed by J. Hatcher, 'English serfdom and villeinage: towards a reassessment', *Past and Present* 90 (February 1981), 3–39.
2. R.C. van Caenegem, *Royal Writs in England from the Conquest to Glanvill*, Selden Soc. 77 (1959), 216–17.

arisen because there were now new ways of going to law to get a piece of land back, or to dispute the amount or nature of the rent that was being charged for it. The collection of attributes which came to make up the concept of unfreedom, or villeinage as it came to be known, was assembled in the process of defining what constituted free tenure and thus entitlement to access to the courts. From this perspective, villeinage is seen essentially as a judicial by-product of the legal changes of the twelfth century: until there was a system of common law there could be no commonlaw villeinage.

Essential to this view is the belief that the period between the Conquest and the late twelfth century was essentially one of continuity not change in the real, as opposed to the legal, status of the peasantry, there being 'no ... reason to believe that a family whose members were ... regarded as in some sense free in 1100, would have taken on an essentially changed condition by 1200 when ... a later generation was ... rejected by the common law as unfree'.[3] Against this view previous chapters have argued that many families had indeed taken on an essentially changed condition in those years in their relationship to the lords of the manors on which they lived. Far from England having seen no significant change in the real status of the peasantry, large real changes had in fact taken place. Not only had the very foundations of many peasants' lives, their homes and land, been widely subject to great upheaval, but many people had undergone, or were in the process of undergoing, exactly that loss of status that legal historians have attributed to legal change and court process alone. Whether or not Fitzneal, the author of *De legibus*, and Horn were accurate in their account of the circumstances, a real process by which people had formally been granted land on more onerous conditions had taken place. Village plans and field systems are the material witness to this transformation.

To understand the changes in social attitudes and legal status that took place in this period it is important to explore some of the ways in which the law of villeinage drew on divisions, customs and attitudes which were already deeply embedded in rural society before the Conquest. Then we will turn to attitudes that were new in Anglo-Norman England. With this background, villeinage law begins to look less like a 'judicial by-product' of legal change, more like a response to much that had already happened in rural society. One such 'embedded' attitude is that some peasants who were not actually slaves were none the less 'unfree' and of low status, were born to their condition and could not shake it off. While much of the available evidence dates from after the Conquest, there is a sense of continuity between some attitudes of late Anglo-Saxon and early Anglo-Norman England. We can

---

3. Hyams, *King, Lords and Peasants*, 242 following N. Stacey, 'The estates of Glastonbury Abbey *c* 1050–1200' (D.Phil. thesis, University of Oxford, 1971), 204. Milsom, *Legal Framework* has been very influential in this context: Hyams, *Kings, Lords and Peasants*, 243 n. 91.

see this continuity in the concept of serfdom. We have already seen that there was a current of twelfth- and thirteenth-century thought that construed the origins of villein *tenure* as arising from various kinds of contract, *pactio*. Quite a different line is followed when it comes to explaining the origins of unfree personal *status*. Fitzneal said of the class of people he calls *ascripticii* that they can be 'bought and sold and otherwise disposed of' and that they are rightly considered part of the demesne. Horn thought serfdom dated back to the Flood, serfs being descended from the sons of Ham. Serfs in his view were attached to the land, could be beaten and bought and sold by their lords and evicted from their holdings: the serf was so bereft of independence 'that his lord provided for him, and had him in his wardship'.[4] The definitive body of law on the subject of legal status in the thirteenth century is contained in the treatise *De legibus et consuetudinibus Angliae (Concerning the Laws and Customs of England)* associated with Bracton. Though he did not go as far as Horn in assigning the origin of the status of serfs to Biblical times, the author too considered serfdom to be innate and of great antiquity. 'There are serfs or neifs (*servi vel nativi*) before the Conquest, at the Conquest, and since.' Like Fitzneal, he thought that the land held by inland or 'bordland' tenants remained part of the demesne.[5] These descriptions fit very well the dependent tenants of the Anglo-Saxon inland, whose counterparts, as we have seen, played such an important part in the labour force of the Anglo-Norman estate. Norman French had a name for them, *neifs* from Latin *nativi*, which links dependence with birth exactly as did Old English *geboren* and *inbyrdlice*. This was but one term in a European vocabulary of dependence and ownership of persons: people who were particularly dependent were known as *homines proprii*, their lords' 'own men' in France and Catalonia.[6]

We find another idea which spanned the Conquest in the association between certain kinds of work and servility. Spreading human or animal dung on the fields can never have carried much prestige, nor can work suitable for women, children and the unfree. 'Slavework' was a known category in Ine's Wessex. Among views of society which might have been current among educated Anglo-Saxon people we sense as a counterpart to a certain idealization of the peasantry a conviction that manual labour is an essential but degraded occupation. Bede is witness to the low status of agricultural work when he cites the labour of the monks of Lindisfarne as evidence of their piety and humility. Ælfric in

4. *The Mirror of Justices*, ed. W.J. Whittaker, Selden Soc. 7 (1893), 76–81; *Dialogus de scaccario*, ed. and trans. C. Johnson (1950), 56, 101.
5. *Mirror of Justices*, 165. *Henry de Bracton, de legibus et consuetudinibus Angliae*, ed. G.E. Woodbine, re-issued with translation by S.E. Thorne (4 vols, Cambridge, Mass. 1968–77), II, fo 7 at 37.
6. M. Bloch, *Feudal Society*, trans. L.A. Manyon (2 vols, 1961), 269–70; P. Bonnassie, *From Slavery to Feudalism in South-Western Europe*, trans. J. Birrell (1991), 221–4; G. Duby, *Rural Economy and Country Life in the Medieval West*, trans. C. Postan (1968), 189–90.

his *Colloquy* singled out the ploughman as the most important member of society because 'he feeds us all', and Alfred, who famously divided of the members of society into the equally important 'those who work, those who fight and those who pray' – a model which was to become very popular in western Europe – envisaged that those who worked should support the rest of society; but the tripartite schema is no prescription for social equality.[7]

The general Latin term most commonly used in the eleventh and twelfth centuries to denote unfreedom and low status, as distinct from pure slavery, is *rusticus*, and one of the characteristics of the *rusticus* seems to lie in the kind of labour rent that he owed. 'Rustic work' appears occasionally in Domesday. One of Ramsey Abbey's eleventh-century abbots, for instance, 'made many men free of rustic services and made Derling, a *rusticus*, into a free man'. At about the same time the register of the Benedictine abbey of Bury St Edmunds drew a distinction between 'free men' and *rustici*.[8] Services owed by free people are contrasted with those owed by *rustici* by the administrators of the Cistercian house of Kirkstall.[9]

Roman law and unfree status

The legal doctrine of villeinage drew on a whole range of ideas about the status of the peasantry, but one intellectual current in particular was very influential, the Roman law on slavery. Here too continuities can be found. Educated Englishmen had, like their continental counterparts, always been steeped in the writings of Isidore of Seville, and his work provided a continuing though very defective acquaintance with vulgar Roman law terms such as *colonus*, which we have seen used to indicate servile status in the tenth century.[10] *Ascripticius*, the term which Fitzneal used for a servile tenant tied to the manor, could very well have been applied to the people 'written into' Pyrton by charter in 887.[11] From the mid-twelfth century Roman law began to be studied in England from proper legal texts, and canon law from collections which made a dialectical and analytic approach possible. The enormous work of synthesis and analysis of the *De legibus* brought jurisprudential analysis to bear on the assembled recorded case law in order to establish legal principles, and one of its models for the unfree *villanus*, the 'villein', was the Roman slave. Nor were these scholarly disciplines altogether remote from the world of rural social relations. The *familia*

---

7. G. Duby, *The Three Orders: feudal society imagined*, trans. A Goldhammer (Chicago 1980), 99–110.
8. *Cartularium monasterii de Rameseia*, ed. W.H. Hart and P.A. Lyons, Rolls Series (3 vols, 1884–93), II, 271; D.C. Douglas, 'A charter of enfeoffment under William the Conqueror', *EHR* 42 (1927), 245–7 at 247.
9. *Coucher Book of the Cistercian Abbey of Kirkstall*, ed. W.T. Lancaster and W.P. Baildon, Thoresby Society 8 (1904), 112.
10. See pp. 80–1 above.

of abbot or bishop, to which his superior estate administrators belonged, and to which many disputes may have been referred which never came into court, 'contained experts trained in the Roman and canon law'.[12]

An important aspect of status at all levels of society was the freedom physically to move about without permission from one's superior. Here too we find social attitudes which spanned the Conquest. Slaves had never had the right, and probably very seldom the chance, to escape from their owners: it is symbolic that a slave set free 'at the crossroads' was given the freedom to travel wherever he wished. A general suspicion of lower-class people on the move, of people who were not accountable by virtue of being part of a family group, appears in the early Anglo-Saxon laws. Ine had ruled that anyone who left a village, or possibly a seigneurial *curia* (the word he used is *boldgetæl*, or handful of dwellings) to take service under another lord must have the ealdorman's permission, and Alfred incorporated this law in his own code, although he changed the wording. The lordless man was one who had no superior who was responsible for his good behaviour, and the laws of Æthelstan guard against this.[13] Limiting mobility had an economic aspect too. Lords whose economy depended on the rents and labour of their inland tenants must always have been anxious to hold onto them. In this respect the prior of Spalding, who made a careful list of his 'serfs' and their children in the thirteenth century, was not doing anything very different from the administrators of the abbot of Ely or the bishop of Rochester whom we have seen drawing up similar lists of their *geburas* in the eleventh.[14] Powerful landlords like the bishop of Worcester had probably always been quite capable of locating and retrieving their fugitive serfs without recourse to the law courts. Those of the bishop's *nativi* who were *fugitivi* living away from his estate were listed in 1170.[15]

What the Anglo-Norman state contributed to this situation was a

---

11. The interest taken in the *Etymologies* appears from the large number of surviving copies and from the appearance of whole blocks of words taken therefrom in Anglo-Saxon vocabulary lists and glossaries. I have analysed these in an unpublished paper. *Colonus* is glossed as *gebur* in Aldhelm, *De virginitate*: BL MS Philips Cheltenham i.8071 and the 'Corpus Glossary': W.M. Lindsay, ed., *An Eighth Century Latin-Anglo-Saxon Glossary (Cambridge, Corpus Christi College m.s. 144)* (1921). Pyrton: BCS 541 (S 217), and see pp. 80–1 above.
12. The influence of Roman law on the common-law doctrine of villeinage is treated throughout Hyams, *King, Lords and Peasants*; the influence of canon law especially in appendix II, 169–72. For canon law and continental social theory, see P. Michaud-Quantin, *Etudes sur la vocabulaire philosophique du moyen âge* (Rome 1970), ch. 9; J. Gilchrist, 'The medieval canon law on unfree persons: Gratian and the decretist doctrines c.1141–1234', *Studia gratiana* 19 1971), 271–301.
13. Liebermann, I, 70, 151: Alfred 37; III Æthelstan 7; II Æthelstan 2.
14. See pp. 181–4 above; H.E. Hallam, 'Some thirteenth-century censuses', *EcHR*, 2nd series 10 (1957–8), 340–61.
15. C.C. Dyer, *Lords and Peasants in a Changing Society: the estates of the bishopric of Worcester 680–1540* (1980), 104.

legal means of retrieving fugitive serfs and of proving their dependent status. The executive writ, a written order from the king, was already becoming an effective instrument of government in late Anglo-Saxon England. After the Conquest the writ *de nativo habendo* brought the whole executive machinery of the sheriff and his staff to the aid of landlords by bringing back fugitives with their goods and chattels. If a prudent lord like the abbot of Abingdon wished to take this course – and there must have been many who preferred self-help and brute force – he would provide himself with general writs *de nativis habendis*. Addressed in the king's name to all the king's sheriffs and one to the sheriff of Oxford, these ordered them to return to the abbot fully and justly 'all his fugitives, with all his possessions and chattels, wherever they shall be found and I forbid that anyone unlawfully keep them or his possessions to himself'.[16] In origin merely executive – ordering sheriffs to take a certain course of action – after about 1160 these writs became judicial. These developments were important in making villeinage a legally definable condition by bringing cases about the legal status of individual peasant tenants into court. Some people thus pursued began to object that they should not be treated in this way, and by the time that the legal writer Glanville wrote the treatise known by his name in 1187 it was possible to bring a counter writ, *de libertate probanda*, claiming free status and to bring the whole process before the king's justices. Once he came to court, much hung on the fugitive's personal status. Precedent was crucial in this respect, how had he and his family been treated in the past? The simplest method was to bring his relatives into court and have them admit their servile status, by means of bribery if necessary.[17] That he or any members of his family were 'natives' of the manor, or proof that a relative had been bought and sold, as many were, was enough to sink his claim to freedom, for *rustici* were people who could lawfully be sold 'like oxen and cows'.

To be bought and sold, for his goods to be considered to belong to his lord, to be unable to leave the manor where he was born, for his children to inherit these disabilities, would have been recognized all over early medieval Europe as marking out the serf. As P.R. Hyams has shown, many peasants' cases were immediately thrown out of the royal courts because they were obviously servile people. Many more were simply stopped by the defendant bringing an 'exception of villeinage' – a bald statement that the plaintiff was his villein – and the further details which would have revealed to us what criteria were being

---

16. *Chronicon monasterii de Abingdon*, ed. J. Stevenson, Rolls Series (2 vols, 1858), II, 81–2. My translation of *catallo suo* as 'his chattels' assumes the chancery clerks were using correct Latin; the more usual translation, 'their chattels', assumes that they were ignorant of the distinction between *suus* and *eius*. Van Caenegem, *Writs*, 336–45; Hyams, *Kings, Lords and Peasants*, 233.
17. Hyams, *King, Lords and Peasants*, 3; 'The proof of villein status in the common law', *EHR* 89 (1974), 721–49; H. Cam, 'Pedigrees of villeins and freemen in the thirteenth century' in H. Cam, *Liberties and Communities in Medieval England: collected studies in local administration and topography* (1944), 124–35 at 131–5.

applied are not recorded, if indeed they were stated in court at all. Some tenants of the abbot of Peterborough were fined a mark in 1170 for their temerity in seeking to bring a case 'as free men and they were *rustici*'.[18]

It is likely that serfs by birth, *nativi*, indeed all inland tenants, would have fallen wholesale into this general category of unfree *rustici*. Were serfs, *nativi* and *rustici* the same as villeins? This was thought to be an important question. Horn believed passionately that it 'is an abuse to count villeins as serfs', and the author of the *De legibus* drew a distinction between 'serfs or neifs' (*servi vel nativi*) who had existed since before the Conquest, and tenants in villeinage.[19] Popular opinion agreed: as late as the fifteenth century it was known in many villages which families were *nativi*, personally unfree by birth, and which were 'customary' tenants who held their land by villein tenure.[20] Nevertheless in the body of the *De legibus* the terms *nativus, servus* and *villanus* are used interchangeably, and this came to be common usage: most lawyers by the late thirteenth century recognized no distinction between people they called *rustici* or *nativi* and the people they called *villani*. In court, the important dividing line came to be that drawn between the free and the unfree, not within the ranks of the unfree. As far as personal status was concerned, both *nativi* and *villani* were unfree in the eyes of the law and if there had ever been a difference, it no longer mattered. Modern historians agree that 'villeinage was a kind of serfdom law'.[21]

Yet if *villanus* had come to mean 'serf', this was to use an old term in a new way. Here we encounter a real gulf between Anglo-Saxon and Anglo-Norman England. Change in the meaning of the terms *villanus* and *villenagium* is a crucial indicator of the changing status of the peasantry in Anglo-Norman England. Early twelfth-century usage of the term *villenagium* seems generally to indicate land held by the peasants, not land held by any particular kind of tenure. *Terra villanorum* in Domesday is simply land which is not demesne.[22] We have repeatedly seen that *villanus* in Domesday could cover a very wide range of people, from minor thegns and *geneats* to the predecessors of the customary tenants we encounter in the surveys. The exceptional development of the common law in England meant that 'villeinage' as a legal concept was a purely English phenomenon.

---

18. Hyams, *Kings, Lords and Peasants*, 249–50; Milsom, *Legal Framework*, 21–2; *Pipe Roll 16 Henry II*, Pipe Roll Soc. 15 (1892), 149.
19. *Mirror of Justices*, 165; *Bracton, de legibus*, II, fo 7 at 37.
20. Dyer, *Lords and Peasants*, 104–5; R.J. Faith, 'Debate: seigneurial control of women's marriage', *Past and Present* 99 (May 1983), 133–48 at 147–8.
21. Hyams, *Kings, Lords and Peasants*, 233.
22. For *villani* in Domesday: p. 86 above; for *terra villanorum*: F.M. Stenton, 'Introduction to Domesday Survey', *VCH Oxfordshire*, I (1939), 373–428 at 394, and p. 198 above. F. Joüon des Longrais, 'Le vilainage anglais et le servage réel et personel', *Recueils de la Sociéte Jean Bodin*, II, *Le servage* (2nd edn, Brussels 1959), 201–242.

But that *villanus* came to stand for an unfree person needs to be seen in a wider European context. The Anglo-Norman landlord class, clerical and lay, came from a society where relations between lords and peasants were undergoing change so severe that it has come to be described as a 'feudal transformation', and this was to make its mark on English peasants as on French.[23]

In one important way English society diverged from the European path. What has come to be known as 'banal lordship' (from *bannum*, order, and thence the district within which the lord had control) was the jurisdictional counterpart of the concentration of power round an aristocratic centre. The institutions of *seigneurie banale*, the privileges of monopoly control of markets, mills and ovens, though known in England (and listed as manorial assets in Domesday Book), were less of a profitable reality than they were in France. Most important of all from the point of view of the development of the legal doctrine of villeinage, the foundations laid by the late Anglo-Saxon state were built on by a royal judicial system in England that was able more effectively to circumscribe seigneurial justice than in France.[24]

As landlords, however, the Anglo-Norman landowning class shared many characteristics with its European counterparts. Before the eleventh century many French estates had been run on much the same mixed servile labour force as had late Anglo-Saxon ones. Norman Domesday clerks had no difficulty in finding for English slaves, cottagers and servile inland tenants the familiar French terms *esclave, cottier* and *bordier* and the Latin *servi, cotarii* and *bordarii*.

Tension between lords and tenants was an integral part of the culture of the class from which England's new landlords were drawn. In order to profit from the proceeds of peasant agriculture and to ensure that their tenants remained on the land where their labour and incomes were readily available, Norman lords, in common with those in other parts of Europe, began to impose a 'new servitude' on their tenants. What were known all over Europe as 'new customs' or 'bad customs' began to be demanded from the peasantry in addition to rent in cash, kind or labour. Briefly summarized, the principal exactions

---

23. G. Duby, *The Early Growth of the European Economy: warriors and peasants from the seventh to the twelfth century*, trans. H.B. Clarke (1974), 158ff.; *The Three Orders*, ch. 13; *Rural Economy*, ch. 2; J.-P. Poly and E. Bournazel, *The Feudal Transformation 900–1200*, trans. C. Higgitt (New York 1991); G. Bois, *The Transformation of the Year One Thousand: the village of Lournand from antiquity to feudalism*, trans. J. Birrell (1992); G. Fourquin, 'La nouvelle stratification' in *Histoire de la France rurale*, ed G. Duby (4 vols, 1975), I, 476–514; Bonnassie, *From Slavery to Serfdom*, chs 7, 9 and 10; T.N. Bisson, 'The feudal revolution', *Past and Present* 142 (February 1994), 6–42.

24. R. Holt, *The Mills of Medieval England* (1988), chs 3 and 4; G. Duby, *La société aux xi* et xii* siècles dans la région maconnaise* (Paris 1953), ch. 6; *Rural Economy*, 186–96; F. Ganshof and A. Verhulst, 'Medieval agrarian society in its prime: France, the Low Countries and Western Germany' in *Cambridge Economic History of Europe*, I, *The Agrarian Life of the Middle Ages* (2nd edn, 1966), ed. M.M. Postan, 291–659 at 333–4; Poly and Bournazel, *Feudal Transformation*, 25–39.

were a tax on inheritance, limitations on the right to marry off the lord's land or into a different legal category, limitations on the right to move, sometimes commuted into a 'head tax' or yearly payment, limitations on the right to convey property. 'Rustic servitudes' such as these were beginning to burden the inheritances, the land transactions and the marriages of the peasantry of western Europe from Catalonia to Flanders from around the year 1000 on. These were not signs of slavery but new impositions on peasants who were legally free. They came to play a leading part in the creation of the legal condition which was between slavery and freedom, that of serfdom.[25] It was in part in reaction to these marks of serfdom that in 996 the Norman peasantry rose in revolt, in a rising imbued with ideas of peasant freedom and equality. Knowledge of this past episode was part of Norman culture, for it was described by the poet Wace in the twelfth century in his poem *Le Roman de Rou* and commented on by the chronicler William of Jumièges.[26]

Birth and status

The definition of serfdom was part of an increasing interest in, and sensitivity about, birth and status at all levels of society. The late Anglo-Saxon text *Geðynคðo* is often deployed to construct a picture of Anglo-Saxon England as an exceptionally mobile society. This is true to the extent that the Anglo-Saxon aristocracy, though valuing family and birth, had been an 'open elite' in the sense that it recruited the upwardly mobile to its ranks. A *ceorl* who prospered to become the kind of small seigneur described earlier, with his defended curia and five hides of his own, was entitled to the rank of thegn. A thegn 'who prospered so that he served the king and rode in his household on his missions, if he himself had a thegn who served him possessing five hides' gained greater legal standing in the courts. The concentration of power from the tenth century in the hands of a single family, the royal house of Wessex, and the sophisticated power of the late Anglo-Saxon

---

25. For customs indicative of unfree status in England: Vinogradoff, *Villainage*, 81–2, 153–64; Pollock and Maitland, *History of English Law*, I, 368–76; Hyams, *King, Lords and Peasants*, 186–94. 'Customs' in France: M. Bloch, 'Personal liberty and servitude' in *Slavery and Serfdom in the Middle Ages: selected papers by Marc Bloch*, trans. and ed. W.R. Beer (Berkeley, 1975), 33–91; *Feudal Society*, chs 19, 20. Bloch's view of the growth of serfdom was challenged by L. Verriest, *Institutions médiévales: introduction au corpus des records de coutumes et des lois des chefs-lieux de l'ancien comté de Hainaut* (Mons 1946), I, 201–19. Poly and Bournazel, *Feudal Transformation*, 132; in south-west France: Bonnassie, *From Slavery to Feudalism*, 218–21. G. Duby, *Early Growth*, 227, regards them as a sign of greater liberty for *homines de corpore*. Against this view: Bonnassie, *From Slavery to Feudalism*, 316–17, 322–8, 330.
26. R.H. Hilton, *Bond Men Made Free: medieval peasant movements and the English rising of 1381* (1973), 70–1; Poly and Bournazel, *Feudal Transformation*, 136–7; Bonnassie, *From Slavery to Feudalism*, 309–12.

state made for a political situation which allowed for advancement through service.[27]

In the post-Conquest world the inflexible attributes of blood and birth were beginning to count for more. It was becoming more common for members of the continental aristocracy to identify themselves by toponymic names, to trace their pedigrees, to expect an unchallenged succession to the land of the family by members of the family. This was not unknown in England before the Conquest, and many aristocratic Anglo-Saxon names contained elements which identified their bearers as descended from a particular individual. But the family property and the family name played a much more important part in the culture of the new Anglo-Norman aristocracy than it had for the Anglo-Saxon. This was beginning to lead towards the concept of inheritance by a single heir.[28] R. Fleming has described how alien to the Normans were the complex familial landholding networks of the English landowners: the Conquest brought a 'widespread destruction of Old English lordships and kindreds which altered the tenurial fabric of England'.[29]

A new emphasis on rank and birth lies behind the investment in building and display, a more refined, luxurious and self-consciously 'gentle' lifestyle in a suitably impressive setting which we have seen made such a mark on post-Conquest England. The growing articulation of the idea of the mounted knight not simply as an efficient fighting machine but as an idealized social type – all that is summed up in the idea of 'chivalry' – brought as its counterpart a more clearly defined non-knightly ideal type. An increased emphasis on 'gentle' birth and refined behaviour required notions of uncouthness as their essential counterpart. In this process low birth became associated with rusticity, a process which progressively debased the public image of the peasant. The language of the romances contrasted *vilain* with *courtois*. *Vilain* became associated not only with low birth but with cowardice and crime: 'culvert', base and cowardly, derived from the *collibertus*, the demesne worker who was born a slave.[30] In the world of the romances

27. See pp. 155–9 above; *EHD* I, 432 (*Geþyncðo*); F.M. Stenton, 'The thriving of the Anglo-Saxon *ceorl*' in *Preparatory to Anglo-Saxon England: being the collected papers of Frank Merry Stenton*, ed. D.M. Stenton (1970), 383–93 at 388–9; W.G. Runciman, 'Accelerating social mobility: the case of Anglo-Saxon England', *Past and Present* 104 (August 1984), 3–30; P. Stafford, *Unification and Conquest: a political and social history of England in the tenth and eleventh centuries* (1989), 155–61, 74.
28. J.C. Holt, 'Feudal society and the family in early medieval England', I, 'The revolution of 1066', *TRHS* 5th series 32 (1982), 193–212, II, 'Notions of patrimony', *ibid.* 33 (1983), 193–212; Duby, *Early Growth*, 169ff.; Bloch, *Feudal Society*, chs 2, 24; E. Searle, *Predatory Kinship and the Creation of Norman Power 840–1066* (Berkeley and Los Angeles 1988), 161ff.
29. R. Fleming, *Kings and Lords in Conquest England* (1991), 138–45 at 145.
30. M. Bloch, 'The *colliberti*: a study on the formation of the servile class' in Bloch, *Slavery and Serfdom in the Middle Ages*, 93–149. For attitudes to the peasantry: A. Murray, *Reason and Society in the Middle Ages* (1978), 237–44; M. Keen, *Chivalry* (New Haven, CT, 1984), ch. 8.

the two ranks could not meet as equals, even as enemies: 'He let them go, judging them unworthy of his sword on account of their rusticity and low birth.' Geoffrey of Monmouth, who was responsible for introducing into European culture many of the enduring themes of medieval romance, seems to be contradicting this notion when he asks 'are not men born with the order of society reversed, so that a knight is begotten by a rustic and a rustic by a knight?'. But the assumption which underpins his question is that in a properly ordered society a gulf should separate the peasant from the knight.[31]

Fiefs and manorial courts

The impact of Norman seigneurial culture in England can best be understood in the context of the fief. After 1066 all title was deemed to stem from the Conquest and William was able to insist that all land held in England was held ultimately from the crown. The language of control over land and people became imbued with the language of the 'fee' of land held from a superior lord by a tenant who swore an oath of personal loyalty to him and owed him service.[32] The concepts of feudal tenure began to pervade the way that the relationship between manorial lords and their peasant tenants was conceived. We have already encountered Horn's description of the post-Conquest settlement as a time when 'contracts were made by our first conquerors, when the counts were enfeoffed of counties ... the knights of knights' fees, the villains of villainages ... some received fees ... to hold by villain custom to plough, lead loads, drive droves, weed, reap, mow, stack'.[33] The setting where this relationship was most clearly displayed to both parties was the lord's court. Lords at every level were entitled to summon their tenants to a court. It is only from the middle of the thirteenth century that records survive of the courts held by manorial lords for their tenants, but the bishop of Winchester was holding a court for the tenants on the episcopal estates at the beginning of the century, and there is some evidence that by that date these courts had probably been in existence for at least a century and a half. The author of the *Leges Henrici Primi* early in the twelfth century seems to assume that lords will hold courts in their halls, *halimota* or hall-moots, which are distinct from the courts of sokes and hundreds.[34] It is likely that by

---

31. Geoffrey of Monmouth, *Historia regum Britanniae*, ed. A. Griscom (1929), VI, ch. 2. For similarities between the military nobility of late Anglo-Saxon England and the Norman knightly class, see N.P. Brooks, 'Arms, status and warfare in late Anglo-Saxon society' in *Ethelred the Unready: papers from the Millenary Conference*, ed. D. Hill, BAR British Series 39 (1978), 81–103.
32. S. Reynolds, *Fiefs and Vassals: the medieval evidence reinterpreted* (1994) has recently drastically challenged this view. Regretably, I have not been able to take her arguments into account here.
33. *Mirror of Justices*, 80; p. 220 above.
34. *Leges Henrici Primi*, ed. L.J. Downer (1972), 9.4, 57.6, 78.2, *pace* Downer, *ibid.* 319, 364, 395.

the end of the twelfth century landowners who were subject to, and members of, the honorial courts of their own lords began to impose the same controls, and perhaps some of the same procedures, that operated there on their peasant tenants in their own manorial courts. Manorial courts provided a body of local law that was much more in touch with local conditions than was the common law. They were useful to peasants as a place where much of the business that concerned them could be dealt with: farming matters and stock control, debt and trespass, the transfer of land, and they continued to be used by them for centuries. In the last analysis, however, they were the lords' courts. By the thirteenth century the manor court had come to be regarded as the proper forum for manorial tenants to settle affairs with the lord from whom they held their land, just as the honorial court was the right place for him to settle his own business with his feudal superior.

It was in the nature of the feudal bond that lords at every level expected to intervene in the lives of those who held land from them, including their peasant tenants. Perhaps the most important event that took place in the manorial court was the admission of a tenant. This was a moment which the seigneurial class was anxious to invest with the meanings which in its own world surrounded investiture with land. The ceremony by which a lord of any kind gave 'seisin' of land to his tenant – that is, put him in possession of it – was reproduced in the procedure for the transfer of holdings in the manorial court. A peasant holding could only change hands by one party surrendering it 'into the lord's hand' and the other party being formally 'admitted' to it. That the ceremony was symbolized by transfer of nothing more impressive than a rod in no way detracted from its self-conscious legalism, which conferred on it the element of solemn agreement, *pactio*. Like all who held land from a superior lord, peasant tenants did fealty when they took over a tenancy, swearing an oath that bound them to be 'justiciable' in the lord's court. Homage, the pledge to be 'his man', was possibly given a peasant counterpart also.[35] Heads bore a symbolic load: *capitagium* or *chevage*, head money, was a payment owed as a sign of continuing dependence by tenants who had physically left the lordship. Originally a payment connected with attendance at the public courts, it became a sign of serfdom: 'they shall be serfs for ever, paying fourpence a year' swore King John of military draft-dodgers in 1205.[36]

At the seigneurial level seisin could only be given to an individual. C. Fell associates the favouring of the male heir among the upper ranks of society with 'the impact of 1066', but the imposition of

---

35. Hyams, *King, Lords and Peasants*, 11–14; Vinogradoff, *Villainage*, 164–5; Bloch, 'Personal liberty', 37–8, 70, 78–9.
36. Bloch, 'Personal liberty', 37–8; Hyams, *King, Lords and Peasants*, 34–6, quotation at 36; Vinogradoff, *Villainage*, 157–8; for another interpretation: N. Neilson, *Customary Rents* in Oxford Studies in Social and Legal History 2 (1910), 166–77; Pollock and Maitland, *History of English Law*, I, 424 n. 6.

primogeniture on the descent of peasant holdings may have been a more gradual process which began with insisting on a single male heir, and it never universally supplanted the older custom of joint or partible tenure.[37] None the less seigneurial interest in selecting or approving a suitable tenant was brought to bear at the level of the peasant tenancy as it had been among the upper ranks of society. Lords of all kinds were eager and able to profit from the desire of a tenant's heir to take over his parent's land. The relief paid by the incoming heir to an aristocratic inheritance had its equivalent in the 'entry-fine' or *gersuma* paid by a peasant on taking over the family holding.

The importance of marriage as a point at which property was transferred to another family, through dowries in land and goods, and which might bring another family's interest into the lordship or transfer a tenant out of it, meant that it was seen as the lord's concern at every level: very few people in medieval society would have expected to marry without the permission of some superior or other, at least where property was involved. Some kind of control over the marriage of dependents in Anglo-Saxon England is indicated by laws which carefully regulated the act of betrothal (the wedding itself was not seen as the important act). Lords of small pre-Conquest *scirs* could demand *merchet* fines when their people married and there are instances of *merchet* in Domesday Book, but it seems not to have been a regular obligation on peasant tenants until the late twelfth century.[38]

As the entry of a tenant into a holding, at any level of society, was an opportunity for seigneurial intervention, so too was his departure from it. The French *mainmorte* and the Catalonian *intestia* represented the lord's right to the goods of a tenant dying intestate. The aristocratic term 'heriot', from the Anglo-Saxon term for the armour given by a lord to his follower and returnable at his death, was given to the levy from the goods of a dead tenant in England. Very large sums and treasures had accrued to Anglo-Saxon kings from this source, particularly from their bishops. It is possible that reliefs took the place of this tax on aristocratic inheritance, while heriot became confined to the peasantry, and eventually to the unfree peasantry. There could be no clearer demonstration of the dominance of a French-speaking aristocracy than the debasement of the English term for this inheritance levy. In France the proportion allowed could amount to the whole, but by the time that the parallel custom is recorded for

---

37. See pp. 135–7 above; C. Fell, *Women in Anglo-Saxon England and the Impact of 1066* (1984), 148–52. P.D.A. Harvey, introduction to *The Peasant Land Market in Medieval England*, ed. P.D.A. Harvey (1984); R.J. Faith, 'Peasant families and inheritance customs in medieval England', *AgHR* 14 (1966), 77–95 at 84–5.
38. Bloch, 'Personal liberty', 37–40; P. Petot, 'Licences de mariage et formariage des serfs dans les coutumiers français au moyen âge', *Annales d'histoire de droit* ii (Poznan 1949), 199–208; E. Searle, 'Seigneurial control of women's marriage: the antecedents and functions of merchet in England', *Past and Present* 82 (February 1979), 3–43; P. Brand, P. Hyams, R.J. Faith, E. Searle, 'Debate: seigneurial control of women's marriage', *ibid.* 99 (May 1983), 123–60.

England, the lord's right to 'heriot' had become limited to the best of the family's draught stock.[39]

The role of the private manorial court as the setting for these seigneurial interventions in the lives of peasant families needs to be seen in the context of their dwindling right to participate in the business of the public courts.[40] The comparative independence of the peasants of the warland had been, since before the Conquest, very closely involved with the obligation of attending a certain court, 'owing suit' to it.[41] By the late eleventh century, suit to the hundred court was beginning to be less of a general right than a special duty limited to holders of over a minimum amount of land, typically 30 acres – by that date a sizeable peasant holding – or attached to particular tenancies. Only some of the better-off Ramsey tenants in the twelfth century still owed suit of court to shire and hundred, which was no longer an assembly of all free men. 'He has attended the county court and been free', it was said of one Ramsey tenant, as if this were something remarkable for such a person, and holding at least 30 acres was coming increasingly to be seen as a rough and ready qualification for attendance. Only sokemen were obliged – and thus entitled – to attend the 'sokemanmoot' or hundred court.[42] Thus the lower ranks of the peasantry were finding themselves gradually excluded from the more important local court, the county, which was coming to be seen as a meeting of the 'county community' of landowners, so important a group in later medieval society. The author of the *Leges Henrici Primi* described who should be summoned to its sessions: village reeves are as low down the social scale as his list goes. Peasants were not specifically excluded but he considered 'villeins or cottars or farthing-men or base and poor persons of this kind' unfit to be included 'among the judges of the laws' as 'holders of free lands' were.[43] The term *rusticus*, peasant, was itself beginning to take on some legal connotations, to gain a new precision, and was beginning to stand for a class with legal disabilities which were becoming more defined. A Colchester cartulary contains a writ debarring the *rustici* from suing for their land. *Rustici* were debarred from sitting on juries, were submitted to a different form of judicial ordeal from the free. From early in the twelfth century, if the author of the *Leges* was

---

39. *Mainmorte* and *intestia*: Bloch, 'The *colliberti*', 106–8; Bonnassie, *From Slavery to Feudalism*, 234–5. Heriot: Neilson, *Customary Rents*, 87–9.
40. For exclusion of the unfree from public courts: Bloch, 'Personal liberty', 88–91; Joüon des Longrais, 'Le vilainage anglais', 213–22; S.F.C. Milsom, *Historical Foundations of the Common Law* (1969), 11–13. The role of the process of exclusion in the evolution of the theory of villeinage underlies Hyams, *King, Lords and Peasants*.
41. See pp. 116–21 above.
42. For example, *DB* II, 130b (Fersfield, Norfolk); *Cartularium monasterii de Rameseia*, III, 274, 257; F.W. Maitland, 'The suitors of the county court', *EHR* 3 (1888), 417–21; H.M. Cam, 'Suitors and *scabini*,' in Cam, *Liberties and Communities*, 47–63 at 62; Neilson, *Customary Rents*, at 157–66.
43. *Leges Henrici Primi*, 7.1, 29.1, 1a.

representative of current thought, the proper place for their business was the lord's own manorial court, the hall-moot.[44]

Royal justice and the peasantry

The legal reforms which began to be introduced from the 1160s made the business of going to the royal court to recover land a much more speedy and cheap matter. Peasants had much business that needed settling: services that had been unreasonably demanded, land lost in the anarchy of Stephen's reign, a whole range of complaints against their lords and their neighbours. One in particular of the new legal remedies seemed ideally suited to their needs and they were among the first to use it. S.F.C. Milsom concluded on the basis of his analysis of the early plea rolls that peasants were enthusiastic users of the new writ of novel disseisin, the writ by which a tenant could recover land from which he had been evicted without due process. Substantial peasant holdings, yardlands and carucates, predominate in the examples of the writs appropriate to property actions in the text book *Glanvill*.[45]

It is the voices of a relatively small category of peasants, who had always been regarded, and regarded themselves, as free and thereby entitled to access to the law, that can be heard in the plea rolls. Analysis of the background of peasant litigants has not so far proceeded very far, but it is striking how many appear to have come from the ranks of the warland peasantry. This can be deduced from the fact that, as they apparently readily admitted, they held their land in return for services which, though agrarian, were fixed. When their labour rent is mentioned, it is typical of warland agrarian service: 'some ploughings and reapings', 'three days' ploughing and three days' reaping' and so on.[46] In a case at Grendon, Northamptonshire, brought by William Ketel and other men of the manor against their lord, the plaintiffs admit to owing two ploughings and providing one man at harvest for one day, the lord providing food, and one man another day providing his own food.[47] The right to have food provided by the lord was evidently considered a further proof of free status, and the right to eat at his table at Christmas was often brought forward as if this too

44. Juries: Hyams, *King, Lords and Peasants*, 153–6. Ordeal: R. Bartlett, *Trial by Fire and Water: the medieval judicial ordeal* (1986), 32–3; Hyams, *King, Lords and Peasants*, 156.
45. *Treatise on the Laws and Customs of England, Commonly Called Glanvill*, ed. G.D.G. Hall (1965); S.F.C. Milsom, Ford Lectures, Oxford 1987. Theoretically, lords could have used the royal court to secure the services owed them and there was an early writ 'of customs and services' which was apparently designed for just this purpose, though seldom used.
46. P. Vinogradoff, 'Agricultural services', *Economic Journal* 10 (1900), 308–22.
47. *Placitorum ... abbreviatio*, Record Commission (1811), 177; *Bracton's Note Book*, ed. F.W. Maitland (3 vols, 1887), 1819.

should count as a sign of freedom. Baldwin Young claimed that the lady of the manor had unjustly disseized him of what he claimed was his free tenement in Halliford. He ploughs the usual three acres for her, mows with his fellows and carries hay to her barn, for which they are entitled to the best wether from her flock. They look back to a time when these boons were freely given rather than demanded as of right: 'they say that in the old days, *antiquitus*, at harvest time the lord used to ask for aid and they used to aid him'.[48] Often a group of tenants will bring a claim together, and if it fails they all sink together: this happened to the men of Lecton, Bedfordshire, tenants of Lecton Priory which belonged to the abbey of Fontevrault. They were found, on consulting the survey which the abbot's bailiff had had drawn up, to owe the usual three ploughings and so on, but more servile work as well, muck spreading and liming. That sunk them.[49]

Nevertheless, juries did not always agree that 'fixed and certain' obligations signified freedom. One problem was that boon works were not only owed by free men, and were not in themselves a mark of free status: it was owing *only* boons that characterized warland obligations. A tenant of the Templars in Becclesham, Berkshire, who owed them three days' reaping, acknowledged that he was their villein.[50] Peter, son of Ailwin, brought a case concerning land he held in Thorney in 1203. Peter said that he held frecly: he willingly admitted that besides his rent in cash he had to do two boon works at which the lord provided him with food. The jury were at a loss to know whether his holding was free or not. Henry de Burton, bringing a case in Yorkshire in 1212, claimed that his holding was free: like his father and grandfather before him he owed his lord two ploughings and three reapings, at all of which he had to be provided with food. He was allowed to proceed and won his case.[51]

The reason that these peasant litigants readily admitted to their obligations was because in their view, far from being incompatible with free status, they marked it. The great divide that had always existed between the dependent peasants of the inland and the independent peasants of the warland had to a certain extent been obscured by the widespread granting of tenancies that had taken place at and after the Conquest. Nevertheless, a strong sense of this divide evidently remained in the minds of the peasants themselves. The development of common-law remedies gave the question of status a new and more legal urgency. As part of their own view of their status, the warland peasantry evidently considered that they were entitled to sue in the royal courts. The services that they owed were in their eyes good testimony to this entitlement.

---

48. *Placitorum abbreviatio*, 117.
49. *Curia Regis Rolls preserved in the Public Record Office* (1922–), VI, 326–7.
50. *Placitorum abbreviatio*, 177.
51. *Three Early Assize Rolls for the County of Northumberland, saec. XIII*, ed. W. Page, Surtees Society 88 (1890), nos. 789, 793; *Curia Regis Rolls*, VI, 335.

The evolving body of law that defined 'villeinage' seems to have taken these divisions between the peasantry into account, indeed to a very large extent it was based on them. The criteria of villein tenure were not plucked out of the air, or from the texts of Roman law alone – although the Roman slave undoubtedly provided a model – but from real life. The view came to be incorporated into the common law that villein tenure was determined not by the performance of labour service but by the terms under which it was performed. What came to be a decisive criterion of unfree tenure was to owe labour rent which was 'uncertain' or 'unfixed' (*incerta*). In the famous words of the *De Legibus*, tenure in pure villeinage is 'where one cannot know in the evening the service to be rendered in the morning, that is, where one is bound to do whatever he is bid'. The 'uncertain' work which you do not know until the bailiff orders you to do it was week-work, the regular obligation to work so many days a week at unspecified tasks.[52] People who were personally free who had entered into tenancies under some kind of written 'pact' or agreement imposing on them this most servile kind of work posed problems for the courts. They held their land in a servile way: 'And those hold villeinage who until the present day perform villein and unfixed customs and whatever they are ordered to do, as long as it is legal and decent.' Some had charters some not, but all held their land by an agreement or covenant in which what they owed was 'named and expressed'. Legal opinion differed as to what kind of legal processes were open to them, but free men who had agreed by a written 'convention' to pay even the most servile kind of labour rent for their holding were not considered personally unfree. New names, 'villein socage' and 'villein sokemen', were evolved to describe these people and their tenure. Often considered to be an anomalous group found only on the 'ancient demesne', or lands entered as the king's in Domesday Book, they were probably a much larger and more significant class, and can be found in large numbers in the Hundred Rolls. If the account given above of the widespread depression of the sokemen is anywhere near the truth, they had once been numerous indeed. They are Bracton's 'free men who held their holdings by free services or free customs' before the Conquest and later 'took the same holdings up again to hold in villeinage, doing work for them which was servile, but set and specified, *certa et nominata*'.[53]

---

52. *Bracton, de legibus*, III, 208b at 131. Vinogradoff, 'Agricultural services', 315–16; *Villainage*, 167–77; Pollock and Maitland, *History of English Law*, I, 370–2.
53. See p. 220 above. *Henry de Bracton, de legibus*, II, fo 7 at 37 (for tenants on royal land; Thorne has inserted a redundant *there* after *there were also ...*) and III, fo 208b at 131 (not specifically on royal lands); Pollock and Maitland, *History of English Law*, I, 292; Hyams, *King, Lords and Peasants*, 194–5 considers that this class of 'privileged villeins' was confined to royal lands, where they were entitled to a particular form of legal procedure. R.S. Hoyt, *The Royal Demesne in English Constitutional History 1066–1272* (Ithaca, N.Y. 1950), 8; *Rotuli Hundredorum*, Record Commission (2 vols, 1812–18), I. For later appeals to ancient demesne status: R.J. Faith, 'The "great rumour" of 1377 and peasant ideology' in *The English Rising of 1381*, ed. T.H. Aston and R.H. Hilton (1984), 43–73.

They have been described as 'freemen who having been manorialized after the conquest are transformed into a class possessing remnants of their former condition', and the writer considers that 'the invention of ancient demesne cannot account entirely for either the villein sokemen or their protection'.[54]

Legal opinion considered holdings from the demesne to be particularly servile, and this must have severely affected the numerous holders of small 'worklands' described earlier. Tenants who held land *from* the demesne were sometimes described as being themselves *part of* the demesne and land thus held could be recalled by the lord at will 'in and out of season', *tempestive et intempestive*. The Bractonian interpretation of 'bordars' and 'bordland', 'what a person has privately for his table, as are Bordlands in English', was useful here. Nevertheless, the *De Legibus* drew a distinction between serfs 'from the Conquest' and tenants who had taken on land *de dominico* by agreement by servile but fixed services.[55]

Given the complexity and variety of the tenures with which courts had to deal, it is perhaps not surprising that the test of services came to be found inadequate. This was particularly so when traditional labour rents began to be commuted for money payments. Besides, tighter definitions of legal status were felt necessary because economic changes were upsetting traditional boundaries. The tremendous pressure on land from people of all classes began to break up the standard regular tenancies granted out for labour rent – often the longest worked and best cultivated arable in an area. Standard holdings began to be fragmented among a host of eager takers who were not by any means all small peasant farmers. A lively, though mostly unofficial market in landholdings thrived. At Peterborough the abbey and its tenants alike competed in a land market of a peculiar intensity with their own freeholding tenants, ill-provided knights, and an acquisitive peasantry. There were no early barriers to this. The law defined land not by who held it but by *how* it was held, whether 'in frank fee', 'by knight service', 'in free pure and perpetual alms', 'in villeinage', 'in serjeanty'. At every level a tenurial spider's web criss-crossed the land. People of the status of the abbot of Eynsham, who in 1279 held land in villeinage in Finstock, Oxfordshire, and by a host of prosperous peasants who by no means thought of themselves as 'villeins', all held land in villeinage.[56] In these confused conditions it was often difficult to define who was a villein and who was not. Lords claiming men or women as their villein tenants encountered complicated family networks. Peasants tended to choose spouses from the same social rank as their own, but were apparently comparatively indifferent to their legal status. A great deal hung on blood relationships and legal 'proof of kin', with witnesses on each side,

---

54. C.A. Joy, 'Sokeright' (Ph.D. thesis, University of Leeds, 1972), 346.
55. *Dialogus de scaccario*, 56; *Bracton, de legibus*, III, fo 263 at 273.
56. *Rotuli Hundredorum*, I, 709.

and the crafty might exploit the situation to their advantage, claiming now to be one, now another.[57] Inter-marriage meant that Norman blood was not always a guarantee of free status by the thirteenth century: in 1269 the lord of Ralph Lorimer claimed him as his villein in spite of the fact that Ralph's grandfather had come over from Normandy and he and his father before him had always been free men. It was worth while to press such a suit: the lord claimed that he had lost £40 from Ralph's holding since his flight seven years before.[58]

The confused tenurial situation, and the impossibility of deciding what services were incontrovertibly unfree, encouraged an emphasis on personal status rather than the terms of tenure as the criterion of freedom. Indicators of personal dependence became increasingly important. The 'new customs' fitted the bill admirably: the most commonly cited were the obligation to pay fines agreed to be of servile nature: '*merchet*' to have permission to marry off one's daughter and the arbitrary payment known as 'tallage' or 'aid'. One of these in particular, the payment of fines in connection with marriage, apprenticing sons or sending them to school, became the test of villeinage *par excellence*. 'There is no service in the world which so quickly proves a man to be a villein as making a fine for marriage', was the opinion of the experienced Chief Justice Belknap in the mid-fourteenth century.[59]

Tenants who had taken up standard holdings by agreement were particularly vulnerable to this approach. Many peasant plaintiffs who were unwilling to admit that they were anything but free men did succeed in bringing cases concerning their holdings to court. Many who came into the royal courts declared that though they had held their land by labour services, nevertheless they were 'free men'. To prove that they were not, that they were villeins, their lords brought against them the evidence of just these 'bad customs': having paid to marry a daughter, to have been tallaged 'high and low', or to be related by blood to someone who had, was enough to sink a peasant's claim to free status. That similar dues had been imposed on holdings which had formerly been held for services and rent alone, we have the witness of the tenants themselves in the thirteenth century. One recurrent complaint – and one that could have been heard all over Europe – was that servile customs such as *merchet* had recently been imposed on them. Some of this protest has been collected by R.H. Hilton.[60] Hilton's view that this protest was indicative of a 'feeling of immediate loss' has been challenged by Hyams, who thought that little had

57. Z. Razi, *Life, Marriage and Death in a Medieval Parish: economy, society and demography in Halesowen 1270–1400* (1980), 92; P.R. Hyams, 'The proof of naifty in the common law', *EHR* 89 (1974), 721–49; Cam, 'Pedigrees of villeins and freemen'.
58. *Three Early Assize Rolls*, 159.
59. Faith, 'Seigneurial control of women's marriage', 133.
60. R.H. Hilton, 'Freedom and villeinage in England', *Past and Present* 31 (1965), 3–19.

changed in the real economic and social status of the peasantry in the eleventh and twelfth centuries.[61] Horn supports Hilton's view that the 'bad customs' were a development subsequent to the establishment of regular tenancies. 'And afterwards ... many of these villeins were driven by tortious distress (i.e. unlawful distraint) to do their lords the service of blood-ransom and many other customs to bring them into serfage and the power of their lords'.[62]

Manorial records give support to the view that 'customs' were a recent imposition in the late twelfth century. The obligation to pay *merchet*, dues on the sale of livestock, the liability to tallage and chevage are recorded in monastic surveys of the late twelfth century as regular obligations on standard villein tenancies. That they were a standard feature of villein tenure in the thirteenth appears from the plentiful manorial court rolls which survive for many estates from the 1230s on. To be an effective mark of status, the 'customs' needed to be routinely exacted: this may be one reason why lords had their stewards write these terms into the descriptions of their tenants' services in the manorial surveys of the late twelfth century, and to make sure that every peasant who had left the manor paid a small yearly sum as chevage or 'head-money' as a sign of their continuing attachment to it. Yet even very detailed surveys of the early twelfth century do not record them and we have no means of finding out when they were first imposed. The surveys of St Paul's manors, for instance, which minutely detailed tenant obligations in 1222, make no mention of these customs, yet an enquiry of *c.* 1290 was ordered to be made 'concerning the customary tenants, how many there are, and who, how much rent each owes ... what works and customs he owes ... what and how much he shall give for marrying his daughter to her equal (*pari suo*) within the manor or outside it ... who can be tallaged at the lord's will and who not'.[63] Customs such as *merchet* seem to have been extended to entire groups of tenants, without regard to their personal histories. In the Hundred Rolls of 1279 in manor after manor, tenant after tenant (some of wealthy peasant families) was recorded as holding his land 'by redeeming his blood' or paying for permission to give his daughter in marriage. 'Redemption' money was the very term that was used for payments exacted from the peasants of Catalonia, the *remensas*, to buy their freedom if they wished to leave their lord's territory.[64]

---

61. *Ibid.*, 14; Hyams, *King, Lords and Peasants*, 242.
62. *Mirror of Justices*, 80.
63. W.H. Hale, ed., *The Domesday of St Paul's of the year MCCXXII or registrum de visitatione maneriorum per Robertum decanum*, Camden Society 69 (1858), 153–6; E. Searle, *Lordship and Community: Battle Abbey and its banlieu 1066-1538* (Toronto 1974), 188–9; R.H. Hilton, 'Lord and peasant in Staffordshire in the middle ages', in his *The English Peasantry in the Later Middle Ages* (1975), 215–43 at 235.
64. *Rotuli Hundredorum, passim.* 'Redeeming his blood' is generally taken to mean liability to pay *merchet*, but the term may also mean that the person in question needed to pay for permission to live off the manor. *Remensas*: Hilton, *Bond Men Made Free*, 117.

The exceptional development of the common law in England briefly held out the prospect of litigation in a public court to peasants who, had they been French, would have been much more subject to their lord's justice. It was the process of preventing a large proportion of the peasantry from suing their lords over their holdings in the royal courts that eventually led to the rules about tenure and status. To that extent the evolution of legal villeinage was indeed, as legal historians have described it, a 'by-product' of the legal reforms of Henry II and his judges, and a specifically English phenomenon. But the 'customs' which provided the criteria of villeinage were European phenomena. The obligations which were evolved as criteria of unfreedom were a widespread phenomenon on the estates of Europe. European phenomena too were the contributions of canon and civil law. The learned laws helped to shape a new and more schematized view of rank and status, and provided the lawyers with the Roman slave as a model of unfreedom. In France and Germany and Catalonia, as on English manors, lords were taking a closer interest in expanding the profitability of their estates and profiting from the peasant economy through 'banal' monopoly rights and control over the lives of their peasants. In the words of Marc Bloch: 'the conceptions evolved by juridical opinion to develop the new idea of servitude belonged to the common heritage of feudal Europe.'[65]

---

65. Bloch, *Feudal Society*, 273.

Epilogue

The developments in rural social relations studied in the course of this book took place over such an immense period and encompassed such a wide variety of changes that it would be absurd to try to sum them up. Instead, the last word will be given to their view of the past held by some survivors of the warland peasantry, typical of the 'villein sokemen' and other peasants who appeared in the public courts apparently convinced of their free status. The evidence comes from a period rather later than that studied here, but it has something in common with the views of Horn and Fitzneal and this suggests that it may have been part of a more generally held medieval view of the history of the peasantry.

A series of abortive uprisings by the tenants on many great ecclesiastical estates in the southern counties which began in the late thirteenth century came to a head in the summer of 1377 and petered out in the early years of the fifteenth century. The peasants involved in these episodes shared a view common to many peasant uprisings of the middle ages: that their ancestors had enjoyed a freedom now lost to them. They associated this earlier freedom with being tenants of the king, their present serfdom with being tenants of the church. The era of better times, as they saw it, was that of the tenth-century kings of Wessex.[1] It was the belief of the tenants of Ottery St Mary, Devon, in 1377 that they too were tenants in 'ancient demesne' of the king. It was no more true of them than of the many other peasants who took part in the rising of that year – Ottery had been given away by Edward the Confessor and by the late fourteenth century belonged to a college of priests. Ottery has a long and well-documented history of tenant unrest, however, and in this enables us to learn a little more about what fourteenth-century peasants considered to be marks of ancient free status. In the light of what we have learned of the relationships between peasants and lords in Anglo-Saxon England, they are highly significant, for they were all services typical of the warland peasantry. The Ottery peasants claimed that they were free men 'because [they] held originally by ploughing the king's lands, plashing his hedges and

---

1. R.J. Faith, 'The "great rumour" of 1377 and peasant ideology' in *The English Rising of 1381*, ed. T.H. Aston and R.H. Hilton (1984), 43–73 at 56–7.

providing part of the maintenance of his household'.[2] A great historical divide separated this 'honourable dependence', a faint echo of the old 'extensive lordship' of the *scir*, from the relationship between lord and peasant at the heart of common law villeinage.

2. F. Rose-Troup, 'Medieval customs and tenures in the manor of Ottery St Mary', *Report and Transactions of the Devonshire Association* 66 (1934), 211-33 at 225 n. 2.

Appendix 1

Domesday Book references to inland *ipso nomine:*

Kent: DB I, 2b.
Oxfordshire: ibid., 155b(4), 155c, 155d(2), 156d, 158a, 158b, 159a.
Huntingdonshire: ibid., 204d.
Northamptonshire: ibid., 219c(3).
Warwickshire: ibid., 242d, 243b.
Shropshire: ibid., 254c.
Yorkshire: ibid., 301b, 301c, 301d(2), 303d, 309c, 312a, 317a(3), 320a(2), 321d, 329d, 330b, 374b.
Lincolnshire: ibid., 336b, 337d, 338d(2), 339a, 339d, 340d(2), 341b, 342c, 344a, 350a, 350b, 350d, 352a, 352b(3), 352c, 352d(2), 353a, 353b, 353c(2), 353d(2), 354c, 354d(2), 355a, 355b, 357b, 358c, 359a, 360a(2), 361c(2), 361d(2), 362a, 363d, 364d, 367a(2), 369c, 369d, 370a, 370c, 370d(2), 377a(2).

Examples of Domesday Book references to geld-free areas:

Dorset
At *Sherborne* 'the bishop has *in dominio* sixteen carucates of land. This never was divided by hides nor ever paid geld ... In the said Sherborne the monks hold from the said bishop nine and a half carucates of land which were never divided into hides or ever paid geld' (*DB* I, 77a).
Church of Glastonbury: at Sturminster Newton, fourteen carucates 'which never gelded' (*DB* I, 77c).

Essex
Hamo Dapifer at Colchester. Hall, curia and one hide, now held from him by burgesses, were always geld-free (*DB* II, 106a).

Gloucestershire
St Peter's Gloucester: the entire barton manor of (Abbot's) Barton, and the entire manor of Hinton on the Green were traditionally exempt from geld and all royal service (*DB* I, 165c).
Church of Winchcombe: entire manor of Frampton; entire manor of Charlton Abbots; ten out of 30 hides at Sherborne which 'belong to the *curia*' (*DB* I, 163d, 165d(2)).

Archbishop of York: entire manor of Oddington with its berewick (*DB* I, 164c).

Church of St Evroul: manor of Roel, which had been *terra regis*, (royal land) (*DB* I, 166c).

Church of Malmesbury: two and a half out of five hides at Littleton on Severn (*DB* I, 165b).

Hampshire

Lands for provisions of the monks of Winchester (de victu monacorum): Chilcombe manor of 68 plough teams assessed at one hide. Twelve plough teams *in dominio* (*DB* I, 41a).

Appendix 2

Aggregated numbers of bordars, cottars, *coscets, geburs, buri,* and slaves as a percentage of total enumerated population by county, from H.C. Darby, *Domesday England* (1986 edn), appendix 3.

10–19 per cent: Rutland, Hunts., Lincs.

20–29 per cent: Derbyshire, Leicestershire, Notts.

30–39 per cent: Cheshire (now in England), Lancs., Northants., Staffs., Suffolk, Sussex, Yorks.

40–49 per cent: Beds., Bucks., Devon, Glos. (now in England), Hereford (now in England), Kent, Middx, Norfolk, Oxon., Shropshire (now in England), Surrey, Warw.

50–59 per cent: Berks., Cambs., Cheshire (now in Wales), Hampshire, Herts., Shropshire (now in Wales), Somerset, Worcs.

60–69 per cent: Cornwall, Dorset, Essex, Glos. (now in Wales), Wilts.

Bibliography

Abels, R.P., *Lordship and Military Obligation in Anglo-Saxon England* (1988).

Addyman, P.V., 'The Anglo-Saxon house', *Anglo-Saxon England* 1 (1972), 273–307.

Alcock, L., 'The activities of potentates in Celtic Britain' in *Power and Politics in Early Medieval Britain and Ireland*, ed. S.T. Driscoll and M.R. Nieke (1988), 22–46.

Anderson, P., *Passages from Antiquity to Feudalism* (1974).

Anglo-Saxon and Old English Vocabularies, ed. T. Wright and R.P. Wullcker (2 vols, 1884).

Applebaum, S., 'Peasant economy and types of agriculture', in *Rural Settlement in Roman Britain*, ed. C. Thomas, CBA Report 7 (1966), 99–107.

———'Roman Britain' in *Ag. Hist.* I.II, 3–277.

Arnold, C. J., *An Archaeology of the Early Anglo-Saxon Kingdoms* (1988).

———'Territories and leadership: frameworks for the study of emergent polities in early Anglo-Saxon southern England' in *Power and Politics in Early Medieval Britain and Ireland*, ed. S.T. Driscoll and M.R. Nieke (1988), 111–27.

Arnold-Forster, F., *Studies in Church Dedications* (3 vols, 1899).

Astill, G., 'Fields' in *The Countryside of Medieval England*, ed. G. Astill and A. Grant (1988), 62–85.

———'Rural settlement: the toft and the croft' in *The Countryside of Medieval England*, ed. G. Astill and A. Grant (1988), 36–61.

Astill, G. and Grant, A., eds, *The Countryside of Medieval England* (1988).

Aston, M., 'The towns of Somerset' in *Anglo-Saxon Towns in Southern England*, ed. J. Haslam (1984), 167–247.

———'Rural settlement in Somerset: some preliminary thoughts', in *Medieval Villages: a review of current work*, ed. D. Hooke, Oxford University Committee for Archaeology Monograph 5, (1985), 81–9.

———'The development of medieval rural settlement in Somerset' in *Landscape and Townscape in the South West*, ed. R. Higham (1989), 19–40.

———'A regional study of deserted settlements in the west of England' in *The Rural Settlements of Medieval England*, ed. M. Aston, M. Austin and C.C. Dyer (1989), 105–28.

——'Medieval settlement sites in Somerset' in *The Medieval Landscape of Wessex*, ed. M. Aston and C. Lewis (1994), 219–37.

Aston, M. and Lewis, C., eds, *The Medieval Landscape of Wessex* (1994).

Aston, T.H., 'The origins of the manor in England', *TRHS* 5th series 8 (1958), 59–83, reprinted with 'The origins of the manor in England: a postscript' in T.H. Aston, P.R. Coss, C. Dyer and J. Thirsk, eds, *Social Relations and Ideas: essays in honour of R.H. Hilton* (1983), 1–43.

F.L. Attenborough, *The Laws of the Earliest English Kings* (1922).

Austin, D., 'The excavation of dispersed settlement in medieval Britain', in *The Rural Settlements of Medieval England*, ed. M. Aston, M. Austin and C.C. Dyer (1989), 231–46.

Backhouse, J., Turner, D.H., Webster, L., eds, *The Golden Age of Anglo-Saxon Art* (1984).

Baker, A.R.H. and Butlin, R.A., *Studies of Field Systems in the British Isles* (1973).

Banham, D., 'The knowledge and use of food plants in Anglo-Saxon England' (Ph.D. thesis, University of Cambridge, 1990).

Baring, F., 'Domesday Book and the Burton Cartulary', *EHR* 11 (1896), 98–102.

Barker, E., 'Sussex Anglo-Saxon charters', *Sussex Archaeological Collections* 86 (1947), 42–101.

Barker, K., 'Sherborne in Dorset: an early ecclesiastical settlement and its estate', *ASSAH* III (1984), 1–33.

Barrow, J., 'A Lotharingian in Hereford: Bishop Robert and the reorganisation of the church of Hereford 1079–1095' in *Hereford: Proceedings of the 1990 British Archaeological Association Conference*, ed. D. Whitehead (forthcoming).

Barrow, G.W.S., *The Kingdom of the Scots: government, church and society from the eleventh to the thirteenth century* (1973).

Bartlett, R., *Trial by Fire and Water: the medieval judicial ordeal* (1986).

Bassett, S., 'Beyond the edge of excavation: the topographical context of Goltho' in *Studies in Medieval History presented to R.H.C. Davis*, ed. H. Mayr-Harting and R.I. Moore (1985), 21–39.

——ed., *The Origins of Anglo-Saxon Kingdoms* (1989).

——'In search of the origins of Anglo-Saxon kingdoms' in *idem*, ed., *The Origins of Anglo-Saxon Kingdoms* (1989), 3–27.

——'Churches in Worcester before and after the conversion of the Anglo-Saxons', *Antiquaries Journal* 69 (1989), 225–56.

——'Church and diocese in the west midlands: the transition from British to Anglo-Saxon control' in *Pastoral Care Before the Parish*, ed. J. Blair and R. Sharpe (1992), 13–40.

Bates, D., *Normandy before 1066* (1982).

Baudoin, E., *Les grandes domaines dans l'empire romain* (Paris 1899).

Bede, *Historia abbatum auctore Baeda* in C. Plummer, ed., *Venerabilis Baedae opera historica* (1896).

——*Bede's Ecclesiastical History of the English People*, ed. B. Colgrave and R.A.B. Mynors (1969).

Beech, G.T., *A Rural Society in Medieval France: the Gatine of Poitou in the Eleventh and Twelfth Centuries* (Baltimore 1964).

Bell, M., 'Environmental archaeology as an index of continuity and change in the medieval landscape' in *The Rural Settlements of Medieval England*, ed. M. Aston, D. Austin and C. Dyer (1989), 269–86.

Beresford, G., *Goltho: the development of an early medieval manor c 850–1150*, Historical Buildings and Monuments Commission for England (1987).

Beresford, M. W. and St Joseph, J.K.S., *Medieval England: an aerial survey* (1958).

Biddick, K., *The Other Economy: pastoral husbandry on a medieval estate* (Berkeley 1989).

Birrell, J. R., 'Medieval agriculture', *VCH Staffordshire*, VI (1979), 1–48.

——'Deer and deer farming in medieval England', *AgHR* 40 (1992), 112–26.

Bishop, M.W., 'Multiple estates in late Anglo-Saxon Nottinghamshire', *Trans. Thoroton Society* 85 (1981), 37–47.

Bishop, T.A.M., 'Assarting and the growth of the open fields', *EcHR* 1st series 6 (1935), 13–29.

Bisson, T.N., 'The feudal revolution', *Past and Present* 142 (February 1994), 6–42.

Blair, J., 'Local churches in Domesday Book and before' in *Domesday Studies*, ed. J. Holt (1987), 265–78.

——ed., *Minsters and Parish Churches: the local church in transition 950–1200*, Oxford University Committee for Archaeology Monograph 17 (1988), 1–19.

——'An introduction to the Surrey Domesday' in *The Surrey Domesday* (1989), 1–17.

——*Early Medieval Surrey: landholding, church and settlement before 1300* (1991).

——'Anglo-Saxon minsters, a topographical review' in *Pastoral Care Before the Parish*, ed. J. Blair and R. Sharpe (1992), 226–66.

——'Hall and chamber: English domestic planning 1000–1250' in *Manorial Domestic Buildings in England and Northern France*, ed. G. Meirion-Jones and M. Jones, Society of Antiquaries of London Occasional Paper 15 (1993), 1–21.

——*Anglo-Saxon Oxfordshire* (1994).

Blair J. and Sharpe, R., eds, *Pastoral Care Before the Parish* (1992).

Bloch, M., *Feudal Society*, trans. L.A. Manyon (2 vols, 1961).

——*Slavery and Serfdom in the Middle Ages: selected papers by Marc Bloch*, trans. and ed. W.R. Beer (Berkeley, 1975).

Bois, G., *The Transformation of the Year One Thousand: the village of Lournand from antiquity to feudalism*, trans. J. Birrell (1992).

Boldon Book: Northumberland and Durham, ed. D. Austin (1982).

Bolton, J.L., *The Medieval English Economy 1150–1500* (1980).

Bond, C. J., 'Medieval Oxfordshire villages and their topography' in *Medieval Villages: a review of current work*, ed. D. Hooke, Oxford University Committee for Archaeology Monograph 5 (1985), 101–23.

——'Church and parish in Norman Worcestershire', in *Minsters and Parish Churches: the local church in transition 950–1200*, ed. J. Blair, Oxford University Committee for Archaeology Monograph 17 (1988), 119–58.

——'Grassy hummocks and stone foundations: field work and deserted medieval settlements in the south-west midlands 1945–1985' in *The Rural Settlements of Medieval England*, ed. M. Aston, M. Austin and C.C. Dyer (1989), 129–48.

Bonnassie, P., *From Slavery to Feudalism in South-Western Europe*, trans. J. Birrell (1991).

Boserup, E., *The Conditions of Agricultural Growth* (1965).

Bourne, J., 'Kingston place-names: an interim report', *Journal of English Place-Name Soc.* 20 (1987–8), 10–37.

Bowen, H.C. and Fowler, P.J., eds, *Early Land Allotment in the British Isles*, BAR British Series 48 (1978).

Bracton's Note Book, ed. F.W. Maitland (3 vols, 1887).

Brand, P., Hyams, P., Faith, R.J. and Searle, E., 'Debate: seigneurial control of women's marriage', *Past and Present* 99 (May 1983), 123–60.

Brandon, P., *The Sussex Landscape* (1974).

Brandon, P. and Short, B., *The South East from AD 1000* (1990).

Bridbury, A. R., 'Domesday Book: a re-assessment', *EHR* 105 (1990), 284–309.

Bridgeman, C.G.O., 'Staffordshire pre-Conquest charters', *Collections for a History of Staffordshire* (William Salt Archaeological Society 1918 for 1916), 67–137.

——'The Burton Abbey twelfth century surveys', *Collections for a History of Staffordshire*, (William Salt Archaeological Society 1918 for 1916), 209–300.

Britnell, R.H., *The Commercialisation of English Society 1000–1500* (1993).

Brooks, N. P., 'The development of military obligations in eighth and ninth century England', in *England before the Conquest: studies in primary sources presented to Dorothy Whitelock*, ed. P. Clemoes and K. Hughes (1971), 69–84.

——'Arms, status and warfare in late Anglo-Saxon society' in *Ethelred the Unready: papers from the Millenary Conference*, ed. D. Hill, BAR British Series 59 (1978), 81–103.

——'Ninth century England: the crucible of defeat', *TRHS* 5th series 29 (1979), 1–20.

——*The Early History of the Church at Canterbury: Christ Church from 597 to 1066* (1984).

——'The creation and early structure of the kingdom of Kent' in *The Origins of Anglo-Saxon Kingdoms*, ed. S. Bassett (1989), 55–74.

——'Rochester Bridge, AD 43–1381' in *Traffic and Politics: the construction and management of Rochester Bridge AD 43–1993*, ed. N. Yates and J. M. Gibson (1994), 1–40.

Brooks, N.P. and Cubitt, C., eds, *St Oswald of Worcester: life and influence* (1996).

Bruneaux, J.L., *The Celtic Gauls: gods, rites and sanctuaries*, trans. D. Nash (1988).

Bullough, D.A., 'Early medieval social groupings: the terminology of kinship', *Past and Present* 45 (November 1969), 3–18.

Cadman, G. and Foard, G., 'Raunds, manorial and village origins' in *Studies in Late Anglo-Saxon Settlement*, ed. M.L. Faull (1984), 81–100.

Cam, H.M., '*Manerium cum hundredo*: the hundred and the hundredal manor', *EHR* 47 (1932), 353–76.

——*Liberties and Communities in Medieval England: collected studies in local administration and topography* (1944).

——'The community of the vill' in *Medieval Studies presented to Rose Graham*, ed. V. Ruffer and A.J. Taylor (1950), 1–14.

Campbell, B., 'Population and the genesis of commonfields on a Norfolk manor', *EcHR* 2nd series 33 (1980), 174–92.

Campbell, J., 'Bede's words for places' in *Places, Names and Graves*, ed. P.H. Sawyer (1979), 34–53.

——*Bede's Reges and Principes* (Jarrow 1979).

——*Essays in Anglo-Saxon History* (1986).

——'Some agents and agencies of the late Anglo-Saxon state' in *Domesday Studies*, ed. J. Holt (1987), 201–18.

Campbell, J., John, E. and Wormald, P., *The Anglo-Saxons* (1982).

Campey, L.H., 'Medieval village plans in County Durham: an analysis of reconstructed plans based on medieval documentary sources', *Northern History* 25 (1989), 60–87.

Carabie, R., 'La propriété foncière dans le très ancien droit normand (xie–xiiie siècles), *Bibliothèque d'histoire du droit normand*, 2nd series 5 (Caen 1943).

Cartularium monasterii de Rameseia, ed. W.H. Hart and P.A. Lyons, Rolls Series (3 vols, 1884–93).

Cartulary and Terrier of the Priory of Bilsington, ed. N. Neilson, British Academy Records of the Social and Economic History of England and Wales 7 (1928).

Cartulary of the Knights of St John of Jerusalem in England: Secunda Camera, Essex, ed. M. Gervers (1982).

Chadwick, H., *Studies on Anglo-Saxon Institutions* (1905).

Chapelot, J., 'Le font de cabane dans le habitat rural ouest-européen: état des questions', *Archaeologie Médiévale* 10 (1980), 5–57.

Chapelot, J. and Fossier, R., *The Village and House in the Middle Ages*, trans. H. Cleeve (1985).

Charles-Edwards, T.M. 'Kinship, status and the origins of the hide', *Past and Present* 56 (1972), 3–33.

——'Native political organization in Roman Britain and the origin of MW *brenhin*', in *Antiquitates indo-germanicae*, ed. M. Mayrhofer *et al.* (1974), 35–45.

——'The distinction between land and moveable wealth in Anglo-Saxon England' in *English Medieval Settlement*, ed. P.H. Sawyer (1979), 97–104.

——'Early medieval kingships in the British Isles' in *The Origins of Anglo-Saxon Kingdoms*, ed. S. Bassett (1989), 28–39.

——'The pastoral role of the church in the early Irish laws', in *Pastoral Care before the Parish*, ed. J. Blair and R. Sharpe (1992), 63–80.

Chibnall, M., ed., *Charters and Custumals of the Abbey of Holy Trinity Caen*, British Academy Records of Social and Economic History, new series 5 (1982).

——*Anglo-Norman England* (1986).

Chronicon monasterii de Abingdon, ed. J. Stevenson, Rolls Series (2 vols, 1858).

Chronicon petroburgense, ed. T. Stapledon, Camden Society 47 (1849).

Clarke, H.B., 'Domesday slavery (adjusted for slaves)', *Midland History* 1.4 (1972), 37–46.

——'The early surveys of Evesham Abbey: an investigation into the problem of continuity in Anglo-Norman England' (Ph.D. thesis, University of Birmingham 1978).

Clausing, R., *The Roman Colonate: the theory of its origin* (New York 1925).

Corcos, N.J., 'Early estates on the Poldens and the origins of settlement at Shapwick', *Proc. Somerset Archaeological and Natural History Society* 127 (1984), 47–54.

Costen, M., *The Origins of Somerset* (1992).

——'Huish and worth: Old English survivals in a later landscape', *ASSAH* 5 (1992), 65–83.

——'Settlement in Wessex in the tenth century: the charter evidence' in *The Medieval Landscape of Wessex*, ed. M. Aston and C. Lewis (1994), 97–107.

Coucher Book of the Cistercian Abbey of Kirkstall, ed. W.T. Lancaster and W.P. Baildon, Thoresby Society 8 (1904).

Cunliffe, B., *Iron Age Communities in Britain* (1974).

Curia Regis Rolls preserved in the Public Record Office (1922–), VI.

Currie, C.R.J., 'Larger medieval houses in the Vale of the White Horse', *Oxoniensia* 57 (1992), 167–71.

Custumale roffensis ed. J. Thorpe (1788).

Darby, H.C., *The Domesday Geography of Eastern England* (1957).

——*Domesday England* (1986 edn).

Davenport, F.G., *The Economic Development of a Norfolk Manor 1086–1565* (1906).

Davies, W., *An Early Welsh Microcosm: studies in the Llandaff charters* (1978).

——'Roman settlements and post-Roman estates in SE Wales' in *The End of Roman Britain*, ed. P.J. Casey, BAR British Series 71 (1979), 153–73.

———*Wales in the Early Middle Ages* (1982).

Davies, W. and Vierck, H., 'The contents of the Tribal Hidage: social aggregates and settlement patterns', *Frühmittelalterliche Studien* 8 (1974), 223–93.

De necessariis observantiis scaccarii dialogus, ed. A. Hughes, C.G. Crump and C. Johnson (1902).

Demarest, E.B., '*Inter Ripam et Mersham*', *EHR* 38 (1923), 161–70.

Devroey, J.P., 'Les premiers polyptyques remois, viie–viiie siècles', reprinted from *Le grand domaine aux époques mérovingienne et carolingienne*, ed. A. Verhulst (Ghent 1985) in J.P. Devroey, *Etudes sur le grand domaine carolingien* (1993), 78–97.

Dialogus de scaccario, ed. and trans. C. Johnson (1950).

Dodgshon, R.A., 'The landholding foundations of the open-field system', *Past and Present* 67 (May 1975), 3–29.

———*The Origins of British Field Systems: an interpretation* (1980).

Dodgson, J.M., 'The significance of the distribution of English place-names in *-ingas, -inga* in south-east England', *Medieval Archaeology* 10 (1966), 1–29.

Dodwell, B., 'Holdings and inheritance in medieval East Anglia', *EcHR* 2nd series 20 (1967), 53–66.

Doehaerd, R., *The Early Middle Ages in the West: economy and society*, trans. W. G. Deakin (1978).

Douglas, D.C., 'A charter of enfeoffment under William the Conqueror', *EHR* 42 (1927), 245–7.

———*The Social Structure of Medieval East Anglia'*, Oxford Studies in Social and Legal History 9 (1927).

———'Some early surveys from the abbey of Abingdon', *EHR* 44 (1929), 618–25.

Douglas, D.C. and Greenaway, G.W., eds, *English Historical Documents*, II, 1042–1189 (1953).

du Boulay, F.R.H., *The Lordship of Canterbury: an essay on medieval society* (1966).

Duby, G., *La société aux xie et xiie siècles dans la région maconnaise* (Paris, 1953).

———*Rural Economy and Country Life in the Medieval West*, trans. C. Postan (1968).

———*The Early Growth of the European Economy: warriors and peasants from the seventh to the twelfth century*, trans. H.B. Clarke (1974).

———*The Three Orders: feudal society imagined*, trans. A. Goldhammer (Chicago, 1980).

Dugdale, W., *Monasticon anglicanum* (6 vols, 1817–30).

Dumville, D., 'Sub-Roman Britain: history and legend', *History* 62, 205 (June 1977).

———'The origins of Northumbria: some aspects of the British background' in *The Origins of Anglo-Saxon Kingdoms*, ed. S. Bassett (1989), 213-22.

———'The Tribal Hidage: an introduction to its texts and their history' in *The Origins of Anglo-Saxon Kingdoms*, ed. S. Bassett (1989), 225–30.

Dyer, C.C., *Lords and Peasants in a Changing Society: the estates of the bishopric of Worcester 680–1540* (1980).

——'The rise and fall of a medieval village: Little Aston (in Aston Blank), Gloucestershire', *Trans. Bristol and Gloucestershire Arch. Soc.* 105 (1985), 165–81.

——'Power and conflict in the medieval English village' in *Medieval Villages: a review of current work*, ed. D. Hooke Oxford University Committee for Archaeology Monograph 5, (1985), 27–32.

——'Towns and cottages in eleventh-century England', in *Studies in Medieval History presented to R.H.C. Davis*, ed. H. Mayr-Harting and R.I. Moore (1985), 91–106.

——'Social structure: the west midlands' in *Ag. Hist.* II, 660–75.

——'Dispersed settlements in medieval England: a case study of Pendock, Worcestershire', *Medieval Archaeology* 34 (1990), 97–121.

——*Hanbury: settlement and society in a woodland landscape* (1991).

——'St Oswald and 10,000 west midland peasants' in *St Oswald of Worcester: life and influence*, ed. N. Brooks and C. Cubitt (1996), 174–93.

Ecclesiastical History of Orderic Vitalis, ed. and trans. M. Chibnall, IV (1969).

Eddius (alias Stephanus), Life of Bishop Wilfrid, ed. B. Colgrave (1927).

Edwards, N. and Lane, A., eds, *The Early Church in Wales and the West* (1992).

Ellison, A., *Medieval Villages in South-East Somerset*, Western Archaeological Trust Survey 6 (1983).

Esmonde Cleary, S., *The Ending of Roman Britain* (1989).

Everett, S., 'The Domesday geography of three Exmoor parishes', *Proc. Somerset Archaeological and Natural History Society* 112 (1968), 54–60.

Everitt, A., *Continuity and Colonization: the evolution of Kentish settlement* (1986).

Everson, P.L., Taylor, C.C. and Dunn, C.J., *Change and Continuity: rural settlement in north-west Lincolnshire* (1991).

Eyton, R.W., *A Key to Domesday* (1878).

Faith, R.J., 'Peasant families and inheritance customs in medieval England', *AgHR* 14 (1966), 77–95.

——'Debate: seigneurial control of women's marriage', *Past and Present* 99 (May 1983), 133–48.

——'The "great rumour" of 1377 and peasant ideology' in *The English Rising of 1381*, ed. T.H. Aston and R.H. Hilton (1984), 43–73.

——'Tidenham, Gloucestershire, and the origins of the manor in England', *Landscape History* 16 (1994), 39–51.

——'Demesne resources and labour rent on the manors of St Paul's Cathedral 1066–1222', *EcHR* 47 (1994), 657–78.

——'The topography and social structure of a small soke in the middle ages: The Sokens, Essex', *Essex Archaeology and History* 27 (1997), 202–13.

Farrer, W., ed., *Early Yorkshire Charters* (3 vols, 1914–16).

Fell, C., *Women in Anglo-Saxon England and the Impact of 1066* (1984).

Fentress, J. and Wickham, C., *Social Memory* (1992).

Finberg, H.P.R., *Early Charters of the West Midlands* (1961).

——*Lucerna: studies of some problems in the early history of England* (1964).

——*The Early Charters of Wessex* (1964).

——*Tavistock Abbey: a study in the social and economic history of Devon* (1969).

——'Anglo-Saxon England to 1042' in *Ag. Hist.* I.II, 385–525.

Finn, R.W., *The Domesday Inquest and the Making of Domesday Book* (1960).

——*The Norman Conquest and its Effects on the Economy* (1970).

Fleming, R., *Kings and Lords in Conquest England* (1991).

Fleuriot, L., 'Les très anciennes lois bretonnes: leur date, leur texte' in *Landevennec et la monachisme breton dans le haut moyen âge* (Landevennec 1985).

Foard, G., 'The administrative organisation of Northamptonshire in the Saxon period', *ASSAH* 4 (1985), 185–222.

Fossier, R., 'Land, castle, money and family in the formation of the seigneuries' in *Medieval Settlement: continuity and change*, ed. P. H. Sawyer (1976), 159–68.

Fourquin, G., 'La nouvelle stratification' in *Histoire de la France rurale*, ed. G. Duby (4 vols, 1975), I, 476–514.

Fowler, P.J., 'Agriculture and rural settlement' in *The Archaeology of Anglo-Saxon England*, ed. D.M. Wilson (1976), 23–48.

——*The Farming of Prehistoric Britain* (1983), first published as 'Later prehistory' in *Ag. Hist.* I.I (1981), 63–298.

Fox, H.S.A., 'Approaches to the adoption of the midland system' in *The Origins of Open-Field Agriculture*, ed. T. Rowley (1981), 64–111.

——'The people of the wolds in English settlement history', in *The Rural Settlements of Medieval England*, ed. M. Aston, D. Austin and C.C. Dyer (1989), 77–101.

Freeman, E.A., *The Norman Conquest: its causes and its results* (6 vols, 1867–79).

Fustel de Coulanges, N.D., *Histoire des institutions de l'ancienne France* (6 vols, 1888–92), I, *La Gaule romaine*.

Ganshof, F. and Verhulst, A., 'Medieval agrarian society in its prime: France, the Low Countries and western Germany' in *Cambridge Economic History of Europe*, I, *The Agrarian Life of the Middle Ages*, ed. M. M. Postan (2nd edn, 1966), 291–659.

Gardiner, M., 'Some lost Anglo-Saxon charters and the endowment of Hastings College', *Sussex Archaeological Collections* 127 (1989), 39–48.

Garmonsway, G.N., ed., *Ælfric's Colloquy* (2nd edn, 1947).

Garnsey, P. and Sellar, R., *The Roman Empire: economy, society and culture* (1987).

Geary, P.J., *Before France and Germany: the creation and transformation of the Mediterranean world* (1988).

Gelling, M., *The Place-Names of Berkshire*, EPNS 49 (1973).
——*Signposts to the Past* (1978).
——*The West Midlands in the Early Middle Ages* (1992).
Gem, R., 'The English parish church in the eleventh and early twelfth centuries: a great rebuilding?' in *Minsters and Parish Churches: the local church in transition 950–1200*, ed. J. Blair, Oxford University Committee for Archaeology Monograph 17 (1988), 21–30.
Gent, H. and Dean, C., 'Catchment analysis and settlement hierarchy: a case study from pre-Roman Britain' in *Central Places, Archaeology and History*, ed. E. Grant (1986), 13–26.
Geoffrey of Monmouth, *Historia regum Britanniae*, ed. A. Griscom (1929).
Gibbs, M., ed., *The Early Charters of the Cathedral Church of St Paul, London*, Camden 3rd series 53 (1939).
Gilchrist, J., 'The medieval canon law on unfree persons: Gratian and the decretist doctrines *c*. 114–1234', *Studia gratiana* 19 (1971), 271–301.
Goebel, J., *Felony and Misdemeanor: a study in the history of English criminal procedure* (New York 1937).
Goetz, H.W., 'Serfdom and the beginnings of a "seigneurial system" in the Carolingian period: a survey of the evidence', *Early Medieval Europe* 2.1 (1993), 29–51.
Goffart, W., *Rome's Fall and After* (1989).
Gomme, G.L., *Primitive Folk-Moots or Open-Air Assemblies in Britain* (1880).
——*The Village Community* (1890).
Gras, N.S.B. and Gras, E.C., *The Economic and Social History of an English Village (Crawley, Hampshire AD 909–1928)* (Cambridge MA, 1930).
Gregson, N., 'The multiple estate model: some critical questions', *Journal of Historical Geography* 11, 4 (1985), 339–51.
Grundy, G.B., *Saxon Charters and Field Names of Gloucestershire*, Bristol and Gloucestershire Archaeological Society (2 parts, 1935–6).
Guidoni, E., *Primitive Architecture*, trans. E. Wolf (1975).
Haddan, A.W. and Stubbs, W., eds, *Councils and Ecclesiastical Documents Relating to Great Britain and Ireland* (4 vols, 1871).
Hadley, D., 'Danelaw society and institutions: east midlands phenomena' (Ph.D thesis, University of Birmingham, 1992).
——*Early Medieval Social Structure: the Danelaw* (forthcoming).
Hale, W.H., ed., *The Domesday of St Paul's of the year MCCXXII or registrum de visitatione maneriorum per Robertum decanum*, Camden Society 69 (1858).
Hall, D., *Medieval Fields* (1982).
——'Late Saxon topography and early medieval estates' in *Medieval Villages: a review of current work* ed. D. Hooke, Oxford University Committee for Archaeology Monograph 5, (1985), 61–9.
——'An introduction to Northamptonshire Domesday' in *The Northamptonshire and Rutland Domesday* (1987), 1–17.

——'The late Saxon countryside: villages and their fields' in *Anglo-Saxon Settlements*, ed. D. Hooke, (1988), 99–122.

Hallam, H. E., 'Some thirteenth–century censuses', *EcHR* 2nd series 10 (1957–8), 340–61.

——'England before the Norman Conquest' in *Ag. Hist.* II, 45–136.

——'Population movements in England 1086–1350' in *Ag. Hist.* II, 508–93.

——'New settlement: southern England', in *Ag. Hist.* II, 203–24.

Hamerow, H., *Excavations at Mucking*, II, *The Anglo-Saxon Settlement*, English Heritage Archaeological Report 21 (1991).

Hamshere, J.D., 'The structure and profitability of the Domesday estate of the church of Worcester', *Landscape History* 7 (1985), 41–52.

——'Domesday Book: estate structures in the west midlands' in *Domesday Studies*, ed. J. Holt (1987), 155–82.

Harding, A., *The Law Courts of Medieval England* (1973).

Harley, J.B., 'Population trends and agricultural developments from the Warwickshire Hundred Rolls of 1279', *EcHR* 2nd series 11 (1958), 8–18.

Harmer, F.E., *Anglo-Saxon Writs* (1952).

Hart, C.R., *The Early Charters of Eastern England* (1966).

Hartley, B.R. and Fitts, R.L., *The Brigantes* (1988).

Harvey, B.F., *Westminster Abbey and its Estates in the Middle Ages* (1977).

Harvey, M.A., 'Planned field systems in eastern Yorkshire: some thoughts on their origin', *AgHR* 31 (1983), 91–103.

Harvey, P.D.A., *A Medieval Oxfordshire Village: Cuxham 1240 to 1400* (1965).

——'The Pipe Rolls and the adoption of demesne farming in England', *EcHR*, 2nd series 27 (1974), 345–59.

——(ed.), *The Peasant Land Market in Medieval England* (1984).

——'Initiative and authority in settlement change' in *The Rural Settlements of Medieval England*, ed. M. Aston, D. Austin and C. Dyer (1989), 31–43.

——'*Rectitudines singularum personarum* and *Gerefa*', *EHR* 426 (1993), 1–22.

Harvey, S.P.J., 'The knight and the knight's fee in England', *Past and Present* 49 (November 1970), 3–43, reprinted in *Peasants, Knights and Heretics*, ed. R.H. Hilton (1976), 133–73.

——'Domesday Book and its predecessors', *EHR* 86 (1971), 753–73.

——'Domesday Book and Anglo-Norman governance', *TRHS* 5th series 25 (1975), 175–93.

——'Evidence for settlement study: Domesday Book', in *English Medieval Settlement*, ed. P.H. Sawyer (1979), 105–9.

——'The extent and profitability of demesne agriculture in England in the later eleventh century' in *Social Relations and Ideas: essays in honour of R.H. Hilton*, ed. T.H. Aston, P.R. Coss, C. Dyer and J. Thirsk (1983), 45–72.

——'Taxation and the ploughland in Domesday Book' in *Domesday Book: a reassessment*, ed. P.H. Sawyer (1985), 86–103.

——'Taxation and the economy' in *Domesday Studies*, ed. J. Holt (1987), 249–64.

——'Domesday England' in *Ag. Hist.* II, 45–136.

Hase, P., 'The mother churches of Hampshire' in *Minsters and Parish Churches: the local church in transition 950–1200*, ed. J. Blair, Oxford University Committee for Archaeology Monograph 17 (1988), 45–66.

——'The church in the Wessex heartlands' in *The Medieval Landscapes of Wessex*, ed. M. Aston and C. Lewis (1994), 47–81.

Hatcher, J., 'English serfdom and villeinage: towards a reassessment', *Past and Present* 90 (February 1981), 3–39.

——'New settlement: south western England' in *Ag. Hist.* II, 234–45.

Hawkes, S.C., 'The early Saxon period' in *The Archaeology of the Oxford Region*, ed. G. Briggs, J. Cook and T. Rowley (1986), 64–108.

Heighway, C., 'Saxon Gloucester' in *Anglo-Saxon Towns in Southern England*, ed. J. Haslam (1984), 359–83.

——'Anglo-Saxon Gloucester, *c* 680–1066' in *VCH Gloucestershire*, IV (1988), 5–12.

Henry de Bracton, de legibus et consuetudinibus Angliae, ed. G. E. Woodbine, reissued with translation by S. E. Thorne (4 vols, Cambridge MA, 1968–77).

Herbert, N.M., 'Longtree hundred' in *VCH Gloucestershire*, IX (1976), 152–5.

——'Medieval Gloucester' in *VCH Gloucestershire*, IV (1988), 13–22.

Herlihy, D., 'The Carolingian *mansus*', *EcHR* 2nd series 13 (1960), 79–89.

Higham, N., *The Northern Counties to AD 1000* (1986).

——*Rome, Britain and the Anglo-Saxons* (1992).

——*The Origins of Cheshire* (1993).

——*An English Empire: Bede and the early Anglo-Saxon kings* (1995).

Hill, D., ed., *An Atlas of Anglo-Saxon England* (1981).

Hill, M.C., *The Demesne and the Waste: a study of medieval enclosure on the manor of High Ercall 1086–1399* (1984).

Hill, P.H. and Kucharski, K., 'Early medieval ploughing at Whithorn and chronology of plough pebbles', *Trans. Dumfriesshire and Galloway Natural History and Antiquarian Society*, 3rd series 65 (1990), 73–83.

Hilton, R.H., 'Freedom and villeinage in England', *Past and Present* 31 (July 1965), 3–19.

——*Bond Men Made Free: medieval peasant movements and the English rising of 1381* (1973).

——'Lord and peasant in Staffordshire in the middle ages' in his *The English Peasantry in the Later Middle Ages* (1975), 215–43.

——*English and French Towns in Feudal Society: a comparative study* (1992).

Hingley, R., *Rural Settlement in Roman Britain* (1989).

Hinton, D., 'The topography of Sherborne: early Christian?', *Antiquity* 55 (1981), 222–3.

Hoare, C., *The History of an East Anglian Soke: studies in the original documents* (1918).

Hodges, R., *The Anglo-Saxon Achievement: archaeology and the beginnings of English society* (1989).

Holt, J.C., 'Feudal society and the family in early medieval England', I, 'The revolution of 1066', *TRHS* 5th series 32 (1982), 193–212, II, 'Notions of patrimony', *ibid.* 33 (1983), 193–212.

Holt, R., *The Mills of Medieval England* (1988).

Homans, G.C., *English Villagers of the Thirteenth Century* (Cambridge, Mass., 1941).

——'The Frisians in East Anglia', *EcHR* 2nd series 10 (1957–8), 189–206.

Hooke, D., *Anglo-Saxon Landscapes of the West Midlands: the charter evidence*, BAR British Series 95 (1981).

——ed., *Medieval Villages: a review of current work*, Oxford University Committee for Archaeology Monograph 5 (1985).

——'Anglo-Saxon settlements in the Vale of the White Horse', *Oxoniensia* 52 (1987), 129–43.

——'Pre-Conquest woodland: its distribution and usage', *AgHR* 37 (1989), 113–29.

——'Early medieval estate and settlement patterns: the documentary evidence' in *The Rural Settlements of Medieval England*, ed. M. Aston, D. Austin and C.C. Dyer (1989), 9–30.

——'The administrative and settlement framework of early medieval Wessex' in *The Medieval Landscape of Wessex*, ed. M. Aston and C. Lewis (1994), 83–95.

Hoskins, W.G., *The Making of the English Landscape* (1955).

Howell, C., *Land, Family and Inheritance in Transition: Kibworth Harcourt 1280–1700* (1983).

Howkins, A., *Reshaping Rural England: a social history 1850–1925* (1991).

Hoyle, R., 'Tenant right in north–western England in the sixteenth century', *Past and Present* 116 (August 1987), 24–55.

Hoyt, R.S., *The Royal Demesne in English Constitutional History 1066–1272* (Ithaca, N.Y. 1950).

——'Farm of the manor and community of the vill in Domesday Book', *Speculum* 30 (1955), 147–69.

Hudson, W.H., 'Traces of primitive agricultural organisation as suggested by a survey of the manor of Martham, Norfolk (1101–1292)', *TRHS* 4th series 1 (1918), 28–58.

——'The status of *villani* and other tenants in Danish East Anglia in pre–Conquest times', *TRHS* 4th series 4 (1921), 23–48.

Huggins, P.J., 'Anglo-Saxon timber building measurements: results', *Medieval Archaeology* 35 (1991), 1–28.

Hurnard, N., *The King's Pardon for Homicide Before A.D. 1307* (1969).

Hurst, J. G., 'Rural building in England and Wales', *Ag. Hist.* II, 854–98.

Hyams, P.R., 'The proof of villein status in the common law', *EHR* 89 (1974), 721–49.

——*King, Lords and Peasants in Medieval England: the common law of villeinage in the twelfth and thirteenth centuries* (1980).

Isidore of Seville, *Etymologies: Isidori hispalensis episcopi etymologiarum sive originum libri XX*, ed. W.D. Lindsay (2 vols, 1911).

James, E., 'The origins of barbarian kingdoms: the continental evidence' in *The Origins of Anglo-Saxon Kingdoms*, ed. S. Bassett (1989), 40–52.

James, S., Marshall, A. and Millett, M., 'An early medieval building tradition', *Arch. Journal* 141 (1984), 182–215.

Jenkins, R.C., *Some Account of the Church of St Mary and St Eadburg in Lyminge* (1859).

——*The Chartulary of the Monastery of Lyminge* (1889).

Jenner, H., 'The manumissions in the Bodmin gospels', *Journal of the Royal Institution of Cornwall* 21 (1922), 235–60.

Jocelin of Brakelond, Chronicle of the Abbey of Bury St Edmunds, ed. D. Greenaway and J. Sayers (1989).

John E., *Land Tenure in Early England: a discussion of some problems* (1960).

——*Orbis Britanniae* (1966).

Jolliffe, J., 'Northumbrian institutions', *EHR* 41 (1926), 1–42.

——*Pre-Feudal England: the Jutes* (1933).

Jones, A., 'Harvest customs and labourers' perquisites in southern England 1150–1350: the corn harvest', *AgHR* 35, I (1977), 14–22.

——'Harvest customs and labourers' perquisites in southern England 1150–1350: the hay harvest', *AgHR* 35, I (1977), 98–107.

Jones, A.H.M., 'The Roman colonate', *Past and Present* 13 (April 1958), 1–13.

——*The Later Roman Empire AD 284–602: a social, economic and administrative survey* (2nd edn, 2 vols 1973).

Jones, G.R.J. 'Early territorial organization in England and Wales' *Geografiskar Annaler* 43 (1961), 174–81.

——'Basic patterns of settlement distribution in Northern England', *Advancement of Science* 18 (1961), 191–200.

——'Post-Roman Wales', in *Ag. Hist.* I.II, 299–349.

——'Multiple estates and early settlement' in *English Medieval Settlement*, ed. P.H. Sawyer (1979), 11–40.

——'Nucleal settlement and its tenurial relationships: some morphological implications' in *Villages, Fields and Frontiers: studies in rural settlement in the medieval and early modern periods*, ed. B.K. Roberts and R.E. Glasscock, BAR International Series 85 (1985), 153–70.

——'Multiple estates perceived', *Journal of Historical Geography* 11 (1985), 325–63 at 354.

——'The portrayal of land settlement in Domesday Book' in *Domesday Studies*, ed. J.C. Holt (1987), 185–6.

Joy, C.A. 'Sokeright', (Ph.D. thesis, University of Leeds, 1972).

Joüon des Longrais, F., 'Le vilainage anglais et le servage réel et personel', *Recueils de la Societé Jean Bodin*, II, *Le servage* (2nd edn, Brussels 1959), 201–242.

Kalendar of Abbot Samson of Bury St. Edmunds and Related Documents, ed. R.H.C. Davis, Camden 3rd series 84 (1954).

Kapelle, W.E., *The Norman Conquest of the North: a region and its transformation 1000–1135* (1979).

Karras, R.M., *Slavery and Society in Medieval Scandinavia* (1988).

Keen, L., 'The towns of Dorset' in *Anglo-Saxon Towns in Southern England*, ed. J. Haslam (1984), 203–47.

Keen, M., *Chivalry* (New Haven CT, 1984).

Kenyon, D., *The Origins of Lancashire* (1991).

Kerridge, E., *Agrarian Problems in the Sixteenth Century and After* (1968), 42–59.

Keynes, S. and Lapidge, M., eds, *Alfred the Great: Asser's life of King Alfred and other contemporary sources* (1983).

King, E., 'The Peterborough *Descriptio militum* (Henry I)', *EHR* 84 (1969), 84–101.

——*Peterborough Abbey 1086–1310: a study in the land market* (1973).

King, V., 'St Oswald's tenants' in *St Oswald of Worcester: life and influence*, ed. N. Brooks and C. Cubitt (1996), 100–16.

Kirby, D.P., ed., *Saint Wilfrid at Hexham* (1974).

Knowles, D., *The Monastic Order in England* (2nd edn, 1962).

Kosminsky, E.A., *Studies in the Agrarian History of England in the Thirteenth Century*, trans. R. Kisch (1956).

Kristensen, A.K.G., 'Danelaw institutions and Danelaw society in the Viking Age: *sochemanni, liberi homines* and *königsfrei*', *Medieval Scandinavia* 8 (1975), 27–85.

Lancaster, L., 'Kinship in Anglo-Saxon society', *British Journal of Sociology* 9 (1958), 230–50, 359–77.

Langdon, J., *Horses, Oxen and Technological Innovation: the use of draught animals in English farming from 1066 to 1500* (1986).

Lapsley, G.H., 'Boldon Book', *VCH Durham*, I (1905), 259–321.

Larson, L.M., 'The king's household in England before the Norman conquest: a thesis', *Bulletin of the University of Wisconsin* 100 (1904).

Law of Hywel Dda: law texts from medieval Wales, trans. and ed. D. Jenkins (1986).

Lawson, M.K., *Cnut: the Danes in England in the early eleventh century* (1993).

Leges Henrici Primi, ed. L.J. Downer (1972).

Lennard, R.V., 'The economic position of the bordars and cottars of Domesday Book', *Economic Journal* 61 (1951), 342–71.

——'The demesnes of Glastonbury Abbey in the eleventh and twelfth centuries', *EcHR*, 2nd series 8 (1956), 355–63.

——*Rural England 1086–1135: a study of social and agrarian conditions* (1959).

Levett, A.E., 'The financial organization of the manor', *EcHR* 1 (1927), 65–86.

——*Studies in Manorial History* (1938).
Levy, E., 'The vulgarization of Roman law in the early middle ages' *Medievalia et Humanistica* 1 (1943), 14–40.
Liber eliensis, ed. E.O. Blake, Camden 3rd series 92 (1962).
Liber Henrici de Soliaco, ed. J.E. Jackson (1882).
Lindsay, W.M., ed., *An Eighth Century Latin-Anglo-Saxon Glossary, (Cambridge, Corpus Christi College m.s. 144)* (1921).
Loyn, H.R., 'Gesiths and thegns in Anglo-Saxon England from the seventh to the tenth century', *EHR* 70 (1955), 529–49.
——*The Governance of Anglo-Saxon England 500–1087* (1984).
Lyth, P., 'The Southwell charter of 956: an exploration of its boundaries', *Trans. Thoroton Society* 85 (1981), 49–61.
McDonald, J. and Snooks, G.D., *Domesday Economy: a new approach to Anglo-Norman history* (1986).
McGovern, J.G., 'The meaning of "gesette land" in Anglo-Saxon land tenure', *Speculum* 46 (1971), 589–96.
McIntosh, M., *Autonomy and Community: the royal manor of Havering 1200–1500* (1986).
Maddicott, J.R., 'Trade industry and the wealth of King Alfred', *Past and Present* 123 (May 1989), 3–51.
Maitland, F.W., 'The suitors of the county court', *EHR* 3 (1888), 417–21.
——'Northumbrian tenures', *EHR* 5 (1890), 625–32.
——*Domesday Book and Beyond: three essays in the early history of England* (1960 edn).
Michaud-Quantin, P., *Etudes sur la vocabulaire philosophique du moyen âge* (Rome, 1970).
Miles, D., *Archaeology at Barton Court Farm, Abingdon, Oxon.*, Council for British Archaeology Research Report 50 (1986).
Miller, E., *The Abbey and Bishopric of Ely: the social history of an ecclesiastical estate from the tenth to the early fourteenth century* (1951).
——'La société rurale en Angleterre (x^e au xiie siècles)' in *Agricoltura e mondo rurale in occidente nell' alto medioevo*, Settimane di studio del Centro Italiano di Studi dell' Alto Medioevo 13 (Spoleto 1966), 111–34.
——'England in the twelfth and thirteenth centuries: an economic contrast?', *EcHR*, 2nd series 24 (1971), 1–14.
——'Social structure: Northern England' in *Ag. Hist.* II, 685–98.
Miller, E. and Hatcher, J., *Medieval England: rural society and economic change 1086–1348* (1978).
Millett, M., *The Romanization of Britain: an essay in archaeological interpretation* (1991).
Milsom, S.F.C., *Historical Foundations of the Common Law* (1969).
——*The Legal Framework of English Feudalism* (1976).
Mirror of Justices, ed. W.J. Whittaker, Selden Society 7 (1893).
Moore, J.S., 'Domesday slavery', *Anglo-Norman Studies* 11 (1988), 191–220.

Morland, S.C., *Glastonbury, Domesday and Related Studies* (1991).

Morris, J., *The Age of Arthur* (3 vols, 1977).

Morris, P., *Agricultural Buildings in Roman Britain*, BAR British Series 70 (1979).

Morris, R., *Churches in the Landscape* (1989).

Murray, A., *Reason and Society in the Middle Ages* (1978).

Murray, A.C., *Germanic Kinship Structure: studies in law and society in antiquity and the early middle ages* (1983).

Mussuet, L., 'La tenure en bordage, aspects normands et manceaux', *Revue historique de droit français et étranger* 4th series 28 (1950), 140.

——'Réflexions sur *alodium* et sa significance dans les textes normands', *Revue historique de droit français et étranger* 4th series 47 (1969).

Nash, D., 'Celtic territorial expansion and the Mediterranean world' in *Settlement and Society: aspects of West European prehistory in the first millennium BC*, ed. T.C. Champion and J.V.S. Megaw (1985).

Neilson, N., *Customary Rents* in Oxford Studies in Social and Legal History 2 (1910).

——'English manorial forms', *American Historical Review 34* (1929), 725–39.

O'Donovan, M.A., *The Charters of Sherborne* (1988).

Oosthuizen, S., 'Isleham: a medieval inland port', *Landscape History* 15 (1993), 29–35.

Palliser, D.M., 'An introduction to the Yorkshire Domesday' in *The Yorkshire Domesday* (1992), 1–38.

Palmer, J.J., 'The Domesday manor' in *Domesday Studies*, ed. J.C. Holt (1987), 139–53.

Pearce, S.M., 'Estates and church sites in Dorset and Gloucestershire: the emergence of a Christian society' in *The Early Church in Western Britain and Ireland: studies presented to C. A. Ralegh Radford*, BAR British Series 102, ed. S.M. Pearce (1982), 117–37.

Pelteret, D.A.E., 'The *coliberti* of Domesday Book', *Studies in Medieval Culture* 12 (1978), 43–54.

——'Slavery in Anglo-Saxon England' in *The Anglo-Saxons: synthesis and achievement*, ed. J.D. Woods and D.A.E. Pelteret (Waterloo, Ontario, 1985), 117–33.

——'Two Old English lists of serfs', *Mediaeval Studies* 48 (1986), 470–513.

——'Slavery in the Danelaw' in *Social Approaches to Viking Studies*, ed. R. Samson (1991), 179–88.

Percival, J.C., 'Seigneurial aspects of late Roman estate management', *EHR* 84 (1969), 449–73.

Perrin, C.E., 'Seigneurie rurale en France et en Allemagne du début du ixe à la fin du xiie siècle' (Paris, n.d.).

Petot, P., 'Licences de mariage et formariage des serfs dans les coutumiers français au moyen âge', *Annales d'histoire de droit* ii (Poznan 1949), 199–208.

Pipe Roll 16 Henry II, Pipe Roll Society 15 (1892).
Placitorum ... abbreviatio, Record Commission (1811).
Platt, C., *The Monastic Grange in Medieval England: a reassessment* (1969).
Pollock, F. and Maitland, F.M., *The History of English Law before the time of Edward I* (2 vols, 1968 edn).
Poly J.P. and Bournazel, E., *The Feudal Transformation 900–1200,* trans. C. Higgitt (New York, 1991).
Postan, M.M., *The Famulus: the estate labourer in the twelfth and thirteenth centuries, EcHR* Supp. 2 (1954).
——*The Medieval Economy and Society* (1972).
——'The chronology of labour services' and 'Glastonbury estates in the twelfth century: a reply' in M.M. Postan, *Essays on Medieval Agriculture and General Problems of the Medieval Economy* (1973), 89–106, 249–77.
——'A note on the farming out of manors' *EcHR* 2nd series 31 (1978), 521–5.
Preston–Jones, A., 'Decoding Cornish churchyards' in *The Early Church in Wales and the West,* ed. N. Edwards and A. Lane (1992), 104–24.
Pretty, K., 'Defining the Magonsaete' in The *Origins of Anglo-Saxon Kingdoms,* ed. S. Bassett (1989), 171–83.
Price, H., 'Ecclesiastical wealth in early medieval Wales' in *The Early Church in Wales and the West,* ed. N. Edwards and A. Lane (1992), 22–32.
Raban, S., *The Estates of Thorney and Crowland: a study in medieval monastic land tenure* (1977).
Rackham, O., *The History of the Countryside* (1986).
Raftis, J.A., *The Estates of Ramsey Abbey* (1957).
——'Social structure: the east midlands' in *Ag. Hist.* II, 634–50.
Rahtz, P., 'Buildings and rural settlement' in *The Archaeology of Anglo-Saxon England,* ed. D. M. Wilson (1976), 49–98.
Ravenhill, W.L.D., 'Cornwall' in *The Domesday Geography of South-West England,* ed. H.C. Darby and R.W. Finn (1967), 296–308.
Ray, J.E., 'The church of SS Peter and Paul, Bexhill', *Sussex Archaeological Collections* 53 (1910), 61–108.
Razi, Z., *Life, Marriage and Death in a Medieval Parish: economy, society and demography in Halesowen 1270–1400* (1980).
Red Book of Worcester, ed. M. Hollings, Worcestershire Historical Society (4 vols, 1934–50).
Register of St Augustine's Abbey, Canterbury, Commonly Called the Black Book, ed. G.J. Turner and H.E. Salter, British Academy Records of Social and Economic History (2 parts 1915, 1924).
Reid, R., 'Barony and thanage', *EHR* 35 (1920), 161–99.
Reuter, T., 'Plunder and tribute in the Carolingian empire', *TRHS* 5th series 35 (1985), 75–94.
Reynolds, S., *Kingdoms and Communities in Western Europe 900–1300* (1984).

———'Bookland, folkland and fiefs', *Anglo-Norman Studies* 14 (1992), 211–27.

———*Fiefs and Vassals: the medieval evidence reinterpreted* (1994).

Richter, M., *Medieval Ireland: the enduring tradition* (1988).

Rippon, S., 'Medieval wetland reclamation in Somerset' in *The Medieval Landscape of Wessex*, ed. M. Aston and C. Lewis (1994), 239–53.

Rivet, A.L.F., ed., *The Roman Villa in Britain* (1969).

Roberts, B.K., 'Village plans in Co. Durham: a preliminary statement', *Medieval Archaeology* 16 (1972), 33–56.

———'Field systems of the west midlands' in *Studies of Field Systems in the British Isles*, ed. A.R.H. Baker and R.A. Butlin (1973), 188–231.

———*Rural Settlement in Britain* (1977).

———*The Making of the English Village* (1987).

———'Nucleation and dispersion: distribution maps as a research tool' in *The Rural Settlements of Medieval England*, ed. M. Aston, D. Austin and C. Dyer (1989), 59–75.

Roffe, D., 'From thegnage to barony: sake and soke, title and tenants-in-chief', *Anglo-Norman Studies* 12 (1989), 157–76.

———'Domesday Book and northern society: a reassessment', *EHR* 105 (April 1990), 310–36.

Roper, M., 'Wilfrid's landholdings in Northumbria' and 'The donation of Hexham' in *Saint Wilfrid at Hexham*, ed. D.P. Kirby (1974), 61–79, 169–71.

Rose-Troup, F., 'Medieval customs and tenures in the manor of Ottery St Mary', *Report and Transactions of the Devonshire Association* 66 (1934), 211–33.

Rosener, W., *Peasants in the Middle Ages*, trans. A. Stutzer (1992).

Rosser, G., *Medieval Westminster 1200–1540* (1989).

Rostovtzeff, M., *The Social and Economic History of the Roman Empire* (2nd edn, 1963).

Rotuli Hundredorum, Record Commission (2 vols, 1812–18).

Round, J.H., 'The Domesday of Colchester', *The Antiquary* 6 (1882), 5–9, 95–100, 251–6.

———'Danegeld and the finance of Domesday' in *Domesday Studies*, ed. P.E. Dove (2 vols, 1888, 1891), I, 77–142.

———*Feudal England: historical studies on the xith and xiith centuries* (1895).

———'Introduction to the Northamptonshire Domesday', *VCH Northamptonshire* I (1902), 257–98.

———'The Domesday survey' in *VCH Essex* I (1903), 333–425.

Rowley, T., ed., *The Origins of Open-Field Agriculture* (1981).

Runciman, W.G., 'Accelerating social mobility: the case of Anglo-Saxon England', *Past and Present* 104 (August 1984), 3–30.

Salway, P., *Roman Britain* (1981).

Sato, S., 'Les implantations monastiques dans la Gaule du nord: un facteur de la croissance agricole au viie siècle? quelques elements d'hypothèse concernants les régions de Rouen et de Beauvais', in

La croissance agricole du haut moyen âge: chronologie, modalités, géographie, Centre Culturel de l'Abbaye de Flaran (Auch 1990), 169–77.

Sawyer, P.H., *Medieval Settlement: continuity and change* (1976)

——ed., *From Roman Britain to Norman England* (1978)

——ed., *English Medieval Settlement* (1979)

——ed., *Names, Words and Graves: early medieval settlement* (1979)

——'The royal *tun* in pre-Conquest England' in *Ideal and Reality in Frankish and Anglo-Saxon Society*, ed. P. Wormald, D. Bullough and R. Collins (1983), 273–99.

——ed., *Domesday Book: a reassessment* (1985).

Schofield, P.R., 'Land, family and inheritance in a later medieval community: Birdbrook, 1292–1412' (D.Phil. thesis, University of Oxford, 1992).

Scull, C., 'Archaeology, early Anglo-Saxon society and the origins of Anglo-Saxon kingdoms', *ASSAH* 6 (1993), 1–18.

Searle, E., 'Hides, virgates and tenant settlement at Battle Abbey', *EcHR* 2nd series 16 (1963–4), 290–300.

——*Lordship and Community: Battle Abbey and its banlieu 1066–1538* (Toronto 1974).

——'Seigneurial control of women's marriage: the antecedents and functions of merchet in England', *Past and Present* 82 (February 1979), 3–43.

——*Predatory Kinship and the Creation of Norman Power 840–1066* (Berkeley and Los Angeles 1988).

Seebohm, F., *The English Village Community* (1896).

Shanin, T., ed., *Peasants and Peasant Societies* (1971).

Sheppard, J.A., 'Field systems of Yorkshire' in *Studies of Field Systems in the British Isles*, ed. A.R.H. Baker and R.A. Butlin (1973), 145–87.

——'Medieval village planning in northern England: some evidence from Yorkshire', *Journal of Historical Geography* 2 (1976), 3–20.

Smith, J.T., 'Romano-British aisled houses', *Archaeological Journal* 120 (1963), 1–30.

——'Villas as a key to social structure' in *Studies in the Romano-British Villa*, ed. M. Todd (1978), 149–85.

Smith, R.A.L., *The Estates of Canterbury Cathedral Priory: a study in monastic administration* (1943).

Smith, R.B., *Blackburnshire* (1961).

Smith, R.M., 'Human resources' in *The Countryside of Medieval England*, ed. G. Astill and A. Grant, (1988), 188–212.

Stacy, N.E., 'The estates of Glastonbury Abbey *c.* 1050–1200' (D.Phil. thesis, University of Oxford, 1971).

Stafford, P., 'The farm of one night and the organisation of King Edward's estates in Domesday Book', *EHR* 33 (1980), 491–52.

——*The East Midlands in the Early Middle Ages* (1985).

——*Unification and Conquest: a political and social history of England in the tenth and eleventh centuries* (1989).

Stenton, F.M., *Types of Manorial Structure in the Northern Danelaw* in Oxford Studies in Social and Legal History 2 (1910).

——*Documents Illustrative of the Social and Economic History of the Danelaw from Various Collections*, British Academy Records of the Social and Economic History of England and Wales 5 (1920).

——'Domesday survey', *VCH Oxfordshire*, I (1939), 373–428.

——*Anglo-Saxon England* (1947).

——*The Latin Charters of the Anglo-Saxon Period* (1955).

——'The thriving of the Anglo-Saxon *ceorl*' in *Preparatory to Anglo-Saxon England: being the collected papers of Frank Merry Stenton*, ed. D. M. Stenton (1970), 383–93.

Stephenson, C., '*Firma unius noctis* and the customs of the hundred', *EHR* 39 (1924), 161–74.

Stevenson, W.H., 'A contemporary description of the Domesday survey', *EHR* 22 (1907), 72–84.

Taylor, C.C., *Village and Farmstead: a history of rural settlement in England* (1984).

——'The regular village plan: Dorset revisited and revised' in *The Medieval Landscape of Wessex*, ed. M. Aston and C. Lewis (1994), 213–8.

Thacker, A., 'Monks, preaching and pastoral care' in *Pastoral Care Before the Parish*, ed. J. Blair and R. Sharpe (1992), 137–70.

Thirsk, J., 'The common fields', *Past and Present* 29 (December 1964), 3–25.

Thomas, C., ed., *Rural Settlement in Roman Britain*, Council for British Archaeology Report 7 (1966).

Thornton, C.C. 'The demesne of Rimpton 938 to 1412: a study in economic development', (Ph.D. thesis, University of Leicester, 1988).

——'The determinants of land productivity on the bishop of Winchester's demesne of Rimpton, 1208 to 1403' in *Land, Labour and Livestock: historical studies in European agricultural productivity*, ed. B.M.S. Campbell and M. Overton (1991), 183–210.

Three Early Assize Rolls for the County of Northumberland, saec. XIII, ed. W. Page, Surtees Society 88 (1890).

Todd, M., ed., *Studies in the Romano-British Villa* (1978).

——*The South-West to AD 1000* (1987).

Toubert, P., *Les structures de Latium* (2 vols, Rome, 1973).

——'La part du grand domaine dans le décollage économique de l'occident (viiie–xe siècles)' in *La croissance agricole du haut moyen âge* (Auch 1990).

Treatise on the Laws and Customs of England, Commonly Called Glanvill, ed. G.D.G. Hall (1965).

Tribe, K., *Land, Labour and Economic Discourse* (1978).

Twinch, C., *In Search of Walstan: East Anglia's Enduring Legend* (1995)

Uhlig, H., 'Old hamlets with infield and outfield systems in western and central Europe', *Geografiska Annaler* 43 (1961), 285–307.

Van Caenegem, R.C., *Royal Writs in England from the Conquest to Glanvill*, Selden Society 77 (1958–9).

Verriest, L., *Institutions médiévales: introduction au corpus des records de coutumes et des lois des chefs-lieux de l'ancien comté de Hainaut* (Mons 1946).

Vinogradoff, P., *Villainage in England: essays in English mediaeval history* (1892).

——'Agricultural services', *Economic Journal* 10 (1900), 308–22.

——*English Society in the Eleventh Century: essays in English mediaeval history* (1908).

——*The Growth of the Manor* (2nd edn, 1911).

Walmesley, J.F.R., 'The *censarii* of Burton Abbey and the Domesday population', *North Staffordshire Journal of Field Studies* 8 (1968), 72–80.

——'The estate of Burton Abbey from the 11th to the 14th centuries' (Ph.D. thesis, University of Birmingham, 1972).

Wareham, A.F., 'The aristocracy of East Anglia c930–1154' (Ph.D. thesis, University of Birmingham, 1992).

Warner, P., *Greens, Commons and Clayland Colonization: the origins and development of green-side settlement in east Suffolk* (1987).

Warren, W.L., *The Governance of Anglo-Norman and Angevin England 1086–1272* (1987).

Watson, C.E., 'The Minchinhampton custumal and its place in the story of the manor', *Transactions Bristol and Gloucestershire Arch. Soc.* 54 (1932), 203–308.

Webster, G., *The Cornovii* (1975).

Welch, M., *The English Heritage Book of Anglo-Saxon England* (1992).

Whitelock, D., *Anglo-Saxon Wills* (1930).

——*The Beginnings of English Society* (1952).

——*The Will of Æthelgifu: a tenth century Anglo-Saxon manuscript* (1968).

——, Brett, M. and Brooke, C.N.L., eds, *Councils and Synods with Other Documents relating to the English Church* (2 vols, 1981).

Wickham, C., 'The other transition: from the ancient world to feudalism', *Past and Present* 103 (May 1984), 3–36.

Wightman, W.E., *The Lacy Family in England and Normandy 1066–1196* (1966).

William of Malmesbury, *De antiquate glastoniensis ecclesie* in T. Hearne, ed., *Adami de Domerham historia de rebus gestis glastoniensibus* (2 vols, 1727).

William of Malmesbury's Chronicle of the Kings of England, ed. and trans. J.A. Giles (1847).

Williams, A., 'The knights of Shaftesbury Abbey', *Anglo-Norman Studies* 8 (1985–6), 214–37.

——' "A bell-house and a *burhgeat*": lordly residence in England before the Norman Conquest' in *The Ideals and Practice of Medieval Knighthood*, ed. C. Harper-Bill and R. Harvey (1986), 221–40.

——'An introduction to the Gloucestershire Domesday', *Domesday Gloucestershire* (1989), 1–39.

Williamson, J., 'Norfolk: thirteenth century' in *The Peasant Land Market in Medieval England*, ed. P.D.A. Harvey (1984), 31–105.

Williamson, T., *The Origins of Norfolk* (1993).

Wilson, D.M., ed., *The Archaeology of Anglo-Saxon England* (1976).

Winchester, A.J.L., 'The distribution and significance of "bordland" in medieval Britain', *AgHR*, 34 (1986), 129–39.

——*Landscape and Society in Medieval Cumbria* (1987).

Witney, K.P., *The Kingdom of Kent* (1982).

——'The economic position of husbandmen at the time of Domesday Book: a Kentish perspective', *EcHR* 2nd series 37 (1984), 23–34.

Wormald, J.M., *Lords and Men in Scotland: bonds of manrent 1442–1603* (1985).

Wormald, P.J., 'The age of Bede and Æthelbald' in *The Anglo-Saxons*, ed. J. Campbell, E. John, P. Wormald (1982), 70–100.

——*Bede and the Conversion of the English: the charter evidence* (Jarrow 1984).

——'Conclusion' in *The Settlement of Disputes in Medieval Europe*, ed. W. Davies and P. Fouracre (1986), 215–19.

——'Lordship and justice in the early English kingdom: Oswaldslow revisited' in *Property and Power in Early Medieval Europe*, ed. W. Davies.

Wrathmell, S., 'Peasant houses, farmsteads and villages in north–east England' in *The Rural Settlements of Medieval England*, ed. M. Aston, D. Austin and C. Dyer (1989), 247–67.

Yorke, B., *Kings and Kingdoms of Early Anglo-Saxon England* (1990).

——*Wessex in the Early Middle Ages* (1996).

Index

All English places are given their pre-1974 county affiliations. Numbers in *italics* refer to figures.

peasant and worker, 67–9, *68*, 73, 76, 130–2, *131*, 201
sunken-featured buildings, 67, *68*, 69
tuguria, 69
housecarls, 199
Hoyt, R.S., 54
Hudson, J., 220 n.62
Hudson, W., 189
Hundon, Suffolk, 156
hundreds, 8, 101, 118
hundred courts, 255, 258–9
hunting, 102–3, 111–12, 168, 207
services connected with, 94, 102–3, 111–2
Huntingestone hundred, Huntingdonshire, 52, 114
Hurtsbourne Priors, Hampshire, 66–7, 77, 86, 167, 113
husbandlands, 228–9
Hyams, P., 246, 250–1, 264
Hyde Farm, Marcham, Berkshire, 139, *140*
Hyde Farm, Pimperne, Dorset, 97–8

infield, 236
ingas, 133–4
inland, *inlanders*; 14, ch. 2, 3, 163, 188–9, 192, 196–202, 209–10, 221–2, 238, 240, 242–3, 247, 251–2, 262; *see* also bordland, demesne,
inheritance
peasant, 129–30, 135–7, 207, 257–8
seigneurial, 137, 159–61, 181, 257–8
Ipswich, Suffolk, 73
Isidore of Seville, *Ten Books of Etymologies*, 62, 81, 249
Isleham, Cambridgeshire, 71
Isleworth, Middlesex, 141
Islingham, Kent, 104
Iudnerth, 81
Iwerne, Dorset, 18

Jarrow, Northumberland, 28–9
Jolliffe, J., 10, 46, *46*, 95, 113, 134, 190
Jones, G.R. 11–14, 28, 46–7
judges, 116–17
juries, 259

Kapelle, W.E. 111, 190, 195–7, 214–15, 217, 227
Keen, L., 19, *20*, 21 n.21
Kempsey, Worcestershire, 37, 111, 170–1, 212, 240–1
Kenilworth, Warwickshire, prior of, 207
Kent, 28
'Custom of Kent', 135, 207
Ketel, will of, 63
Ketel, William, litigant, 259
Kettering, Northamptonshire, 214
Kibworth Harcourt, Leicestershire, 231
King, E., 187
kings
Æthelstan, 22, 38, 249
Alfred, 96, 99, 106, 248, 249
Cædwalla, 29, 40, 104
Cenwalh, 18–19, 34, 41, 112
Eadwig, 134, 155
Edgar, 94, 98, 118, 121, 167
Edwin, 62–3
Edward the Confessor, 63
Edward the Elder, 117, 99
Edwin, 74
Egfrith, 29, 35
Ethelbert, 62
Ethelred Unræd, 21
Guthrum, 67, 106
Harold Harefoot, 105
Henry I, 54
Henry II, 119, 245
Ine, 38–9, 40, 76, 103, 119–20, 155–6, 249
Offa, 39
Osric, 25
Oswiu, 28, 35, 39
William I, 54, 55, 91, 188, 219
kingship, 5–8
Kings Worthy, Hampshire, 40
kingston, 32 and n.66, 42, 150
Kingston, Surrey, 42
Kingstone, Herefordshire, 112
Kirby, Essex, *92*, 115
Kirkstall, Yorkshire, 248
Knighton, 158–9
Knighton on Teme, Worcestershire, 170
knights, 97–8
fees, 179, 198, 220
Kosminsky, E.A., 169, 207